Modular Knitting

Pat Ashforth | Steve Plummer

Modular Knitting

SIMPLE MODULAR TECHNIQUES FOR MAKING WONDERFUL GARMENTS AND ACCESSORIES

SEARCH PRESS

A Quarto book

Published in 2006 by Search Press Ltd.
Wellwood
North Farm Road
Tunbridge Wells
Kent
TN2 3DR

ISBN-10: 1-84448-138-7

QUAR.CZK

Conceived, designed and produced by
Quarto Publishing plc
The Old Brewery
6 Blundell Street
London N7 9BH

EDITOR Donna Gregory
DESIGNER Elizabeth Healey
ASSISTANT ART DIRECTOR Penny Cobb
PICTURE RESEARCHER Claudia Tate
TEXT EDITOR Eleanor Holme
PROOFREADER Diana Chambers
PHOTOGRAPHER Martin Norris
ILLUSTRATORS Kuo Kang Chen, Terry Evans, Luise Roberts
PROJECTS Luise Roberts

ART DIRECTOR Moira Clinch
PUBLISHER Paul Carslake

Manufactured by Modern Age Repro House Ltd,
Hong Kong
Printed by SNP Leefung Printing International Ltd, China

Contents

Introduction

Modular Knits will enable you to look at garment shapes in a new way, then make small shapes to create whatever you want without a pattern. There are suggestions for a great deal of experimenting and also complete projects for those who still require a little more guidance.

Start at the beginning, and after reading the first few pages, you will have learned enough to make a sweater or jacket using the simplest modular techniques. After that, there are many points where you may feel compelled to stop and make something. This book could last a knitting lifetime.

Over time, you can work through all the extra information, but you should also be prepared to abandon the book and "do your own thing" when your own ideas start to take over.

The individual modules require very basic knitting skills and are guaranteed to fit together using

your own choice of yarn. The challenge lies in looking at the shapes of garments and other items in a new way to see how they can be broken down into modules.

Creations can be very economical to make, as scraps, odd balls and small quantities of exotic yarns can all be used to good effect.

This is an inexpensive way of working as you can use any yarns and any needles. If you have already been knitting for some time, you probably won't need to buy anything, but you will find tips for buying and making yarns that you might not have thought of before. If you are new to knitting, you will be able to start with a couple of balls of basic yarn.

The knitting requires very basic techniques, but the methods for creating designs will prove equally exciting for novice and experienced knitters alike.

What is modular knitting?

Modular knitting is a fun way to make unique garments, and fashion and home accessories – without knitting patterns.

It will change the way you look at shapes and how they combine to create an infinite variety of items, all using your own choice of yarns. This approach appeals to new and experienced knitters alike, as there are no difficult stitches to learn. Best of all, this method guarantees that anything you knit will fit, whether you're knitting for a baby, a friend or your partner. You'll never need another knitting pattern again, but beware – modular knitting can be addictive!

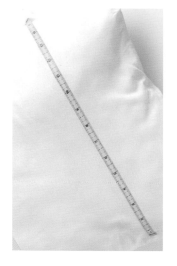

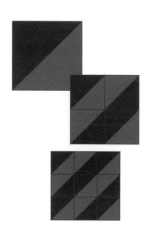

1 Arm yourself with yarn and needles
⇨ **See pages 12–13**

You can use any yarn and any needles. If you are already a knitter, you will probably have plenty of suitable yarns. If you are a beginner, buy a couple of balls of inexpensive plain DK yarn and the needles suggested on the ball band.

2 Take measurements
⇨ **See pages 64–65**

Arm yourself with a tape measure. Depending on what you want to knit, find an existing item whose size and shape you want to re-create (for example, a favourite sweater or a sofa cushion). Use the existing item to decide how big you want the modular item to be. Measure its length and width, and add or take off the amount needed to make it the size you want.

3 How many squares?
⇨ **See pages 65**

Do you want large square blocks or small square blocks, half-square blocks or a mixture? The choice is yours. Figure how many of your chosen block size will fit into the width and length of the item you measured in stage 2. You'll need a calculator for this stage, but this part isn't difficult.

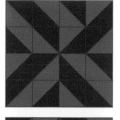
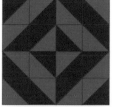
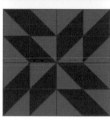

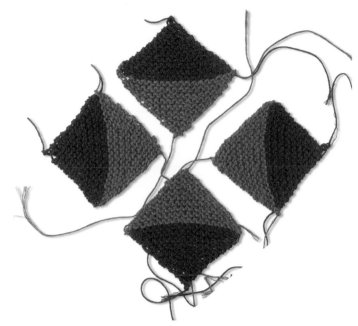

4 **Draw the squares**
⇨ **See pages 66–67**
Draw a scaled-down version of what you plan to knit and mark in the square blocks that will fill the shape. Draw one full-size square to use as a measure or template.

5 **Knit the squares**
⇨ **See pages 20–21**
Start with one stitch at the corner and increase at the beginning of every row until the knitting fits the widest part of the template, then decrease at the end of every row until all the stitches have gone.

6 **Join the squares**
⇨ **See pages 22–27**
Place two squares face to face and oversew (whip stitch) them together using a large sewing needle and the yarn you have been knitting with. Stitch all the squares for each row, then stitch the rows together.

7 **Finished knit**
A knitted cushion made in a simple garter stitch using coordinating colours.

CHAPTER ONE

modular knitting basics

Materials and equipment

The most important ingredients for modular knits are imagination and a sense of adventure. You need an open mind and a willingness to look at shapes in a new way.

You can't go out and buy these ingredients, but you can buy beautiful, practical yarns and equipment to start you on your way to modular knitting. You may well already have favourite yarns and tools, and these can be added to as you go along. Don't be afraid to experiment with yarns, and you will soon discover great new combinations of colours, shapes and textures!

Bulky (chunky) wool/acrylic

Aran-weight Shetland wool

Aran-weight cotton/angora

Fingering-weight wool

Sport-weight cotton/acrylic

DK-weight wool/acrylic

Bulky (chunky) wool

Aran-weight wool

DK-weight cotton

Fingering-weight wool

Yarn

Let your imagination take over. There are thousands of yarns to choose from, but you can mix and match them to your heart's content. Use two or three colours for a subtle effect; try a dozen shades of one colour; perhaps use twenty or thirty colours from your collection, with a neutral or contrast to tie them all together; choose one beautiful colour and create interest and variety by using different textures; experiment with a variegated or self-striping yarn for unique effects. Choose any yarn in any thickness or fibre, bearing in mind two simple rules:

■ Although it is possible to mix the weights of yarn used, the instructions in this book assume that you will be using the same weight throughout a project. For example, use all DK-weight yarn.

■ Your finished garment must be washed according to the most gentle instructions on any of the ball bands.

Yarns for free

Tie short lengths of yarn together to make a unique and unpredictable yarn of your own. Choose each new length in a colour close to the previous one to achieve a subtle effect.

Recycle yarn from worn out or outgrown garments. Unravel the garments, wind the yarn into small hanks, wash and allow to dry so that the kinks drop out, then wind into balls for knitting. As you will mostly be creating small pieces of knitting, it won't matter if the balls are much smaller than you would normally work with.

Yarn storage

Store unused balls and scraps of yarn away from dust and dampness in transparent plastic bags or boxes, sorting them by weight, fibre content and colour. An organized collection of odd balls and remnants is a modular knitter's best friend.

Needles

The range of knitting needles available is enormous and you can use almost any type for modular knitting, according to your particular preference. Much of the time you will be working with only a small number of stitches, so very small needles, like those intended for children, are perfect for some knitters. These have the advantage of being small enough to carry a project with you for working on in odd moments.

Circular needles are equally useful. They don't have to be used for knitting "in the round". They are just as good for flat knitting and there is never any fear of losing a needle. These needles are very versatile as you can also use them when you want to work on the same item with a larger number of stitches, such as for bands and edgings.

Any straight needles can be used, but remember that small pieces need to be turned very frequently and long needles have more chance of getting tangled when you turn.

You might find double-pointed needles useful if you are experienced with them, but novices should take care

not to lose stitches off the unprotected ends.

Most yarns now carry information on their bands recommending sizes (thickness) of needles, and it is best to be guided by this to start with. However, as you get more adventurous, you may decide to disregard it entirely.

Whatever size you choose, you will often need one needle two or three sizes bigger for casting off loosely.

Needle care
- Needles should be kept clean and dry, stored flat with the points protected.
- Plastic and aluminium needles may be washed in warm water if necessary.
- Damaged needles will snag the yarn as you knit – replace them.

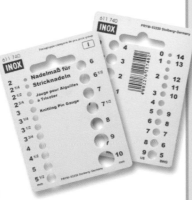

Equivalent needle sizes

Needles are sized in the US from 0 to 50, and in Europe from 2 mm to 15 mm or more. There is not an exact match between the two systems, but if you always check your gauge, you can use either size type, as available.

US	EUROPE	US	EUROPE
0	2 mm	9	5.5 mm
1	2.25 mm	10	6 mm
3	3.25 mm	10½	6.5 or 7 mm
4	3.5 mm	11	8 mm
5	3.75 mm	13	9 mm
6	4 mm	15	10 mm
7	4.5 mm	17	12 or 13 mm
8	5 mm	19	15 mm

Other equipment

If you are already a knitter, you probably own most of the equipment you need. If you are a beginner, there are a few extras you may wish to acquire along the way, though it is probable that you already have basic tools such as scissors, pins (non-rusting) and safety-pins.

Crochet hook

A crochet hook with similar thickness to your needles may be useful at times, especially for joining shapes together (see page 24).

Sewing-up needles

Look for needles with large eyes and blunt tips to prevent splitting strands of yarn. They are sold as "yarn needles" or "tapestry needles," and are available in a wide range of sizes to suit any type of yarn.

Stitch markers

These can be bought or you can use loops of contrasting yarn to mark points you may need to locate later.

Large-headed pins

Use these to hold knitted pieces together. Large heads prevent the pins from being lost between the stitches.

Tape measure and ruler

Buy a new tape measure from time to time, as old ones stretch with use and become inaccurate. A ruler is useful for accurately measuring dimensions.

Small sharp scissors

Always use scissors for cutting yarn; never break it between your fingers.

Stitch holders

These are like huge safety-pins. Use them for temporarily holding stitches, such as the neckband stitches on a sweater.

Equivalent weights and measures

US	UK & EUROPE
¾ ounce	20 grams
1 ounce	28 grams
1¾ ounces	50 grams
2 ounces	60 grams
3½ ounces	100 grams
1 inch	2.5 centimetres
4 inches	10 centimetres
39½ inches	1 metre
1 yard	91.5 centimetres

Basic techniques

The basic techniques that you will need in order to start knitting take only minutes to learn, and they will serve you for a lifetime of knitting. Use the techniques shown here, or ask someone to show you how to get started.

Slip knot

Most pieces of knitting begin with a slip knot.

1 Unwind about 12 inches (30 cm) of yarn from the ball and place the tail to your left and the ball to your right. Wind the ball end clockwise around two fingers of your left hand.

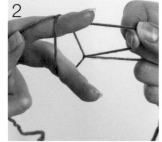

2 Pull a loop from the ball end through the loop on your fingers, from behind.

3 Slip the tip of one needle through the new loop from front to back. Tighten the knot by pulling on the tail and the ball end at the same time. This is the first stitch for many cast-on methods.

Holding yarn and needles

There are many ways to hold your yarn and needles, so it's up to you to use whichever method you prefer. Here are just two ways: the English method is the one used for the photographs in this book, but you may find holding the yarn in your left hand (the Continental method) more comfortable.

The English (right-hand) method

1 Hold the needle with the stitches in your left hand. Your forefinger should be close to the needle tip, with the other three fingers supporting the needle. Put the little finger of your right hand behind the yarn, twist your hand to loop the yarn around your little finger, then lift the yarn with your forefinger, as shown.

2 Pick up the empty needle with your right hand and hold it with your forefinger close to the tip and the other three fingers supporting the needle from below. To wrap the yarn for a stitch, move your right forefinger forwards without completely letting go of the needle.

The Continental (left-hand) method

1 Hold the needle with the stitches in your right hand, with your forefinger close to the needle tip, and your other fingers supporting the needle. Put your left little finger behind the yarn, turn your hand to loop the yarn around your little finger, then lift the yarn with your forefinger, as shown.

2 Transfer this needle to your left hand, and pick up the empty needle in your right hand. Both needles are held with the forefinger near the tip and the other three fingers underneath. Rather than wrap the yarn for a stitch, you catch it with the right needle tip, turning your hands slightly with the palms towards you.

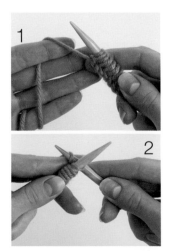

Cable cast-on

1 Make a slip knot (see page 15). Hold the needle with the knot in your left hand and the other needle in your right. Insert the tip of the right needle into the front of the loop from left to right. Wind the ball end of yarn counterclockwise around the tip of this needle, as indicated by the arrow.

2 Pull the new loop towards you, through the old loop.

3 Insert the tip of the left-hand needle into the new loop from right to left, and let the new loop slip off the right needle onto the left needle. Now you have two stitches on the left needle.

4 Insert the tip of the right needle under the left needle, between the stitch you have just made and the one before. Wind the yarn counterclockwise around the right needle.

5 Pull the new loop through and slip it onto the left needle. Now you will have three stitches on the left needle.

6 Repeat steps 4 and 5 until you have the correct number of stitches.

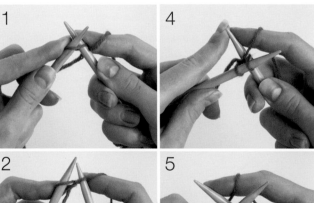

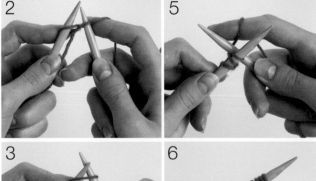

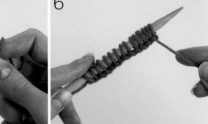

Tip

■ If you require a firmer edge, such as when beginning a garment with garter stitch, work the two-needle cable cast-on as given, then work the first row through the back loops of the stitches instead of the front. This tightens the stitches by twisting them.

Knit a row

If you knit every stitch of every row or purl every stitch of every row, the result is garter stitch. This is the easiest way to knit your shapes.

1 Slip the right needle tip from left to right into the first stitch on the left needle, below the tip of the left needle and in front of the yarn held in your right hand. Take care not to split the stitch with the point of the needle.

2 For the English method, use your right forefinger to carry the yarn counterclockwise around the right needle and between the two needles from left to right. (For the Continental method, catch the yarn from the right with the right needle tip.)

3 Use the right needle tip to pull the loop of yarn towards you, through the first stitch on the left needle.

4 Slip the first stitch off the left needle. One knit stitch is on the right needle.

5 Repeat steps 1, 2, 3 and 4. Every few stitches, push the stitches on the right needle down from the tip to prevent them bunching together in your right hand, and push the stitches on the left needle up towards the tip. When all the stitches from the left needle have been knitted onto the right needle, you have made one row of knit stitches. Move the needle with the stitches to your left hand to begin the next row.

Buttonholes

Buttonholes are often worked by casting off a group of stitches on one row (see page 19), then casting the same number on again on the next row (see page 16). When casting on the new stitches, before you slip the last one onto the left needle, bring the yarn between the needles, to the side of the work facing you, then transfer the last cast-on stitch to the left needle. This will tighten the stitch and make a neater buttonhole.

Purl a row

1 Hold the needle with the stitches in your left hand and the empty needle in your right hand, as before. Hold the yarn in front of the right needle and insert the right needle tip into the first stitch on the left needle, from right to left, in front of the left needle.

2 Use your right forefinger to wrap the yarn counterclockwise around the right needle tip as shown. (For the Continental method, use your left forefinger to wrap the yarn counterclockwise.)

3 With the right needle tip, pull the loop of yarn away from you, through the first stitch.

4 Slip the first stitch off the left needle. One purl stitch is on the right needle.

5 Repeat steps 1 to 4 until all the stitches from the left needle have been worked onto the right needle. You have made one row of purl stitches. Notice how the purl row forms a row of loops on the side of the work facing you. Move the needle with the stitches to your left hand to begin the next row.

1
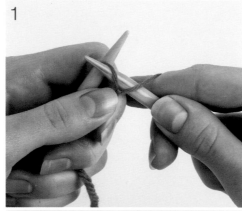

2

3

4

Stitch increases

There are several ways of creating extra stitches but this increase will produce the smoothest edge to the basic square.

1 Knit to the position of the increase, knit into the next stitch on the left-hand needle as usual but without slipping it off the needle.

2 Insert the right needle into the same stitch again, but this time into the back of the stitch and complete the stitch as if to knit. Slip the stitch off the left-hand needle.

Knit two together (abbr. K2tog)

By knitting two stitches together, you create a right-slanting decrease.

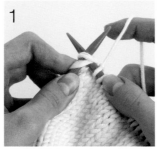

1 Insert the right needle through the fronts of two stitches on the left needle from left to right. Wrap the yarn in the usual way for a knit stitch.

2 Draw the new loop through and drop both stitches together from the left needle.

Purl two together (abbr. P2tog)

Worked on a wrong side row, this decrease also creates a right-slanting decrease on the right side of the work.

1 Insert the tip of the right needle from right to left through two stitches on the left needle.

2 Wrap the yarn in the usual way for a purl stitch.

3 Draw the new loop through, away from you, and allow both stitches to drop from the left needle.

Casting off

Casting off links stitches together at the end of a piece of knitting. You might need to cast off all the stitches, or just a certain number (for example, for an armhole shaping or a buttonhole). A bound-off edge should not be too loose or too tight. It should stretch by about the same amount as the rest of the piece. If you need a looser, more elastic edge, for example, on a neckband, change to a needle one or two sizes larger than used to knit the previous rows.

1 Knit the first two stitches in the usual way onto the right needle. Insert the tip of the left needle from left to right into the front of the first stitch you knitted.

2 Lift the first stitch over the second stitch and off the right needle. One stitch remains on the right needle. You have cast off one stitch. Knit the next stitch. There

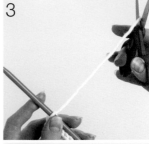

are now two stitches on the right needle. Repeat step 2 as required.

3 When you have cast off all the stitches, you will be left with one stitch on the right needle. Cut the yarn, leaving a tail of at least 6 inches (15 cm).

4 Wrap the tail around the right needle, lift the last stitch over it and pull the tail through to make a neat finish.

How to knit squares

By knitting diagonally, it is very easy to make perfect squares, of the size you want in any yarn. The squares are guaranteed to fit together even when they are made by two or more knitters working on different needles and at a different tension. You can forget about working to a particular tension and use a variety of yarns. The squares will still be the correct size. With yarn, needles and a paper template, you can't go wrong.

The perfect square lies flat so you can measure it easily, has no loopy edges that make it difficult to join, and has nothing to spoil its appearance.

template

Checklist for the perfect square

First, decide on the size you want the square and make a paper template to these dimensions.

1 Knit in garter stitch and have your paper template nearby.
2 On every row knit to the end of the row and knit the last stitch twice to increase the stitches.
3 A triangle starts to appear.
4 Check the triangle against the template.
5 Don't cheat! Don't stretch! When the ends of the triangle match your template, you can start decreasing the stitches.
6 On every row, knit to the last two stitches, then knit the last two together.
7 When you have only two stitches left, knit them together and cast off.
8 You have the perfect square.

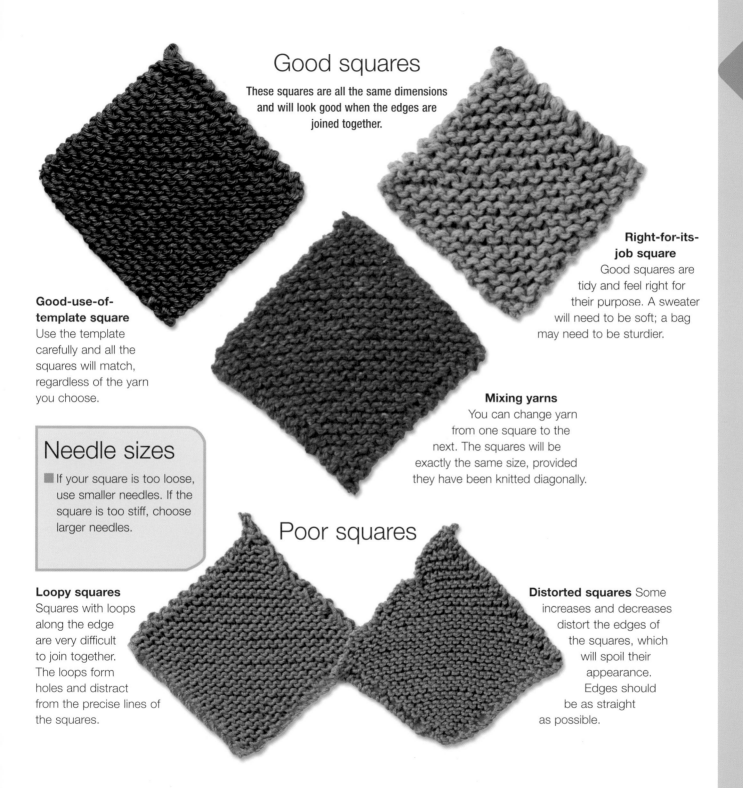

Good squares

These squares are all the same dimensions and will look good when the edges are joined together.

Good-use-of-template square
Use the template carefully and all the squares will match, regardless of the yarn you choose.

Right-for-its-job square
Good squares are tidy and feel right for their purpose. A sweater will need to be soft; a bag may need to be sturdier.

Mixing yarns
You can change yarn from one square to the next. The squares will be exactly the same size, provided they have been knitted diagonally.

Needle sizes

■ If your square is too loose, use smaller needles. If the square is too stiff, choose larger needles.

Poor squares

Loopy squares
Squares with loops along the edge are very difficult to join together. The loops form holes and distract from the precise lines of the squares.

Distorted squares Some increases and decreases distort the edges of the squares, which will spoil their appearance. Edges should be as straight as possible.

Joining shapes

In most conventional knitting patterns, the pieces have extra stitches at the edges for making seams. The shapes in this book do not. They lie edge-to-edge, which is why you can be sure you will finish with the size you want. The edges must not be allowed to overlap at all. There will be no bulky seams and the back of the work will look almost as good as the front.

Coaxing squares into shape

Garter stitch is usually very good-natured. The edges never curl and it will need little blocking to form perfect squares. In many cases a good tug is enough to form a perfect shape. The main exception to this are yarns that have a flat cross-section, such as chenille or ribbon. These may require more coaxing.

Blocking your shapes using an iron in the usual way is not recommended as it will flatten the bumps in the garter stitch and destroy the texture you have created. If you have to block the shapes, try the gentlest methods first.

Spraying and shaping

If you plan to block many shapes, consider making a padded board covered with a check fabric where the shapes can be lined up with the pattern on the fabric. The padding can be old blankets, polyester wadding, foam or anything else suitable for sticking pins into.

Small pieces can be shaped very successfully on a piece of polystyrene packaging. Use your knitting template to mark the same size on the polystyrene. Spray the shape with water (or immerse in water and remove the excess in a towel, if no spray is available). Place the shape on the polystyrene template and insert a pin at each corner. Place the pins at an angle leaning out from the shape. Add extra pins at the centre of each side, and more pins between these, if necessary. Allow to dry.

Steaming and shaping

Very firm shapes may need stronger treatment. Pin the shape in the way just described above and use a steam iron to give blasts of steam to the shape, without actually touching it with the iron. If you have a steam iron with a built-in spray, you can combine the spraying and steaming processes.

Blocking with heat

If all other methods fail to produce perfect squares, use your iron over a clean cloth or absorbent paper towels to press the edges of the square lightly. Be aware that heat will damage some yarns, so pay special attention to any information on the ball bands. Do not use heat if you have used polystyrene or any other plastic for your blocking template.

Joining by stitching

Garter stitch squares and other shapes are very easy to stitch together because the edges are always flat. Even if you normally dislike sewing up a completed garment, do not be afraid to join many small pieces together. The two main methods of stitching are from the back and from the front. Whip stitch is extremely easy, especially for novice sewers. Mattress stitch has the advantage of your being able to see the outcome of every stitch you make.

Whip stitch

This method of sewing from the back is also known as overcasting.

1 Place two squares together with their right sides facing and their corners matching exactly. If you have long lengths of yarn at the corners of your shapes, use them for stitching. Otherwise, use a length of yarn to match one of the squares and attach it firmly to the first corner.

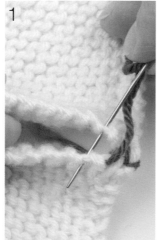

2 Whip stitch over the edge of both squares, working far enough into the squares to make sure they are secure, but not far enough to stop them from lying flat, side by side, when you open them up.

Mattress stitch

Place the two shapes side by side. If they are large pieces, or have special points that must be linked, you may want to use safety-pins to hold them loosely together.

1 Use any connected yarns or securely attach a new length of yarn. Start at the bottom edge and pass the needle through the top of the first stitch on one square, then through the bottom of the matching stitch on the other square.

2 Work a few stitches in this way, then pull the yarn gently until the stitches close together, giving an almost-invisible join. Continue until the whole seam is closed, then bind off.

Tips for joining

■ The order in which you join the squares will vary from one project to another. Some ways might be easier than others, but the end result will be the same. It is particularly important to match corners, whether they point inward or outward. Sometimes the corners seem to need more stretching than other parts. Flatten or smooth them out as you stitch rather than allowing them to form bulges or hollows.

■ When all of the shapes are squares it is generally easier to join them into rows first and then to join the rows together.

Joining by crochet

Crocheting shapes together is a dual-purpose method. It joins the shapes and gives a decorative finish. It is not a good idea to put the pieces back-to-back and crochet through both pieces. This creates a seam that falls to one side or the other, and can distort your item or make it look unbalanced.

1 Place the squares side by side and work with the joining yarn at the back and the hook at the front. Make a slip knot and pull it through to the front with the hook.

2 Insert the hook into the corresponding stitch on the other square, pull a loop of yarn through the block, and then loop on the hook.

3 Continue in this way, alternating between the squares, pulling through a loop each time. When you get to the end, break off the yarn, pull the end through the last loop, and fasten it securely by pulling the end through a few of the stitches at the back.

Two sample squares joined together using crochet. A contrast yarn is used for clarity.

Diagonal	Edge	Diagonal	Edge
10	7	25	18
11	8	26	18
12	8	27	19
13	9	28	20
14	10	29	21
15	11	30	21
16	11	31	22
17	12	32	23
18	13	33	23
19	13	34	24
20	14	35	25
21	15	36	25
22	16	37	26
23	16	38	27
24	17	39	28

This chart tells you the number of stitches you need for the side of the square, when you know the number of stitches in the diagonal.

Joining shapes as you work

There are many instances where a new shape can be knitted directly onto an existing shape and you will need to pick up stitches from the first shape. There are three ways to do this: picking up stitches from the edge of diagonally knitted square; picking up stitches along the edge of a straight piece of knitting, or picking up one stitch at a time from an existing shape.

Picking up stitches from the edge of a diagonally knitted square

Work out the number of stitches you need to pick up from the edge of the square by using the chart on page 26. Pick up these stitches, taking care to get the first and last stitches at the corners, as follows:

1 With the right side of the shape facing, insert only one needle into the firm part of the knot at the end of the ridge. Pull through a loop of yarn and keep it on the right-hand needle to create the first stitch. Repeat in the second ridge.

2 In the same way, pick up a stitch in the end of the furrow before the next ridge, pulling the yarn through the firmest part so that you don't create a hole. If you have difficulty picking up the stitches with your knitting needle, pull each loop of yarn through using a crochet hook and slip the loops onto your knitting needle as you go.

3 Pick up one stitch from each of the third and fourth ridges. As in step 2, pick up a stitch in the end of the furrow before the next ridge, pulling the yarn through the firmest part. Pick up one stitch. You should now have seven stitches. Repeat for each set of five ridges.

The ridges formed from the pick-up stitches will create a horizontal ridged square.

Picking up stitches from a straight edge

The width of one stitch, in garter stitch, is equal to the height of one garter ridge. (A ridge is made up of two rows.) If your knitting has a completely straight edge, pick up one stitch from the end of each of the ridges.

1 Pick up one stitch from each of the cast-off stitches.

2 You should now have picked up all the stitches.

3 This shows the beginning of the new square, from the picked-up stitches.

The ridges on the new square are in the same direction as the first.

1

2

3

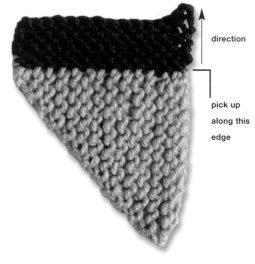

direction

pick up along this edge

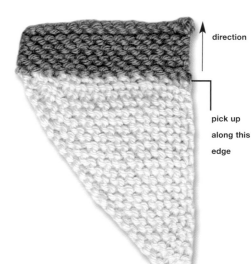

direction

pick up along this edge

Picking up one stitch at a time from an existing shape

There are three different circumstances when you might want to use this technique.

1 You need an extra stitch. Instead of increasing at the end of the row in the usual way, pick up the extra stitch from the corresponding ridge of the existing shape.

2 You need to keep the same number of stitches as before. Pick up one stitch from the existing piece. (You now have one more stitch than you need.) At the start of the next row, knit two together. Using this method, the join on the wrong side looks as good as that on the right side.

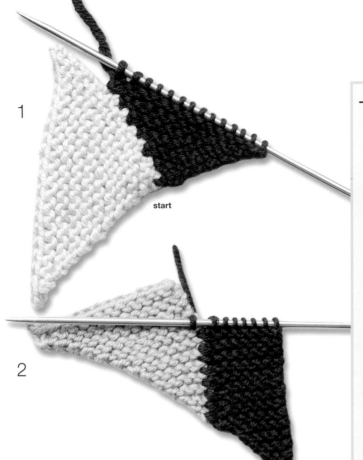

1

start

2

start

3

start

3 You need to decrease by one. Knit together the last two stitches of the row, where it is about to join the existing piece. Pick up one from the existing piece. (You now have the same number of stitches as before.) At the start of the next row, slip the first stitch, knit the second stitch, and pass the slipped stitch over. In some yarns this join can be rather bulky and may be better left unjoined, then stitched later.

Tip

As a general rule, every five ridges of garter stitch has to produce seven stitches. Five of these are from the ends of the ridges and the others from between ridges 1 and 2, and ridges 4 and 5.

GETTING THE CORRECT NUMBER OF STITCHES

Divide the number of stitches you had at the widest part (the diagonal) of your square by 1.4. Round the answer to the nearest whole number. This is the number of stitches needed along the side of the square.

Square variations

Squares don't have to be plain and uninteresting. Spectacular designs can be made by using two or more colours in each square and then arranging the squares in different ways. You will be surprised by the number of patterns you can create with a batch of similar squares. Try various arrangements with your squares before you reach a final decision about your design.

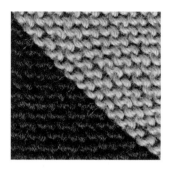

Make the first half of the square, increasing one stitch at the end of every row. Break off the yarn, leaving a long end for seaming. Using the second colour, knit one row even. Complete the square by decreasing at the end of every row.

Sawtooth – *all squares in the same orientation.*

Windmills – *repeated block of four squares.*

Large pinwheel – *rotated block of four squares.*

Eight-pointed star – *rotated block of four squares.*

Arrowheads – *rotated block of four squares.*

Light and shadow – *block of four in two orientations.*

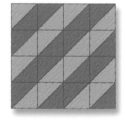

Stripes – *alternate up and down squares.*

Butterflies – *rotated block of four squares.*

Zigzags – *repeated block of four squares.*

Parallelograms – *rotated block of four squares.*

Square in square – *rotated block of four squares.*

Pinwheels – *repeated block of four squares.*

Table and chairs – *rotated block of four squares.*

Using the first colour, begin the square as before. Continue until you have half the number of stitches needed at the widest point. Change to the second colour and complete the first half of the square. Using the first colour, work one row even, then decrease on every row and complete as for a plain square.

Hidden windmill – *rotated block of four squares.*

Make the first half of the square as above. Change to the first colour. Knit one row even, then decrease on every row until you have the same number of stitches as when you changed colour on the first half. Complete the square in the second colour.

Candy stripes – *all squares in the same orientation.*

Shadow Xs – *repeated block of four squares.*

X – *block of eight squares and rotation.*

Honeycomb – *repeated block of four squares.*

Catherine wheel – *rotated block of four squares.*

Split chevrons – *repeated block of two squares.*

Tip

 Always change colour on the same side of the work.

making other shapes

In this chapter...

How to knit triangles

A square can be cut in half diagonally to form two identical triangles. The angles of this triangle will always be the same size regardless of the length of the sides.

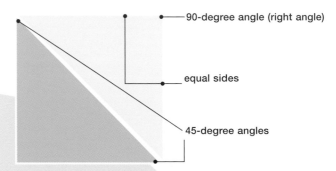

90-degree angle (right angle)

equal sides

45-degree angles

Template

Three methods of knitting a triangle

The first half of the basic square
- Make a slip knot and knit into it twice.
- **Every row**: knit to the last stitch; knit into the last stitch twice.
- Continue until the triangle is the size you want; then cast off loosely, using a larger needle. (The edge must not pull tight and distort the triangle.)

Reverse method
If you know how wide the triangle has to be, work the triangles in reverse, starting from the widest part.
- Cast on, or pick up, the required number of stitches.
- **Every row**: knit to the last two stitches; knit two together.
- Continue until two stitches remain. Knit two together.
- Cast off.

Ridges at right angles to half basic square
- Make a slip knot and knit into it twice.
- **Next row**: knit.
- **Next row**: knit to the last stitch; knit into the last stitch twice.
- Repeat these two rows until you reach the half-way point of the triangle.
- **Next row**: knit.
- **Next row**: knit to the last two stitches; knit two together.
- Repeat these two rows until two stitches remain. Knit two together. Cast off.

finish   direction   start

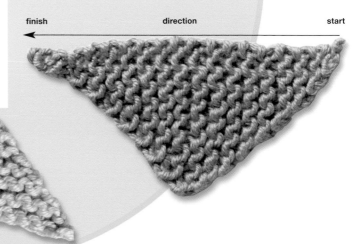

finish

direction

start

Increase at one side and keep the other side straight

- ■ Make a slip knot and knit into it twice.
- ■ **Next row**: knit.
- ■ **Next row**: knit to the last stitch; knit into the last stitch twice.
- ■ Repeat these two rows until the triangle is the size you want. Cast off loosely.

Reverse method

If you know how wide the triangle has to be, work the triangles in reverse, starting from the widest part.
- ■ Cast on the required number of stitches.
- ■ **Next row**: knit.
- ■ **Next row**: knit to the last two stitches; knit two together.
- ■ Repeat these two rows until two stitches remain. Knit two together. Cast off.

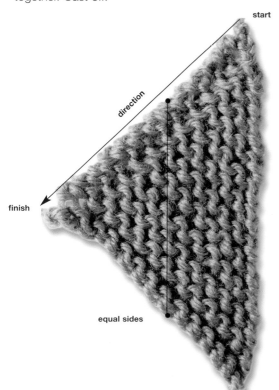

start

direction

finish

equal sides

Combining triangles

Triangles can be combined to form squares. When knitted in different directions, the textures and shadows created by garter stitch ridges create an interesting texture.

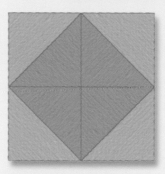

Looking in – four rotated squares.

Pinwheels – four rotated squares.

Arrows – four squares in the same orientation.

Corners – four squares rotated.

Criss-cross – four squares in the same orientation.

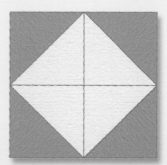

Looking out – four squares rotated.

33

Simple shapes with four sides

Many four-sided shapes can be made very easily, using the same simple methods as for making squares. These shapes can be fitted together without any further calculations or complicated shaping. Learn to make these basic shapes and you will be able to combine them in arrangements of your own.

Patterns made by fitting small shapes together are known as tessellations. Once you know how to create the shapes, have fun creating different patterns.

In order to use four-sided shapes, you may need some information about each of them and to know which can be made using the methods learned so far.

Four-sided shapes

A four-sided shape is also called a quadrilateral. The four-sided shapes dealt with in this book are detailed below.

*A **square** has four equal sides and four 90-degree angles (right angles). It has two pairs of parallel sides. See page 20.*

*A **rectangle** has four right angles and two pairs of parallel sides. See page 36.*

*A **lozenge** has four equal sides and two pairs of parallel sides with angles of 45 and 135 degrees. See page 41.*

*A **diamond** is simply a square or rhombus turned to stand on its point.*

*A **parallelogram** has two pairs of parallel sides, with angles of 45 and 135 degrees. It is like a rectangle that has been pushed over. See page 40.*

*A **trapezoid** has one pair of parallel sides. The other two sides can slope inward, outward or straight up, at angles of 45, 90 or 135 degrees. See page 38.*

Which shapes can you make?

For ease of fit, and to make use of the methods learned so far, use only shapes that have 45- and 90-degree angles.

Squares – any size.

Rectangles – any size.

Rhombuses – any size but only with 45-degree angles.

Parallelograms – any size but only with 45-degree angles.

Trapezoids – any size but only with 45- and 90-degree angles.

Stick to these shapes and it is just as easy to make a random pattern as it is to make a repeating pattern.

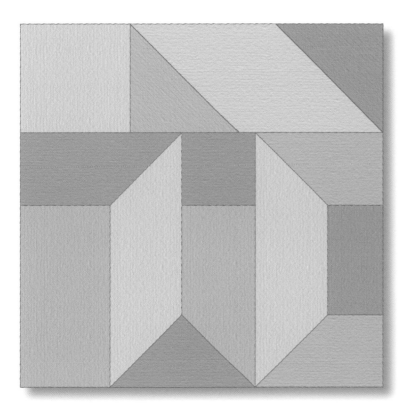

It is very easy to combine all these different shapes. All that matters is that you should make each shape slope in the right direction to fit with the others. The diagrams show how to determine the techniques needed.

Designing other shapes

You already know all the techniques needed to start creating other shapes. There are only three possibilities at each side of the shape: straight, increase, decrease.

The diagrams show all the combinations.

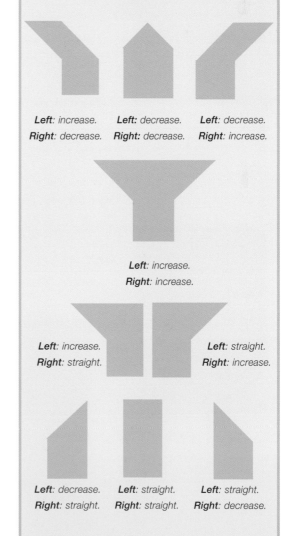

Left: *increase.*
Right: *decrease.*

Left: *decrease.*
Right: *decrease.*

Left: *decrease.*
Right: *increase.*

Left: *increase.*
Right: *increase.*

Left: *increase.*
Right: *straight.*

Left: *straight.*
Right: *increase.*

Left: *decrease.*
Right: *straight.*

Left: *straight.*
Right: *straight.*

Left: *straight.*
Right: *decrease.*

How to knit rectangles

A rectangle is a simple block shape with four square corners and two pairs of parallel sides. A square is a special kind of rectangle, so most of the rules for knitting a rectangle are the same as those for knitting a square.

Knitting a rectangle

- Increase at the end of every row, as for the beginning of a square, until the short sides of the triangle are the size you want for the width of your rectangle, finishing at the right-hand side.
- **Next row**: knit to the last stitch; knit into the last stitch twice.
- **Next row**: knit to the last two stitches; knit two together.
- (The left-hand edge continues to slope as before; the right-hand

edge starts to slope in the same direction, creating the parallel sides.)
- Repeat these two rows until the longest edge of the shape is the height of the rectangle you want, finishing at the right-hand side.
- **Next row**: knit to the last two stitches; knit two together.
- Repeat this row until there are two stitches remaining. Knit two together and cast off.

Adding interest
To add textural interest, you may want the garter stitch ridges running in the opposite direction. If you are working with plain rectangles, you can simply turn them over to get the texture you want.

For multicoloured rectangles, reverse all shaping.

start

start

start

start

finish

finish

finish

finish

▲▶ *Identical rectangles facing opposite ways.*

◀▲ *Two-colour rectangles with shaping reversed.*

Fitting rectangles together

Rectangles can be any width and any length. Those that are twice as high as they are wide fit together very well in different directions.

Use rectangles in groups of two to create squares.

Stagger rectangles to create a step pattern.

Two- and three-colour rectangles

Use two colours in each rectangle to make more patterns.

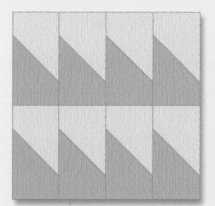

Identical rectangles.

Rectangles made in different directions.

The same rectangles with some turned around.

Add stripes to create even more possibilities.

Rectangles with coloured corner and stripe.

Similar rectangles in off-set pattern.

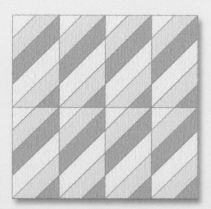

Striped rectangles facing the same way.

How to knit trapezoids

A trapezoid has one pair of parallel sides. The other two sides can go in any direction. Using the rules of this book, there is a limit to the number of variations that can be made, though each can be turned round or over. They can be made to any length and width you want. There are two main types:

1 Trapezoids with right angles
2 Trapezoids without right angles

Each type can be knitted in any of three directions, as detailed here.

start

finish

start

finish

start

finish

start

Methods for knitting trapezoids with right angles

Starting at the 45-degree point (right, top)

■ Make a slip knot and knit into it twice.
■ **Next row**: knit.
■ **Next row**: knit to the last stitch; knit into the last stitch twice.
■ Repeat these two rows until you have the width you want for the trapezoid.
■ Knit straight until you have the size you want.
■ Cast off loosely.

Reverse method

■ If you know how wide the trapezoid is to be, it can be made starting from the widest part.
■ Cast on the required number of stitches.

■ Knit straight until you reach the point where the slope should begin.
■ **Next row**: knit to the last two stitches; knit two together. Repeat these two rows until two stitches remain. Knit two together.
■ Cast off.

Starting at the 90-degree point (right, centre)

■ Increase at the end of every row, as for the beginning of a square, until the short side of the triangle is the size you want for the width of your trapezoid.
■ At one edge, continue increasing in the same way.
■ At the other edge, knit two together at the end of the row. (One edge continues to slope as before; the other edge starts to form a line parallel to it.)

■ Repeat these two rows until the longest edge of the shape is the height of the trapezoid you want.
■ Cast off loosely.

Reverse method

■ Cast on the number of stitches required for the sloping edge and reverse all shaping.

Starting at one of the parallel sides (right, below)

■ Cast on the number of stitches needed for the straight edge.
■ Knit straight at one side and increase or decrease, depending on whether the shape is to get wider or narrower, on alternate rows at the other edge.

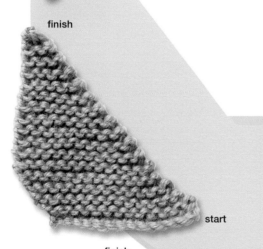

finish

start

finish

start

finish

start

Methods for knitting trapezoids without right angles

Starting at the 45-degree point (left, top)
■ Work as for a right angle trapezoids but do not cast off.
■ Continue knitting with no shaping at the straight edge and decreasing on alternate rows on the other edge.

Starting at a sloping side (left, centre)
■ Cast on the number of stitches needed. Increase at one side and decrease at the other until the short side is the correct length.
■ Continue to decrease at one side, knit straight at the other until two stitches remain. Knit two together and cast off.

Starting at one of the parallel sides (left, below)
■ Cast on the number of stitches needed. Increase or decrease at the end of every row, depending on whether the shape is to get wider or narrower.

Mixing shapes

This arrangement is particularly useful because the addition of a small square will create a larger square. These can then be put together to give interesting effects.

How to knit parallelograms and lozenges

A parallelogram has two pairs of parallel sides. Using the methods learned so far, parallelograms can be any length or width but will all slope at the same angle – 45 degrees. A lozenge is simply a parallelogram with all four sides of equal length. For our purposes, we will only use lozenges and parallelograms with 45-degree angles. Both shapes are very useful for tessellating.

Knitting a parallelogram

Starting at any of the sides
- Cast on the number of stitches needed for the straight edge.
- **Next row**: knit to the last stitch; knit into the stitch twice.
- **Next row**: knit to the last two stitches; knit two together.
- Repeat these two rows until the parallelogram is the height you want.
- Cast off loosely.

Starting at the point
- Knit straight at one edge; increase at the end of alternate rows at the other edge.
- When the parallelogram is the width you want, knit straight until the longer edge is the length you want.
- Continue knitting straight at the shorter edge and decreasing at the other edge.
- Continue until two stitches remain. Knit two together. Cast off.

finish

start

finish

start

Mixing shapes

Some interesting arrangements can be made using identical lozenges . . . or add squares or triangles in the spaces to make larger motifs.

Rose made entirely from lozenges.

Star with lozenges and squares.

The same design with four of the squares changed to triangles.

Knitting a lozenge

Starting at any of the sides

■ Work as for a parallelogram. To find the height: divide the number of cast on stitches by 1.4 (see table on page 44). The answer tells you the number of garter ridges to knit. Remember that one ridge is two rows of garter stitch.

Starting at the point

■ Work as for a parallelogram. When the rhombus is the width you want, count the number of stitches on the needle. Divide this number by 1.4. Knit even for this number of ridges, then decrease at the opposite edge from where you increased, knitting straight at the other edge.

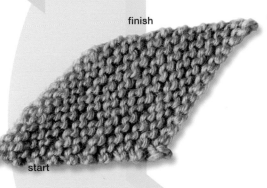

finish

start

start

Using lozenge strips

■ Narrow strips are useful because you can keep adding more if you change your mind about the size of the garment you are making, and you can use up scraps of yarn.

■ These strips can also be used as a bias binding for edging a garment. They are less bulky than straight strips and can add interest.

■ Take care not to stretch strips. Narrow pieces are much more likely than wider pieces to stretch during construction.

Tessellating parallelograms

Parallelograms and lozenges can easily become plain or colourful strips, with a variety of uses.

A continuous strip of small parallelograms. Use two or more colours for a repeating pattern.

Reverse the shaftings on alternate strips.

Start and end with a triangle to make a long rectangle.

Pick up stitches along the edge of the strip to knit in another direction, or add a border.

How to knit hexagons

It is not possible to make a regular hexagon using the rules learned so far, but you can make an elongated hexagon. The shape is like the two halves of a square with a straight piece in between. It can be any length and any width. The height of each of the points is half the width of the hexagon.

A hexagon is essentially a square or rectangle with a triangle at each end.

Methods for knitting hexagons

Starting at a point
■ Start with a slip knot and increase at the end of every row until the hexagon is the width you want.
■ Knit straight until the hexagon is the height you want, remembering that the second point will add extra height.
■ Decrease at the end of every row until two stitches remain. Knit two together and cast off.

finish

start

Starting at an edge parallel to the diagonal between the points
■ Cast on the required number of stitches. Increase at the end of every row until the hexagon is the width you want.
■ Decrease at the end of every row until you have one more stitch than you had at the start. Cast off, knitting the last two stitches together as you go.

finish

start

Note
■ You could knit a hexagon starting at an edge at right angles to a point, but this method is complicated as it varies, depending on the proportions of the hexagon.

finish

start

An elongated hexagon can make an interesting centre for a square

- To add textural interest and to make the square symmetrical, it is best to start at a point.
- The total height (from point to point) of the hexagon is the same as the length of the diagonal of the square it is to fit in.
- The width of the square will be this measurement divided by 1.4. Calculate the number of stitches that would be needed for the diagonal of the square. Make the hexagon by starting at the point. Increase until you have the width you want. Count the stitches on the needle. Subtract this number from the number calculated for the diagonal of the square. Knit straight for this number of garter ridges. Decrease to make the other point.
- To complete the square: pick up one stitch from each of the straight garter stitch rows and decrease at the end of every row. Repeat on the other side of the hexagon.

Using hexagons as a basis for other shapes

Hexagons can be used as starting shapes. There are many ways to include them in a design.

Vary the width of the hexagons and fit the squares together.

 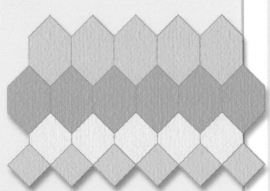

An arrangement of identical hexagons in a range of colours can be very dramatic and good for using up scraps of yarn.

Try mixing hexagons of different heights, and perhaps some squares.

Turning hexagons at right angles to each other will form a square frame that can be filled in with more hexagons or other shapes.

How to knit octagons

The simple methods used to create shapes so far work because they have been based on using multiples of 1.4. The same methods can be used to make an octagon, combining it with the measurements of a straight square. Octagons are wonderful for adding a little flair to a pattern.

Method for knitting octagons

This shape is a little more difficult to make because all eight sides have to be the same length. The 1.4 rule is very important. Try making this small octagon before you venture on to making other octagons.

Make a practice octagon

- Cast on 10 stitches.
- Knit to the last stitch; knit into the last stitch twice.
- Repeat this row until you have knitted 7 ridges (because 10 divided by 1.4 is 7).
- You will now have 24 stitches.
- Knit straight for 10 ridges (this matches the number of cast-on stitches).
- **Next row:** knit to the last two stitches; knit two together.
- Repeat this row until you have 11 stitches (one more than the number of cast-on stitches).
- Cast off, knitting the last two stitches together as you go.

Making your own octagon

- To make an octagon to the size you require, the only calculation you need to do is to divide the number of cast-on stitches by **1.4**. On the diagram this is called **a/1.4**. The number of cast-on stitches is called **a**. Substitute the numbers from your own calculation or use the chart.

- Cast on your chosen number of stitches (**a** from the diagram).
- Knit **a/1.4** ridges, knitting twice into the last stitch of every row.
- Knit straight for **a** rows.
- Continue, knitting two together at the end of every row until you have one more stitch than you cast on. Cast off, knitting the last two stitches together.

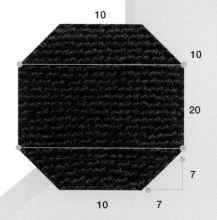

a (cast-on stitches)	a/1.4 (cast-on stitches divided by 1.4)
10	7
11	8
12	8
13	9
14	10
15	11
16	11
17	12
18	13
19	13
20	14
21	15
22	16
23	16
24	17
25	18
26	18
27	19
28	20
29	21

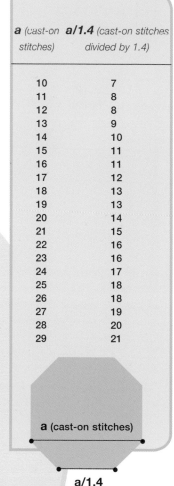

a (cast-on stitches)

a/1.4
(cast-on stitches divided by 1.4)

Note

- 2 rows of garter stitch make 1 ridge.
- 1 ridge is the same width as 1 stitch.

Fitting octagons

Octagons will not fit on their own, but they can be joined to two other shapes.

Edge-to-edge

When you join the octagons edge-to-edge, you need squares to fill the spaces.

The squares are **a** stitches across their straight edges or **1.4** times **a** across their diagonals.

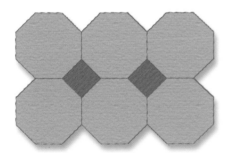

Point-to-point

Join octagons point-to-point and the holes that are left are four-pointed stars.

The angles at the points of the star are 45 degrees, but it is extremely difficult to make the star in one piece (if using only the methods learned so far). However, it can be split into a small square surrounded by four trapezoids.

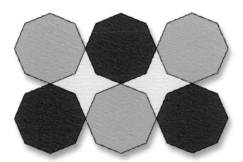

Stars with a square and four trapezoids

It is possible to begin the star with the square, then pick up the stitches for the trapezoid, but the easier way of getting the correct size is to make the pieces separately and stitch them together.

- Make the four trapezoids first.
- Use your calculations for the octagon.
- The straight sides will be **a** ridges, the width will be **a/1.4**.
- Make a slip knot and knit into it twice.
- **Next row:** knit.
- **Next row:** knit to the last stitch; knit twice into the last stitch.
- Repeat these two rows until you have **a/1.4** stitches.
- Knit straight until the total number of ridges is **a**. Cast off loosely.
- Stitch the four trapezoids as shown on the completed star, matching ridges from one with stitches from the next.
- Knit a small basic square to fit the remaining hole. Sew in place.

Note

Octagons cover more space when joined point-to-point. The width from point-to-point is 2.6 times the length of one side.

Making octagons from shapes

The octagons can be made up from combinations of other shapes.

A square surrounded by rectangles and triangles.

This large square touches the edges of the octagon. The extra shapes are trapezoids.

A square, four triangles, and four lozenges give the impression of a rotating star within an octagon.

45

Alternative ways of creating squares

The method you have learned for making a square is probably the easiest, especially for a beginner, but it certainly isn't the only way.

Using the same basic method, there are many ways of increasing and decreasing at the beginning or end of rows. A good knitting "encyclopedia" will show you lots of methods you might like to try, including slightly holey, lacy edges.

Some people dislike constantly turning the work when making small pieces. Using very short needles sometimes helps. Cut down a longer pair of needles, if necessary. Another solution is to learn to knit backwards so you never need to turn the work.

Other ways to create a square

Straight square

■ Cast on the number of stitches you need.
■ Knit straight for the same number of garter ridges.
■ Cast off.

For this method, you need to know the gauge that will give you the right size square before you begin.

1

2

3

Square on double-pointed needles

1 Working in rounds, knitting every round does not result in garter stitch. It creates stocking stitch and the proportions of the stitches will not be the same. The square will quickly stop lying flat. If you want to try it, you will need extra increases.

2 You can work around and around if you knit one round and purl the next. The result will be garter stitch.

3 Cast on eight stitches and join them into a ring. If using double-pointed needles, put two stitches on each of four needles and knit with a fifth. Increase at both ends of each needle until the square is the size you want. If working on circular needles, divide the stitches with markers.

Magic or mitred squares

There are many books
available where mitred
squares are explained in
detail. They can be knitted
from the outside in or from
the centre. Starting at the
outside reveals the magic of
the squares as a straight
row of knitting gradually
turns into a square. It is also
very easy to connect
squares together by picking
up stitches from one to start
the next. Starting from the
centre has the advantage
that you can adjust the size
without having worked out
your tension first.

From the outside in

1 Cast on an even number
of stitches and put a
marker between the two
centre stitches.

2 **Row 1**: knit, knitting two
together at each side of
the marker.
Row 2: knit. Repeat these
two rows until two stitches
are left. Knit two together
and cast off.

From the centre out

1 Cast on two stitches and put a
marker between them. Knit every row,
increasing in the stitch immediately before
the marker.

2 Continue in this way until the square
is the size you want. Cast off loosely,
or keep the stitches on a spare needle if
you intend to knit another shape directly
onto them.

Raised shapes

You will want to produce a tidy outline shape to fit your overall plan for the item you are making (see pages 64–67), but within that outline you can add raised shapes.

If the shape stands out too far from the background, it may sag and get pushed around as you wear your garment. The tighter you knit, the less likely this is to happen.

Generally, the shapes need to be surrounded and supported by some firm, flat shapes. In order to decide how to make these raised surfaces, it is best to think of the hole you need to fill and what the outside of it looks like.

Creating raised shapes

Make a raised shape using different thicknesses of yarn

1 Using bulky yarn, cast on 10 stitches and knit a triangle that is straight on one side and sloping at 45 degrees at the others. This triangle will be more flexible if you knit quite loosely.

Using a thinner yarn, pick up 14 stitches along the sloping edge. Next row: knit to last stitch; knit twice into last stitch. Repeat until you have 20 stitches. Next row: knit to last two stitches; knit two together. Repeat until all stitches are worked off.

2 Using a thinner yarn, pick up 10 stitches from the cast-on stitches of the triangle and 7 stitches from the shorter edge of shape 2 (17 stitches total). Knit straight for 4½ ridges. Cast off loosely on the wrong side.

3 Using thinner yarn, pick up 7 stitches from the other short edge of shape 2, 10 stitches from the ends of the ridges of shape 1, and 5 stitches from the ends of the ridges of shape 3 (22 stitches). Knit straight for 4½ ridges. Cast off loosely on the wrong side.

1

2

3

Other ways to create raised shapes

There are many other ways to make raised shapes. Here are two ideas for distorting the surface within a shape.

Irregular shaping

1 Knit backwards and forwards at random.

2 Knit a few stitches. Turn. Knit back a few stitches. Turn. Repeat this process as often as you want. Whenever you decide to knit to the edge of the shape, remember to do the normal shaping.

More regular shaping

1 Knit twice into some of the stitches. Knit straight on the next row. On the next row either increase again or decrease, depending on the effect you want to create.

2 The effects will differ according to your yarn and the size of the shape you are making. Experimentation is the best way to find an effect you like.

Tips for raised shapes

■ Always knit at least two rows at the start, with only the normal shaping.

■ Never use the first two or last two stitches as part of the distortion.

■ Never have fewer stitches than you would have in the "normal" shape.

■ Whenever you reach the edge of the shape, remember to do the normal shaping.

1

2

1

2

Combining shapes to fit

In order to join shapes together around a point, all the angles of the corners must add up to 360 degrees. To keep things simple, all of the shapes used so far are made from 45-, 90-, and 135-degree angles. Shapes with these angles can be in any order around the point. It is worth thinking about this at an early stage in your design.

Joining the shapes around a point

Where shapes meet around a point, there can be a minimum of three shapes and a maximum of eight.

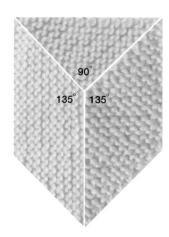

Joining three pieces together

If three shapes meet at a point, two of them must have 135-degree angles and the other one must be 90 degrees. No other combination will result in the 360 degrees needed to make a full circle around the point.

Joining four pieces together

There are three different possible combinations of angles when four shapes meet at a point.

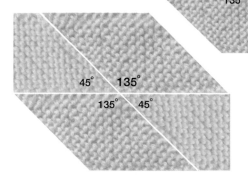

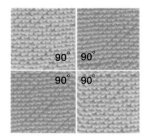

Joining five pieces together

There are two combinations using five shapes.

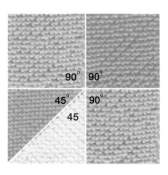

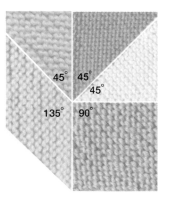

Joining six pieces together

There are two combinations of six shapes.

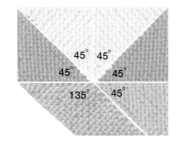

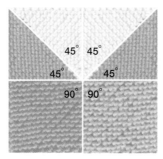

Joining seven or eight pieces together

There is only one possible combination each for joining seven and eight shapes.

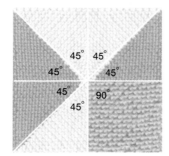

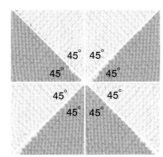

Using small shapes to make a block

Combine any small shapes to make a block. Ensure that the angles at each point add up to 360 degrees. Make several identical blocks and arrange them in different ways.

Swapping the order

There are many possibilities if you change the arrangement of the blocks and even more when you start to change the colours.

Turn individual blocks.

The block can be repeated with all blocks facing the same way . . .

. . . or some rows can be turned the opposite way.

Turning the whole design on its side makes it look different again.

51

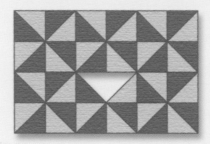

colour and design

In this chapter...

Colour

The use of colour is a very personal choice. Everyone has likes and dislikes, often for reasons that can't be explained. A good way of choosing colour combinations is to base them on something you have seen and liked. For instance, a peach or nectarine is not peach-coloured. The skin can be made up of flecks of many shades, ranging from pale orange to the deepest red. The colours work well in nature; they work equally well in yarns.

Choosing colours from pictures

If you don't see anything around you, look at the photographs in a magazine for inspiration. Make a small card frame and place it over different parts of the picture so that you are seeing only colours, not the subject. Cut out and keep any areas that appeal to you.

There will often be several very close shades in a

chosen area and you might want to work with these, not just the obvious main colours. Use roughly the same proportion of each colour in your item as there is in the picture.

There are a huge number of plain yarns available, even before you start to consider other variables such as thickness and fibre. Most yarn manufacturers produce shade cards.

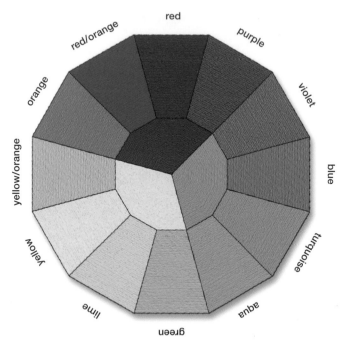

red

red/orange

purple

orange

violet

yellow/orange

blue

yellow

turquoise

lime

aqua

green

▲ *The colour wheel shown above is an arrangement of colours that demonstrates the basic elements of colour theory. This standard wheel displays the primary colours (red, yellow, and blue) on the inside circle, with secondary colours on the outside circle.*

▲▶ *Choose colours from within the same palette. Shown above, a pastel palette, and right, a brighter palette.*

◀ *When looking in magazines for inspiration, use a card frame to isolate key colours.*

You can find every colour in a wide range of shades and textures. Create your own shade card or use the manufacturer's.

Same yarn, with direction changed.

Different yarns from the same manufacturer.

Assorted yarns provide contrast.

Using the same yarn

The same yarn worked in different directions usually looks as though you have used closely matched shades. The light is reflected at various angles to give different impressions. This is particularly true of textured stitches like garter stitch.

Using different types of yarn from the same manufacturer

Choose yarns from the same manufacturer in the same shade but different fibres. For example, a woollen yarn will look slightly different from a cotton yarn dyed with the same colour, because the fibres absorb and reflect light differently. Some people might consider this to be a matter of texture, not colouring. It can be difficult to separate the two, but it really doesn't matter as long as you like the effect you get.

Using different types of yarn from different manufacturers

Combine yarns from various manufacturers. Many ranges of yarn change with fashion trends and you will find that manufacturers often include very similar colours. A good yarn shop will stock several ranges and you can mix and match from them.

Tips for combining yarn

■ Stick to standard thicknesses of yarn because the novelty yarns often work to a different tension from others. You will not be able to create shapes in regular sizes when the yarns don't match.

■ When you wash your finished item, follow the instructions for the yarn that needs the most gentle treatment.

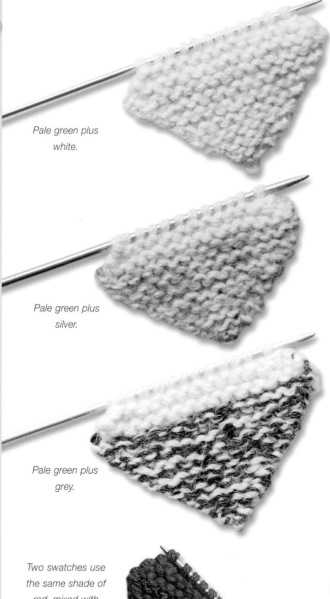

Pale green plus white.

Pale green plus silver.

Pale green plus grey.

Make your own subtle yarns

Use one basic yarn throughout and mix a variety of thinner yarns with it to change the overall appearance. There are so many possible combinations, it is impossible to say what effect you will get in each case. It is a matter of experimentation.

A pale colour needs very little extra colour to change it. For example, if you are working with a pale green yarn and add a white yarn in some shapes, a silver-grey yarn in others and a darker grey in the rest, you will have three noticeably different shades. The added yarn can be of any thickness, but it is best if it is thinner than the starting yarn. You must add a second strand to all shapes. Do not make any in the original yarn by itself. Treat the combined yarns as one.

Dark blue yarn mixed with three different reds will give three shades of purple in much the same way as mixing paint. Try twisting the yarns together to get an idea of the result.

Note

■ When you are assessing colours, half-close your eyes so you are seeing the overall effect. You will immediately spot anything that looks out of place. When you have mixed yarns, you will see a tweedy, flecked effect close-up and a more blended effect from further away. You don't have to be subtle!

Two swatches use the same shade of red, mixed with blues. Two use the same shade of blue; one mixed with red, the other with brown.

Experimenting and using other colours

You will find many books about colour in the arts and crafts sections of your library. It is not necessary to know or use the technical terms. Some people find them helpful; others prefer to work with what they already know. Everyone understands words such as light, dark, bright, dull, vibrant and muted, and they are particularly easy to use as comparisons. We can all say whether one yarn is darker or paler than another without having to explain how or why. Use your own instincts.

If you are making garments for yourself, you know which colours suit you best. That doesn't mean you can't ever use other colours though – just use them in smaller amounts, away from your face.

Neutral colours

We tend to think of white/cream/beige shades as neutral, but these are often too insignificant and make a design look washed out. Very dark shades can also be considered to be neutral. The darkest shades of navy, brown, purple or green are the perfect foil for many colour schemes.

Harmonious effect

When you want colours to blend together, choose all pale, or all dark, or all bright, and so on. Alternatively, choose several shades from the same area of a colour wheel. Squint at your chosen colours and reject any that stand out from the rest.

Contrasting colours

Choose contrasting colours to add vivacity and vibrancy to your design.

Harmonious effect, achieved by using complementary colours, gives a calm feel to the design.

Contrasting effect, producing a more vibrant feel.

The same shade of pink mixed with two different blues.

How many colours do you need?

The number of colours depends very much on your design and the effect you are trying to create. If the object is to colour a pattern without any adjacent pieces being the same, you will never need more than four colours. Of course, you can choose to use more.

A chequerboard design needs only two colours.

A staggered design needs three.

Experiment with the colours you happen to have. You may be surprised by the results.

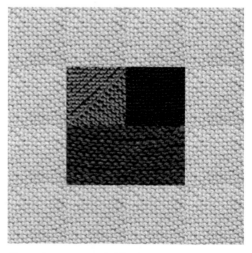

Four colours are needed for this complex design.

Arranging the colours

These strips show you some of the possibilities for arranging colour. Unless you are knitting scarves, you are not likely to be making strips of squares.

When you have two colours, you can make two different patterns (although you might argue that this is the same pattern turned around).

When you add a third square, it can go behind, between or in front of the existing squares, making a total of six possible combinations.

When a fourth colour is added, it can go in any of four positions, in each of the six existing patterns – a total of twenty-four.

Again, you might see some of these combinations as being the same, but starting in a different place or going in the opposite direction. We all look at the world differently!

The same colour in another place will vary the effect.

The appearance of a particular colour is strongly affected by the colours around it. It can also be affected by the light. You should never take separate balls of yarn and assume that because you like them individually, you are certain to like them together. Look at them together, with eyes half-closed, under as many lighting conditions as possible. If you like the combination in all circumstances, you will almost certainly like the finished item.

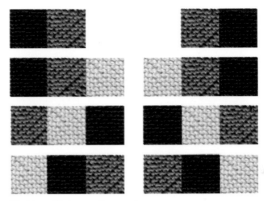

Working with two or three colours.

These are all the possible combinations of four colours arranged in a line.

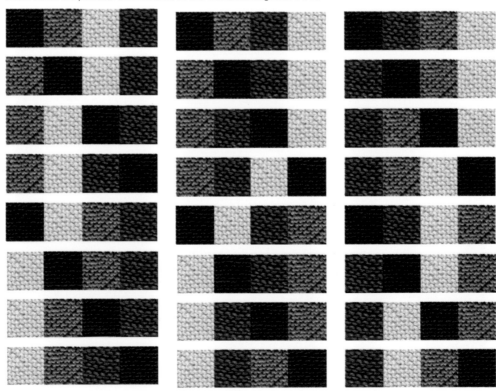

Visual effects – optical illusions using colour

These effects are all created by colouring the design in different ways. The flower design is probably seen in the same way by everyone, but all the others will be interpreted according to what the onlooker perceives them to be.

Optical illusions can easily be created in repeating patterns such as these. When looking at a darker shade, the eye may tell the brain that it is an area of shadow. A brighter shade could be one where the light is falling directly onto it. A pale shade could be a semi-shadow. Putting all this information together may give the illusion of boxes, steps or houses. Merely changing the positions of two colours gives a new effect.

A multicoloured random version gives the brain lots of conflicting information, which some people see as confusing, while others see it as exciting.

Visual effects – optical illusions using shape
It is easiest to create optical illusions with repeated motifs. They can confuse without giving the brain too much information at once.

Cubes?
These 4 sets of cubes (below) look very different.

Do you see cubes or a star?

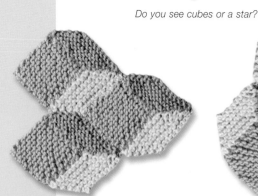

1 A set of 3 cubes, created by using lozenges to shadow squares.

2 The same set of cubes turned 90 degrees clockwise.

3 The same set of cubes, turned 180 degrees.

4 The same set of cubes, turned 90 degrees counterclockwise.

They are actually identical – the block has merely been turned around. Brown is always on top of and below the blue square. Cream is always to left and right. The position of the lightest shape suggests the direction of light on a cube.

Focus on looking at any one block and you will begin to see the cubes "move". Any colours could be used to create the cubes – the effect will always work. The colours determine how the brain sorts out the information it is receiving.

Now look at the larger pattern on the left, which is made up of the same colours used in a slightly more complex design. The squares no longer make such an obvious pattern – perhaps they are making two patterns at once, and some people see cubes while others see a star.

These two blocks are identical but the relative position of the light squares to the other shapes changes the illusion.

Squares?
Each square has a trapezoid on two of its sides, making a new square. When these new squares are put together, they begin to create the illusion of looking through a series of windows. Turning the shapes through 90 degrees changes the illusion slightly, as the windows appear to be pointing in a different direction.

Optical illusion designs

At the design stage (see pages 64–67), play around with colours within your design – there's an infinite array of effects you could achieve!

A two-colour repeating windmill or cube pattern.

The same design in two different shades of the same colour.

Highlight the windmills by working with one colour per windmill.

Use a random colour sequence to confuse the eye.

For a subtle effect, highlight just one element of the repeating pattern in a different colour.

Create a chevron effect.

Create a wavy step effect by using three colours.

Using yarn with dramatic changes.

Visual effects – mixed colours and textures

There are many multicoloured yarns on the market. They come in many variations and are created by a variety of dyeing techniques. Some have very subtle colour changes over a long length; some change colour very frequently; some are bright; some are softly toning. You could even try mixing your own multicoloured yarn!

Using yarn with subtle changes.

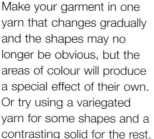

Combining yarn and fabric.

Combining textured or flecked yarns

Textured yarns are available in all kinds of fibres. A smooth yarn is the perfect foil for some of the textures.

The simplest yarn with flecks of another colour could be a good starting point. The flecks may be in a colour you might not normally use, but if the combination of colours works in the yarn, it will also work if you pick out the second colour for some of your other shapes.

Using yarn with subtle changes

Make your garment in one yarn that changes gradually and the shapes may no longer be obvious, but the areas of colour will produce a special effect of their own. Or try using a variegated yarn for some shapes and a contrasting solid for the rest.

Using yarn with dramatic changes

Using a brightly coloured, frequently changing yarn could be too overwhelming to use for a whole garment, but could be wonderful if used for a few shapes surrounded by other solid-coloured shapes, picking out the colours from the mixture.

Unconventional yarns

Texture can be far more than using a ready-made textured yarn. You can knit with anything that can be made into strands and is not sharp or dangerous. Perhaps you already have string or garden twine that is flexible enough to knit with, though it might be hard and should only be used for pieces that will not irritate the skin. You must remember to be especially careful when choosing yarn to create children's garments.

Self-striping yarns

Some yarns are self-striping, but these only work if you have the correct number of stitches on each row – knitting to a different width will produce irregularly shaped areas of colour. Allow shapes to evolve naturally. If you try to make them all identical, any that don't quite match will look out of place.

Combining yarn and fabric

Fabric shapes can be used to complement your knitted pieces. Cut the shape the same size as a knitted piece, then stitch all around the edges using a serger, or blanket stitch by hand. Join to other shapes by picking up stitches from the loops of thread created by the serger. Very firm fabrics can have stitches picked up through holes punched at intervals.

What else is there?

Check a department store or craft shop for ribbon, lace, binding or paper. Unless you can buy these on large rolls, they could be very expensive for making more than a few shapes.

Recycle plastic bags by cutting them into strips. Cut off the handles, then cut in a spiral using as much of the bag as possible. This yarn would probably be too hot and sticky for a sweater, but good for a hat, bag or garden cushions. Plastic bags come in a huge range of colours and will cost you little or nothing.

Almost any fabric can be cut into strips. Some will fray, but you might like this effect. Very fine fabrics might look squashed when knitted and completely different from the starting fabric. Stretch fabrics can pull stitches very tight and be difficult to work with. Printed fabrics are often much paler on the back than on the front and it is very difficult always to keep this side out of sight. Give a new lease of life to old clothes by ripping the seams and using the fabric.

There are some fabrics specifically intended for other purposes that can be used to good effect, such as waterproof kite-making fabric or crunchy netting.

Knitting with plastic bags.

Knitting with recycled fabric.

How to recycle fabric

To get the maximum length either:

- Cut in a continuous spiral from one corner; or
- Fold the fabric in half, make cuts as shown, then cut across the fold on all sections except those at the end. You will have a huge loop that can be wound into a ball.

Practise the technique first with a small piece of paper.

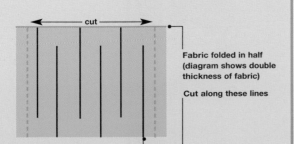

cut

Fabric folded in half (diagram shows double thickness of fabric)

Cut along these lines

Have you accidentally felted your favourite sweater?

Cut it into shapes and use it to make a new sweater. Use the paper template you had for your squares (or other shape) and cut shapes from your felted fabric. They should be exact size of the template. Do not allow for turning under or seaming.

Stitch around all edges of the shapes with a serger or zigzag sewing-machine.

If you do not have a sewing-machine, then blanket stitch the edges.

Blanket stitch around a fabric square and then join to a knitted square.

Planning your design

The size of your new sweater, cardigan, or jacket might be very different from your actual measurements. Commercial patterns allow a certain amount of "ease". The amount can vary enormously between designs.

You will have to decide for yourself how much ease you need for your own design – but there is an easy way to do this.

Basic shape

The basic shape of the front and back will usually be a rectangle; however, there may be some shaping for the waist and chest, or a band at the bottom which has gathered the garment in. Try to establish the size of the key measurements shown on the diagram below by pulling the garment flat.

You don't have to take all the measurements from one garment. If the length, sleeves, etc. are not quite right, find other garments that are the size you want. Take the width from one, the length from another, and the sleeves from another to get your ideal shape.

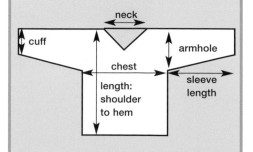

neck

cuff

armhole

chest

length: shoulder to hem

sleeve length

Taking measurements from an original garment

It doesn't matter whether you work in inches or centimetres, as long as you are consistent. Use a diagram, like the one below, to record your measurements.

Necklines vary a great deal and at this stage all you need to know is the size of the hole you want to leave. Ignore any collar or band, and measure the size of the neck you want from the main part of the garment.

1 Find an old sweater or cardigan that fits widthwise the way you want your new garment to fit. It doesn't matter if it's a little too small, as you can adjust the measurements later. Lay this out on a flat surface, and fasten any zips or buttons.

2 Measure the garment's width. If the garment you are measuring is also the correct length, or has the right-sized armholes, neck or sleeves, take these measurements too. You can take measurements from more than one garment and use only the desired dimensions from each item. Sleeves and lower edges may have been gathered and these will have to be gently stretched to find the knitted dimensions, assuming you want the same amount of fullness.

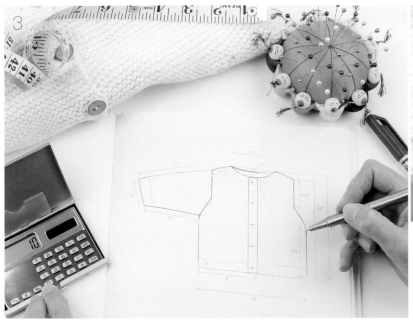

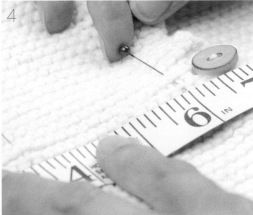

3 Make a note of these measurements onto a scale drawing. This will help you to put the measurements in context, and to work out how many shapes will fit into the garment's dimensions.

4 Working across the garment, pin out your initial ideas of how the shapes fit. It is a good idea to use the width as a guide as there is often more flexibility in the length, but if this is not the case, start with the most important dimension.

5 It is useful to bring together yarn samples, buttons and even fabrics, so that you can find good yarns to fit your design. Knit some sample blocks and lay them out to gauge their effect.

Sizing your squares

Try different sizes of squares without having to knit them by simply dividing into the total number of stitches. The smaller the square, the greater the number of squares you will fit onto your garment. The example below has 120 stitches across the width of the sweater. This total has been divided by convenient numbers to establish the best options for the sizes of the squares. Choosing a convenient measure makes it easier to check the depth and width of the individual blocks, and to press the pieces later.

Sweater width 120 sts	Sweater width 120 sts	Sweater width 120 sts	Sweater width 120 sts
2 squares of 60 sts	3 squares of 40 sts	4 squares of 30 sts	6 squares of 20 sts

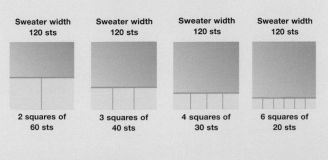

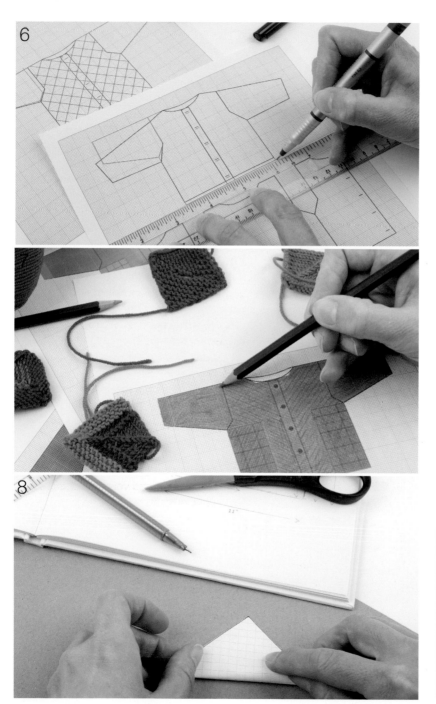

6 Once a basic unit or block size has been established, draw out the garment to scale on graph paper, simplify the angles to 45 and 90 degrees, and make any adjustments for ease or block size.

7 Make several copies of the drawing made on graph paper and draw various ideas over the top – experiment with colour and geometric shapes. Knit sample blocks based on the basic unit you worked out previously.

Making paper templates

Once you are happy with the design, it is time to make paper templates. It is worth taking the time to make actual-size templates of all the major shapes in your design. This will allow you to check that they fit together to the correct size. Any fairly stiff paper can be used and squared paper will make the template easier to draw out.

8 Start with one of the more basic shapes whose width and depth can easily be marked on squared paper. Draw and cut out the shape. Not all the shapes need to be drawn out – sometimes folding existing templates can create another shape in the design.

Tip

A quilter's rule can be an aid to drawing templates on plain paper. The block divisions and marked angles make it possible to draw out complex shapes by positioning the ruler over lines already made.

9 If the template dimensions are based on convenient measurements, then simply make a note of stitch counts before increases and decreases. This can be done on the template so they are easily to hand.

10 Once the size of the first template has been established, draw the remaining shapes onto squared paper. Start with an adjacent shape and check any dimensions you can with a template or templates you have already made.

Bringing it together

Now is the time to get ready to start knitting. This is the most satisfying stage so far, as you start to see the garment take shape before your eyes. Remember that the best thing about modular knitting is the flexibility it affords – if something in your design looks as if it isn't working, simply amend your plan as you knit.

11 Draw out a knitting plan or diagram of the garment on graph paper. Make notes so you remember your decisions; these notes can be considered and developed as you knit, which will help with this garment and your next design. Make yourself a stencil of frequently used shapes.

12 Follow your knitting plan, but remember you are gaining experience about the yarn and the pattern as you knit. So, check and double-check crucial dimensions, and make any additional notes and adjustments as you work.

Designing sleeves

The easiest way for a beginner to shape the edges of a sleeve is with wedge shapes made from rows of straight knitting. In the example shown here, the squares have a diagonal of 28 stitches, so the number of stitches to be picked up along the edge is 20.

1 Use a completed square or a template to measure the distance from the square to the edge of the sleeve at the top of the wedge. In this example, the extra piece needed is three-quarters of the square's width, so will need 15 ridges.

2 Measure the distance at the bottom of the wedge in the same way. Here, it is half the width of the square, so needs 10 ridges. This means that 15 ridges are needed at one end, but only 10 at the other, so 5 stitches must be lost evenly. The edge of the adjacent square is 20 stitches high. Divide the number of rows by the number of stitches you need to lose. In this case, 20 divided by 5 equals 4. This means that the stitches have to be in groups of 4.

3 Knit the 10 ridges that you need for all stitches, ending at the narrow end of the wedge. Turn and cast off 4 stitches. Knit to the wide end, then back towards the narrow end. Cast off 4 stitches at the start of every row at the narrow end, until all stitches have gone.

4 If the sleeve has the same slope all the way down, you will need to lose the same number of stitches on each wedge. Shaping will be the same, regardless of the size of the wedge. The top of one wedge will have the same number of ridges at its widest point as the one above had at its narrowest.

Alternative method

As an alternative, simple method, the pieces can be knitted parallel to the top and bottom of the square. In the example, you will need 15 stitches at the top of the larger wedge and 10 stitches at the bottom. Therefore, you need to lose 5 stitches in 20 ridges of knitting. Decrease one stitch at the end of every fourth ridge. Shape other wedges in the same way.

4

Tapered sleeves

Shape **1** is the same width as a square along the top edge, so (starting at the top left corner) the number of increases along the top edge will be the same as for the other squares. The other side of the shape does not spread out as much as for a square, so will need fewer increases. Shapes **2** and **3** have the slope going in the same direction but the top edges are very much smaller. Shape **4** is exactly the same as shape 1 – it is one square wide at the top and has the same slope. Shape **5** has a complete half-square before you need to start the shaping. The shaped edge makes the shape less than a square, so the stitches need to disappear more quickly. Extra decreases will be needed. Shape **8** is identical to shape 5. Similar principles apply to shapes **6** and **7**.

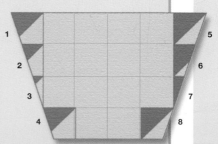

Edgings and bands

So far, you have learned the basics that you need to create your garment. However, to finish your garment to perfection, you will need to think about edgings, bands, **buttonholes, trimmings and necklines. These details will add another unique element to your design and you are still free to change your mind as you go along.**

You could introduce some ribbing into edging modules to help grip.

Edgings

At the edges of your garment there is nothing to keep the edges in place, so you will usually need at least one row of extra knitting to prevent movement.

"Edgings" refers to the lower edges, sleeves or armholes, necklines, pockets and openings of any other kind in a garment. In cushions, bags and afghans, it refers to any of the outside edges.

Wherever the edgings may be, the rules for a straight edge are the same. If you want the pieces to stay flat, pick up the same number of stitches across each shape as you would when adding another small shape.

Straight edges

If you want nothing more than an edge to keep the shapes firm, cast off knitwise on the next row.
In order not to pull in the edge, make this cast off loose, possibly using a larger-size needle than you used for the knitting. You could use your preferred method of casting off.

For a wider flat band, knit as many rows of garter stitch as you need, then cast off as before. Straight edges work particularly well on blankets and cushions, although they can also be used to good effect on garments.

Button and buttonhole bands

These are no different from any other bands. Make these a little wider than the buttons. You do not have to space buttons evenly – they could line up with various parts of your design. Consider zips, ties, snaps, and other fastenings instead of buttons.

- Work the button side first so that you can mark the places for the buttons. Make the buttonhole band to match, lining up the buttonholes with the marked positions.

- Knit to one stitch before the marked position, cast off 2 stitches and continue to next position. On the next row, cast on two above the cast-off stitches. For large buttons, you may need to cast off more stitches.

- For a child's garment, the button and buttonhole bands could be across the shoulders. This should be completed before the sleeves are made.

Tip

If you are making a wall-hanging, create a channel for a hanging pole by knitting the top edging twice as wide as the others. Fold over and stitch into place, leaving the ends open.

Flared edges

Edgings don't have to pull inwards and hold the garment to your shape. They can be decorative and flare out, such as on the hat shown below. This can also be used on the bottom edge or collar of a sweater.

Pick up the number of stitches you need in the normal way and knit at least one row even. Knit more than one row even

for a narrow flat band before the start of the flare.

Increasing makes the band flare. (See page 18 for instructions.) Note that when all increases go in the same direction, the band may appear to twist.

Increases in the same place on successive rows will result in small points. This could be a design feature, but avoid increasing in the same place if you want a softer flare.

Fitted bands

The bottom edges of your sweater may need a fitted band. Garter stitch does not grip as well as a rib would, so take care to make the band the actual size required.

To work out the number of stitches, measure your hips or wrists and work out how many of your starting squares would fit into this measurement. Multiply the number of squares by the

number of stitches needed at the edge of one square. Pick up this total number of stitches, distributing them proportionally across the shapes.

If your band has far fewer stitches than the bottom edge of your shapes, pick up twice as many stitches as you calculated, then knit two together all across the next row. This will make a smoother fit.

Embellishing your edgings

To pull a garment together and add flair, try adding beads into your design, as shown on the hat below. Other ideas include using a lacy trim, tassels, or pompoms. Refer to a good knitting encyclopedia for new ideas.

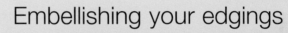

See also Embellishments on pages 84–91

Necklines and collars

Some of your designs will need nothing more than one row of knitting to hold all the edges in place, but generally your garments will benefit from a simple neckline or collar. There are three simple neckline shapes – square, V-neck, and round. Once you know how to create these, you can adapt them to fit any of your designs.

Drawing your neckline on a grid

As for the sleeve, the easiest way to design a collar is to create a template of the shape you want. This can be based either on a garment you already have, or on draping fabric around your shoulders and cutting it to shape. Unfortunately, because the shape of the neckline will determine the shape of the collar, this decision cannot be entirely left until the body of the garment has been completed. The following are only suggestions – there are many more possibilities.

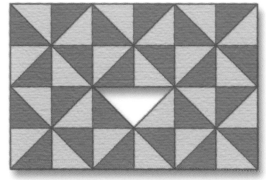

V-neck follows the pattern in the squares.

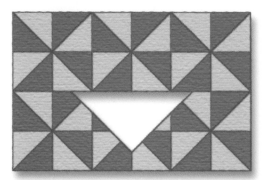

A larger V-neck cuts across some shapes.

A large rectangular neckline cuts across some shapes. All edges are parallel to the sides or top and bottom.

Rectangle follows lines of squares.

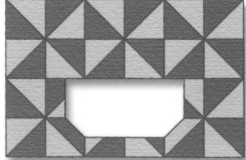

A series of short straight edges will distort into a curve without any noticeable effect on the overall design.

1. RUFFLE COLLAR This collar can be added to most neckline shapes. Measure around the neckline, including any facings. Divide this evenly into convenient lengths. Knit a rectangle whose shorter edge is the same depth as the desired ruffle and longer edge matches the divided length. Then knit the first half of a basic square to create a right-angle triangle until the edges match that of the ruffle depth. Knit alternate rectangles and triangles, joining them as you knit, until the desired lengthis reached. Stitch the collar in place.

2. OFF-THE-SHOULDER COLLAR Measure and divide the neckline as for the polo neck, but knit a trapezoid starting at the 90-degree point instead of a rectangle. The width matches the divided length and will attach to the neckline; the longest edge is the depth of the collar. Sew together as mirrored pairs and attach to the neckline. Keep the points as a feature or knit right-angle triangles to fill the gaps.

6. POLO NECKS This collar is usually added to a rounded neckline. Start by measuring around the neckline and dividing the distance evenly by a number that can be divided by two and about 1½ inches (3.7 cm) wide. Knit a rectangle whose shorter edge matches the divided length and the longest edge is the depth of the collar. Sew together as mirrored pairs and attach to the neckline. See also off-the-shoulder collar.

3. SIMPLE EDGING This edging can act as a collar on most necklines. Pick up stitches along the neckline, using the table on page 24 as a guide, and knit one, two or more rows back and forth or around and around before casting off. If applied to a v-neck, knit two stitches together at the point of the v.

4. SHAWL COLLAR This collar is usually added to a v-neckline. Knit a trapezoid starting at the 90-degree point, increasing at both edges until the width is the desired depth of the collar. Then continue as directed on page 38 until the shorter edge equals half the neckline measurement. Cast off. Make a second collar piece. Join the two pieces together along the shortest edges with the points to the outside. Stitch the collar in place.

5. PETER PAN COLLAR This collar is usually added to a round neckline. Cast on enough stitches for approximately half the collar depth. Knit, increasing into the last stitch of each row, until the number of ridges knitted equals the number of stitches cast on divided by 1.4. Knit without shaping until the edges equal that of half the neckline. Cast off. Make a second collar piece. Without joining the collar pieces together, stitch them in place. There will be a v-shaped gap at the centre back.

Pockets

Pockets can be added anywhere that you can leave a shape unstitched or can apply a patch. There are two types of pocket: the inset pocket that lies behind the knitted fabric and the patch pocket, which is applied to the surface of the fabric. Functional pockets should be larger than your hand and positioned within comfortable reach, but decorative pockets can be smaller. It is best to plan for pockets at the design stage, although patch pockets can be added later.

Tip

If the outer edge of a pocket opening shows any signs of stretching out of shape, pick up a row of stitches (following the usual rules) and cast off again, knitwise, on the next row.

Patch pockets

Patch pockets should be decorative as they will be in full view. They can be added as an afterthought by either making another shape (or shapes), matching the shapes on the garment or by knitting a contrasting shape or rectangle. The new shape can be sewn on top of the old leaving one side open for access. Patch pockets can also be planned at the start and knitted with the other shapes.

Stitching patch pockets onto a garment

Attach a pocket by using mattress stitch. For added strength, the bottom of this pocket has been attached to the backing by picking up stitches on both pieces and casting them off on the wrong side.

Knitting patch pockets into a garment

1 Knit the front pocket shape and the backing as two separate pieces. Do not be tempted to knit them as one and fold them, as the fold will add bulk to the pocket.

2 Hold the two pieces together and pick up stitches through both layers. Knit the new shape as usual. These pockets are very firmly attached and become an integral part of the design, so cannot be removed later.

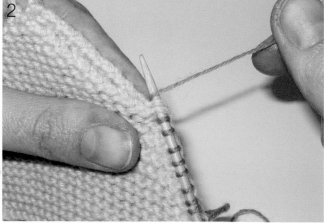

Decorative patch pockets

These two small pockets appear to sit on the surface of the fabric, but they are added at the original construction stage by knitting them into the garment. They show identical pockets added in different ways. Patch pockets look best when applied in pairs to a garment.

The pocket and backing have ridges going at 90 degrees to each other. The shapes are the same as those in the example opposite.

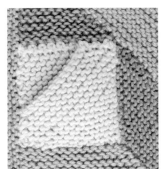

The pocket and backing have ridges going in the same direction as each other, which makes the pocket less conspicuous.

A pocket has been inset behind the blue trapezoid. The top layer is incomplete so that the pocket can be seen. The finished pocket would be completely hidden, as the top edge would be finished in the tan yarn.

Inset pockets

If you don't wish to make a feature of the pocket, then knit an inset pocket, which can be made to be almost invisible. The opening can appear between two shapes or be created within a shape. For an opening between two shapes, simply leave the shapes either entirely or partially unattached. If the opening must appear within a shape, make sure the shape is big enough to have a margin of stitches about 1 inch (2.5 cm) either side of the opening.

Work to the position of the opening, knit the required number of stitches across the top of the pocket, place them onto a stitch holder, and continue to the end of the row. On the next row, work to the position of the opening and cast the same number of stitches as were put onto the stitch holder. The stitches on the stitch holder can later be knitted or cast off.

Create a pocket either by knitting an extra shape large enough to lie behind the opening, or by picking up stitches along the cast-on edge and knitting these stitches down to make the back of the pocket. The backing will not be seen, so it can be any colour that will not show through the garment. Catch the pocket backing to the inside of the garment through the ridges or garter stitches. Take care not to let the stitches show on the outside.

Developing ideas

Now that you know the basic methods, don't restrict yourself to sweaters – adapt the ideas to make anything. Create a patchwork of modules to make a blanket; use scraps of yarn to make toys for a baby; or design a bag to go with your favourite outfit. Keep in mind the principles of modular knitting, but let your imaginaiton run wild!

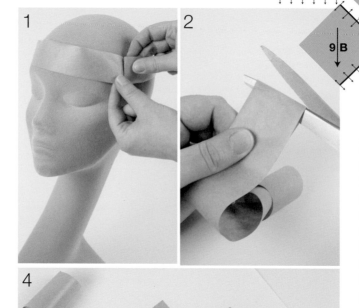

To match your sweater you could make a hat with eight squares (or more complex shapes) attached to an octagon. You don't even need to do any measuring.

Method for basic hat

1 Take a strip of gummed paper, wrap it tightly around your head, and cut it to the size of your head. (It is easier to have a friend do this for you.)

2 Cut the strip exactly in half and throw one half away.

3 Cut the other half exactly into four and stick these four pieces on a sheet of paper to form a square.

4 Use the square you have created as your template.

5 Increase as for the first half of a square until the work fits across the diagonal inside the square. You must make a note of the number of stitches. Complete by decreasing for the second half of the square. Eight squares like this joined together will go around your head.

6 Make the top of the hat as explained in making an octagon (see page 44) and stitch the pieces together.

7 Add a band to stop the edge from stretching. If required, thread shirring elastic through the edge.

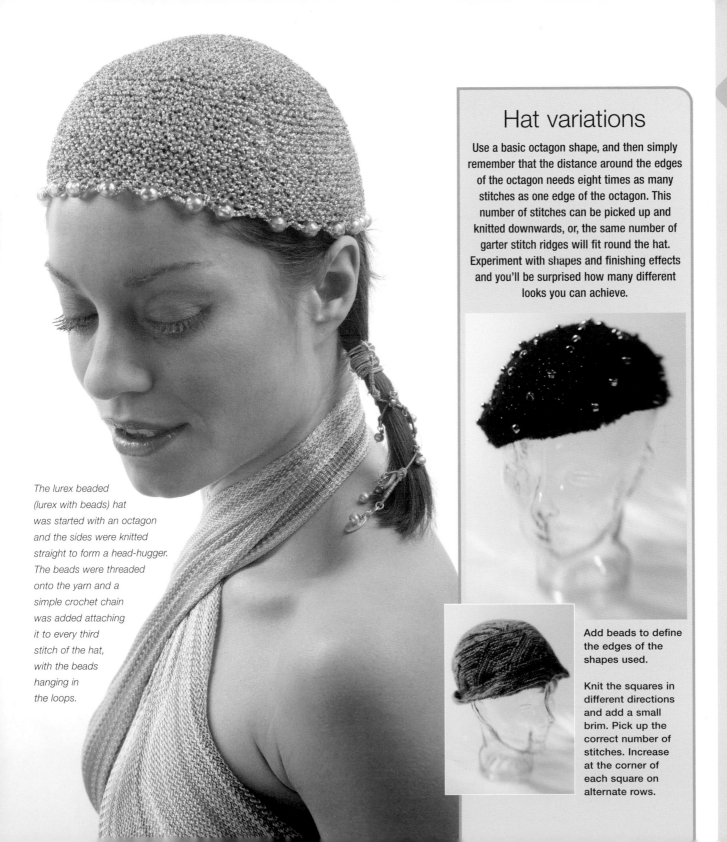

The lurex beaded (lurex with beads) hat was started with an octagon and the sides were knitted straight to form a head-hugger. The beads were threaded onto the yarn and a simple crochet chain was added attaching it to every third stitch of the hat, with the beads hanging in the loops.

Hat variations

Use a basic octagon shape, and then simply remember that the distance around the edges of the octagon needs eight times as many stitches as one edge of the octagon. This number of stitches can be picked up and knitted downwards, or, the same number of garter stitch ridges will fit round the hat. Experiment with shapes and finishing effects and you'll be surprised how many different looks you can achieve.

Add beads to define the edges of the shapes used.

Knit the squares in different directions and add a small brim. Pick up the correct number of stitches. Increase at the corner of each square on alternate rows.

▼ Bags

You can't have enough bags. Just one colour or texture can link one to a sweater or scarf to make an ensemble. Bags come in all shapes and sizes, and a trip to a department store will fuel your imagination. One bag was inspired by a corded quilt pattern and the second by a Japanese purse in a local decorative arts museum. Finding the perfect button looked as if it was going to be a major problem and the idea of painting a perfectly shaped button seemed to be the solution.

Tip

A wooden button will absorb any pigment from a marker pen and will not necessarily need to be varnished. It may fade, but then you can just quickly paint it again.

◄ Cushion

This is my favourite design for a cushion. It is just one of a thousand block designs that can be found in patchwork or maths books. They can be used as single blocks or as part of a design of one or more blocks. It is a good idea is to draw and cut out smaller versions of the blocks you think you might use to try out some ideas.

Tip

The secret of making a good cushion is to use a filling slightly larger than the cover so that the cushion is well rounded.

► Shawl

Shawls and ponchos are perfect for trying out your own designs because they don't have to fit in the way a sweater does. Be as traditional or eccentric as you wish.

Useful information

Knitting and sewing patterns will give you a good idea of sizing, but these figures should only ever be a guide and used when you can't get measurements for the person you wish to knit for.

Here are a few general notes for your reference:

The average head circumference for a:
baby – 15 in. (38 cm)
12-year-old – 18 in. (45 cm)
woman – 20 in. (50 cm)
man – 22 in. (55 cm)

The average foot length for a:
newborn – 3¾ in. (9 cm)
6-month-old – 4 in. (10 cm)
1-year-old – 4½ in. (11.5 cm)

▼ Scarf

Scarves are a great vehicle for trying out new ideas and colour schemes. A maths book and a childhood obsession with the graphic artist Escher inspired this scarf. As you can see from the work sheet, using the scarf flat was a happy accident; initially, it was intended to resemble a chain of paper lanterns. Maybe that idea will still see the light of day.

▶ Mittens

Rather than knitting the thumb separately, it is possible to knit a mitten in two pieces with a seam around the top and sides of the hand. Perhaps next time a cuff of rib will be used to help keep them on and keep out the cold. To make a custom pair of mittens, draw around your hand on squared paper and adjust the shapes so an outline is made up of angles of 45 or 90 degrees. Do not make the shape any bigger than your hand. The mittens will stretch to fit.

Alternative ideas

You can make literally anything as a modular toy – if the child you are knitting for has a passion for dinosaurs, trains or birds, try breaking down the overall sketch into shapes that you can knit and then join together. Squared paper is helpful for this.

►Toys

Children's toys are the perfect excuse to use your imagination. They allow artistic licence and need not resemble anything in particular. Remember that safety is vital. Do not use toxic substances and secure elements firmly using strong materials. And, if we are talking of a wish list, being washable is useful, although felted wool has its own attraction. Try making this caterpillar from a string of octagons.

Modules for babies and toddlers

The two main advantages of this method of knitting are that you can make a garment any size you want, and that there are none of the usual **seams to cause any irritation. These make it ideal for even the smallest baby garment. If you need to make a cardigan for a premature baby with a 12-inch (30-cm) chest, the planning is the same but there will be fewer shapes to make.**

To avoid bulk, consider using finer yarns for a baby than you would for an adult. The rules remain the same whatever the size of the shapes and the thickness of the yarn.

Because baby items are so small, using a lot of different shapes might make the garment look too busy. A repeating or symmetrical design is often best.

These diagrams show the layouts for some of the effects you could achieve using simple, diagonally divided squares. They also show what you would see once the front and back were joined. Bands and edgings can be added later.

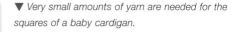

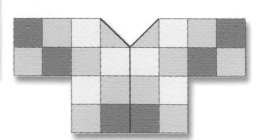

▼ *Very small amounts of yarn are needed for the squares of a baby cardigan.*

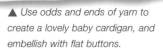

▲ *Use odds and ends of yarn to create a lovely baby cardigan, and embellish with flat buttons.*

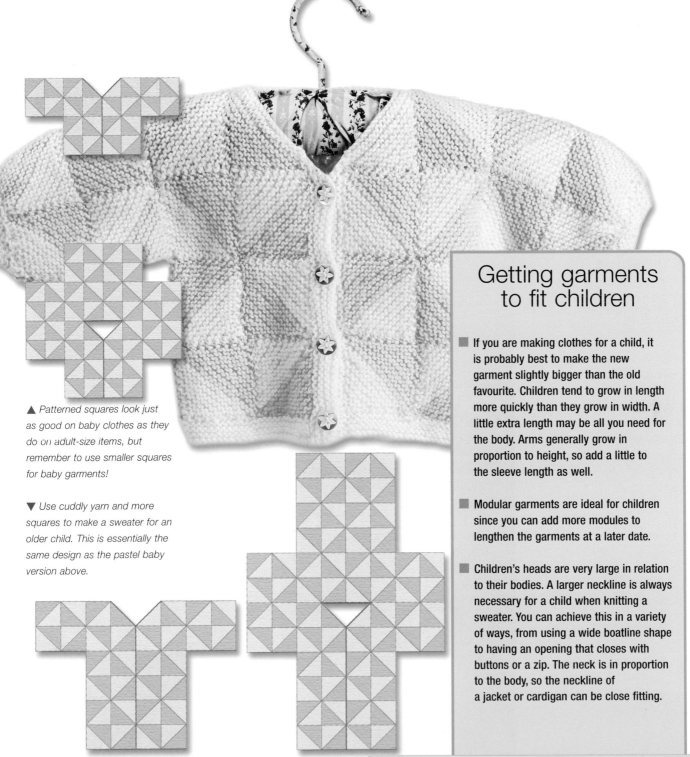

▲ Patterned squares look just as good on baby clothes as they do on adult-size items, but remember to use smaller squares for baby garments!

▼ Use cuddly yarn and more squares to make a sweater for an older child. This is essentially the same design as the pastel baby version above.

Getting garments to fit children

■ If you are making clothes for a child, it is probably best to make the new garment slightly bigger than the old favourite. Children tend to grow in length more quickly than they grow in width. A little extra length may be all you need for the body. Arms generally grow in proportion to height, so add a little to the sleeve length as well.

■ Modular garments are ideal for children since you can add more modules to lengthen the garments at a later date.

■ Children's heads are very large in relation to their bodies. A larger neckline is always necessary for a child when knitting a sweater. You can achieve this in a variety of ways, from using a wide boatline shape to having an opening that closes with buttons or a zip. The neck is in proportion to the body, so the neckline of a jacket or cardigan can be close fitting.

Embellishments

There are many ways to add extra interest, either during construction or afterwards. Whether you need to insert buttonholes or want to add embellishments such as fringe, tassels, loops, i-cords or pompoms for that final touch, here are some simple techniques that require only small amounts of yarn.

Fringe

A fringe can add a wonderful finishing touch to the edge of a garment. A fringe looks lovely when added to the edge of a collar and can be embellished further by adding beads.

Knitted fringe

This fringe is sewn on once the knitted piece is completed and is worked in garter stitch.

1 Cast on the number of stitches that, when knitted, make approximately one-fifth the length of the required fringe. Work in garter stitch until the band is the required length. Cast off the first four or five stitches.

2 Unravel the remaining stitches to create the fringe. This may be left as loops or trimmed.

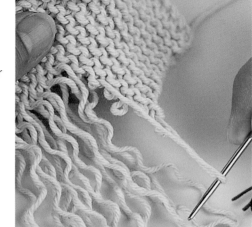

▲ *A knitted fringe can be the perfect finishing touch.*

Tip

■ A few yarns do not lend themselves to tassels or fringe. Slippery yarns may not stay in place, heavily textured yarns might be difficult to pull through, and some yarns will start to unravel.

▼ *The fringe here consists of one strand knotted through the end of every garter stitch ridge. Use more strands or other spacing for a different effect.*

Tassels

You will need a piece of cardboard, scissors and a tapestry needle.

1

2

3

4

5

6

2 Cut the yarn, leaving a tail of about 10 inches (25 cm) and thread this tail into the needle.

3 Slip the yarn off the cardboard and wind the tail tightly around it, about ½ inch (½ cm) from one end. Cast tightly with several turns.

4 Slip the needle underneath the turns and bring it out at the top.

5 Pass the needle through all the small loops at the top of the tassel.

6 Knot the tail tightly at the top of the loop. Don't cut it off.

7 Cut through all of the strands at the bottom of the tassel and trim to ensure that all are even.

1 Decide how long you want the tassel to be. Cut a piece of cardboard about ½ inch (1.2 cm) wider than this measurement. Wind the yarn around the cardboard as many times as you want.

Pompoms

Pompom making is a popular pastime for small children and is a great way to introduce them to yarns and the concept of knitting. Pompoms can look lovely hanging from shelves or a Christmas tree, and are particularly attractive on cushions and winter hats. You can buy a ready-made pompom maker, but circles of cardboard work just as well. Cut two circles bigger than the required diameter of the pompom, with a smaller hole at the centre.

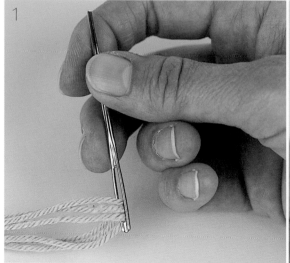

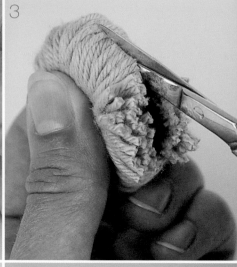

1 Thread a large sewing needle or bodkin with as many ends of yarn as it will take. The yarn ends should be approximately 3 ft (1 m) long.

2 Hold the two discs of the pompom maker together and thread the needle through the centre, around the outside and back through the centre from the front, holding the tail end of yarn in place with your thumb if necessary. Continue to do this until the centre hole is full.

3 Using a sharp pair of scissors, cut around the pompom, between the discs.

4 Tie a piece of yarn or sewing cotton around the centre of the pompom as tightly as possible and remove the discs. Trim the pompom to form a ball.

Loops

Loops can be functional, used as buttonholes or used simply as decoration. Either way, they are an easy way to add flair.

Sewn buttonhole loop

Sewn buttonhole loops are very effective when used for buttons that have a shank. They are made by sewing around a small loop of yarn.

1 Mark the position of the buttonhole using pins. Thread a large needle with the yarn and make a loop by bringing the yarn through the knitted piece from back to front and in by one stitch at the first pin.

2 Take the yarn back through the work at the second pin and then through near the first pin for a second time. Work buttonhole or blanket stitch around the loop until complete.

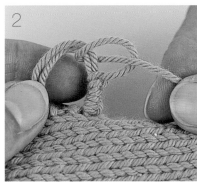

Loopy trim

A knitted, loopy trim works only in small areas, since it may distort the shape.

1 To work the loops, knit into the stitch in the normal way but do not let it slip off the left-hand needle.

2 Bring the yarn to the front and wrap a loop round your thumb close to the needle, take the yarn to the back and knit into the back of the stitch you kept on the needle. Repeat in every stitch.

i-cord

This cord is a knitted tube, useful for ties and handles. You will need two double-pointed needles, two or three sizes smaller than the size recommended for your yarn.

1 Cast on 3, 4 or 5 stitches. Knit one row in the usual way.

2 Without turning the work around, pass the needle with the stitches to your left hand. Push the stitches along to the right end of the needle. Pass the yarn across the back of the stitches and pull tight to bunch the stitches together. Use the empty needle to knit another row from right to left.

3 Repeat to the length required. The knitting forms a small tube.

Adding beads

Beads can be used in many different ways and can be applied as the knitting is progressing or added later.

▲ *Highlight the different directions of knitting by adding beads along the diagonal of your squares.*

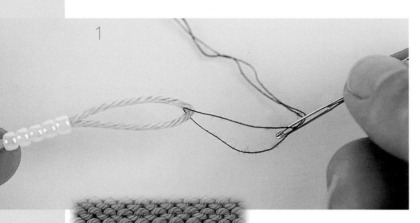

Adding beads while knitting

1 To add beads while knitting, thread them onto your yarn before you begin. Keep pushing them down out of the way until you reach the place where you want to attach a bead.

2 Slide the bead as close as you can to the knitting and work a very tight stitch, then continue as normal.

All beads and other trims must be washable if they are knitted into the design as it will not be possible to remove them. Also be aware that extra weight can distort the precision of your shapes. Use beads to define lines in your shapes or to add any pattern you want. Sequins could be used in the same way, but must have holes big enough to thread them onto the yarn.

▶ *Use coordinating beads at the corners of squares.*

Attaching by sewing

If you are unsure about the positioning of beads, wait until the item is complete before making a decision. Stitching them on is a long process, but they can be more easily removed this way.

A simple chequerboard pattern is enhanced by beads to tone with both colours. Use them at the corners or seams between shapes, in the middle of shapes or hanging down to create a fringed effect.

To make the beads hang down in this way, a tiny gold ring was used beneath each bead. Using a sewing needle small enough to go through your beads, fasten the yarn securely on the back side of the knitted item, bring it to the front, pass the needle through the bead, through the ring and up through the bead before fastening off.

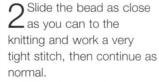

Holes and spaces

Holes and spaces in your knitted pieces can create an attractive pattern. You could leave small spaces between shapes and fill them in some other way. (Large holes might allow the garment to stretch.) You could line your garment with a contrasting lining and the colour will show through the holes.

Knitted holes

Small holes can be used to make patterns within a shape. Choose the spacing according to the pattern you want to make. If you can't visualize it, draw your shape on squared paper, using one square per stitch. Colour the squares that will be holes.

1 Make the holes by your preferred method. A hole is created by knitting two stitches together, followed by bringing the yarn forwards or around the needle to create a new stitch and maintain the same number of stitches.

2 The two stitches knitted together must include the one that is to be the hole. If it is the first of the two stitches, make the extra stitch in front of it. If it is the second stitch, make the extra stitch after it.

Holes should be used in moderation as too many will cause a shape to stretch.

▼ *Sew around the edge of a small curtain ring using buttonhole or blanket stitch, and then use the covered ring to support the structure of a larger hole.*

Crocheted holes

This is a small crochet square surrounded by garter stitch to make it the right size to fit with other shapes. The square consists of alternate trebles and chains. Two stitches were picked up from the edge of each square.

Any ready-made fabric with holes can be used in a similar way. Look for curtain net or any other mesh fabric. A very small length of an exotic gold or silver mesh can provide the centre for many shapes. Picking up stitches from any fabric will be a trial-and-error process until the work lies flat. One favourite is sequin waste (the strip that is left when sequins are punched out), although it is difficult to work with because the rows of holes form 60-degree angles. Stitches can be picked up easily from one pair of edges, but need to zigzag on the other edges.

Stitch patterns

Other stitches, such as stocking stitch, can be used inside the garter stitch shapes to create textured effects. Remember that the tension of stocking stitch and other variations is different from garter stitch, so you will need to keep this in mind when you knit. In both of these blocks, stocking stitch has been used within a garter stitch "frame" to create an interesting visual effect. Using an alternative stitch within a garter stitch shape should enable you to easily retain your original shape.

3-D embellishment

Finish a shape in the usual way, then add another shape, wherever you want, by picking up another set of stitches along any vertical or horizontal line of bumps and working as for other shapes. One side will show bumps of the wrong colour where you have picked up stitches. Make sure this is on the side that is to be out of sight.

This two-colour square had another row of stitches picked up along the colour change row. The third triangle is the same size as the underlying triangle.

Weaving

One of the delights of garter stitch is that the stitches are evenly spaced, obvious and easy to count. This makes it ideal for adding yarn as an embellishment. This weaving is a plain dark square with two colours of yarn woven under alternate bumps of garter stitch. The yarn was used double. There are many ways to vary this technique:

■ Work the lines at any angle by counting across and up in a regular pattern.

■ Take the yarn to the back and bring up again where required. In a two-colour design, use the same two s for the weaving.

■ Use novelty yarns – only small quantities are needed. Weaving will not distort your shape but could add noticeably to the weight of the garment if there is a lot of it.

Parallelograms

The parallelograms for the base of this shape are alternately blue and pink. Stitches were picked up along the colour change and the new parallelograms were knitted so they slope in the opposite direction. This creates an unusual visual effect, confusing the brain.

Experiment with adding new shapes on top of the old. If you don't like them, pull them out and no damage will have been done.

Embroidery

Many pieces can be enhanced with the addition of a little embroidery. Try adding a simple motif or monogram on a few shapes, or use embroidered buttons.

Dorset buttons

Dorset buttons can be made in almost endless permutations of colour or just one colour. Dorset buttons are especially effective on cushions and garments that require larger buttons since small ones can be tricky to make.

1 Using a long length of yarn, sew around the edge of a small curtain ring using buttonhole or blanket stitch. Holding the tail end of the yarn close to the ring, sew around both the ring and the tail until it has disappeared. Secure once the ring is full and turn the hem edge of the blanket stitch to the inside of the ring.

2 Using a second yarn, sew around the ring to create a web effect. Using two or three stitches, overcast the centre of the spokes and secure the yarn.

3 Using a third yarn, thread the needle through from the back to the front of the button, close to the centre of the web, between two spokes. Fill in the ring's centre by working backstitch around the spokes. Cast off the yarn.

Embroidered buttons

You can buy button kits that consist of a two-part button: one side acts as the front and the other side has a slot that holds the shank in place. Fabric is placed over the front of the button and clipped into place with the second piece.

Monogram

The monogram below is embroidered in chain stitch, using a smooth cotton yarn. Use any yarn, any stitches and any design. The squareness of garter stitch makes it ideal for cross-stitch patterns. Embroidery will not distort the shapes.

91

CHAPTER FOUR

projects

In this chapter…

KEY

◎ = Degree of difficulty on a scale of 1–3

Booties

These booties use so little yarn that an investment in luxury yarns such as cashmere and silk will make them a joy to knit. Even with a strenuous laundry regime, they will last as long as they will fit the baby.

Template

Use this template to check the size of blocks A, B, C and D.

For the suggested yarns, the number of stitches on the needle before decreasing should be: 17 stitches for blocks A, B, C and D.

Blocks

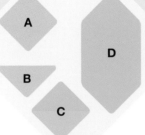

Size

0–3 months

To adjust the size, photocopy the template to the width of the foot plus ¼ inch (6 mm) on each side.

Materials

- For each of the two colours:
  ½ oz. (15 g) of fingering-weight yarn.
- A firm but soft tension is required.

For the booties shown:

Rowan cashcotton 4-ply 1¾ oz. (50 g) balls

pink	1
green	1

- A selection of ribbons, buttons and embroidery silks to embellish the booties.
- 1 pair of US 5 (3.75 mm) needles.

Blocks

Each bootie is made up of four different blocks, one of which is a basic square.

Block A is a basic square; see page 20.

Make a slip knot and increase at the end of every row until the sides of the square match the template (right). Work one row with no increases. Knit two stitches together at the end of every row until no stitches remain.

Block B is half a basic square, or a right-angle triangle; see page 32. Make a slip knot and increase at the end of every row until the sides of the square match the template. Cast off.

Block C is a two-colour basic square with eyelets. Make a slip knot and increase at the end of every row until the sides of the square match the template (left). Cut the yarn of the first colour 4 inches (10 cm) from the needles and join in the second colour. Count the number of stitches on the needle.

IF A MULTIPLE OF 3 STS

Eyelet row: K3 sts * yo, K2tog, K1 *, rep from * to * until the end of the row.

IF A MULTIPLE OF 3 STS PLUS 2 STS

Eyelet row: K2 sts, * yo, K2tog, K1 *, rep from * to * until the end of the row.

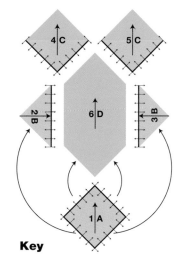

Key

Pink

Green

1|A Block number and direction of knitting

Sew this edge to the edge of the block indicated

IF A MULTIPLE OF 3 STS PLUS 1 ST

Eyelet row: K2 sts, * yo, K2tog, K1 *, rep from * to * until the last 2 sts, K2tog.

Continue to work in the second colour and knit two stitches together at the end of each row until none remain.

Block D is an elongated basic hexagon; see page 42.

Make a slip knot and increase at the end of every row until the lower edges of the hexagon match the template (see page 94).

Work rows without increases or decreases until the vertical edges match the width of block B.

Knit two stitches together at the end of every row until no stitches remain.

Knitting a bootie (make two)

The blocks should be knitted separately using the chart (page 95) as a guide to the number and shape of the pieces.

Finishing

With the wrong side facing, pin out the pieces onto a blocking board or towel using the template as a guide. Check the pressing instructions on the ball band and, with a cool iron and a pressing cloth, gently press the pieces.

Join the pieces together using whip stitch (see page 23) or crochet (see page 24), following the order shown on the chart. The flatter the seams, the more comfortable they will be for the baby.

Thread the ribbon through the eyelets.

Variations

The basic bootie shape can be embellished in a number of ways. It is important to ensure that anything attached to the bootie is secured firmly and cannot be pried off by inquisitive fingers or gums.

Variation 1: with buttons and ribbon

Twist one end of a 2-inch (5-cm) length of ribbon and sew it to the other to create a figure of eight. Attach to block A and cover the join with a button or in this case two buttons, one over the top of the other.

Variation 2: with attach-later bobbles

Secure three attach-later bobbles to block A of the bootie.

TO MAKE AN ATTACH-LATER BOBBLE:
Make a basic square with sides measuring ⅞ inch (2 cm).

Cut the yarn leaving a 4-inch (10-cm) tail and thread it through a yarn needle. Using small running stitches, sew around the edges of the square. Pull the yarn tight and draw the edges together.

TO MAKE THE TIE:
Using the main colour, cast on enough stitches for a 10-inch (25-cm) length. On the next row, cast the stitches off. Thread the tie through the eyelets.

Variation 3: with satin stitch

Using a dressmaker's marker transfer a design onto interfacing. Iron the interfacing to the reverse of the block A. Embroider block A of the bootie with stitches such as satin stitch, lazy daisy, and French knots. Thread ribbon through the eyelets.

Patchwork ball

The crazy patchwork style of this soft ball is a very useful way to hide less-than-perfect seams. Using random embroidery stitches within the blocks will add to the charm. This ball can also be worked in scraps left over from other projects.

Size
Height: 6 inches (15 cm)

Materials
- For each of the five colours:
  ½ oz. (25g) of sport-weight yarn.
- Use needles one size smaller than those suggested on the ball band to produce a firm tension.

For the ball shown:
Rowanspun 4-ply ⅞ oz. (25 g) balls
- lime green   1
- red   1
- orange   1
  Work using the yarn double throughout.
- Rowan felted tweed 1¾ oz. (50 g) balls
  - slate blue   1
- Jaeger matchmaker merino DK 1¾ oz. (50 g) balls
  - flamingo pink   1
- A selection of embroidery silks and cottons in complementary colours.
- Washable soft toy filler.
- 1 pair of US 3 (3.25 mm) needles.

Templates
Use this template to check the size of blocks A and B.

**For the suggested yarns, the number of stitches on the needle before decreasing should be:
14 stitches for blocks A and B.**

Blocks

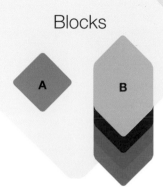

Blocks
The ball is made up of two different blocks.

Block A is a basic square; see page 20. Make a slip knot and increase at the end of every row until the sides of the square match the template (below, left).
   Work one row with no increases.
   Knit two stitches together at the end of every row until no stitches remain.

Block B is a basic hexagon; see page 42. Make a slip knot and increase at the end of every row until the lower edges of the hexagon match the template (left).
   Work rows without increases or decreases until the vertical edges match the length of the lower edges of the hexagon.
   Knit two stitches together at the end of every row until no stitches remain.

Centre strip is a strip that joins the two halves of the ball.
   Calculate the number of stitches required to make the strip half the width of the edge of block A, using the table on page 25. Cross-reference the number of diagonal stitches on block A before decreasing begins, with the edge stitch count given, halve this number and, if necessary, round it up to the nearest whole number. Cast on this number of stitches using the cable method.

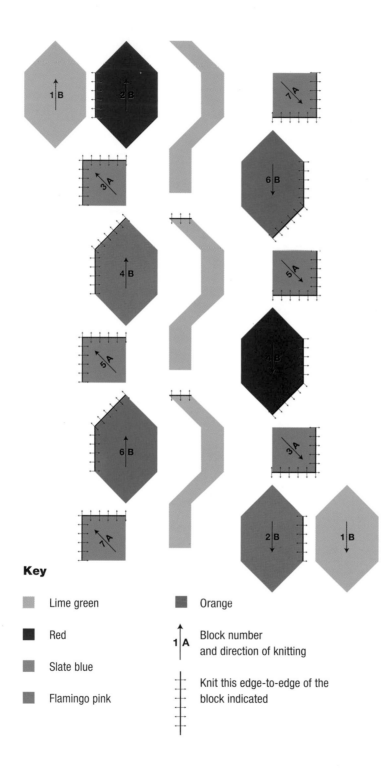

Key

Lime green

Red

Slate blue

Flamingo pink

Orange

1|A Block number and direction of knitting

Knit this edge-to-edge of the block indicated

* STRAIGHT SECTION
Work rows without increases or decreases until the vertical edges match the length of one of the edges of block A.

RIGHT SLOPING SECTION
Row 1: Inc, k to the end of the row.
Row 2: Knit.
Row 3: Inc, k to the end of the row.
Row 4: K2togtbl, k to the end of the row.
Repeat the last two rows until the edges match the length of one of the edges of block A.
    Repeat the straight section.

LEFT SLOPING SECTION
Row 1: Knit
Row 2: Inc, k to the end of the row.
    Repeat the last two rows.
Row 3: Knit
Row 4: K2togtbl, k to the end of the row.
Row 5: K2togtbl, k to the end of the row.
Row 6: Inc, k to the end of the row.
Repeat the last two rows until the edges match the length of one of the edges of block A.
Next row: K2togtbl, k to the end of the row.
Next row: Knit
    Repeat the last two rows.*
    Repeat from * to * twice more.

Attach-later bobble is a basic square with the edges drawn together; see page 96. Knit two in each of the block B colours.

Firmly secure the bobbles to the centre of each block B.

Knitting the ball

The ball is worked in two halves with a centre strip. The blocks can be knitted separately and joined by whip stitch, (see page 23), or crochet (see page 24), following the order shown on the chart (see page 98).

To knit the shapes together, see Joining shapes as you work, page 25. Start with block 1 and join the shapes to those to the left by picking up a stitch from the edge of the other square. Blocks 2–7 all join to the last block knitted and block 1.

Finishing

With the wrong side facing, pin out the pieces in sections to a blocking board or towel using the templates as a guide. Then check the pressing instructions on the ball bands and, starting with a cool iron and a pressing cloth, gently press the pieces.

Leaving one seam, join the pieces together using mattress stitch; see page 23. Stuff the ball with washable filler and close the last seam.

Embellish the seams and surface of the ball using complementary colours, and feather, lazy daisy, and chain stitch.

Blue and white

Size

Cushion one: 12 inches (30 cm) × 12 inches (30 cm)

Cushion two: 16 inches (40 cm) × 16 inches (40 cm)

Afghan: 40 inches (1 m) × 54 inches (1.37 m)

Materials

■ Cushion one, for each colour:
3½ oz. (100 g) balls of a double knitting-weight yarn.

■ Cushion two, for each colour:
5 oz. (140 g) balls of a double knitting-weight yarn.

■ Afghan for each colours:
15 oz. (420 g) balls of a double knitting weight yarn.

■ To create a firm tension in the chosen yarn, use needles one or two sizes smaller than those suggested on the ball band.

For the two cushions and afghan shown:

Jaeger aqua cotton 1¾ oz. (50 g) balls

white	19
blue	19

■ Four ½-inch (12-mm) buttons.

■ 1 pair of US 6 (4 mm) needles.

Blocks

These cushions and afghan are made up of five different blocks, but only three different constructions.

Blocks A and B are the same construction, but block B is larger.

Blocks C and D are the same construction, but block D is larger.

The basic square and the two-colour basic square lend themselves to many traditional quilting patch designs. These patches can either be used singly or grouped to create a variety of designs.

Templates

Use the smaller template to check the size of blocks A and C, and the larger template to check the size of blocks B, D and E.

For the suggested yarns, the number of stitches on the needle before decreasing should be:

23 stitches for block A,

44 stitches for block B,

16 stitches for centre square of block C,

32 stitches for centre square of block D.

The number of stitches to be picked up along the edge should be:

11 stitches for blocks C,

23 stitches for blocks D and E.

Blocks

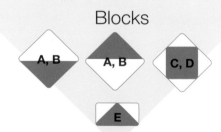

Blocks A and B are two-colour basic squares; see page 20. Make a slip knot and increase at the end of each row until the sides of the square match the template (below, left). Cut the yarn of the first colour and join the second.

Work one row with no increases. Continue to work in the second colour and knit two stitches together at the end of every row until none remain.

Blocks C and D are smaller squares with stitches picked up along each edge and knitted to create a square the same size as blocks A or B.

Starting with the centre square, calculate the number of diagonal stitches, using the table on page 25. Find the number of diagonal stitches on block A or B before decreasing begins the edge stitch count is the total number of diagonal stitches.

Make a slip knot and increase at the end of every row until the calculated diagonal stitch count is reached.

*Work one row with no increases. Knit two stitches together at the end of every row until no stitches remain.

Calculate the number of stitches along each edge using the table on page 25 and pick up the stitches in the second colour, see page 25.

Knit two stitches together at the end of every row until no stitches remain.

Repeat for each edge.

Block E is half of block C or D. Work as for block C or D from *, but casting on the number of diagonal stitches.

Knitting cushion one

FRONT

The blocks can be knitted separately and whip stitched (see page 23) or crocheted (see page 24) together later, following the order shown on the chart (below).

To knit the shapes together, see Joining shapes as you work, page 25. Start with block 1 and join the shapes to those to the left by picking up a stitch from the edge of the other square.

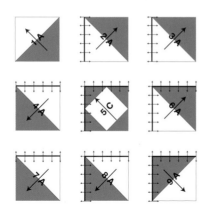

Key

 Blue

White

 Block number and direction of knitting

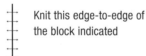 Knit this edge-to-edge of the block indicated

BACK

The back is made up of two rectangles joined together to make a square the same size as the front.

To knit a rectangle, see page 30.

FIRST RECTANGLE

** Make a slip knot in blue and increase at the end of every row for 8 rows.

Join in the second colour and work the following stripe sequence.

*2 rows white
4 rows blue
2 rows white
2 rows blue
2 rows white
4 rows blue
2 rows white
8 rows blue *

From * to * forms the pattern; repeat throughout.

Continue increasing at the end of each row until the edge measures 6 inches (15 cm).**

Next row: K to the last st, inc.

Next row: K to the last 2 sts, K2tog. Repeat the last two rows until the side of the rectangle measures 12 inches (30 cm).

Knit two stitches together at the end of every row until no stitches remain.

SECOND RECTANGLE

Work as for first rectangle from ** to **.

Next row: K to the last 2 sts, K2tog.

Next row: K to the last st, inc.

Continue, following the stripe sequence and repeat the last two rows until the side of the rectangle measures 12 inches (30 cm)

Knit two stitches together at the end of every row until no stitches remain.

BACK FLAP

The back flap is a single right-angle triangle knitted to the width of the cushion with a single buttonhole 1 inch (2.5 cm) from the slip knot.

Make a slip knot in blue and increase at the end of every row for 1 inch (2.5 cm), ending with an odd number of stitches on the needle.

Buttonhole row: Knit to the centre 3 sts, cast off 3 sts, and continue to the end of the row, increasing into the last stitch.

Next row: Knit to the bound-off stitches, cast on 3 sts to complete the buttonhole, and continue to the last stitch, increase.

Continue increasing at the end of each row until the width of the work is 12 inches (30 cm), and cast off.

Finishing

With the wrong side facing, pin out the pieces onto a blocking board or towel using the template as a guide. Check the pressing instructions on the ball band and, with a cool iron and a pressing cloth, gently press the pieces.

Join the front blocks if they have not been knitted together and weave all the ends into the seams.

Join the back pieces together using mattress stitch (see page 23) taking care to match the stripes.

Join the front side and bottom edges to the back by using mattress stitch.

Join the back flap to the front using whip stitch (see page 23).

Attach a button to the back to align with the buttonhole on the back flap.

Knitting cushion two

FRONT

Follow instructions for cushion one, using the chart below.

Block E is used in pairs and each can either be knitted separately or the upper block can be knitted by picking up the number of stitches to be cast on along the top edge of the lower block.

It takes practice to pick up stitches and knit on from a shape and to get sharp corners. Block E can also be divided in two vertically to make two blocks of A.

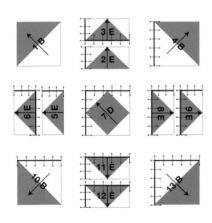

Key

Blue

White

Block number
and direction of knitting

Knit this edge-to-edge of
the block indicated

BACK

The back is made up of a slip stitch pattern knitted with shaping as for the basic square.

Make a slip knot in white and increase at the end of every row until there are 7 sts on the needle.

Pattern row 1: *K1, sl1 purlwise* repeat from * to * to the last st, inc.

Pattern row 2: K2 *yf sl1 purlwise, yb, K1* repeat from * to * to the last 2 sts, yf sl1 purlwise, yb, inc.

Pattern rows 3–4: Knit.

Repeat these 4 rows until the edge measures 16 inches (40 cm).

Keeping the pattern correct, knit two stitches together at the end of every row until no stitches remain.

BACK FLAP

The back flap is a single right-angle triangle knitted to the width of the cushion with three buttons up the centre.

Make a slip knot in blue and increase at the end of every row for 1 inch (2.5 cm), ending with an odd number of stitches on the needle.

***Buttonhole row:** Knit to the centre 3 sts, cast off 3 sts, and continue to the end of the row, increasing into the last stitch.

Next row: Knit to the bound-off stitches, cast on 3 sts to complete the buttonhole, and continue to the last stitch, increase.

Continue increasing at the end of each row until the distance from the last buttonhole is 2½ inches (6 cm), ending with an odd number of stitches on the needle.*

Repeat from * to *.

Repeat the buttonhole row and next row once more.

Continue increasing at the end of each row until the width of the work is 16 inches (40 cm), and cast off.

Finishing

As for cushion one but there is only one back piece.

Variations

The blocks used for the Blue and White projects can be created using beads to create the contrast colour.

Thread the yarn with beads.

Every other row before working each stitch, slide a bead along the yarn so it is tight against the right needle.

The pattern used for the back of cushion two slips a stitch purlwise over two rows. This can give the illusion of more than one colour being used along a row. In the example below, the first stitches and the first two pattern rows were worked in red, then the next two rows were worked in white and finally the next two rows were worked in blue.

Knitting an afghan

Both cushions one and two can be used to create a matching afghan. In the diagram (right) cushion two front sections have been edged with blocks half the size of block B.

Joining shapes as you work (see page 27) will make the wrong side of the afghan less obvious. Start with blocks at the top left and join the shapes to those to the left by picking up a stitch from the edge of the other square.

For a more portable project, knit the blocks separately.

Finishing

Block and press as for cushion one.

Join the blocks together and weave all the ends into the seams.

EDGING

With the blue yarn and right side facing, pick up and knit 11 rows along a long edge, inc in the last st of each row. Cast off.

Repeat along the opposite edge.

Repeat for top and bottom edges of the afghan, but do not include the edging on the long edges.

Sew the border edges together at the corner, working from the inside out, and easing them together.

Geometric scarf

Size

30 inches (84 cm) × 9½ inches (24 cm)

Materials

For each of the three colours:

- 1 × 1¾ oz. (50 g) balls of a worsted-weight yarn.
- To create a soft drape in the chosen yarn, use needles one or two sizes larger than those suggested on the ball band.

For the scarf shown:

- Rowan kid classic 1¾ oz. (50 g) balls
  - dark grey   1
  - pink   1
- Jaeger luxury tweed 1¾ oz. (50 g) balls
  - grey   1
- 1 pair of US 9 (5.5 mm) needles.

Blocks

This scarf is made up of three different square or half-square blocks.

A scarf is a good introduction to modular knitting. Think of all those lovely alpacas, mohairs, and cashmeres that feel so good against the skin! Buy as much luxury yarn as you can and supplement it with odd remnants.

Template

Use this template to check the size of blocks A, B and C.

For the suggested yarns, the number of stitches on the needle before decreasing should be 11 stitches for blocks A and C, and 22 sts for block B

Blocks

Block A is a right-angle triangle; see page 32. Make a slip knot and increase at the end of every other row, starting with the second row, until the sides of the triangle match the template (below, left). End with a row with an increase. Work one row with no increase.

Knit two stitches together at the end of every other row until no stitches remain.

Block B is a two-colour basic square with a slip-stitch pattern on the decrease rows. Make a slip knot in the first colour and increase at the end of every row until the sides of the square match the template (left). Cut the first colour and join in the second colour.

Work one row with no increases. Continue to work in the second colour.

Row 1 (RS): Knit to the last 2 sts, K2tog.

Row 2: * K1, yf, sl1 knitwise, yb * Rep from * to * to the last 2 sts, K2tog.

Row 3: Knit to the last 2 sts, K2tog.

Row 4: * K2, yf, sl1 knitwise, yb * rep from * to * to the last 2 sts, K2tog.

Repeat rows 1–4 until no stitches remain.

Block C is a one-colour vertical half-square similar to block A. Make a slip knot and increase at the end of every other row, starting with the first row, until the sides of the triangle match the template (left). End with a row with an increase.

Work one row with no increase.

Knit two stitches together at the end of every other row until none remain.

Knitting the scarf

The blocks can be knitted separately and whip stitched (see page 23) or crocheted (see page 24) together later, following the order shown on the chart (right).

To knit the shapes together and produce a neater reverse side, see Joining shapes as you work, page 25. Start with block 1 and join the shapes to those to the left by picking up a stitch from the edge of the other square.

Finishing

With the wrong side facing, pin out the pieces to a blocking board or towel using a copy of the templates as a guide. Then check the pressing instructions on the ball bands and, starting with a cool iron and a pressing cloth, gently press the pieces.

Join the blocks if they have not been knitted together and weave all the ends into the seams.

Make and cut the pom-pom (see page 86). Cut a piece of card the same length as the tassel plus a ½ inch (1.2 cm). Wrap the tassel yarn around the card until the skirt is the desired thickness. Secure the tassel near the top edge with a length of yarn. Tie this then round the centre of the pom-pom. Trim the tassel skirt. Repeat five times.

Attach the tassels to the on-point squares on the ends of the scarf.

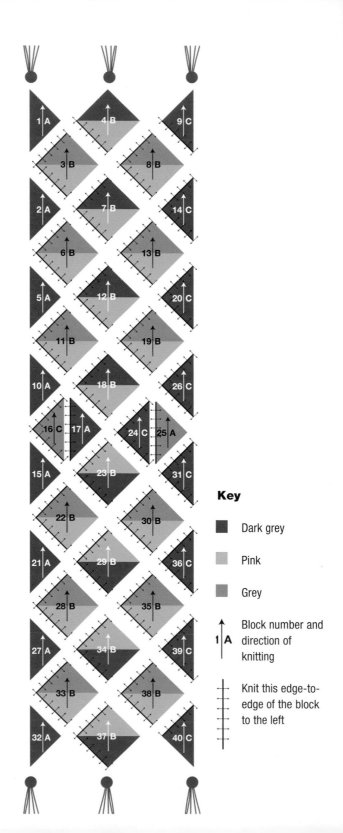

Key

- ▇ Dark grey
- ▇ Pink
- ▇ Grey

↑
1|A Block number and direction of knitting

Knit this edge-to-edge of the block to the left

Baby hats

The crown is made up of radiating kite shapes in stocking stitch. Create your own design by using any stitch with a short stitch and row repeat. Be careful if you use a pattern such as a twist as it may cause the crown to peak and sit high on the head. This can be avoided by knitting an extra round of basic square blocks.

Size
Head circumference
Baby: 16 inches (40.5 cm)

Materials
- For each of the colours:
  1½ oz. (42 g) of a sport-weight yarn.
- To create a medium drape in the chosen yarn, use needles suggested on the ball band and experiment until the correct tension has been achieved.

For the baby hat shown:
- Rowan cashcotton 4-ply 1¾ oz. (50 g) balls

pink	1
green	1

- 1 pair of US 5 (3.75 mm) needles.
- US 2 (2.75 mm) circular needle.

Blocks
This hat is made up of two different shapes: a kite, and a half-square block.

Block A is a kite shape which uses the different stitch proportion of stocking stitch to create a different triangle shape. The kite shape is knitted partially in stocking stitch and partially in garter stitch.
Cast on 3 sts.
Row 1: Knit.
Row 2: Purl.
Row 3: K1, M1, K1, M1, K1.
Work 3 rows in stocking stitch.
Row 7: K2, M1, K1, M1, K2.
   Repeat the last 4 rows, increasing

either side of the centre stitch every fourth row, until the sides of the kite match the template (below, left).
   End with a knit (RS) row.
Working in garter stitch, knit two stitches together at the end of every other row until no stitches remain.

Block B is a half-square or a right-angle triangle; see page 29.
Make a slip knot and increase at the end of every row until the sides of the square match the template.
   Cut yarn, leaving a 4-inch (10-cm) tail.

Knitting the baby hat
Use the larger needles. The blocks can either be knitted separately or whip stitched (see page 23), following the order shown on the chart (on page 110). To knit the shapes together, see Joining shapes as you work, page 25. Start with block 1 and join the shapes to those to the left by picking up a stitch from the edge of the other square.
   When each block B is completed, transfer the stitches onto the slightly smaller sized circular needle.
RIM
Count the number of stitches on the circular needle. If there is an odd number, knit two stitches together somewhere in the following row.
   Using the green yarn, work ½ inch (12 mm) in stocking stitch, working back and forth on the needle.

Baby hat templates
Use these templates to check the size of blocks A and B.

For the suggested yarns, the number of stitches on the needle before decreasing should be 17 stitches for blocks A and B.

Blocks

A   B

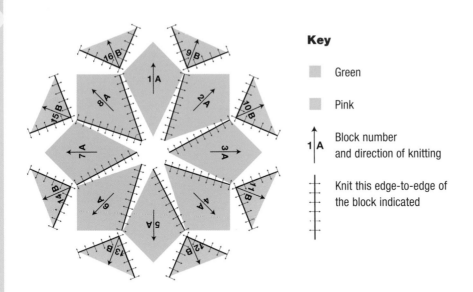

Key

Green

Pink

1|A Block number
and direction of knitting

Knit this edge-to-edge of
the block indicated

Cut the yarn, leaving a 4-inch
(10-cm) tail.

Join in the pink yarn, work 1 row in
pattern as set.

Rejoin the green yarn, work ½ inch
(12 mm) in pattern set.

Work in rib as follows.

Next row: * K1, P1 *, rep from * to * to
the end of the row.

Repeat the last row until the rib
pattern measures 1 inch (2.5 cm).

Cast off loosely.

Finishing

With the wrong side facing, pin out the
pieces onto a blocking board or towel,
using a copy of the template as a
guide. Check the pressing instructions
on the ball band and, starting with a
cool iron and a pressing cloth, gently
press the pieces.

Join the blocks if they have not been
knitted together and weave all the ends
into the seams.

Join the rim seam using mattress
stitch; see page 23.

Knitting the jester hat

This is a variation on the baby hat with
eight shapes in each round, and with a
point added to the crown. Work from
the centre out as follows:

The first round is worked as for the
baby hat with a block similar to block
A, but with the increases every eighth
row. Once the correct width is achieved
the decreases are worked in either
green or orange yarn; alternating
around the crown.

The second round are basic squares
in red. Pick up stitches (see page 27),
along the diagonal of each basic
square using yellow yarn, knit one row

and decrease at the end of each row
until no stitches remain.

The third round is made up of half-
square blocks of alternating orange and
green. Do not cast off the stitches.

RIM

The stitches from the blocks in round
three were transferred onto a circular
needle. They were worked in red
stocking stitch for ½ inch (12 mm) and
then rib as for the baby hat.

To create a second row of points on
round three, use the red yarn to pick
up stitches from one triangle point to
the next. Knit one row and decrease at
the end of each row until no stitches
remain.

Repeat three more times round the
crown; once for each pair of points.

Finishing

Follow instructions for the baby hat.

Adult hat

Hats are the perfect way to use up the odds and ends from your yarn stash. Only small amounts are required for this hat, which will allow you to mix and match different weights and textures to complement your favourite outfit.

Size
Head circumference
Adult: 20 inches (50 cm)

Materials
- For each of the colours:
  1½ oz. (42 g) of a sport-weight yarn.
- To create a medium drape in the chosen yarn, use needles suggested on the ball band and experiment until the correct tension has been achieved.

For the adult hat shown:
- Rowan felted tweed 1¾ oz. (50 g) balls

brown	1
ruby	1
mustard	1

- 1 pair of US 5 (3.75 mm) needles.
- US 2 (2.75 mm) circular needle.

Blocks
This hat is made up of three different shapes: a kite, a square block, and a half-square block.

Block A is a kite shape which uses the stitch proportion of stocking stitch to create a different triangle shape. The kite shape is knitted partly in garter stitch and partly in stocking stitch.
Cast on 3 sts.
Row 1: Knit.
Row 2: Purl.
Row 3: K1, M1, K1, M1, K1.
Work 3 rows in stocking stitch.

Adult hat templates

Use this template to check the size of block A. Use the square template (above, left) to check the size of blocks B and C.

For the suggested yarns,
the number of stitches on the needle before decreasing should be
26 stitches for blocks A, B and C.

Blocks

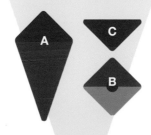

Row 7: K2, M1, K1, M1, K2.
Repeat the last 4 rows, increasing either side of the centre stitch every fourth row, until the sides of the kite match the template (left).
Cut the yarn of the first colour, leaving a 4-inch (10-cm) tail.
Join in the second colour.
Knit 1 row.
Working in garter stitch, knit two stitches together at the end of every other row until no stitches remain.

Block B is two-colour basic square (see page 28), with an attach-later bobble. Make a slip knot and increase at the end of every row until the sides of the square match the template (left), ending with a right side. Cut the yarn of the first colour and join in the second colour.
Work one row with no increases.
Continue to work in the second colour and knit two stitches together at the end of every row until no stitches remain.

TO MAKE AN ATTACH-LATER BOBBLE:
Make a basic square with sides measuring ⅞ inch (2 cm).
Cut the yarn, leaving a 4-inch (10-cm) tail and thread it through a yarn needle. Using small running stitches, sew around the edges of the square. Pull the yarn tight and draw the edges together.
Attach to the centre of the block.

Block C is a half-square or a right-angle triangle; see page 32. Make a slip knot and increase at the end of every row until the sides of the square match the template (on page 111).

Cut yarn, leaving a tail of 4-inches (10-cm).

Knitting the adult hat

Use the larger needles. The blocks can be knitted separately and whip stitched (see page 23), following the order shown on the chart (right). To knit the shapes together, see Joining shapes as you work, page 25. Start with block 1 and join the shapes to those to the left by picking up a stitch from the edge of the other square.

When each block C is completed, transfer the stitches onto a slightly smaller sized circular needle.

RIM

Count the number of stitches on the circular needle. If there is an odd number, knit two stitches together somewhere in the following row.

Using the brown yarn, work ½ inch (12 mm) in stocking stitch, working back and forth on the needles.

Cut the yarn, leaving a 4-inch (10-cm) tail.

Join in the ruby yarn, work 1 row in pattern as set.

Rejoin the brown yarn, work ½ inch (12 mm) in pattern as set.

Work in rib as follows.

Next row: * K1, P1 *, rep from * to * to the end of the row.

Key

■ Brown

■ Ruby

■ Mustard

1|A   Block number and direction of knitting

┼   Knit this edge-to-edge of the block indicated

Repeat the last row until the work measures 1 inch (2.5 cm) from the start of the rib.

Cast off loosely.

Finishing

With the wrong side facing, pin out the pieces onto a blocking board or towel, using a copy of the template as a guide. Then check the pressing instructions on the ball band and starting with a cool iron and a pressing cloth, gently press the pieces.

Join the blocks if they have not been knitted together and weave all the ends into the seams.

Join the rim seam using mattress stitch; see page 23.

Bag

Make this bag in many colours and forms. Add beads between the stitches for an evening style; use looped fur stitch for a more wintry look; or embellish with chain stitch and beads, and team with leather straps for a more ethnic look.

Size
13 inches (32.5 cm) × 9 inches (23 cm)

Materials
For each of the four colours:
- 1 oz. (28 g) of a double knitting-weight yarn.
- To create a very firm tension in the chosen yarn, use needles two sizes smaller than those suggested on the ball band.

For the bag shown:
- Jaeger Extra fine merino DK
  1¾ oz. (50 g) balls
  brown   1
  grey   1
- Rowan kid classic 1¾ oz. (50 g) balls
  rose   1
- Jaeger matchmaker merino DK
  1¾ oz. (50 g) balls
  beige   1
- 8 × 1 inch (24 mm) buttons
- US 3 (3.25 mm) circular needle.
- 1 pair of US 3 (3.25 mm) double-pointed needles.
- 1 pair of US 5 (3.75 mm) needles.

Abbreviations
ML= Insert the right-hand needle into the next stitch on the left-hand needle as if to knit and draw the loop through without dropping the stitch off the left-hand needle. Bring the yarn to the front between the two needles and wind it clockwise round your free thumb. Take the yarn to the back of the work between the needles, knit the stitch again, and then slip it off the left-hand needle. Slip both stitches onto the left-hand needle, give the loop a sharp tug, and work the stitches together through the backs of their loops.

Blocks
The bag is made up of four different square, triangular, or parallelogram blocks.

Block A is a one-colour parallelogram; see page 40. Make a slip knot and increase at the end of every other row, starting with the first row, until the sides of the parallelogram match the template (left). End with a row with an increase.

Work an even number of rows with no increases, until the vertical sides of the parallelogram match the template.

Knit two stitches together at the end of the next row and every other row until no stitches remain.

Block B is a two-colour parallelogram with a slip-stitch pattern. Only one colour is worked at a time; the other is woven in on the reverse side of the work. Make a slip knot, and increase at the end of every other row, starting with the first row, until the sides of the parallelogram match the template (left). End with a row with an increase.

Cut the yarn of the first colour and join in the second colour.

Work an even number of rows with

Template
Use this template to check the size of blocks A, B, C and D.

For the suggested yarns, the number of stitches on the needle before decreasing should be
12 stitches for blocks A and B,
21 sts for block C
23 sts for block D

Blocks
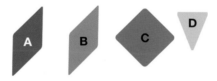

no increases, until the vertical sides of the parallelogram match the template.

Row 1 (RS): In the second colour, yarn B, knit to the last 2 sts, K2tog.

Rejoin the first colour, yarn A.

Row 2: Using yarn A, * K1, yf, sl1 knitwise, yb *, rep from * to * to the last 2 sts, K2tog, weaving yarn B along the row.

Row 3: Using yarn B, knit to the end of the row, weaving yarn A along the row.

Row 4: Using yarn A, * K2, yf, sl1 knitwise, yb *, rep from * to * to the last 2 sts, K2tog, weaving the yarn B along the row.

Repeat rows 1–4 until no stitches remain.

Block C is a basic square (see page 20), with every other row worked in looped fur stitch. Make a slip knot and increase at the end of every row for 6 rows.

Row 7: K1, * ML *, rep to the last stitch, inc.

Row 8: Knit to the last stitch, inc.

Repeat the last two rows until the sides of the square match the template (right).

Work one row as set by the repeat pattern but with no increases.

Continue to ML on every other row as set by the repeat pattern but knit two stitches together at the end of every row until no stitches remain.

The loops can be cut to create a fur texture or left in loops as shown here.

Block D is a 45-degree triangle; see page 32. Make a slip knot and increase at both ends of every fourth row, starting with the first row, until the sides of the parallelogram match the template (on page 114). End with a row with an increase.

Cut the yarn, leaving a 4-inch (10-cm) tail.

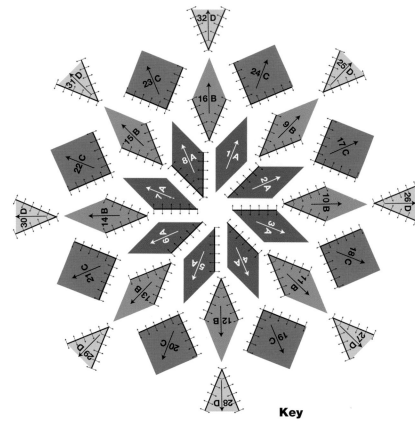

Key

■ Brown

■ Grey and Brown

■ Rose

■ Cream

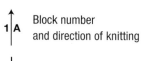

1 A — Block number and direction of knitting

Knit this edge-to-edge of the block indicated

Knitting the bag

Use the larger needles. The blocks can be knitted separately and whip stitched (see page 23), or crocheted (see page 24) together later, following the order shown on the chart (left). For block B, the first colour is grey and the second, brown.

To knit the shapes together, see Joining shapes as you work, page 25. Start with block 1 and join the shapes to those to the left by picking up a stitch from the edge of the other square.

When each block D is completed, transfer the stitches onto a slightly smaller circular needle.

TOP EDGE

Count the stitches on the circular needle and if there is an odd number, knit two stitches together somewhere in the following row as part of the rib. Using the rose yarn.

Next row: * K1, P1 *, rep from * to * to the end of the row.

Repeat the last row until the work measures 3 inches (7.5 cm) from the top of block D.

Cast off loosely.

I-CORD

Cast on 4 sts using brown yarn onto slightly smaller double-pointed needles.

Knit the stitches.

Slide the stitches along the needle until they are at the right-hand end and the yarn is on the left. Stretch the yarn across the back of the work and knit the first stitch of the previous row again, pulling the yarn tight across the back of the work. Continue knitting the remaining stitches on the row.

Repeat from * to * until the cord is 30 inches (75 cm) long.

STRAPS (MAKE TWO)

Cast on 9 sts using beige yarn onto slightly smaller double-pointed needles.

Row 1: Knit.

Row 2: Purl.

Repeat the last two rows until 10 rows have been completed.

Join in the rose yarn.

Work from * to * of the i-cord (left), knitting each row as follows:

Next row: * K1 rose, K1 beige * rep from * to * to the last st, K1 rose. Continue until the work measures 28 inches (70 cm).

Cut the rose yarn 4 inches (10 cm) from the needle.

Repeat the first 10 rows in beige.

Cast off.

Finishing

With the wrong side facing, pin out the pieces onto a blocking board or towel using a copy of the template as a guide. Then, check the pressing instructions on the ball band and, starting with a cool iron and a pressing cloth, gently press the pieces.

Join the blocks if they have not been knitted together and weave all the ends into the seams.

Fold the top edge over to the right side and stitch the top edge to the top edge of the round of block D shapes, leaving a small gap at the front.

Thread the i-cord through the gap and use to draw the bag closed.

Attach the first strap to the top inside edge of the bag 3 inches (7.5 cm) from either side of the front gap.

Flatten the bag slightly with the gap in the top edge to the centre back and attach the second strap to align with the first on the back edge.

For extra security, a length of ¼-inch (6-mm) chain can be threaded and secured through the centre of the i-cord straps.

Sew the buttons to the centre of each block C.

Sweater

This garment is made up of mitred squares that are easy to join together as you knit. Because of the way it is made, this stocking stich mitred square drapes better than the garter stitch basic square. Mitred squares tolerate more stitch combinations; so experiment.

Size

Imperial

CHEST SIZE	SQUARE EDGE	SQUARE DIAGONAL
34 inches	3⅛ inches	4⅜ inches
36 inches	3¼ inches	4½ inches
40 inches	3¾ inches	5⅛ inches
42 inches	4⅞ inches	5⅜ inches

Metric

CHEST SIZE	SQUARE EDGE	SQUARE DIAGONAL
86 cm	8 cm	11 cm
91 cm	8.5 cm	11.5 cm
102 cm	9.5 cm	13 cm
107 cm	10 cm	13.5 cm

Materials

- 1¾ oz. (50 g) balls of a sport-weight yarn.
  Main colour   9 (10, 11, 11)
- To create a soft drape, use needles one size larger than those suggested on the ball band.

For the sweater shown:

- Rowan cashcotton DK 1¾ oz. (50 g) balls
  green   9 (10, 11, 11)
- Size 8 beads 2 oz. (50 g) pack
  cream   1
- 1 pair of US 7 (4.5 mm) needles
- 1 US 3 (3.25 mm) circular needle

Template

Choose the appropriate size square and use the template to check the size of blocks A, B, and C.

For the suggested yarns the number of stitches required for two edges of the square are:

34 inches (86 cm) 33 sts
36 inches (91 cm) 35 sts
40 inches (102 cm) 39 sts
42 inches (107 cm) 41 sts

Blocks

Abbreviations

Sl2tog, K1, Psso = slip two stitches together knitwise, knit 1, pass the slipped stitches over.

PB = place bead. Slide a bead along the yarn so it lies tight against the last stitch knitted, knit the next stitch.

K2togtbl = knit two stitches together through the back of the loops.

Blocks

This sweater is made up of one mitred block with three variations.

Block A is a one-colour mitred square with beads. Thread the ball of yarn with beads. Use the ball band and the experience of your knitting tension to calculate and work a test square to the correct size. Remember these stitches form two edges of the block.

Cast on, or cast on and pick up an odd number of stitches with an even number for each edge and the odd stitch in the center.

Row 1 (WS): Knit.

Row 2 (RS): K to the center 3 sts, sl2tog, K1, psso, k to the end of the row.

Row 3: Purl.

Repeat rows 2–3 until the two edges equal a quarter of the template edge, ending with a RS row and there are an even number of stitches on the needle.

Next row: * K1, PB *, rep from * to * to the last st, K1.

BACK

FRONT

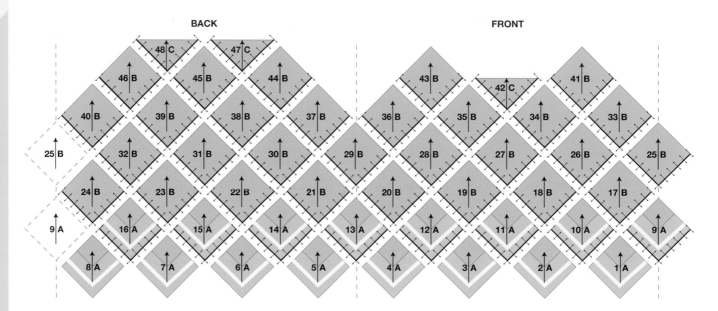

Key

Green

Place bead

Block number and
direction of knitting

Knit this edge-to-edge
of the block to the left

SLEEVE

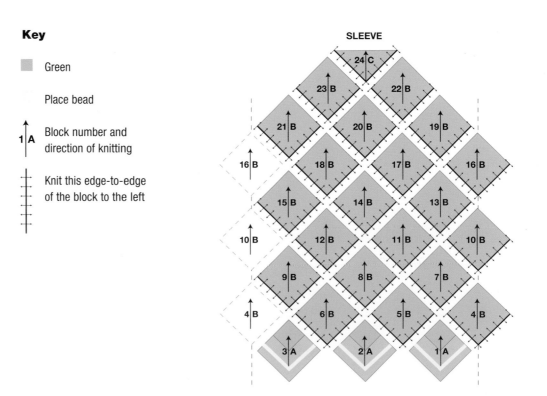

Next row (RS): K1, *yo, K2togtbl*, rep from * to * to the center 3 sts, sl2tog, K1, psso, *K2tog, yo*, rep from * to * to the last st, K1.

Next row: Purl.

Repeat the last 2 rows until the two edges equal half the template edge, ending with a WS row.

Next row: K to the center 3 sts, sl2tog, K1, psso, k to the end of the row.

Next row: Purl.

Repeat the last 2 rows until no stitches remain.

Block B is a one-colour mitred square with no beads.

Cast on, or cast on and pick up an odd number of stitches with an even number for each edge and and the odd stitch in the center.

Row 1: Knit.

Row 2: K to the center 3 sts, sl2tog, K1, psso, k to the end of the row.

Row 3: Purl.

Repeat rows 2–3 until no stitches remain.

Block C is a one-colour mitred half square with no beads. Cast on or cast on and pick up an odd number of stitches with an even number for each edge and the odd stitch in the center.

Row 1: Knit.

Row 2 (RS): K1, K2togtbl, k to the center 3 sts, sl2tog, K1, psso, k to the last 3 sts, K2tog, K1.

Row 3: Purl.

Repeat rows 2–3 until no stitches remain.

Knitting the sweater

The sweater front and back is worked in one cylindrical piece with block 1 on the first row of the front.

Row 1: Work block A 8 times.

Row 2: Start with block 9 and join the shapes to those below. For block 9 pick up half the number of stitches from the top edge of block 8, cast on the odd number stitch and pick up the remaining stitches from the edge of block 1.

Work block 9A.

Repeat for blocks 10–16.

For block 17, pick up half the number of stitches from the top edge of block 9, pick up the odd number stitch from the increase stitch loop of the point of block 1, and pick up the remaining stitches from the edge of block 10.

Work block 17B.

Repeat for blocks 18–48.

Continue to work the blocks as indicated, following the chart above until block 48 has been completed.

Sleeve (make 2)

The sleeve front and back is worked in one cylindrical piece.

Row 1: Work block A 3 times.

Row 2: Start with block 4 and join the shapes to those to the below. For block 4, pick up half the number of stitches from the top edge of block 3, cast on the odd number stitch and pick up the remaining stitches from the edge of block 1.

Work block 4B.

Repeat for block 5–6.

For block 7 pick up half the number of stitches from the top edge of block 4, pick up the odd number stitch from the increase stitch loop of the point of block 1 and pick up the remaining stitches from the edge of block 5.

Work block 7B.

Repeat for blocks 8–24.

Continue to work the sleeve following the chart above until block 24 has been completed, working the blocks as indicated.

BACK

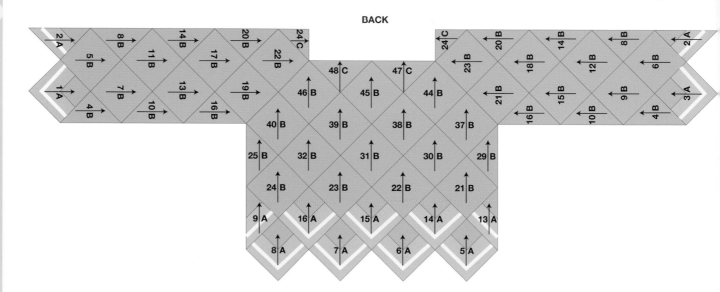

FRONT

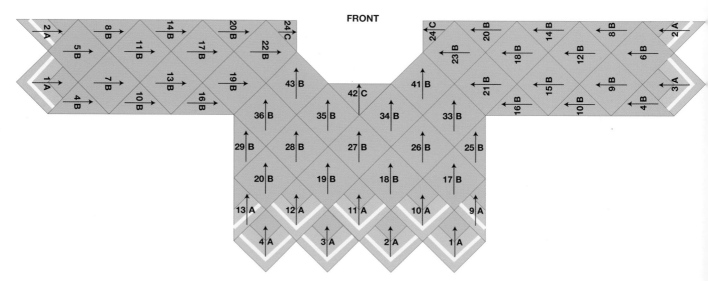

Finishing

With the wrong side facing, lightly press all the pieces.

Join the sleeves to the sweater body using mattress stitch; see page 23, and the diagrams above as a guide.

Using the US 3 (3.25 mm) circular needle, pick up stitches around the neck, picking up an even number of stitches along the edges as before and using the table on page 25 to determine the number of stitches across the top of the B blocks.

Knit 4 rows in the round around the neckline.

Loosely cast off.

Useful information

And, finally, some information that may be useful to have on hand as you explore the ideas in this book.

Yarns

The choice of yarns presented by manufacturers is enormous and enough to make any knitter want to get out her knitting needles. In general, using yarns from a manufacturer that has a reputation for quality will always make knitting a pleasure and the finished result better.

Knitted samples

Yarns used on pages 8–91.

Jaeger Siena 4-Ply
Fingering-weight yarn
100% mercerized cotton
Approx. 153 yds (140 m) per
1³/₄ oz. (50 g) ball

Rowan 4-Ply Cotton
Fingering-weight yarn
100% cotton
Approx. 186 yds (170 m) per
1³/₄ oz. (50 g) ball

Jaeger Matchmaker Merino 4-ply
Fingering-weight yarn
100% merino wool
Approx. 200 yds (183 m) per
1³/₄ oz. (50 g) ball

Rowan Cotton Glacé
Sport-weight yarn
100% cotton
Approx. 125 yds (115 m) per
1³/₄ oz. (50 g) ball

Jaeger Matchmaker Merino DK
Double knitting-weight yarn
100% merino wool
Approx. 131 yds (120 m) per
1³/₄ oz. (50 g) ball

Rowan Wool Cotton
Double knitting-weight yarn
50% merino wool, 50% cotton
Approx. 123 yds (113 m) per
1³/₄ oz. (50 g) ball

Project yarns

Yarns used on pages 94–121.

Jaeger Extra Fine Merino DK
Sport-weight yarn
100% extra fine merino wool
Approx. 137 yds (125 m) per
1³/₄ oz. (50 g) ball

Rowan Felted Tweed DK
Double-knitting-weight yarn
50% merino wool, 25% alpaca, 25% viscose/rayon
Approx. 191 yds (175 m) per
1³/₄ oz. (50 g) ball

Jaeger Luxury Tweed
Double knitting-weight yarn
65% merino lambswool, 35% alpaca
Approx. 197 yds (180 m) per
1³/₄ oz. (50 g) ball

Rowan Kid Classic
Worsted-weight yarn
70% lambswool, 26% kid mohair, 4% nylon
Approx. 153 yds (140 m) per
1³/₄ oz. (50 g) ball

Rowan Classic Yarns Cashcotton 4-Ply
Fingering-weight yarn
35% cotton, 25% polyamide, 18% angora, 13% viscose, 9% cashmere
Approx. 197 yds (180 m) per
1³/₄ oz. (50g) ball

Rowanspun 4ply
Fingering-weight yarn
100% pure new wool
Approx. 162 yds (148 m) per
⁷/₈ oz. (25 g) hank

Rowan Classic Yarns Cash cotton DK
Sport-weight yarn
35% cotton, 25% polyamide, 18% angora, 13% viscose, 9% cashmere
Approx. 130 yds (142 m) per
1³/₄ oz. (50 g) ball

Jaeger Matchmaker Merino DK
Double knitting-weight yarn
100% merino wool
Approx. 131 yds (120 m) per
1³/₄ oz. (50 g) ball

Jaeger Aqua Cotton
Double knitting-weight yarn
100% mercerized cotton
Approx. 116 yds (106 m) per
1³/₄ oz. (50 g) ball

Substituting yarns

The techniques and projects described in this book are particularly suited to the substitution of yarn.

There are several points to consider in order to successfully substitute yarns. First is its potential for wear and tear and the properties of different yarn compositions. Retailers are a rich source of information about their stock and often have sample swatches or finished projects in the store that can be examined. If the substituted yarn is of a similar weight and composition, then the question more often is how much yarn would be

required. The simplest way to calculate this is to work out the total yardage of the yarn specified (number of balls multiplied by yardage of one ball) and divide this by the yardage of one ball of the substituted yarn. Yardage information is given on most ball bands.

However, for all yarn substitutions, it is always a good idea to weigh a ball of yarn and, using the needles suggested on the ball band, knit a sample block. If this block does not feel or look right, adjust the needle size until the desired drape is achieved. Then either weigh the block or, if only one block is knitted, the ball to discover the percentage yardage of yarn used for one block.

Alternatively, unravel the knitted block and measure the length of the yarn used. Multiply this figure by the number of blocks, facings and notions to estimate the amount of yarn required in the pattern. The sooner this is done, the more likely it is to be possible to purchase more of the same yarn or a complementary yarn that may have been produced by the same manufacturer for that season.

Yarn definitions

There are no rules about the use of yarns. Weight terms are simply a way of describing the nature of a yarn to someone who hasn't seen it. Their uses can be mixed and matched, and the recommended needle sizes and gauge information ignored to achieve the desired effect.

Fingering-weight yarn
This is the lightest weight and often used for gossamer shawls or baby clothes. The recommended needle sizes range from US 0–3 and have a gauge of more than 27 stitches over 4 inches (10 cm).

Sport-weight yarn
This yarn is often used for lighter garments and may have the appearance of double knitting yarn, but because of its composition benefits from either being knitted on very fine needles or with a slightly tighter tension. Sport-weight yarns are very good for dense stitch patterns because they don't become unyielding. The recommended needle sizes often range from US 4–6 and have a gauge of 22–26 stitches over 4 inches (10 cm).

Double knitting-weight yarn (DK weight)
This yarn is slightly heavier and denser than sport-weight yarn and produces a denser fabric than sport-weight yarn on simple stitch patterns. The recommended needle sizes often range from US 4–6 and have a gauge of 21–22 stitches over 4 inches (10 cm).

Worsted-weight yarn
This yarn tends to have the appearance of a chunky yarn, but it is spun with a lot of loft. It feels light and soft, and will produce garments that feel quite light but with more warmth than lighter yarn weights. It is excellent for afghans because it knit up quite quickly but doesn't have weight. The recommended needle sizes range from US 7–9 and have a gauge of 16–20 stitches over 4 inches (10 cm).

Chunky-weight yarn
This yarn is quite heavy and dense, and is useful for heavier outdoor garments and afghans. The recommended needle sizes often range from US 9–10^1/$_2$ and have a gauge of 14–15 stitches over 4 inches (10 cm).

Bulky-weight yarn
The bulk of this yarns means that it is often only suitable for simple stitch patterns, and its bulk does not necessarily translate into warmth. It is very quick to knit, with very few stitches for an average garment but the needle sizes mean that they can be unwieldy. The recommended needle sizes often range from US 10 and larger, with a gauge of less than 13 stitches over 4 inches (10 cm).

Abbreviations

Many of these entries appear in this book, though we have included others for reference when experimenting with stitch patterns for your shapes.

alt alternate

beg beginning/begin

cm centimeter

cont continue

Cr2 cross the number stated

C4B cable back the number stated

C4F cable forward the number stated

dec decrease

dp double pointed

foll/folls following/follows

g grams

in. inch

inc increase, knit into the front and back of the next stitch

k knit, see page 17

k2tog knit two stitches together

k2tog tbl knit two stitches together through the backs of the loops

MB make bobble

ML make loop; insert the right-hand needle into the next stitch on the left-hand needle as if to knit, draw the loop through without dropping the stitch off the left-hand needle. Bring the yarn to the front between the two needles and wind it clockwise around your free thumb. Take the yarn to the back of the work between the needles, knit the

stitch again and then slip it off the left-hand needle. Slip both stitches onto the left-hand needle, give the loop a sharp tug, and then work the stitches firmly together through the backs of their loops.

M1 make one; pick up the loop that lies between the stitch just knitted and the next by inserting the right needle from front to back. Transfer onto the left needle and work the stitch by inserting the needle into the back of the stitch.

oz. ounces

p purl, see page 18

patt pattern

PB place bead, using the method stated in the pattern

psso pass slipped stitch over

p2tog purl two stitches together

p2tog tbl purl two stitches together through the backs of the loops

rem remaining

rep/reps repeat/repeats

RS right side of work

sl knitwise slip knitwise; insert the right needle into the st/sts as if to knit but pass onto the right needle without winding the yarn around the needle

sl purlwise slip purlwise; insert the right needle into the st/sts as if to purl but pass onto the right needle without winding the yarn around the needle

sl2tog k1 psso slip two stitches together knitwise, knit 1, pass slipped stitches over

ssk slip, slip, knit 2 stitches together

st/sts stitch/stitches

ST st stocking stitch

tbl through the back of the loop/s

T2B twist 2 back

T2F twist 2 forward

WS wrong side of work

yb yarn back between the needles

yf yarn forward between the needles

yfon yarn forward and over needle to make a stitch

yo yarnover

✱ repeat instructions between ✱ as many times as instructed

[ ] repeat instructions between [ ] as many times as instructed

US and English terms

US	English
Bind off	Cast off
Gauge	Tension
Seed stitch	Moss stitch
Stockinette stitch	Stocking stitch

Conversions
Needle sizes

US size	Metric size	Canadian size
15	10	000
13	9	00
11	8	0
–	7.5 mm	1
10$^{1}/_{2}$	7	2
–	6.5 mm	3
10	6	4
9	5.5 mm	5
8	5	6
7	4.5 mm	7
6	4	8
5	3.75 mm	9
4	3.5 mm	–
3	3.25 mm	10
–	3	11
2	2.75 mm	12
1	2.25 mm	13
0	2	14

Index

Suppliers of Rowan Yarns and Jaeger Handknits

USA
Westminster Fibers Inc.
4 Townsend West
Suite 8
Nashua, NH 03063
Tel: 603 886 5041
Fax: 603 886 1056

Canada
Diamond Yarn
9697 St Laurent
Montreal
Quebec H3L 2N1
Tel: 514 388 6188

Diamond Yarn (Toronto)
155 Martin Ross
Unit 3
Toronto
Ontario M3J 2L9
Tel: 416 736 6111

Australia
Rowan at Sunspun
185 Canterbury Road
Melbourne
Victoria 3126
Tel: 03 9830 1609

UK
Rowan Yarns and Jaeger Handknits
Green Lane Mill
Holmfirth
West Yorkshire
HD9 2DX
Tel: 01484 681881
www.knitrowan.com

QUARTO WOULD LIKE TO THANK: Luise Roberts for designing projects on pages 94–122, and for her advice on other sections.

Heather Esswood for knitting the sweater, and for demonstrating techniques.

Jackie Jones for make up and hair.

Models: Tashi, at Models Direct, Sami Williamson, and Isabelle Crawford.

All photographs and illustrations are the copyright of Quarto Inc. While every effort has been made to credit contributors, Quarto would like to apologize should there have been any omissions or errors.

Staff

Executive Director
Matthew Cahill

Editorial Director
Patricia Dwyer Schull, RN, MSN

Art Director
John Hubbard

Clinical Manager
Judith A. Schilling McCann, RN, MSN

Managing Editor
A. T. McPhee, RN, BSN

Clinical Editors
Ann M. Barrow, RN, MSN, CCRN (project manager), Carla Roy, RN, BSN

Editors
Mary Lou Ambrose, Elizabeth Mauro, Joann Nash, Dianna Sinovic

Copy Editors
Cynthia C. Breuninger (manager), Karen Comerford, Mary T. Durkin, Brenna H. Mayer

Designers
Arlene Putterman (associate art director), Matie Patterson (project manager), Mary Ludwicki (book designer), Joseph Clark

Illustrators
Bot Roda, Judy Newhouse, Mary Stangl, Jackie Facciolo, Dan Fione, Robert Neumann, Cynthia Mason, Michael Reingold, Page Two Inc.

Typography
Diane Paluba (manager), Joyce Rossi Biletz, Phyllis Marron, Valerie Rosenberger

Manufacturing
Deborah Meiris (director), T.A. Landis, Otto Mezei

Production Coordinator
Margaret A. Rastiello

Editorial Assistants
Carol Caputo, Beverly Lane, Mary Madden

Indexer
Barbara Hodgson

© 1997 by Springhouse Corporation. All rights reserved. No part of this publication may be used or reproduced in any manner whatsoever without written permission, except for brief quotations embodied in critical articles and reviews. For information, write Springhouse Corporation, 1111 Bethlehem Pike, P.O. Box 908, Springhouse, PA 19477-0908. Authorization to photocopy items for internal or personal use, or for the internal or personal use of specific clients, is granted by Springhouse Corporation for users registered with the Copyright Clearance Center (CCC) Transactional Reporting Service, provided that the fee of $.75 per page is paid directly to CCC, 222 Rosewood Dr., Danvers, MA 01923. For those organizations that have been granted a license by CCC, a separate system of payment has been arranged. The fee code for users of the Transactional Reporting Service is 0874348870/97 $00.00 + .75.
Printed in the United States of America.
IEECG-031098

A member of the Reed Elsevier plc group

Library of Congress Cataloging-in-Publication Data

ECG interpretation made incredibly easy.
   p. cm.
   Includes index.
   1. Electrocardiography.   I. Springhouse Corporation.
   [DNLM: 1. Electrocardiography—nurses' instruction WG 140 E172 1997]
RC683.5.E5E256   1997
616.1'207547—dc21
DNLM/DLC
ISBN 0-87434-887-0 (alk. paper)   97-2965
                                           CIP

X96 = £18·99
616. 1207547 SPR

Ecg Interpretation

Made Incredibly Easy!™

Springhouse Corporation

heart, or its base, lies just below the second rib; the bottom of the heart, or its apex, tilts forward and down, toward the left side of the body, and rests on the diaphragm.

The heart varies in size depending on the person's body size, but the organ is roughly 5″ (12 cm) long and 3 1/2″ (9 cm) wide, or about the size of the person's fist. The heart weighs 9 to 12 oz (250 to 350 g) and varies depending on the person's size, age, sex, and athletic conditioning. An athlete's heart usually weighs more than the average, and an elderly person's heart weighs less.

Layer upon layer

The heart's wall — the pericardium — is made up of three layers: the epicardium, myocardium, and endocardium. (See *Layers of the heart wall*.) The epicardium is the inner, visceral layer of the pericardium that lines the heart's surface. The myocardium makes up the largest portion of the heart's wall. This layer of muscle tissue contracts with each heartbeat. The endocardium, the innermost layer of the heart's wall, contains endothelial tissue that lines the heart chambers and valves.

A skeleton of connective tissue called the fibrous pericardium surrounds the heart and acts as a tough, protective sac. It contains the serous pericardium, which consists of two layers: the visceral and the parietal. The outer

Layers of the heart wall

This cross section of the heart wall shows its various layers.

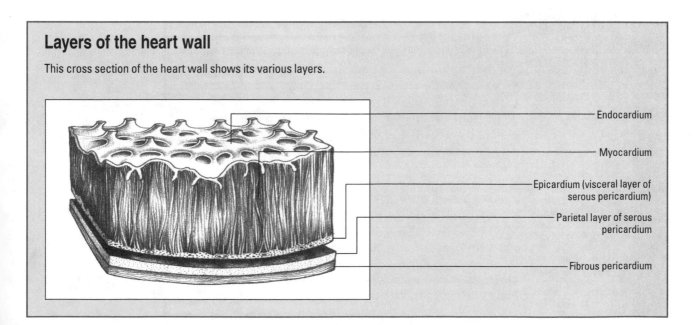

- Endocardium
- Myocardium
- Epicardium (visceral layer of serous pericardium)
- Parietal layer of serous pericardium
- Fibrous pericardium

layer, the parietal, is continuous with the inner visceral layer and adheres to the fibrous pericardium, which helps to hold the heart in place.

Between the layers

The pericardial space separates the visceral and parietal layers and contains 10 to 20 ml of thin, clear pericardial fluid that lubricates the two surfaces and cushions the heart. Excess pericardial fluid, a condition called pericardial effusion, can compromise the heart's ability to pump blood.

Inside the heart

The heart contains four chambers — two atria and two ventricles. (See *Inside a normal heart.*) The right and left atria serve as volume reservoirs for blood being sent into the ventricles. The right atrium receives deoxygenated blood returning from the body through the inferior and superior vena cavas and from the heart through the coronary sinus. The left atrium receives oxygenated blood from the lungs through the four pulmonary veins. The interatrial septum divides the chambers and helps them contract. Contraction of the atria forces blood into the ventricles below.

Pump up the volume

The right and left ventricles serve as the pumping chambers of the heart. The right ventricle receives blood from the right atrium and pumps it through the pulmonary arteries to the lungs, where it picks up oxygen and drops off carbon dioxide. The left ventricle receives oxygenated blood from the left atrium and pumps it through the aorta and then out to the rest of the body. The interventricular septum separates the ventricles and also helps them to pump.

The thickness of a chamber's walls depends on the amount of high-pressure work the chamber does. Because the atria collect blood for the ventricles and don't pump it far, their walls are considerably thinner than the walls of the ventricles. Likewise, the left ventricle has a much thicker wall than the right ventricle because the left ventricle pumps blood against the higher pressures in the body's arterial circulation, whereas the right ventricle pumps blood against the lower pressures in the lungs.

One-way valves

The heart contains four valves — two atrioventricular (AV) valves (tricuspid and bicuspid) and two semilunar valves (aortic and pulmonic). The valves open and close in response to changes in pressure within the chambers they connect and serve as one-way doors that keep blood flowing through the heart in a forward direction.

When the valves close, they prevent backflow, or regurgitation, of blood from one chamber to another. The closing of the valves creates the heart sounds heard through a stethoscope during a physical examination.

The two AV valves, located between the atria and ventricles, are called the tricuspid and bicuspid valves. The tricuspid valve is located between the right atrium and the right ventricle. The bicuspid valve, commonly called the mitral valve, is located between the left atrium and the left ventricle.

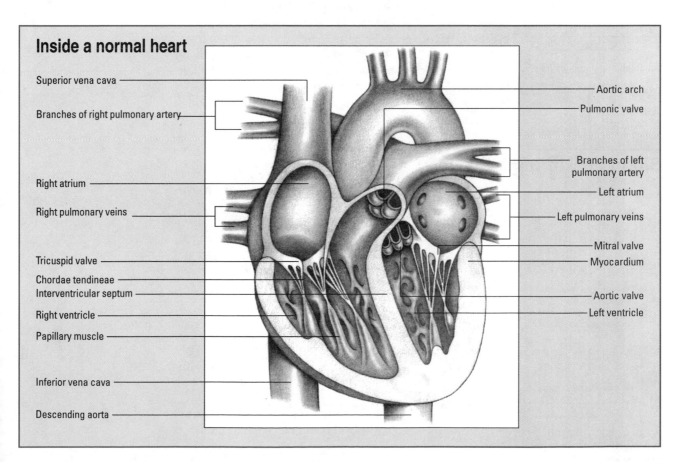

Inside a normal heart

Superior vena cava

Branches of right pulmonary artery

Right atrium

Right pulmonary veins

Tricuspid valve

Chordae tendineae

Interventricular septum

Right ventricle

Papillary muscle

Inferior vena cava

Descending aorta

Aortic arch

Pulmonic valve

Branches of left pulmonary artery

Left atrium

Left pulmonary veins

Mitral valve

Myocardium

Aortic valve

Left ventricle

Cardiac cords

The mitral valve has two cusps, or leaflets, and the tricuspid valve has three. The cusps are anchored to the papillary muscles in the heart wall by fibers called chordae tendineae. These cords work together to prevent the cusps from bulging backward into the atria during ventricular contraction. Damage to them may allow blood to flow backward into a chamber, resulting in a heart murmur.

Cusps of the half-moons

The semilunar valves are the pulmonic valve and the aortic valve. These valves are called semilunar because the cusps resemble three half-moons. Because of the high pressures exerted on the valves, their structure is much simpler than that of the AV valves.

They open due to pressure within the ventricles and close due to the back pressure of blood in the pulmonary arteries and aorta, which pushes the cusps closed. The pulmonic valve, located where the pulmonary artery meets the right ventricle, permits blood to flow from the right ventricle to the lungs and prevents backflow of blood into that ventricle. The aortic valve, located where the left ventricle meets the aorta, allows blood to flow from the left ventricle to the body and prevents backflow of blood into the left ventricle.

Blood flow through the heart

Understanding the flow of blood through the heart is critical for understanding the overall functions of the heart and how changes in electrical activity affect peripheral blood flow. Deoxygenated blood from the body returns to the heart through the inferior and superior vena cavas and empties into the right atrium. From there, blood flows through the tricuspid valve into the right ventricle.

Circuit city

The right ventricle pumps blood through the pulmonic valve into the pulmonary arteries and then into the lungs. From the lungs, blood flows through the pulmonary veins and empties into the left atrium, which completes a circuit called pulmonary circulation.

When pressure rises to a critical point in the left atrium, the mitral valve opens and blood flows into the left ventricle. The left ventricle then contracts and pumps blood through the aortic valve into the aorta, and then throughout the body. Blood returns to the right atrium through the veins, completing a circuit called systemic circulation.

Getting into circulation

Like the brain and all other organs, the heart needs an adequate supply of blood to survive. The coronary arteries, which lie on the surface of the heart, supply the heart muscle with blood and oxygen. (See *The heart's vessels,* page 12.) *Understanding coronary blood flow can help you provide better care for a patient with a myocardial infarction because you'll be able to predict which areas of the heart would be affected by a blockage in a particular coronary artery.*

Open that ostium

The coronary ostium, an opening in the aorta that feeds blood to the coronary arteries, is located near the aortic valve. During systole, when the left ventricle is pumping blood through the aorta and the aortic valve is open, the coronary ostium is partially covered. During diastole, when the left ventricle is filling with blood, the aortic valve is closed and the coronary ostium is open, enabling blood to fill the coronary arteries.

With a shortened diastole, which occurs during periods of tachycardia, less blood flows through the ostium into the coronary arteries. Tachycardia also impedes coronary blood flow because contraction of the ventricles squeezes the arteries and lessens blood flow through them.

That's right, Coronary

The right coronary artery, as well as the left coronary artery (also known as the left main artery), originates as a single branch off the ascending aorta. The right coronary artery supplies blood to the right atrium, the right ventricle, and part of the inferior and posterior surfaces of the left ventricle. In about 50% of the population, the artery also supplies blood to the sinoatrial (SA) node. The bundle of His and the AV node also receive their blood supply from the right coronary artery.

What's left, Coronary?

The left coronary artery runs along the surface of the left atrium, where it splits into two major branches, the left anterior descending and the left circumflex arteries. The left anterior descending artery runs down the surface of the left ventricle toward the apex and supplies blood to the anterior wall of the left ventricle, the interventricular septum, the right bundle branch, and the left anterior fascicle of the left bundle branch. The branches of the left anterior descending artery—the septal perforators and the diagonal arteries—help supply blood to the walls of both ventricles.

Circling circumflex

The circumflex artery supplies oxygenated blood to the lateral walls of the left ventricle, to the left atrium and, in about half of the population, to the SA node. In addition, the circumflex artery supplies blood to the left posterior fascicle of the left bundle branch. This artery circles around the left ventricle and provides blood to the ventricle's posterior portion.

Circulation, guaranteed

When two or more arteries supply the same region, they usually connect through anastomoses, junctions that provide alternative routes of blood flow. This network of smaller arteries, called collateral circulation, provides blood to capillaries that directly feed the heart muscle. Collateral circulation often becomes so strong that even if major coronary arteries become clogged with plaque, collateral circulation can continue to supply blood to the heart.

Veins in the heart

The heart has veins just like other parts of the body. Cardiac veins collect deoxygenated blood from the capillaries of the myocardium. The great cardiac vein, thebesian veins, and other cardiac veins, along with the coronary sinus and its tributaries, return blood to the right atrium, where it continues through the circulation.

A look at cardiac physiology

This discussion of cardiac physiology includes descriptions of the cardiac cycle (See *Phases of the cardiac cycle*), how the cardiac muscle is innervated, how the depolarization-repolarization cycle operates, how impulses are conducted, and how abnormal impulses work.

Phases of the cardiac cycle

The cardiac cycle consists of the following phases.

1. *Isovolumetric ventricular contraction.* In response to ventricular depolarization, tension in the ventricles increases. The rise in pressure within the ventricles leads to closure of the mitral and tricuspid valves. The pulmonic and aortic valves stay closed during the entire phase.

2. *Ventricular ejection.* When ventricular pressure exceeds aortic and pulmonary arterial pressure, the aortic and pulmonic valves open and the ventricles eject blood.

3. *Isovolumetric relaxation.* When ventricular pressure falls below pressure in the aorta and pulmonary artery, the aortic and pulmonic valves close. All valves are closed during this phase. Atrial diastole occurs as blood fills the atria.

4. *Ventricular filling.* Atrial pressure exceeds ventricular pressure, which causes the mitral and tricuspid valves to open. Blood then flows passively into the ventricles. About 70% of ventricular filling takes place during this phase.

5. *Atrial systole.* Known as the atrial kick, atrial systole (coinciding with late ventricular diastole) supplies the ventricles with the remaining 30% of the blood for each heartbeat.

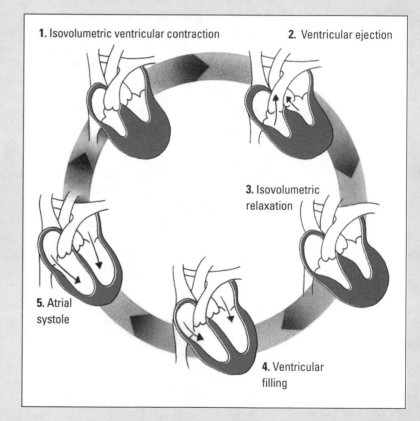

1. Isovolumetric ventricular contraction

2. Ventricular ejection

3. Isovolumetric relaxation

4. Ventricular filling

5. Atrial systole

Cardiac cycle dynamics

During one heartbeat, ventricular diastole or relaxation and ventricular systole or contraction occur.

During diastole, the ventricles relax, the atria contract, and blood is forced through the open tricuspid and mitral valves. The aortic and pulmonic valves are closed.

During systole, the atria relax and fill with blood. The mitral and tricuspid valves are closed. Ventricular pressure rises, which forces open the aortic and pulmonic valves. Then the ventricles contract, and blood flows through the circulatory system.

Atrial kick

The atrial contraction, or atrial kick, contributes about 30% of the cardiac output — the amount of blood pumped by the ventricles in 1 minute. (See *Quick facts about circulation.*) Certain arrhythmias, such as atrial fibrillation, can cause a loss of atrial kick and a subsequent drop in cardiac output. Tachycardia also affects cardiac output by shortening diastole and allowing less time for the ventricles to fill. Less filling time means less blood will be ejected during ventricular systole and less will be sent through the circulation.

Your cycle's output

The cardiac cycle produces cardiac output, measured by multiplying heart rate times stroke volume. (See *Preload and afterload,* page 15.) The term stroke volume refers to the amount of blood ejected with each ventricular contraction and is usually about 70 ml.

Normal cardiac output is 4 to 8 L per minute, depending on body size. The heart pumps only as much blood as the body requires. Three factors affect stroke volume — preload, afterload, and myocardial contractility. A balance of those three factors produces optimal cardiac output.

Preload

Preload is determined by the amount of blood remaining in the left ventricle at the end of diastole. Preload increases with greater venous return to the heart and determines how much cardiac muscle fibers will stretch.

Quick facts about circulation

• It would take about 25 capillaries laid end-to-end to fill 1″ (2.5 cm).

• The body contains about 10 billion capillaries.

• On average, it takes a red blood cell less than 1 minute to travel from the heart to the capillaries and back again.

Where the heart lies

This illustration shows exactly where the heart is located. The heart lies within the mediastinum, a cavity that contains the tissues and organs separating the two pleural sacs. In most people, two-thirds of the heart extends to the left of the body's midline.

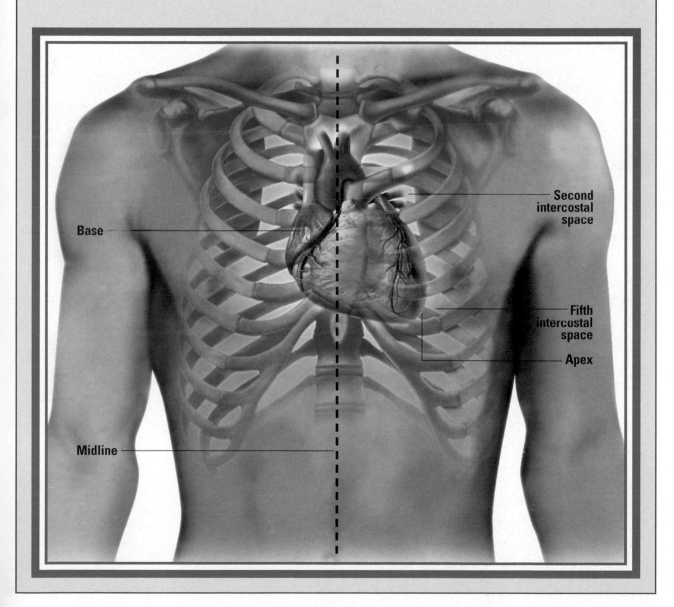

The heart's vessels

The two views shown below detail the great vessels of the heart and some of the major coronary vessels.

ANTERIOR VIEW

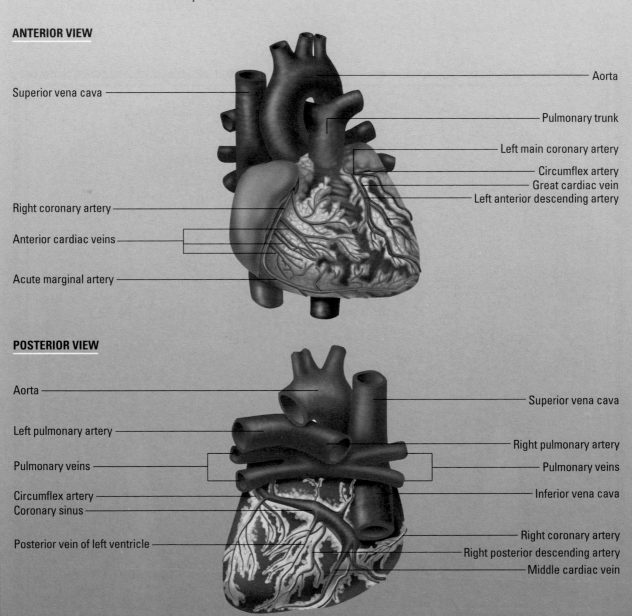

Superior vena cava

Right coronary artery

Anterior cardiac veins

Acute marginal artery

Aorta

Pulmonary trunk

Left main coronary artery

Circumflex artery
Great cardiac vein
Left anterior descending artery

POSTERIOR VIEW

Aorta

Left pulmonary artery

Pulmonary veins

Circumflex artery
Coronary sinus

Posterior vein of left ventricle

Superior vena cava

Right pulmonary artery

Pulmonary veins

Inferior vena cava

Right coronary artery
Right posterior descending artery
Middle cardiac vein

Conducting impulses

The conduction system of the heart, shown below, begins with the heart's pacemaker, the sinoatrial (SA) node. When an impulse leaves the SA node, it travels through the atria along Bachmann's bundle and the internodal pathways on its way to the atrioventricular (AV) node and the ventricles.

After the impulse passes through the AV node, it travels to the ventricles first down the bundle of His, then along the bundle branches and, finally, down the Purkinje fibers.

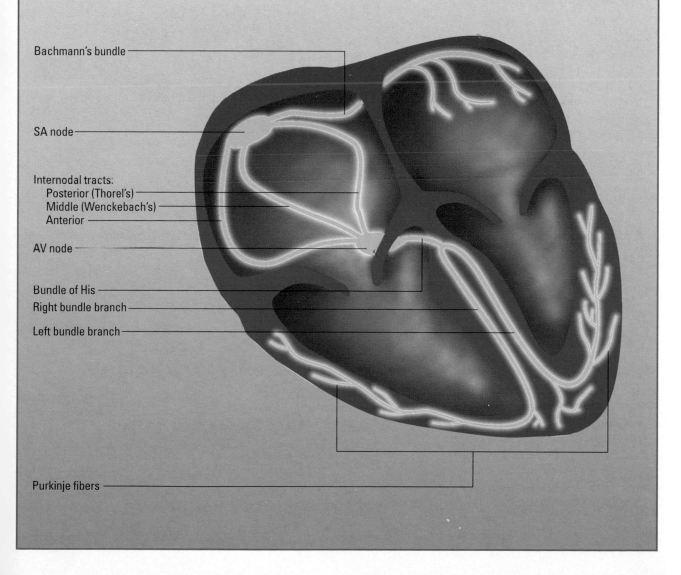

Bachmann's bundle

SA node

Internodal tracts:
    Posterior (Thorel's)
    Middle (Wenckebach's)
    Anterior

AV node

Bundle of His

Right bundle branch

Left bundle branch

Purkinje fibers

How circus reentry develops

Normally, conduction occurs along a single pathway, so circus reentry can't occur. In some people, however, conduction occurs along two pathways—one fast and one slow. The speed and frequency of impulse conduction varies along those paths.

Think of the two pathways as racetracks. One track has a perfect surface for speed. The other meanders through an obstacle course. An impulse starting off stays together until the tracks diverge.

Unidirectional conduction

At that point, the impulse—like a group of runners—splits up, as shown on the right. Half of them take the fast track, and half struggle through obstacles on the slow track. The fast-track runners reach the finish line well ahead of the slow-track runners, which causes the slow-track runners to stop running and disperse.

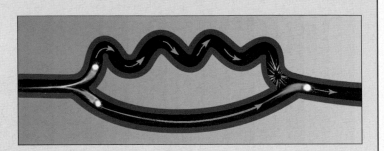

Premature impulse

If an ectopic impulse reaches the tracks earlier than usual, the fast track isn't ready; it's still refractory from the previous conduction. In such cases, shown on the left, the impulse takes the slow track, which can accept "runners" more quickly.

Circus reentry

When the runners reach the bottom of the slow track, as shown on the right, one runner splits off and heads to the finish line. The others are so excited, they head back up the fast track in a kind of victory lap. The impulse then continues around the circuit—down the slow track and up the fast track—repeatedly, sending one runner each time to the finish line and one back up to the starting point. That continuous looping of an impulse through the two pathways is known as circus reentry and can result in tachyarrhythmias.

Afterload

Afterload is the amount of pressure the left ventricle must work against to pump blood into the circulation. The greater this resistance, the more the heart works to pump out blood.

Contractility

Contractility is the ability of muscle cells to contract after depolarization. That ability depends on how much the muscle fibers are stretched at the end of diastole.

Overstretching or understretching these fibers alters contractility and the amount of blood pumped out of the ventricles. Picture trying to shoot a rubber band across the room. If you don't stretch it enough, it won't go far. If you stretch it too much, it'll snap. But if you stretch it just the right amount, it'll go as far as you want it to.

Preload and afterload

Preload refers to a passive stretching exerted by blood on the ventricular muscle at the end of diastole. According to Starling's law, the more the cardiac muscles are stretched in diastole, the more forcefully they contract in systole.

Afterload refers to the pressure that the ventricles need to generate to overcome higher pressure in the aorta. Normally, pressure in the left ventricle at the end of diastole is 5 to 10 mm Hg. In the aorta, it's 70 to 80 mm Hg. That difference means that the left ventricle needs to pump with enough force to pop open the aortic valve.

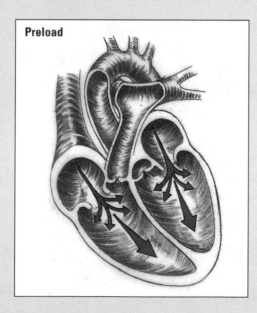

Preload

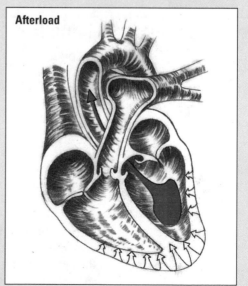

Afterload

Nerve supply to the heart

The heart is supplied by the two branches of the autonomic nervous system — the sympathetic (or adrenergic) and the parasympathetic (or cholinergic).

The sympathetic nervous system is basically the heart's accelerator. Two sets of chemicals — norepinephrine and epinephrine — are highly influenced by this system. Those chemicals increase heart rate, automaticity, atrioventricular conduction, and contractility.

Braking the heart

The parasympathetic nervous system, on the other hand, serves as the heart's brakes. One of this system's nerves, the vagus nerve, carries impulses that slow heart rate and the conduction of impulses through the AV node and ventricles. The vagus nerve is stimulated by baroreceptors, specialized nerve cells in the aorta and the internal carotid arteries. Things that stimulate the baroreceptors also stimulate the vagus nerve to apply its cardiac brakes.

For instance, a stretching of the baroreceptors — which can occur during periods of hypertension or when applying pressure to the carotid artery — stimulates the receptors. In a maneuver called carotid sinus massage, baroreceptors in the carotid arteries are purposely activated in an effort to slow a rapid heart rate.

Transmission of electrical impulses

The heart can't pump unless an electrical stimulus occurs first. Generation and transmission of electrical impulses depend on the automaticity, excitability, conductivity, and contractility of cardiac cells.

Terms revisited

The term automaticity refers to a cell's ability to spontaneously initiate an impulse. Pacemaker cells possess this ability. Excitability results from ion shifts across the cell membrane and indicates how well a cell responds to an electrical stimulus.

Conductivity is the ability of a cell to transmit an electrical impulse to another cardiac cell. Contractility refers to how well the cell contracts after receiving a stimulus.

"De"-cycle and "re"-cycle

As impulses are transmitted, cardiac cells undergo cycles of depolarization and repolarization. (See *Depolarization-repolarization cycle*.) Cardiac cells at rest are considered polarized, meaning that no electrical activity takes place. Cell membranes separate different concentrations of ions, such as sodium and potassium, and create a more negative charge inside the cell. This is called the resting poten-

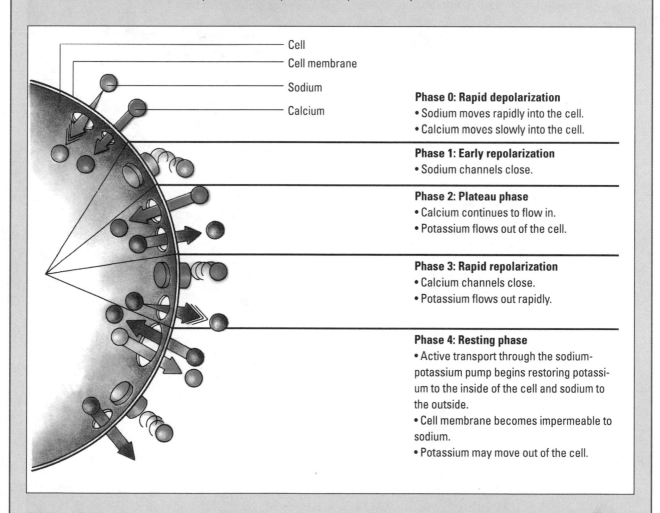

Depolarization-repolarization cycle

Use this illustration to review the five phases of the depolarization-repolarization cycle.

Cell
Cell membrane
Sodium
Calcium

Phase 0: Rapid depolarization
• Sodium moves rapidly into the cell.
• Calcium moves slowly into the cell.

Phase 1: Early repolarization
• Sodium channels close.

Phase 2: Plateau phase
• Calcium continues to flow in.
• Potassium flows out of the cell.

Phase 3: Rapid repolarization
• Calcium channels close.
• Potassium flows out rapidly.

Phase 4: Resting phase
• Active transport through the sodium-potassium pump begins restoring potassium to the inside of the cell and sodium to the outside.
• Cell membrane becomes impermeable to sodium.
• Potassium may move out of the cell.

tial. Once a stimulus occurs, ions cross the cell membrane and cause an action potential, or cell depolarization.

When a cell is fully depolarized, it attempts to return to its resting state in a process called repolarization. Electrical charges in the cell reverse and return to normal.

A cycle of depolarization-repolarization consists of five phases — 0 through 4. The action potential is represented by a curve that shows voltage changes during the five phases. (See *Action potential curve.*)

Many phases of the curve

During phase 0, the cell receives an impulse from a neighboring cell and is depolarized. Phase 1 is marked by early, rapid repolarization. Phase 2, the plateau phase, is a period of slow repolarization.

During phases 1 and 2 and at the beginning of phase 3, the cardiac cell is said to be in its absolute refractory period. *During that period, no stimulus, no matter how strong, can excite the cell.*

Phase 3, the rapid repolarization phase, occurs as the cell returns to its original state. During the last half of this

Memory jogger

To help you remember the difference between depolarization and repolarization, think of the R in repolarization as standing for rest. Remember that repolarization is the resting phase of the cardiac cycle.

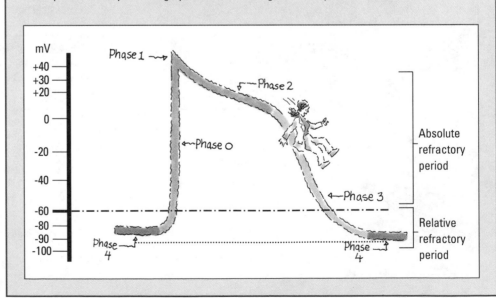

Action potential curve

An action potential curve shows the electrical changes in a myocardial cell during the depolarization-repolarization cycle. This graph shows the changes in a nonpacemaker cell.

phase, when the cell is in its relative refractory period, a very strong stimulus can depolarize it.

Phase 4 is the resting phase of the action potential. By the end of phase 4, the cell is ready for another stimulus.

All that electrical activity is represented on an ECG. *Keep in mind that the ECG represents electrical activity only, not actual pumping of the heart.*

Pathway through the heart

Once depolarization and repolarization occur, the resulting electrical impulse travels through the heart along a pathway called the conduction system. (See *Conducting impulses,* page 13.)

Impulses travel out from the SA node and through the internodal tracts and Bachmann's bundle to the AV node. From there, they travel through the bundle of His, the bundle branches, and finally to the Purkinje fibers.

Numero uno node

The SA node, located in the upper right corner of the right atrium where the superior vena cava joins the atrial tissue mass, is the heart's main pacemaker, generating impulses 60 to 100 times a minute. Once initiated, the impulses follow a specific path through the heart. They usually can't flow in a backward direction because the cells can't respond to a stimulus immediately after depolarization.

Bachmann's bundle of nerves

Impulses from the SA node next travel through Bachmann's bundle, tracts of tissue extending from the SA node to the left atrium. Impulses are thought to be transmitted throughout the right atrium through the anterior, middle, and posterior internodal tracts. Whether those tracts actually exist, however, is unclear. Impulse transmission through the right and left atria occurs so rapidly that the atria contract almost simultaneously.

AV: The slow node

The AV node, located in the inferior right atrium near the ostium of the coronary sinus, is responsible for delaying the impulses that reach it. Although the nodal tissue itself has no pacemaker cells, the tissue surrounding it (called junctional tissue) contains pacemaker cells that can fire at a rate of 40 to 60 times a minute.

The AV node's main function is to delay impulses by 0.04 second to keep the ventricles from contracting too quickly. This delay allows the ventricles to complete their filling phase as the atria contract. It also allows the cardiac muscle to stretch to its fullest for peak cardiac output.

Branch division

The bundle of His, a tract of tissue extending into the ventricles next to the interventricular septum, resumes the rapid conduction of the impulse through the ventricles. The bundle eventually divides into the right and left bundle branches.

The right bundle branch extends down the right side of the interventricular septum and through the right ventricle. The left bundle branch extends down the left side of the interventricular septum and through the left ventricle.

The left bundle branch then splits into two branches, or fascicles: the left anterior fascicle, which extends through the anterior portion of the left ventricle, and the left posterior fascicle, which runs through the lateral and posterior portions of the left ventricle. Impulses travel much faster down the left bundle branch (which feeds the larger, thicker-walled left ventricle) than the right bundle branch (which feeds the smaller, thinner-walled right ventricle).

The difference in the conduction speed allows both ventricles to contract simultaneously. The entire network of specialized nervous tissue that extends through the ventricles is known as the His-Purkinje system.

Those perky Purkinje fibers

Purkinje fibers extend from the bundle branches into the endocardium, deep into the myocardial tissue. These fibers conduct impulses rapidly through the muscle to assist in its depolarization and contraction.

Purkinje fibers can also serve as a pacemaker and are able to discharge impulses at a rate of 20 to 40 times per minute, sometimes even more slowly. (See *Pacemakers of the heart*.) Purkinje fibers usually aren't activated as a pacemaker unless conduction through the bundle of His becomes blocked or a higher pacemaker (SA or AV node) doesn't generate an impulse.

Pacemakers of the heart

Pacemaker cells in lower areas, such as the junctional tissue and the Purkinje fibers, normally remain dormant because they receive impulses from the SA node. They initiate an impulse only when they don't receive one from above, such as when the SA node is damaged from a myocardial infarction.

Firing rates

The illustration shows intrinsic firing rates of pacemaker cells located in three critical areas of the heart.

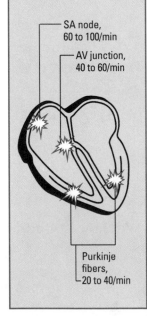

SA node,
60 to 100/min

AV junction,
40 to 60/min

Purkinje
fibers,
20 to 40/min

Abnormal impulses

Now that you understand how the heart generates a normal impulse, let's look at some causes of abnormal impulse conduction, including automaticity, backward conduction of impulses, reentry abnormalities, and ectopy.

When the heart goes on "manual"

Automaticity is a special characteristic of pacemaker cells to generate impulses automatically, without being stimulated to do so. If a cell's automaticity is increased or decreased, an arrhythmia can occur. Tachycardia, for instance, is often caused by an increase in the automaticity of pacemaker cells below the SA node. Likewise, a decrease in automaticity of cells in the SA node can cause the development of bradycardia or an escape rhythm (a compensatory beat generated by a lower pacemaker site).

Out of synch

Impulses that begin below the AV node can be transmitted backward toward the atria. This backward, or retrograde, conduction usually takes longer than normal conduction and can cause the atria and ventricles to beat "out of synch."

Coming back for more

Sometimes impulses cause depolarization twice in a row at a faster-than-normal rate. Such events are referred to as reentry events and can be either circus or focal in origin. In circus reentry, impulses are delayed long enough that cells have time to repolarize. (See *How circus reentry develops,* page 14.) In those cases, the active impulse reenters the same area and produces another impulse.

In focal reentry, cells in the process of repolarizing excite surrounding cells that have already been repolarized. When that happens, the impulse enters the already repolarized cells and causes a second depolarization. Focal reentry happens when repolarization of neighboring cells occurs at different rates within the cells.

Repeating itself

An injured pacemaker (or nonpacemaker) cell may partially depolarize, rather than fully depolarizing. Partial depolarization can lead to spontaneous or secondary depolarization, repetitive ectopic firings called triggered activity.

The resultant depolarization is called afterdepolarization. Early afterdepolarization occurs before the cell is fully repolarized and can be caused by hypokalemia, slow pacing rates, or drug toxicity. If it occurs after the cell has been fully repolarized, it's called delayed afterdepolarization. These problems can be caused by digitalis toxicity, hypercalcemia, or increased catecholamine release. Atrial or ventricular tachycardias may result. You'll learn more about these and other arrhythmias in later chapters.

Quick quiz

1. The term automaticity refers to the ability of a cell to:
    A. initiate an impulse on its own.
    B. send impulses in all directions.
    C. block impulses formed in areas other than the SA node.

Answer: A. Automaticity, the ability of a cell to initiate an impulse on its own, is a unique characteristic of cardiac cells.

2. Parasympathetic stimulation of the heart results in:
    A. increased heart rate and slower AV conduction.
    B. increased heart rate and faster AV conduction.
    C. decreased heart rate and slower AV conduction.

Answer: C. Parasympathetic stimulation of the vagus nerve causes a decrease in heart rate and slowed AV conduction.

3. The normal pacemaker of the heart is the:
    A. SA node.
    B. AV node.
    C. bundle of His.

Answer: A. The SA node is the main pacemaker of the heart, firing at an intrinsic rate of 60 to 100 times a minute.

4. The impulse delay produced by the AV node allows the atria to:
    A. repolarize simultaneously.
    B. contract before the ventricles.
    C. send impulses to the bundle of His.

Answer: B. The 0.04-second delay allows the atria to contract and the ventricles to completely fill, which optimizes cardiac output.

5. The coronary arteries fill with blood during:
   A. atrial systole.
   B. atrial diastole.
   C. ventricular diastole.

Answer: C. The coronary arteries fill with blood when the ventricles are in diastole and filling with blood. The aortic valve is closed at that time, so it no longer blocks blood flow through the coronary ostium into the coronary arteries.

6. When stimulated, baroreceptors cause the heart rate to:
   A. increase.
   B. decrease.
   C. stay the same.

Answer: B. Baroreceptors, when stimulated, cause the heart rate to decrease.

7. The two valves called the semilunar valves are the:
   A. pulmonic and mitral valves.
   B. pulmonic and aortic valves.
   C. aortic and mitral valves.

Answer: B. The semilunar valves are the pulmonic and aortic valves.

8. Passive stretching exerted by blood on the ventricular muscle at the end of diastole is referred to as:
   A. preload.
   B. afterload.
   C. the atrial kick.

Answer: A. The passive stretching exerted by blood on the ventricular muscle at the end of diastole is called preload. It increases with an increase in venous return to the heart.

Scoring

☆☆☆　If you answered all eight items correctly, hooray! You're a happenin', heart-smart hipster!

☆☆　If you answered five to seven correctly, way to go! You're clearly heart smart!

☆　If you answered fewer than five correctly, take heart. Just review this chapter again—and you'll be up to speed.

Obtaining a rhythm strip

Just the facts

An electrocardiogram (ECG) can be used to help diagnose cardiac and noncardiac illnesses and to monitor the effects of medications or electrolyte imbalances. In this chapter, you'll learn:

♦ how important the ECG is for providing effective patient care

♦ how leads and planes function

♦ what types of ECG monitoring are available

♦ how to apply electrodes, select leads, and obtain rhythm strips

♦ how to solve cardiac-monitoring problems.

A look at ECG recordings

The heart's electrical activity produces currents that radiate through the surrounding tissue to the skin. When electrodes are attached to the skin, they sense those electrical currents and transmit them to an ECG monitor. The currents are then transformed into waveforms that represent the heart's depolarization-repolarization cycle.

You might remember that myocardial depolarization occurs when a wave of stimulation passes through the heart and causes the heart muscle to contract. Repolarization is the relaxation phase.

An ECG shows the precise sequence of electrical events occurring in the cardiac cells throughout that process. It allows the nurse to monitor phases of myocardial contraction and to identify rhythm and conduction disturbances. A series of ECGs can be used as a baseline comparison to assess cardiac function.

Leads and planes

To understand electrocardiography, you need to understand leads and planes. Electrodes placed on the skin measure the direction of electrical current discharged by the heart. That current is then transformed into waveforms.

An electrocardiograph records information about those waveforms from different views or perspectives. Those perspectives are called leads and planes.

Take the lead

A lead provides a view of the heart's electrical activity between one positive pole and one negative pole. Between the two poles lies an imaginary line representing the lead's axis, a term that refers to the direction of the current moving through the heart.

The direction of the current affects the direction in which the waveform points on an ECG. (See *Current direction and wave deflection*.) When no electrical activity occurs or the activity is too weak to measure, the waveform looks like a straight line, called an isoelectric waveform.

Plane and simple

The term "plane" refers to a cross-sectional perspective of the heart's electrical activity. The frontal plane, a vertical cut through the middle of the heart, provides an anterior-to-posterior view of electrical activity. The horizontal plane, a transverse cut through the middle of heart, provides either a superior or an inferior view.

Types of ECGs

The two types of ECG recordings are the 12-lead ECG and the single-lead ECG, commonly known as a rhythm strip. Both types give valuable information about heart function.

A dozen views

A 12-lead ECG records information from 12 different views of the heart and provides a complete picture of electrical activity. These 12 views are obtained by placing electrodes on the patient's limbs and chest. The limb leads and the chest, or precordial, leads reflect information from the different planes of the heart.

Different leads provide different information. The six limb leads — I, II, III, augmented vector right (aV_R), augmented vector left (aV_L), and augmented vector foot (aV_F) — provide information about the heart's frontal plane. Leads I, II, and III require a negative and positive electrode for monitoring, which makes those leads bipolar. The augmented leads record information from one lead and are called unipolar.

The six precordial or V leads — V_1, V_2, V_3, V_4, V_5, and V_6 — provide information about the heart's horizontal plane. Like the augmented leads, the precordial leads are also unipolar, requiring only a single electrode. The opposing pole of those leads is the center of the heart as calculated by the electrocardiograph.

Just one view

Single-lead monitoring provides continuous information about the heart's electrical activity and is used to monitor cardiac status. Chest electrodes pick up the heart's electrical activity for display on the monitor. The monitor also displays heart rate and other measurements and prints out strips of cardiac rhythms.

Current direction and wave deflection

The illustration shows possible directions of electrical current, or depolarization, on a lead. The direction of the electrical current determines the upward or downward deflection of an ECG waveform.

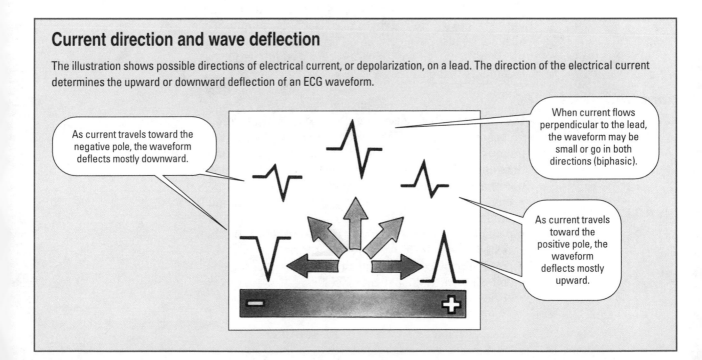

As current travels toward the negative pole, the waveform deflects mostly downward.

When current flows perpendicular to the lead, the waveform may be small or go in both directions (biphasic).

As current travels toward the positive pole, the waveform deflects mostly upward.

Commonly monitored leads include the bipolar leads I, II, and III and two unipolar leads called MCL_1 and MCL_6. The initials *MCL* stand for modified chest lead. These leads are similar to the unipolar leads V_1 and V_6 of the 12-lead ECG. MCL_1 and MCL_6, however, are bipolar leads.

Monitoring ECGs

The type of ECG monitoring system you'll use — hardwire monitoring or telemetry — depends on the patient's condition and the area in which you work. Let's look at each system.

Hardwire basics

With hardwire monitoring, the electrodes are connected directly to the cardiac monitor. Most hardwire monitors are mounted permanently on a shelf or a wall near the patient's bed. Some monitors are mounted on an I.V. pole for portability, and some may include a defibrillator.

The monitor provides a continuous cardiac rhythm display and transmits the ECG tracing to a console at the nurses' station. Both the monitor and the console have alarms and can print rhythm strips to show ectopic beats, for instance, or other arrhythmias. Hardwire monitors can also track pulse oximetry, blood pressure, hemodynamic measurements, and other parameters through various attachments to the patient.

Some drawbacks

Hardwire monitoring is generally used in critical care units and emergency departments because it permits continuous observation of one or more patients from more than one area in the unit. However, this type of monitoring does have drawbacks, among them:
• limited patient mobility because patients are tethered to a monitor by electrodes
• patient discomfort because of the electrodes and cables attached to the chest
• possibility of lead disconnection and loss of cardiac monitoring when the patient moves
• accidental shock to the patient (rare).

Portable points

With telemetry monitoring, the patient carries a small, battery-powered transmitter that sends electrical signals to another location, where the signals are displayed on a monitor screen. This type of ECG monitoring frees the patient from cumbersome wires and cables and protects him from the electrical leakage and accidental shock occasionally associated with hardwire monitoring.

Telemetry monitoring still requires skin electrodes to be placed on the patient's chest. Each electrode is connected by a thin wire to a small transmitter box carried in a pocket or pouch.

Telemetry monitoring is especially useful for detecting arrhythmias that occur at rest or during sleep, exercise, or stressful situations. Most systems, however, can monitor heart rate and rhythm only.

All about leads

Electrode placement is different for each lead, and different leads provide different views of the heart. A lead may be chosen to highlight a particular part of the ECG complex or the electrical events of a specific cardiac cycle.

Although leads II, MCL_1, and MCL_6 are among the most commonly used leads for monitoring, you should adjust leads according to the patient's condition. If your monitoring system has the capability, you may also monitor the patient in more than one lead. (See *Dual lead monitoring,* page 30.)

Going to ground

All bipolar leads have a third electrode, known as the ground, placed on the chest to prevent electrical interference from appearing on the ECG recording.

Heeeere's lead I

Lead I provides a view of the heart that shows current moving from right to left. Because current flows from negative to positive, the positive electrode for this lead is placed on the left arm or on the left side of the chest; the negative electrode is placed on the right arm. Lead I produces a positive deflection on ECG tracings and is helpful in monitoring atrial rhythms and hemiblocks.

Dual lead monitoring

Monitoring in two leads provides a more complete picture than monitoring in one. With simultaneous dual monitoring, you'll generally review the first lead — usually designated as the primary lead — for arrhythmias.

A two-lead view helps detect ectopic beats or aberrant rhythms. Leads II and V_1 are the leads most often monitored simultaneously.

Lead II

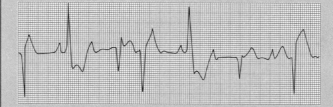

Lead V_1

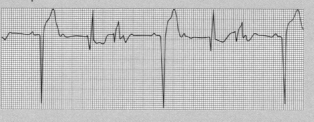

Introducing lead II

Lead II produces a positive deflection. Place the positive electrode on the patient's left leg and the negative electrode on the right arm. For continuous monitoring, place the electrodes on the torso for convenience, with the positive electrode at the lowest palpable rib at the left midclavicular line and the negative electrode below the right clavicle. The current travels down and to the left in this lead. Lead II tends to produce a positive, high-voltage deflection, resulting in tall P, R, and T waves. This lead is commonly used for routine monitoring and is useful for detecting sinus node and atrial arrhythmias.

Next up, lead III

Lead III produces a positive deflection. The positive electrode is placed on the left leg and the negative electrode, on the left arm. Along with lead II, this lead is useful for detecting changes associated with an inferior wall myocardial infarction.

The axes of the three bipolar limb leads — I, II, and III — form a triangle around the heart and provide a frontal plane view of the heart. (See *Einthoven's triangle.*)

The "a" leads

Leads aV_R, aV_L, and aV_F are called augmented leads because the small waveforms that normally would appear from these unipolar leads are enhanced by the electrocardiograph. (See *Augmented leads*, page 32.) The "a" stands for "augmented," and "R, L, and F" stand for the positive electrode position of the lead.

In lead aV_R, the positive electrode is placed on the right arm (hence, the R) and produces a negative deflection because the heart's electrical activity moves away from the lead. In lead aV_L, the positive electrode is on the left arm and produces a positive deflection on ECG. In lead aV_F, the positive electrode is on the left foot and produces a positive deflection. These three limb leads also provide a view of the heart's frontal plane.

Einthoven's triangle

When setting up standard limb leads, you'll place electrodes in positions commonly referred to as Einthoven's triangle, shown here. The electrodes for leads I, II, and III are about equidistant from the heart and form an equilateral triangle.

Axes

The axis of lead I extends from shoulder to shoulder, with the right-arm electrode being the negative electrode and the left-arm electrode positive.

The axis of lead II runs from the negative right-arm electrode to the positive left-leg electrode. The axis of lead III extends from the negative left-arm electrode to the positive left-leg electrode.

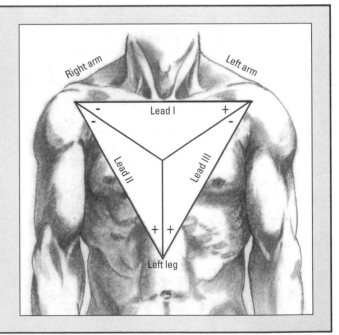

Augmented leads

Leads aV_R, aV_L, and aV_F are called augmented leads. They measure electrical activity between one limb and a single electrode. Lead aV_R provides no specific view of the heart. Lead aV_L shows electrical activity coming from the heart's lateral wall. Lead aV_F shows electrical activity coming from the heart's inferior wall.

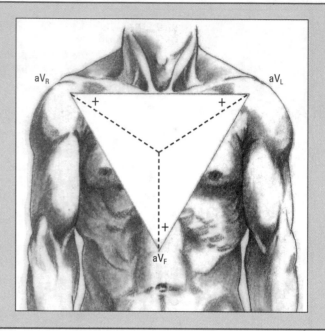

The preeminent precordials

The six unipolar precordial leads are placed in sequence across the chest and give a view of the heart's horizontal plane. (See *Precordial views*.)

Lead V_1. The precordial lead V_1 electrode is placed on the right side of the sternum at the fourth intercostal rib space. This lead corresponds to the modified chest lead MCL_1 and shows the P wave, QRS complex, and ST segment particularly well. It helps to distinguish between right and left ventricular ectopic beats that result from myocardial irritation or other cardiac stimulation outside the normal conduction system. Lead V_1 is also useful in monitoring ventricular arrhythmias, ST-segment changes, and bundle-branch blocks.

Lead V_2. Lead V_2 is placed at the left of the sternum at the fourth intercostal rib space.

Lead V_3. Lead V_3 goes between V_2 and V_4 at the fifth intercostal space. Leads V_1, V_2, and V_3 are biphasic, with both positive and negative deflections. V_2 and V_3 can be used to detect ST-segment elevation.

Precordial views

These illustrations show the different views of the heart obtained from each precordial (chest) lead.

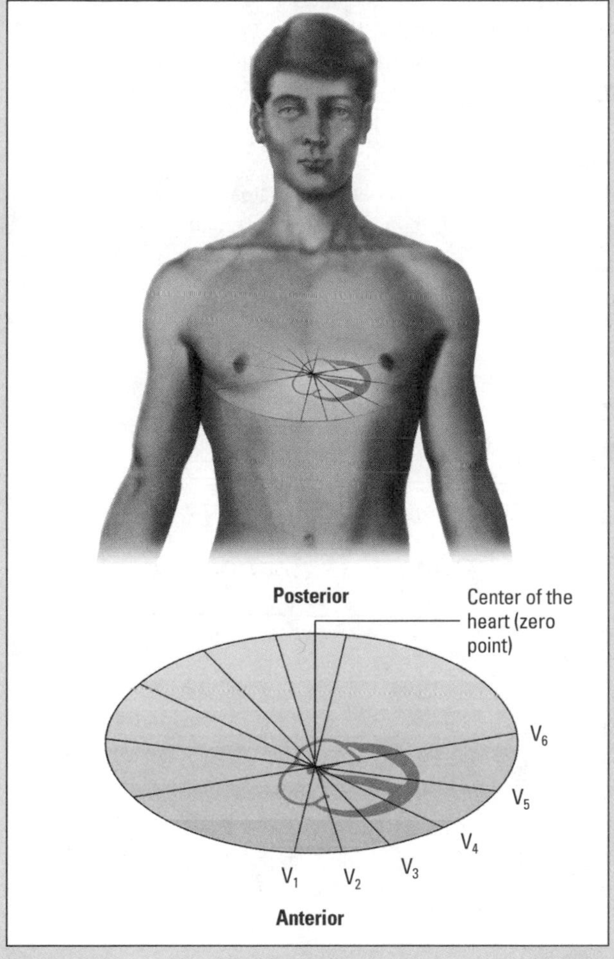

Posterior

Center of the heart (zero point)

V_6

V_5

V_4

V_1 V_2 V_3

Anterior

Lead V_4. Lead V_4 is placed at the fifth intercostal space at the midclavicular line and produces a biphasic waveform.

Lead V_5. Lead V_5 is placed between lead V_4 and V_6 anterior to the axillary line. V_5 produces a positive deflection on the ECG and, along with V_4, can show changes in the ST segment or T wave.

(Text continues on page 36.)

Leadwire systems

This chart shows the correct electrode positions for some of the leads you'll use most often — the five-leadwire, three-leadwire, and telemetry systems. The chart uses the abbreviations RA for the right arm, LA for the left arm, RL for the right leg, LL for the left leg, C for the chest, and G for the ground.

Electrode positions

In the three- and the five-leadwire systems, electrode positions for one lead may be identical to those for another lead. When that happens, change the lead selector switch to the setting that corresponds to the lead you want. In some cases, you'll need to reposition the electrodes.

Telemetry

In a telemetry monitoring system, you can create the same leads as the other systems with just two electrodes and a ground wire.

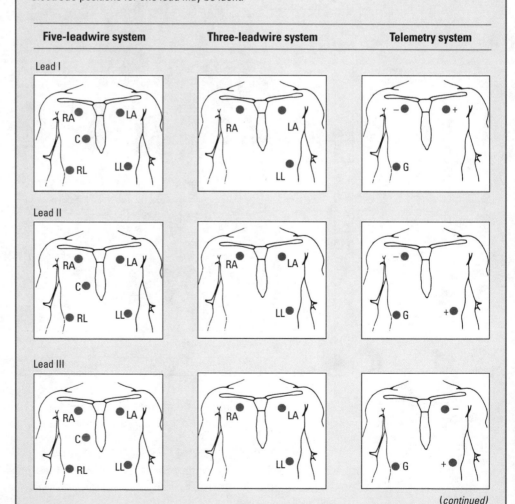

(*continued*)

Leadwire systems *(continued)*

Five-leadwire system	Three-leadwire system	Telemetry system

Lead MCL₁

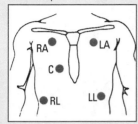 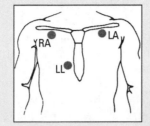 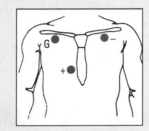

Lead MCL₆

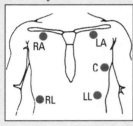 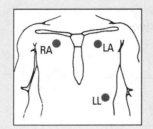 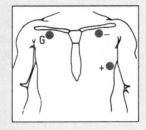

Sternal lead

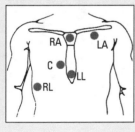 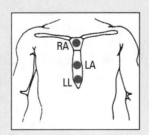 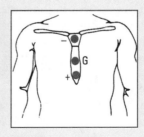

Lewis lead

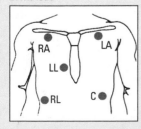 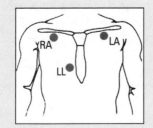 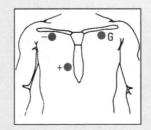

Lead V_6. Lead V_6, the last of the precordial leads, is equivalent to the modified chest lead, MCL_6 and is placed level with V_4 at the midaxillary line. Lead V_6 produces a positive deflection on the ECG.

The modest modified lead

Choose the lead MCL_1 to assess QRS-complex arrhythmias. The equivalent of the MCL_1 lead on the 12-lead ECG is V_1. That lead is created by placing the negative electrode on the left upper chest, the positive electrode on the right of the heart, and the ground electrode usually on the right upper chest.

When the positive electrode is on the right side of the heart and the electrical current travels toward the left ventricle, the waveform has a negative deflection. As a result, ectopic or abnormal beats deflect in a positive direction.

You can use this lead to monitor premature ventricular beats and to distinguish different types of tachycardia, such as ventricular tachycardia and supraventricular tachycardia. Lead MCL_1 can also be used to assess bundle branch defects and P-wave changes and to confirm pacemaker wire placement.

The alternative lead

Lead MCL_6 is an alternative to MCL_1. Like MCL_1, it monitors ventricular conduction changes. The positive lead in MCL_6 is placed in the same location as its equivalent, V_6, for which the positive electrode is placed at the line of the left fifth intercostal space, the negative electrode below the left shoulder, and the ground below the right shoulder.

Lewis and Sternal, the last leads

Two other leads may be used to monitor a patient's cardiac rhythm. The Lewis lead may be viewed with telemetry or hardwire monitoring and helps detect varying P waves associated with atrial arrhythmias.

The sternal lead is used in telemetry because it stabilizes an active patient's ECG pattern. Electrodes are placed directly over the sternum, which hardly moves during activity.

Electrode basics

A three-, four-, or five-electrode system may be used for cardiac monitoring. (See *Leadwire systems*, pages 34 and

Using a five-leadwire system

This illustration shows the correct placement of the leadwires for a five-leadwire system. The chest electrode shown is located in the V₁ position, but you can place it in any of the chest-lead positions. The electrodes are color-coded as follows.

- White — right arm (RA)
- Black — left arm (LA)
- Green — right leg (RL)

- Red — left leg (LL)
- Brown — chest (C)

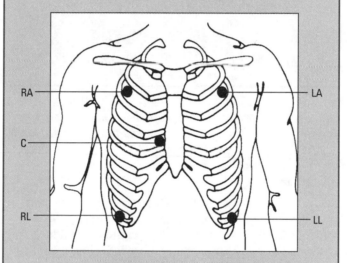

35.) All three systems use a ground electrode to prevent accidental electrical shock to the patient.

A three-electrode system has one positive electrode, one negative electrode, and a ground. A four-electrode system has a right leg electrode that becomes a permanent ground for all leads.

The popular five-electrode system is an extension of the four-electrode system and uses an additional exploratory chest lead to allow you to monitor any six modified chest leads as well as the standard limb leads. (See *Using a five-leadwire system.*) This system uses standardized chest placement. Wires that attach to the electrodes are usually color-coded to help you to place them correctly on the patient's chest.

Also remember your patient's needs when applying chest electrodes. For instance, *if you anticipate defibrilla-*

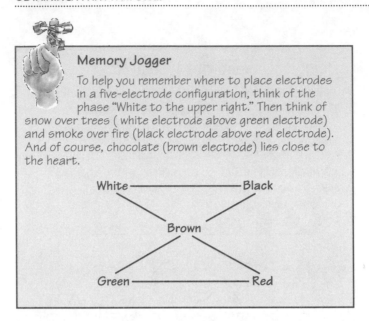

Memory Jogger

To help you remember where to place electrodes in a five-electrode configuration, think of the phase "White to the upper right." Then think of snow over trees (white electrode above green electrode) and smoke over fire (black electrode above red electrode). And of course, chocolate (brown electrode) lies close to the heart.

White ———————— Black

Brown

Green ———————— Red

tion, avoid placing the electrodes to the right of the sternum and under the left breast, where the paddles would be placed.

How to apply electrodes

Before you attach electrodes to your patient, make sure he knows you're monitoring his heart rate and rhythm, not controlling them. Tell him not to become upset if he hears an alarm during the procedure; it probably just means a leadwire has come loose.

Explain the electrode placement procedure to the patient, provide privacy, and wash your hands. Expose the patient's chest, and select electrode sites for the chosen lead. Choose sites over soft tissues or close to bone, not over bony prominences, thick muscles, or skin folds. Those areas can produce ECG artifacts — waveforms not produced by the heart's electrical activity.

Prepare the skin

Next prepare the patient's skin. Use a special rough patch on the back of the electrode, a dry washcloth, or a gauze pad to briskly rub each site until the skin reddens. Be sure not to damage or break the skin. Brisk scrubbing helps to remove dead skin cells and improves electrical contact.

Care about hair

Hair may interfere with electrical contact, so shave densely hairy areas at each site. Dry the areas if you moistened them.

If the patient has oily skin, clean each site with an alcohol sponge, and let it air-dry. This ensures proper adhesion and prevents alcohol from becoming trapped beneath the electrode, which can irritate the skin and cause skin breakdown.

Stick it to me

To apply the electrodes, remove the backing and check to be sure each pregelled electrode is still moist. If an electrode has become dry, discard it and select another. A dry electrode decreases electrical contact and interferes with waveforms.

Apply one electrode to each prepared site using this method:
• Press one side of the electrode against the patient's skin, pull gently, and then press the opposite side of the electrode against the skin.
• Using two fingers, press the adhesive edge around the outside of the electrode to the patient's chest. This fixes the gel and stabilizes the electrode.
• Repeat the procedure for each electrode.
• Every 24 hours, remove the electrodes, assess the patient's skin, and replace the old electrodes with new ones.

Clip, clip, snap, snap

You'll also need to attach leadwires or cable connections to the monitor. Leadwires may clip on or, more commonly, snap on. (See *Clip-on and snap-on leadwires*.) If you're using the snap-on type, attach the electrode to the leadwire before applying it to the patient's chest. You can even do this ahead of time if you know when the patient will arrive. Keep in mind that you may lose electrode contact if you press down to apply the leadwire.

When you use a clip-on leadwire, apply it after the electrode has been secured to the patient's skin. That way, applying the clip won't interfere with the electrode's contact with the skin.

Clip-on and snap-on leadwires

Several kinds of leadwires are available for monitoring. A clip-on leadwire should be attached to the electrode *after* it has been placed on the patient's chest. A snap-on leadwire should be attached to the electrode *before* it has been placed on the patient's chest. Doing so prevents patient discomfort and disturbance of the contact between the electrode and the skin.

Clip-on leadwire

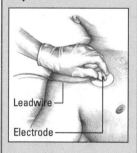

Snap-on leadwire

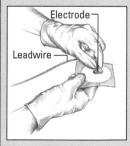

Observing the cardiac rhythm

Once the electrodes are in proper position, the monitor is on, and the necessary cables are attached, observe the screen. You should see the patient's ECG waveform. Although some monitoring systems allow you to make adjustments by touching the screen, most require you to manipulate knobs and buttons. If the waveform appears too large or too small, change the size by adjusting the gain control. If the waveform appears too high or too low on the screen, adjust the position dial.

Verify that the monitor detects each heartbeat by comparing the patient's apical rate with the rate displayed on the monitor. Set the upper and lower limits of the heart rate according to your facility's policy and the patient's condition. Heart rate alarms are generally set 10 to 20 beats per minute higher or lower than the patient's heart rate.

Monitors with arrhythmia detectors generate a rhythm strip automatically whenever the alarm goes off. You can obtain other views of your patient's cardiac rhythm by selecting different leads. You can select leads with the lead selector button or switch.

Printing it out

To get a printout of the patient's cardiac rhythm, press the record control on the monitor. The ECG strip will be printed at the central console. Some systems print the rhythm from a recorder box on the monitor itself.

Most monitors can input the patient's name as a permanent record, but if the monitor you're using can't do this, label the rhythm strip with the patient's name, room number, date, time, and rhythm interpretation. Add any appropriate clinical information to the ECG strip, such as any medication administered or patient activity at the time of the recording. Be sure to place the rhythm strip in the appropriate section of the patient's medical record.

It's all on paper

Waveforms produced by the heart's electrical current are recorded on graphed ECG paper by a heated stylus. ECG paper consists of horizontal and vertical lines forming a grid. A piece of ECG paper is called an ECG strip or tracing. (See *ECG grid*.)

ECG grid

This ECG grid shows the horizontal axis and vertical axis and their respective measurement values.

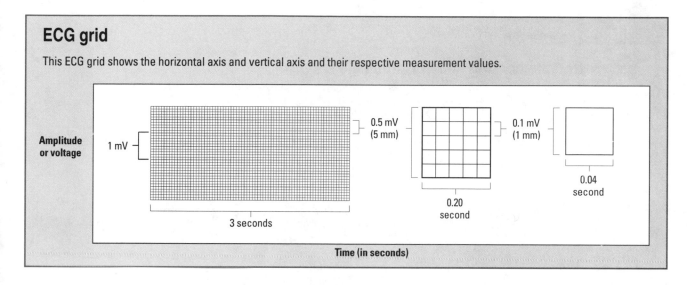

The horizontal axis of the ECG strip represents time. Each small block equals 0.04 second, and five small blocks form a large block, which equals 0.2 second. This time increment is determined by multiplying 0.04 second (for one small block) by 5, the number of small blocks that compose a large block. Five large blocks equal 1 second (5 × 0.2). When measuring or calculating a patient's heart rate, a 6-second strip comprised of 30 large blocks is usually used.

The ECG strip's vertical axis measures amplitude, or electrical voltage in millivolts (mV). Each small block represents 0.1 mV; each large block, 0.5 mV. To determine the amplitude of a wave, segment, or interval, count the number of small blocks from the baseline to the highest or lowest point of the wave, segment, or interval.

Troubleshooting problems

For optimal cardiac monitoring, you need to recognize problems that can interfere with obtaining a reliable ECG recording. (See *Troubleshooting monitor problems,* page 42.) Causes of interference include artifact from patient movement and poorly placed or poorly functioning equipment.

Artifact

Artifact, also called waveform interference, may be seen with excessive movement (somatic tremor). The baseline

Mixed signals

Troubleshooting monitor problems

What you see	What might cause it	What to do about it
Artifact (waveform interference) 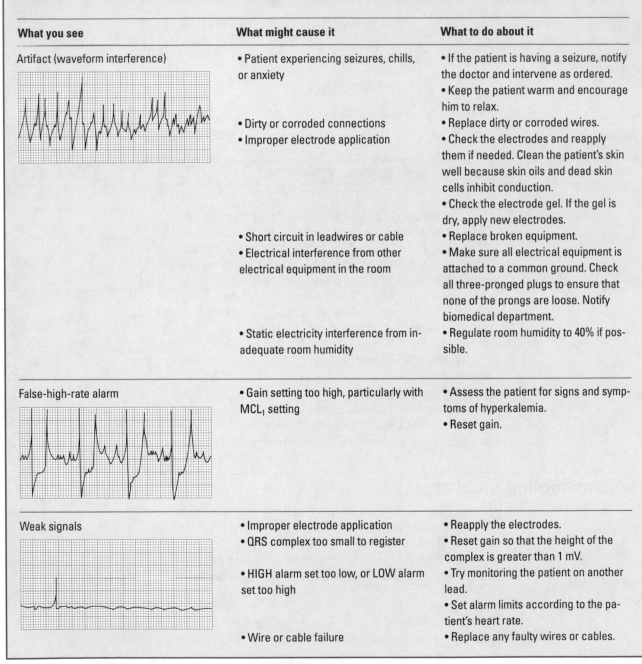	• Patient experiencing seizures, chills, or anxiety	• If the patient is having a seizure, notify the doctor and intervene as ordered. • Keep the patient warm and encourage him to relax.
	• Dirty or corroded connections • Improper electrode application	• Replace dirty or corroded wires. • Check the electrodes and reapply them if needed. Clean the patient's skin well because skin oils and dead skin cells inhibit conduction. • Check the electrode gel. If the gel is dry, apply new electrodes.
	• Short circuit in leadwires or cable • Electrical interference from other electrical equipment in the room	• Replace broken equipment. • Make sure all electrical equipment is attached to a common ground. Check all three-pronged plugs to ensure that none of the prongs are loose. Notify biomedical department.
	• Static electricity interference from inadequate room humidity	• Regulate room humidity to 40% if possible.
False-high-rate alarm	• Gain setting too high, particularly with MCL_1 setting	• Assess the patient for signs and symptoms of hyperkalemia. • Reset gain.
Weak signals	• Improper electrode application • QRS complex too small to register	• Reapply the electrodes. • Reset gain so that the height of the complex is greater than 1 mV.
	• HIGH alarm set too low, or LOW alarm set too high	• Try monitoring the patient on another lead. • Set alarm limits according to the patient's heart rate.
	• Wire or cable failure	• Replace any faulty wires or cables.

Troubleshooting monitor problems (continued)

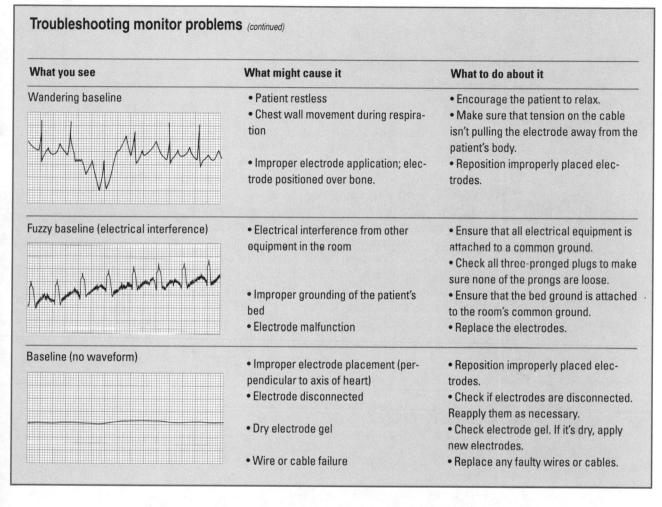

What you see	What might cause it	What to do about it
Wandering baseline	• Patient restless • Chest wall movement during respiration • Improper electrode application; electrode positioned over bone.	• Encourage the patient to relax. • Make sure that tension on the cable isn't pulling the electrode away from the patient's body. • Reposition improperly placed electrodes.
Fuzzy baseline (electrical interference)	• Electrical interference from other equipment in the room • Improper grounding of the patient's bed • Electrode malfunction	• Ensure that all electrical equipment is attached to a common ground. • Check all three-pronged plugs to make sure none of the prongs are loose. • Ensure that the bed ground is attached to the room's common ground. • Replace the electrodes.
Baseline (no waveform)	• Improper electrode placement (perpendicular to axis of heart) • Electrode disconnected • Dry electrode gel • Wire or cable failure	• Reposition improperly placed electrodes. • Check if electrodes are disconnected. Reapply them as necessary. • Check electrode gel. If it's dry, apply new electrodes. • Replace any faulty wires or cables.

of the ECG appears wavy, bumpy, or tremulous. Dry electrodes may also cause this problem due to poor electrical contact.

Interference

Electrical interference, also called 60-cycle interference, is caused by electrical power leakage. It may also occur due to interference from other room equipment or improperly grounded equipment. As a result, the lost current pulses at a rate of 60 cycles per second. This interference appears on the ECG as a baseline that's thick and unreadable.

Wandering baseline

A wandering baseline undulates, meaning that all wave-forms are present but the baseline isn't stationary. This problem is usually caused by movement of the chest wall during respiration, poor electrode placement, or poor electrode contact.

Faulty equipment

Faulty equipment, such as broken leadwires and cables, also can cause monitoring problems. Excessively worn equipment can cause improper grounding, putting the patient at risk for accidental shock.

Be aware that some types of artifact resemble arrhythmias, and the monitor will interpret them as such. For instance, a small movement such as the patient brushing his teeth may be sensed by the monitor as a potentially lethal ventricular tachycardia. So remember to *treat the patient, not the monitor*. The more familiar you become with your unit's monitoring system — and with your patient — the more quickly you can recognize and interpret problems and act appropriately.

Quick quiz

1. On ECG graph paper, the horizontal axis measures:
   A. time.
   B. speed.
   C. voltage.

Answer: A. The horizontal axis measures time and is recorded in increments of 0.04 second for each small box.

2. On ECG graph paper, the vertical axis measures:
   A. time.
   B. speed.
   C. voltage.

Answer: C. The vertical axis measures voltage by the height of a waveform.

3. The leads *not* included in a 12-lead ECG are:
    A. II and III.
    B. V_1 and V_3.
    C. MCL_1 and MCL_6.

Answer: C. The modified chest leads MCL_1 and MCL_6 are equivalent to V_1 and V_6 of the 12-lead ECG, but they're actually bipolar limb leads and aren't included in a 12-lead ECG.

4. A biphasic deflection will occur on an ECG if the electrical current is traveling in a direction:
    A. posterior to the positive electrode.
    B. perpendicular to the positive electrode.
    C. superior to the positive electrode.

Answer: B. A current traveling in a route perpendicular to the positive electrode will generate a biphasic wave, partially above and below the isoelectric line.

5. If a lead comes off the patient's chest, the waveform:
    A. will appear much larger on the monitor.
    B. will appear much smaller on the monitor.
    C. won't be seen at all on the monitor.

Answer: C. Leadwire disconnection will stop the monitoring process, and the waveform won't be seen on the monitor.

6. To monitor lead II, you would place:
    A. the positive electrode at the lowest palpable rib at the left midclavicular line and the negative electrode below the right clavicle.
    B. the positive electrode below the right clavicle at the midline and the negative electrode below the left clavicle at the midline.
    C. the positive electrode below the left clavicle and the negative electrode below the right clavicle at the midclavicular line.

Answer: A. This electrode position is the proper one for monitoring in lead II.

Scoring

☆☆☆   If you answered all six items correctly, superb! We're
ready to go out on a *limb lead* for you!

☆☆   If you answered four or five correctly, great! We hardly
need to *monitor* your progress!

☆   If you answered three or fewer correctly, keep at it! We
like the way your *current* flows!

3

Interpreting a rhythm strip

Just the facts

This chapter explains the rate and rhythm of electrical impulses as they travel through the heart. In this chapter, you'll learn:

♦ what the components of an electrocardiogram (ECG) complex are, along with their significance and variations

♦ how to calculate the rate and rhythm of an ECG recording

♦ what the step-by-step approach to ECG interpretation is

♦ how to identify normal sinus rhythm.

A look at an ECG complex

An ECG complex represents the electrical events occuring in one cardiac cycle. A complex consists of five waveforms labeled with the letters P, Q, R, S, and T. The middle three letters — Q, R, and S — are referred to as a unit, the QRS complex. ECG tracings represent the conduction of electrical impulses from the atria to the ventricles. (See *Normal ECG,* page 48.)

The P wave

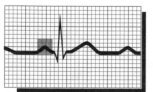

The P wave is the first component of a normal ECG waveform. It represents atrial depolarization — conduction of an electrical impulse through the atria. When evaluating a P wave, look closely at its characteristics, especially its location, configuration, and deflection.

A normal P wave has the following characteristics:
- Location — precedes the QRS complex
- Amplitude — 2 to 3 mm high
- Duration — 0.06 to 0.12 second
- Configuration — usually rounded and upright
- Deflection — positive or upright in leads I, II, aV_F, and V_2 to V_6; usually positive but may vary in leads III and aV_L; negative or inverted in lead aV_R; biphasic or variable in lead V_1.

Normal ECG

This strip shows the components of a normal ECG waveform.

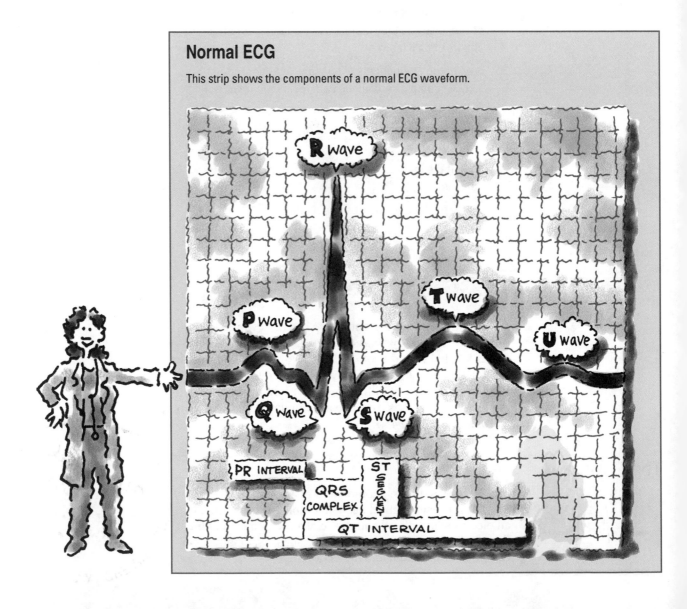

If the deflection and configuration of a P wave are normal — for example, if the P wave is upright in lead II and is rounded and smooth — and if the P wave precedes each QRS complex, you can assume that this electrical impulse originated in the sinoatrial (SA) node. The atria start to contract partway through the P wave, but you won't see this on the ECG. Remember, the ECG records electrical activity only, not mechanical activity or contraction.

The odd Ps

Peaked, notched, or enlarged P waves may represent atrial hypertrophy or enlargement associated with chronic obstructive pulmonary disease, pulmonary emboli, valvular disease, or congestive heart failure. Inverted P waves may signify retrograde or reverse conduction from the atrioventricular (AV) junction towards the atria. *Whenever an upright sinus P wave becomes inverted, consider retrograde or reverse conduction as possible conditions.*

Varying P waves indicate that the impulse may be coming from different sites, as with a wandering pacemaker rhythm, irritable atrial tissue, or damage near the SA node. Absent P waves may signify conduction by a route other than the SA node, as with a junctional or atrial fibrillation rhythm. When a P wave doesn't precede the QRS complex, complete heart block may be present.

The PR interval

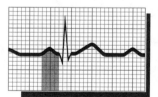

The PR interval tracks the atrial impulse from the atria through the AV node, bundle of His, and right and left bundle branches. When evaluating a PR interval, look especially at its duration. Changes in the PR interval indicate an altered impulse formation or a conduction delay, as seen in AV block.

A normal PR interval has the following characteristics (amplitude, configuration, and deflection aren't measured):
• Location — from the beginning of the P wave to the beginning of the QRS complex
• Duration — 0.12 to 0.20 second.

The short and long of it

Short PR intervals (less than 0.12 second) indicate that the impulse originated somewhere other than the SA node. This variation is associated with junctional arrhythmias and preexcitation syndromes. Prolonged PR intervals (greater than 0.20 second) may represent a conduction delay through the atria or AV junction due to digitalis toxicity or heart block — slowing related to ischemia or conduction tissue disease.

The QRS complex

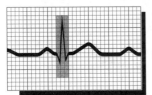

The QRS complex follows the P wave and represents depolarization of the ventricles, or impulse conduction. Immediately after the ventricles depolarize, as represented by the QRS complex, they contract. That contraction ejects blood from the ventricles and pumps it through the arteries, creating a pulse.

Not necessarily mechanical

Whenever you're monitoring cardiac rhythm, remember that the waveform you see represents the heart's electrical activity only. It doesn't guarantee a mechanical contraction of the heart and a subsequent pulse. The contraction could be weak, as happens with premature ventricular contractions, or absent, as happens with pulseless electrical activity. So before you treat the strip, check the patient.

It's all normal

Pay special attention to the duration and configuration when evaluating a QRS complex. A normal complex has the following characteristics:
• Location — follows the PR interval
• Amplitude — 5 to 30 mm high, but differs for each lead used
• Duration — 0.06 to 0.10 second, or half of the PR interval. Duration is measured from the beginning of the Q wave to the end of the S wave or from the beginning of the R wave if the Q wave is absent.
• Configuration — consists of the Q wave (the first negative deflection, or deflection above the baseline, after the P wave), the R wave (the first positive deflection after the Q wave), and the S wave (the first negative deflection after

QRS waveform variety

The illustrations below show the various configurations of QRS complexes. When documenting the QRS complex, use uppercase letters to indicate a wave with a normal or high amplitude (greater than 5 mm) and lowercase letters to indicate one with a low amplitude (less than 5 mm).

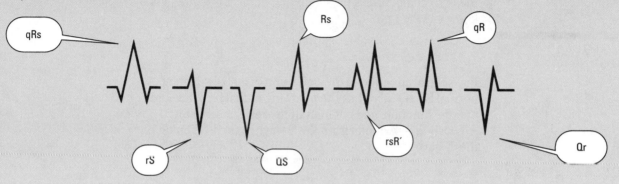

the R wave). You may not always see all three waves. The ventricles depolarize quickly, minimizing contact time between the stylus and the ECG paper, so the QRS complex typically appears thinner than other ECG components. It may also look different in each lead. (See *QRS waveform variety*.)

• Deflection — positive in leads I, II, III, aV_L, aV_F, and V_4 to V_6 and negative in leads aV_R and V_1 to V_3.

Crucial I.D.

Remember that the QRS complex represents intraventricular conduction time. That's why identifying and correctly interpreting it is so crucial. If no P wave appears with the QRS complex, then the impulse probably originated in the ventricles, indicating a ventricular arrhythmia.

Deep and wide

Deep, wide Q waves may represent myocardial infarction. In this case, the Q wave amplitude is 25% of the R-wave amplitude, or the duration of the Q wave is 0.04 second or more. A notched R wave may signify a bundle-branch block. A widened QRS (greater than 0.12 second) may signify a ventricular conduction delay. A missing QRS complex may indicate AV block or ventricular standstill.

The ST segment

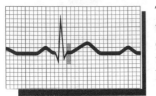

Normal ST

The ST segment represents the end of ventricular conduction or depolarization and the beginning of ventricular recovery or repolarization. The point that marks the end of the QRS complex and the beginning of the ST segment is known as the J point.

Pay special attention to the deflection of an ST segment. A normal ST segment has the following characteristics (amplitude, duration, and configuration aren't observed):
• Location — extends from the S wave to the beginning of the T wave

Changes in the ST segment

Closely monitoring the ST segment on a patient's ECG can help you detect ischemia or injury before infarction develops.

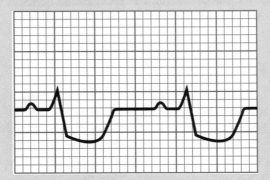

ST-segment depression
An ST segment is considered depressed when it is 0.5 mm or more below the baseline. A depressed ST segment may indicate myocardial ischemia or digitalis toxicity.

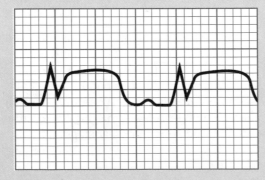

ST-segment elevation
An ST segment is considered elevated when it is 1 mm or more above the baseline. An elevated ST segment may indicate myocardial injury.

• Deflection — usually isoelectric (neither positive nor negative); may vary from − 0.5 to +1 mm in some precordial leads.

Not so normal ST

A change in the ST segment may indicate myocardial damage. An ST segment may become either elevated or depressed. (See *Changes in the ST segment*.)

The T wave

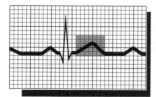

The T wave represents ventricular recovery or repolarization. When evaluating a T wave, look at the amplitude, configuration, and deflection. Normal T waves have the following characteristics (duration isn't measured):
• Location — follows the S wave
• Amplitude — 0.5 mm in leads I, II, and III and up to 10 mm in the precordial leads
• Configuration — typically round and smooth
• Deflection — usually upright in leads I, II, and V_3 to V_6; inverted in lead aV_R; variable in all other leads.

Why is that T so bumpy?

The T wave's peak represents the relative refractory period of ventricular repolarization, a period during which cells are especially vulnerable to extra stimuli. Bumps in a T wave may indicate that a P wave is hidden in it. If a P wave is hidden, atrial depolarization has occurred, the impulse having originated at a site above the ventricles.

Tall, inverted, or pointy Ts

Tall, peaked, or tented T waves indicate myocardial injury or hyperkalemia. Inverted T waves in leads I, II, or V_3 through V_6 may represent myocardial ischemia. Heavily notched or pointed T waves in an adult may mean pericarditis.

The QT interval

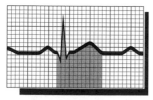

The QT interval measures ventricular depolarization and repolarization. The length of the QT interval varies according to heart rate. The faster the heart rate, the shorter the QT interval. When checking the QT interval, look closely at the duration.

A normal QT interval has the following characteristics (amplitude, configuration, and deflection aren't observed):
• Location — extends from the beginning of the QRS complex to the end of the T wave
• Duration — varies according to age, sex, and heart rate; usually lasts from 0.36 to 0.44 second; shouldn't be greater than half the distance between consecutive R waves when the rhythm is regular.

The importance of QT

The QT interval shows the time needed for the ventricular depolarization-repolarization cycle. An abnormality in duration may indicate myocardial problems. Prolonged QT intervals indicate prolonged ventricular repolarization, meaning that the relative refractory period is longer.

This variation is also associated with certain medications such as type I antiarrhythmics. Prolonged QT syndrome is a congenital conduction-system defect present in certain families. Short QT intervals may result from digitalis toxicity or hypercalcemia.

The U wave

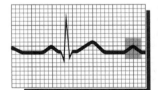

The U wave represents the recovery period of the Purkinje or ventricular conduction fibers. It's not present on every rhythm strip. The configuration is the most important characteristic of the U wave.

When present, a normal U wave has the following characteristics (amplitude and duration aren't measured):
• Location — follows the T wave
• Configuration — typically upright and rounded
• Deflection — upright.

The U wave may not appear on an ECG. A prominent U wave may be due to hypercalcemia, hypokalemia, or digitalis toxicity.

8-step method

Interpreting a rhythm strip is a skill that develops through practice. You can use several methods, as long as you're consistent. (See *Methods of measuring rhythm*.) Rhythm strip analysis requires a sequential and systematic approach, such as the eight steps outlined here.

Methods of measuring rhythm

You can use either of the following methods to determine atrial or ventricular rhythm.

Paper-and-pencil method

Place the ECG strip on a flat surface. Then position the straight edge of a piece of paper along the strip's baseline. Move the paper up slightly so the straight edge is near the peak of the R wave.

With a pencil, mark the paper at the R waves of two consecutive QRS complexes, as shown. This is the R-R interval. Next, move the paper across the strip lining up the two marks with succeeding R-R intervals. If the distance for each R-R interval is the same, the ventricular rhythm is regular. If the distance varies, the rhythm is irregular.

Use the same method to measure the distance between the P waves (the P-P interval) and determine whether the atrial rhythm is regular or irregular.

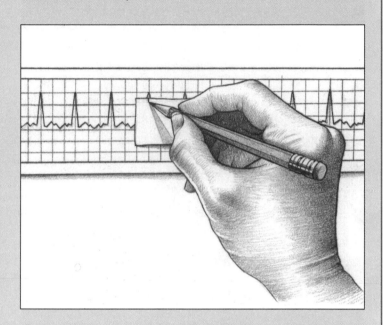

Caliper method

With the ECG on a flat surface, place one point of the calipers on the peak of the first R wave of two consecutive QRS complexes. Then adjust the caliper legs so the other point is on the peak of the next R wave, as shown. This distance is the R-R interval.

Now pivot the first point of the calipers toward the third R wave and note whether it falls on the peak of that wave. Check succeeding R-R intervals in the same way. If they're all the same, the ventricular rhythm is regular. If they vary, the rhythm is irregular.

Using the same method, measure the P-P intervals to determine whether the atrial rhythm is regular or irregular.

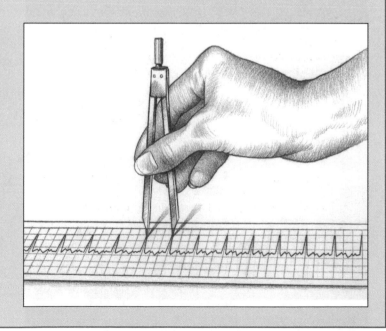

Calculating the heart rate

This table can help make the sequencing method of determining heart rate more precise. After counting the number of boxes between the R waves, use this table to find the rate.

For example, if you count 20 small blocks or 4 large ones, the rate would be 75 beats/minute. To calculate the atrial rate, use the same method with P waves instead of R waves.

Rapid estimation

This rapid-rate calculation is also called the countdown method. Using the number of large boxes between R waves or P waves as a guide, you can rapidly estimate ventricular or atrial rates by memorizing the sequence "300, 150, 100, 75, 60, 50."

Number of small blocks	Heart rate
5 (1 large block)	300
6	250
7	214
8	187
9	166
10 (2 large blocks)	150
11	136
12	125
13	115
14	107
15 (3 large blocks)	100
16	94
17	88
18	83
19	79
20 (4 large blocks)	75
21	71
22	68
23	65
24	63
25 (5 large blocks)	60
26	58
27	56
28	54
29	52
30 (6 large blocks)	50
31	48
32	47
33	45
34	44
35 (7 large blocks)	43
36	41
37	40
38	39
39	38
40 (8 large blocks)	37

Step 1: Check the rhythm

To determine the heart's atrial and ventricular rhythms, use either the paper-and-pencil method or the caliper method.

For atrial rhythm, measure the P-P intervals — the intervals between consecutive P waves. These intervals should occur regularly with only small variations associated with respirations. Then compare the P-P intervals in several cycles. Consistently similar P-P intervals indicate regular atrial rhythm; dissimilar P-P intervals indicate irregular atrial rhythm.

To determine the ventricular rhythm, measure the intervals between two consecutive R waves in the QRS complexes. If an R wave isn't present, use either the Q wave or the S wave of consecutive QRS complexes. The R-R intervals should occur regularly.

Then compare R-R intervals in several cycles. Just like with atrial rhythms, consistently similar intervals mean a regular rhythm; dissimilar intervals point to an irregular rhythm.

Ask yourself: How irregular is the rhythm? Is it slightly irregular or markedly so? Does the irregularity occur in a pattern (a regularly irregular pattern)? Keep in mind that variations of up to 0.04 second are considered normal.

Step 2: Calculate the rate

You can use one of three methods to determine atrial and ventricular heart rate. But remember, don't rely on those methods alone. Always check a pulse to correlate it with the heart rate on the ECG.

- *10-times method.* The easiest way to calculate rate is the 10-times method, especially if the rhythm is irregular. You'll notice that ECG paper is marked in increments of 3 seconds, or 15 large boxes. To figure the atrial rate, obtain a 6-second strip, count the number of P waves on it, and multiply by 10. Ten 6-second strips equal 1 minute. Calculate ventricular rate the same way, using the R waves.
- *1,500 method.* If the heart rhythm is regular, use the 1,500 method, so named because 1,500 small squares equals 1 minute. Count the small squares between identical points on two consecutive P waves, and then divide 1,500 by that number to get the atrial rate. To obtain the ventricular rate, use the same method with two consecutive R waves.
- *Sequence method.* The third method of estimating heart rate is the sequence method, which requires memorizing a sequence of numbers. (See *Calculating the heart rate.*) For atrial rate, find a P wave that peaks on a heavy black line and assign the following numbers to the next six heavy black lines: 300, 150, 100, 75, 60, and 50. Then find the next P wave peak and estimate the atrial rate, based on the number assigned to the nearest heavy black line. Estimate the ventricular rate the same way, using the R wave.

Step 3: Evaluate the P wave

When examining a rhythm strip for P waves, ask yourself: Are P waves present? Do they all have normal configuration? Are they all of similar size and shape? Does every P wave have a QRS complex? (See *Where P waves should be,* page 58.)

Step 4: Check out the P to R

To measure the PR interval, count the small squares between the start of the P wave and the start of the QRS complex; then multiply the number of squares by 0.04 second. Now ask yourself: Is the duration a normal 0.12 to 0.20 second? Is the PR interval constant?

Step 5: Now check out the Q to R to S

When determining QRS duration, make sure you measure straight across from the end of the PR interval to the end of the S wave, not just to the peak. Remember, the QRS has no horizontal components. To calculate duration, count the number of small squares between the beginning and end of the QRS complex and multiply this number by

Where P waves should be

In this 6-second rhythm strip, each P wave is followed by a QRS complex, as it normally would.

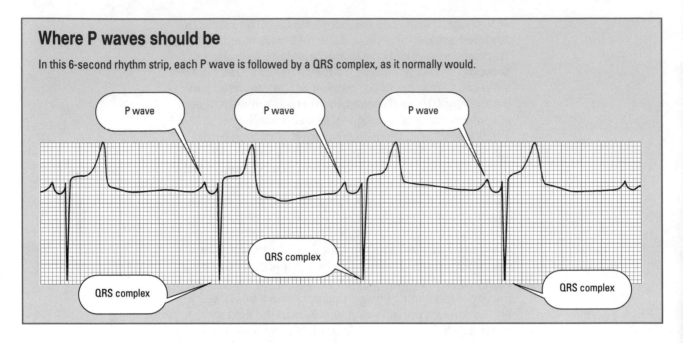

0.04 second. Then ask yourself: Is the duration a normal 0.06 to 0.10 second? Are all QRS complexes the same size and shape? (If not, measure each one and describe them individually.) Does a QRS complex appear after every P wave?

Step 6: Talk to the T wave

Examine the strip for T waves. Then ask yourself: Are T waves present? Do they all have a normal shape? Do they all have a normal amplitude? Do they all have the same amplitude as the QRS complexes?

Step 7: On to the QT...

Count the number of small squares between the beginning of the QRS complex and the end of the T wave, where the T wave returns to the baseline. Multiply this number by 0.04 second. Ask yourself: Is the duration a normal 0.36 to 0.44 second?

Step 8: Oh, yes, and don't forget ...

Check for ectopic beats and other abnormalities. Also check the ST segment for abnormalities, and look for the presence of a U wave. Note your findings, and then interpret them by naming the rhythm strip according to one or all of these findings:

• origin of the rhythm; for example, sinus node, atria, AV node, or ventricles
• rate characteristics; for example, bradycardia or tachycardia
• rhythm abnormalities; for example, flutter, fibrillation, heart block, escape rhythm, or other arrhythmias.

Recognizing normal sinus rhythm

Before you can recognize an arrhythmia, you first need to be able to recognize normal sinus rhythm. Normal sinus rhythm records an impulse that starts in the sinus node and progresses to the ventricles through a normal conduction pathway — from the sinus node to the atria and AV node, through the bundle of His, to the bundle branches, and on to the Purkinje fibers. Normal sinus rhythm is the standard against which all other rhythms are compared. (See *Normal sinus rhythm*.)

Normal sinus rhythm

Normal sinus rhythm, shown below, represents normal impulse conduction through the heart.

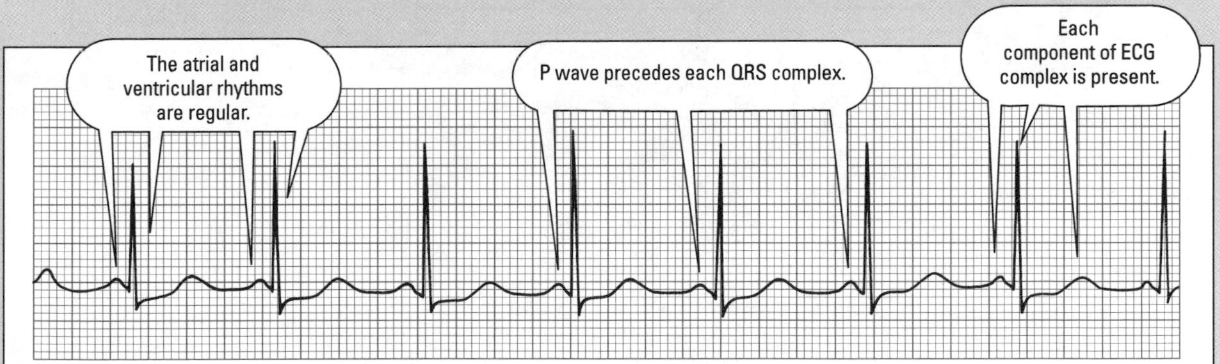

The atrial and ventricular rhythms are regular.

P wave precedes each QRS complex.

Each component of ECG complex is present.

Characteristics of normal sinus rhythm include:

• regular rhythm
• normal rate
• a P wave for every QRS complex; all P waves similar in size and shape

• all QRS complexes similar in size and shape
• normal PR and QT intervals
• normal (upright and round) T waves.

What makes for normal?

Following the eight-step method described above, here are the characteristics of normal sinus rhythm:

• Atrial and ventricular rhythms are regular.

• Atrial and ventricular rates fall between 60 and 100 beats/minute, the SA node's normal firing rate, and all impulses are conducted to the ventricles.

• P waves are rounded, smooth, and upright in lead II, signaling that a sinus impulse has reached the atria.

• The PR interval is normal (0.12 to 0.20 second), indicating that the impulse is following normal conduction pathways.

• The QRS complex is of normal duration (less than 0.12 second), representing normal ventricular impulse conduction and recovery.

• The T wave is upright in lead II, confirming that normal repolarization has taken place.

• The QT interval is within normal limits (0.36 to 0.44 second).

• No ectopic or aberrant beats are occurring.

Quick quiz

1. The P wave represents:
 A. atrial repolarization.
 B. atrial depolarization.
 C. ventricular depolarization.

Answer: B. The impulse spreading across the atria generates a P wave.

2. The normal duration of a QRS complex is:
 A. 0.06 to 0.10 second.
 B. 0.12 to 0.20 second.
 C. 0.36 to 0.44 second.

Answer: A. This time frame — 0.06 to 0.10 second — represents ventricular depolarization.

3. To gather information about impulse conduction from the atria to the ventricles, study the:
 A. P wave.

   B. PR interval.
   C. ST segment.

Answer: B. The PR interval measures the interval between atrial depolarization and ventricular depolarization. A normal PR interval is 0.12 to 0.20 second.

4. The period when myocardial cells are vulnerable to extra stimuli begins with:
   A. the end of the P wave.
   B. the start of the R wave.
   C. the peak of the T wave.

Answer: C. The peak of the T wave represents the beginning of the relative, though not the absolute, refractory period, when the cells are vulnerable to stimuli.

5. Atrial and ventricular rates can be determined by counting the number of small boxes between:
   A. the end of one P wave and the beginning of another.
   B. two consecutive P or R waves.
   C. the middle of two consecutive T waves.

Answer: B. Atrial and ventricular rates can be determined by counting the number of small boxes between two consecutive P or R waves and then dividing that number into 1,500.

Test strips

Now try this test strip. Fill in the blanks below with the particular characteristics of the strip.

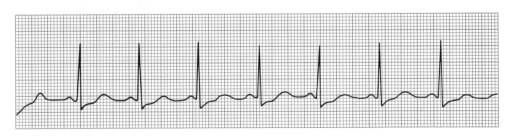

Atrial rhythm: _____   QRS complex: _____

Ventricular rhythm: _____   T wave: _____

Atrial rate: _____   QT interval: _____

Ventricular rate: _____   Other: _____

P wave: _____   **Interpretation:** _____

PR interval: _____

Answers to test strip

Rhythm: both atrial and ventricular rhythms are regular
Rate: atrial and ventricular rates are both 79 beats/minute
P wave: normal size and configuration
PR interval: 0.12 second
QRS complex: 0.08 second; normal size and configuration
T wave: normal configuration
QT interval: 0.44 second
Other: none
Interpretation: normal sinus rhythm

Scoring

☆☆☆   If you answered all five items correctly and filled in all the blanks pretty much as we did, hooray! You can read our rhythm strips anytime!

☆☆   If you answered three or four items correctly and filled in most of the blanks the way we did, excellent! You deserve a shiny new pair of calipers!

☆   If you answered fewer than three items correctly and missed most of the blanks, chin up! You're still tops with us!

Part II

Recognizing arrhythmias

Sinus node arrhythmias

Just the facts

This chapter will help you identify the various sinus node arrhythmias — sinus arrhythmia, sinus brady-cardia, sinus tachycardia, sinus arrest, and sick sinus syndrome. In this chapter, you'll learn:

♦ what role the sinoatrial (SA) node plays in arrhythmia formation

♦ which arrhythmias are generated from the SA node

♦ what causes each arrhythmia and what the signifi-cance, treatment, and nursing implications of each arrhythmia are

♦ which assessment findings are associated with each arrhythmia

♦ how to correctly interpret sinus node arrhythmias on an electrocardiogram (ECG).

A look at sinus node arrhythmias

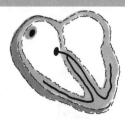

When the heart functions normally, the SA node, also called the sinus node, acts as the primary pacemaker. The sinus node assumes this role because its automatic firing rate exceeds that of the heart's other pacemakers. In an adult at rest, the sinus node has an inherent firing rate of 60 to 100 times per minute.

The SA node's blood supply comes from the right coronary artery and left circumflex artery. The autonomic nervous system richly innervates the sinus node through the vagal nerve, a parasympathetic nerve, and several sympathetic nerves. Stimulation of the vagus nerve de-creases the node's firing rate, and stimulation of the sym-pathetic system increases it.

Sinus arrhythmia

In sinus arrhythmia, the pacemaker cells of the SA node fire irregularly. The cardiac rate stays within normal limits, but the rhythm is irregular and corresponds to the respiratory cycle. Sinus arrhythmia can occur naturally in athletes, children, and older adults, but it rarely occurs in infants. Conditions unrelated to respiration may also produce sinus arrhythmia, including inferior-wall myocardial infarction (MI), advanced age, use of digitalis glycosides or morphine, heart disease, and conditions involving increased intracranial pressure.

How it happens

Sinus arrhythmia, the heart's normal response to respirations, results from an inhibition of reflex vagal activity, or tone. During inspiration, an increase in the flow of blood back to the heart reduces vagal tone, which increases the heart rate. ECG complexes fall closer together, which shortens the P-P interval, the time elapsed between two consecutive P waves.

During expiration, venous return decreases, which in turn increases vagal tone, slows the heart rate, and lengthens the P-P interval. (See *Breathing and sinus arrhythmia.*)

Breathing and sinus arrhythmia

When sinus arrhythmia is related to respirations, you'll see an increase in heart rate with inspiration and a decrease with expiration, as shown here.

Sick sinus

Sinus arrhythmia is usually not significant and produces no symptoms. A marked variation in P-P intervals in an older adult, however, may indicate sick sinus syndrome, a related, potentially more serious phenomenon.

What to look for

When you look for sinus arrhythmia, you'll see that the rhythm is irregular and corresponds to the respiratory cycle. (See *Sinus arrhythmia*.) The difference between the shortest and longest P-P intervals — and the shortest and longest R-R intervals — exceeds 0.12 second.

The atrial and ventricular rates are within normal limits (60 to 100 beats/minute) and vary with respiration — faster with inspiration, slower with expiration. All other parameters are normal, except for the QT interval, which may vary slightly but remain normal.

It's all in the breath

Look for a peripheral pulse rate that increases during inspiration and decreases during expiration. If the arrhyth-

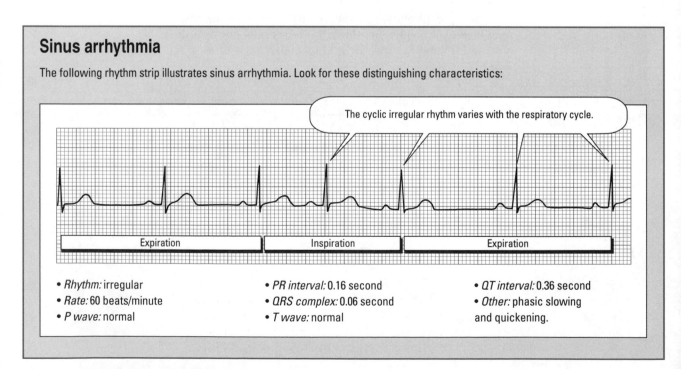

Sinus arrhythmia

The following rhythm strip illustrates sinus arrhythmia. Look for these distinguishing characteristics:

> The cyclic irregular rhythm varies with the respiratory cycle.

Expiration | Inspiration | Expiration

- *Rhythm:* irregular
- *Rate:* 60 beats/minute
- *P wave:* normal
- *PR interval:* 0.16 second
- *QRS complex:* 0.06 second
- *T wave:* normal
- *QT interval:* 0.36 second
- *Other:* phasic slowing and quickening.

mia is caused by an underlying condition, you may note signs and symptoms of that condition.

Sinus arrhythmia is easier to detect when the heart rate is slow; it may disappear when the heart rate increases, as with exercise or after atropine administration. Sinus arrhythmia may be induced during carotid sinus massage and eliminated as a result of a heart transplant.

How you intervene

Unless the patient is symptomatic, treatment usually isn't necessary. If sinus arrhythmia is unrelated to respirations, the underlying cause may require treatment.

When caring for a patient with sinus arrhythmia, observe the heart rhythm during respiration to determine if the arrhythmia is respiratory or nonrespiratory. Be sure to check the monitor carefully to avoid an inaccurate interpretation of the waveform. (See *A longer look at sinus arrhythmia.*)

Keep at it

If sinus arrhythmia is induced by drugs, such as morphine sulfate or other sedatives, the doctor may decide to continue to give the patient those medications. If sinus arrhythmia develops suddenly in a patient taking digitalis glycosides, notify the doctor immediately. The patient may be experiencing digitalis toxicity.

Mixed signals

A longer look at sinus arrhythmia

Don't mistake sinus arrhythmia for other rhythms. At first glance it may look like atrial fibrillation, normal sinus rhythm with PACs, SA block, or sinus pauses.

Observe the monitor and the patient's respiratory pattern for several minutes to determine the rate and rhythm. And, as always, check the patient's pulse.

Sinus bradycardia

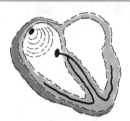

Sinus bradycardia is characterized by a sinus rate below 60 beats per minute and a regular rhythm. It may occur normally during sleep or in a person with a well-conditioned heart — an athlete, for instance. Unless the patient shows symptoms of decreased cardiac output, no treatment is necessary.

How it happens

Sinus bradycardia usually occurs as the normal response to a reduced demand for blood flow. In this case, vagal stimulation increases and sympathetic stimulation decreases. (See *Causes of sinus bradycardia,* page 68.) As a result, automaticity (the tendency of cells to initiate their own impulses) in the SA node diminishes.

A tolerable condition?

Sinus bradycardia often occurs after an inferior wall MI that involves the right coronary artery, which supplies blood to the SA node. It can also result from numerous other conditions and the use of certain drugs.

The clinical significance of sinus bradycardia depends on how low the rate is and whether the patient is symptomatic. For instance, most adults can tolerate a sinus bradycardia of 45 to 59 beats per minute but are less tolerant of a rate below 45.

No symptoms? No problem.

Usually, sinus bradycardia is asymptomatic and insignificant. Many athletes develop sinus bradycardia because their well-conditioned hearts can maintain a normal stroke volume with less-than-normal effort. Sinus bradycardia also occurs normally during sleep as a result of circadian variations in heart rate.

Symptoms? Problem!

When sinus bradycardia is symptomatic, however, prompt attention is critical. The heart of a patient with underlying cardiac disease may not be able to compensate for a drop in rate by increasing its stroke volume. The resulting drop in cardiac output produces such signs and symptoms as hypotension and dizziness. Bradycardia may also predispose some patients to more serious arrhythmias, such as ventricular tachycardia or ventricular fibrillation.

In a patient with acute inferior wall MI, sinus bradycardia is considered a favorable prognostic sign, unless it's accompanied by hypotension. Because sinus bradycardia rarely affects children, it's considered a poor prognostic sign in ill children.

What to look for

In sinus bradycardia, both the atrial and ventricular rhythms are regular, as are their rates, except that they're both under 60 beats a minute. (See *Sinus bradycardia.*) Everything else is normal. You'll see a P wave preceding each QRS complex and a normal PR interval, QRS complex, T wave, and QT interval.

Causes of sinus bradycardia

Sinus bradycardia may be caused by:

• noncardiac disorders, such as hyperkalemia, increased intracranial pressure, hypothyroidism, hypothermia, sleep, and glaucoma

• conditions producing excess vagal stimulation or decreased sympathetic stimulation, such as sleep, deep relaxation, Valsalva's maneuver, carotid sinus massage, and vomiting

• cardiac diseases, such as SA node disease, cardiomyopathy, myocarditis, myocardial ischemia, and heart block; sinus bradycardia can also occur immediately following an inferior wall MI

• certain drugs, especially beta blockers, digitalis glycosides, calcium channel blockers, lithium, and antiarrhythmic medications, such as sotalol, amiodarone, and quinidine.

When CO gets low

As long as a patient is able to compensate for the decreased cardiac output, he's likely to remain asymptomatic. If compensatory mechanisms fail, however, signs and symptoms of declining cardiac output, such as hypotension and dizziness, usually appear. (See *Treating symptomatic bradycardia,* pages 70 and 71.)

Palpitations and pulse irregularities may occur if the patient experiences more ectopic beats, such as premature atrial, junctional, or ventricular contractions. Diminished blood flow to the cerebrum may produce signs of decreased level of consciousness such as confusion. Bradycardia-induced syncope (Stokes-Adams attack) may also occur.

How you intervene

If the patient is asymptomatic and his vital signs are stable, treatment is not necessary. Continue to observe his heart rhythm, monitoring the progression and duration of the bradycardia. Evaluate his tolerance of the rhythm at rest and with activity. Review the drugs he is taking.

(Text continues on page 72.)

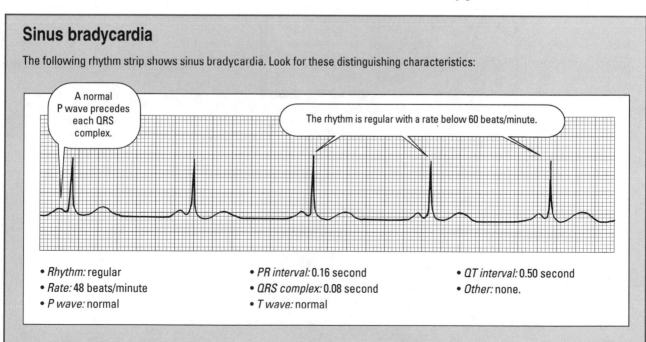

Sinus bradycardia

The following rhythm strip shows sinus bradycardia. Look for these distinguishing characteristics:

> A normal P wave precedes each QRS complex.

> The rhythm is regular with a rate below 60 beats/minute.

- *Rhythm:* regular
- *Rate:* 48 beats/minute
- *P wave:* normal
- *PR interval:* 0.16 second
- *QRS complex:* 0.08 second
- *T wave:* normal
- *QT interval:* 0.50 second
- *Other:* none.

Treating symptomatic bradycardia

The following algorithm shows the steps for treating bradycardia in a patient not in cardiac arrest.

Perform initial assessment and early interventions:
• Assess airway, breathing, and circulation.
• Secure the patient's airway.
• Administer oxygen.
• Start an I.V. line.
• Attach monitor, pulse oximeter, and automatic sphygmomanometer.
• Assess vital signs.
• Review the patient's history.
• Perform a physical examination.
• Order a 12-lead electrocardiogram.
• Order a portable chest X-ray.

If assessment indicates bradycardia, monitor for serious signs, symptoms, and complications, including chest pain, shortness of breath, decreased level of consciousness, low blood pressure, shock, pulmonary congestion, congestive heart failure, and acute myocardial infarction.

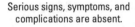

Serious signs, symptoms, and complications are absent.

Serious signs, symptoms, or complications are present.

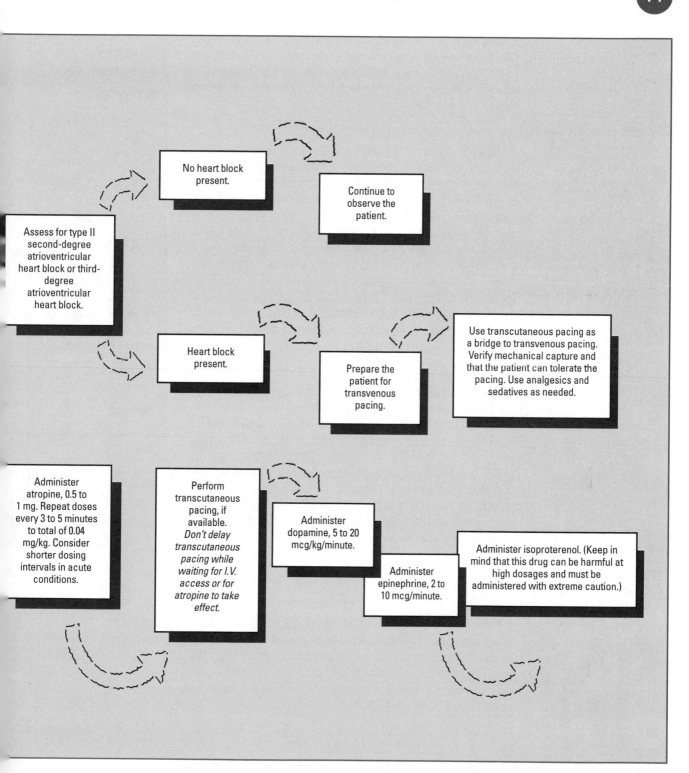

Assess for type II second-degree atrioventricular heart block or third-degree atrioventricular heart block.

No heart block present.

Continue to observe the patient.

Heart block present.

Prepare the patient for transvenous pacing.

Use transcutaneous pacing as a bridge to transvenous pacing. Verify mechanical capture and that the patient can tolerate the pacing. Use analgesics and sedatives as needed.

Administer atropine, 0.5 to 1 mg. Repeat doses every 3 to 5 minutes to total of 0.04 mg/kg. Consider shorter dosing intervals in acute conditions.

Perform transcutaneous pacing, if available. *Don't delay transcutaneous pacing while waiting for I.V. access or for atropine to take effect.*

Administer dopamine, 5 to 20 mcg/kg/minute.

Administer epinephrine, 2 to 10 mcg/minute.

Administer isoproterenol. (Keep in mind that this drug can be harmful at high dosages and must be administered with extreme caution.)

Check with the doctor about stopping any medications that may be depressing the SA node, such as digitalis glycoside preparations, beta blockers, or calcium channel blockers. Before giving those drugs, make sure the heart rate is within a safe range.

Identify and correct

If the patient is symptomatic, treatment aims to identify and correct the underlying cause. Meanwhile, the heart rate must be maintained with such drugs as atropine or isoproterenol (Isuprel) or with a temporary or permanent pacemaker.

Atropine is given as a 0.5- to 1-mg dose by rapid injection. The dose may be repeated every 3 to 5 minutes up to a maximum of 3 mg total. If atropine proves ineffective, isoproterenol may be given cautiously as an I.V. infusion. Isoproterenol increases myocardial oxygen demands and irritability and may cause ventricular arrhythmias. Treatment of chronic, symptomatic sinus bradycardia requires insertion of a permanent pacemaker.

Check the ABCs

If the patient abruptly develops a significant sinus bradycardia, assess his airway, breathing, and circulation (ABCs). If these are adequate, determine whether the patient has an effective cardiac output. If not, he will become symptomatic. (See *Clues to symptomatic bradycardia*.)

When administering atropine, be sure to give the correct dose: Doses lower than 0.5 mg can have a paradoxical effect, slowing the heart rate even further. *Keep in mind that a patient with a transplanted heart will not respond to atropine and may require pacing for emergency treatment.*

> ### Clues to symptomatic bradycardia
>
> If a patient can't tolerate bradycardia, he may develop these signs and symptoms:
>
> • hypotension
>
> • cool, clammy skin
>
> • altered mental status
>
> • dizziness
>
> • blurred vision
>
> • crackles, dyspnea, and an S_3 heart sound, which indicate congestive heart failure
>
> • chest pain
>
> • syncope.

Sinus tachycardia

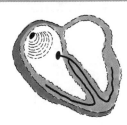

If sinus bradycardia is the tortoise of the sinus arrhythmias, sinus tachycardia is the hare. Sinus tachycardia in an adult is characterized by a sinus rate of more than 100 beats per minute. The rate rarely exceeds 180 except during strenuous exercise; the maximum rate achievable with exercise decreases with age.

How it happens

The clinical significance of sinus tachycardia depends on the underlying cause. (See *Causes of sinus tachycardia*.) The arrhythmia may be the body's response to exercise or high emotional states and of no clinical significance. It may also occur with hypovolemia, hemorrhage, or pain. When the stimulus for the tachycardia is removed, the arrhythmia spontaneously resolves.

When pain hits

Sinus tachycardia can also be a significant arrhythmia with dire consequences. Because myocardial demands for oxygen are increased at higher heart rates, tachycardia can bring on an episode of chest pain in patients with coronary artery disease.

An increase in heart rate can also be detrimental for patients with obstructive types of heart conditions, such as aortic stenosis or idiopathic hypertrophic subaortic stenosis.

Sinus tachycardia occurs in about 30% of patients after acute MI and is considered a poor prognostic sign because it may be associated with massive heart damage. Persistent tachycardia may also signal impending congestive heart failure (CHF) or cardiogenic shock.

What to look for

In sinus tachycardia, atrial and ventricular rhythms are regular. (See *Sinus tachycardia*, page 74.) Both rates are equal, generally 100 to 160 beats a minute. Like sinus bradycardia, the P wave is of normal size and shape and precedes each QRS, but it may increase in amplitude. As the heart rate increases, the P wave may be superimposed on the preceding T wave and difficult to identify.

The PR interval, QRS complex, and T wave are all normal. The QT interval normally shortens with tachycardia.

Pulse check!

When assessing a patient with sinus tachycardia, look for a peripheral pulse rate above 100 beats a minute but with a regular rhythm. Usually, the patient will be asymptomatic. However, if his cardiac output falls and compensatory mechanisms fail, he may experience hypotension, syn-

---

Causes of sinus tachycardia

Sinus tachycardia may be a normal response to exercise, pain, stress, fever, or strong emotions, such as fear or anxiety. It can also occur:

• in certain cardiac conditions, such as congestive heart failure, cardiogenic shock, and pericarditis

• after a heart transplant

• as a compensatory mechanism in shock, anemia, respiratory distress, pulmonary embolism, sepsis, and hyperthyroidism

• when taking such drugs as atropine, isoproterenol, aminophylline, dopamine, dobutamine, epinephrine, alcohol, caffeine, nicotine, quinidine, and amphetamines.

cope, and blurred vision. (See *What happens in tachycardia.*)

He may report chest pain and palpitations, often described as a pounding chest or a sensation of skipped heartbeats. He may also report a sense of nervousness or anxiety. If CHF develops, he may exhibit crackles, an extra heart sound (S_3), and jugular vein distention.

How you intervene

No treatment of sinus tachycardia is necessary if the patient is asymptomatic or if the rhythm is the result of physical exertion. In other cases, the underlying cause of the arrhythmia may be treated. For example, if the tachycardia is due to hemorrhage, treatment consists of stopping the bleeding and replacing blood and fluid.

Slow it down

If tachycardia leads to cardiac ischemia, treatment may include medications to slow the heart rate. The most commonly used drugs include beta blockers, such as metoprolol (Lopressor) or atenolol (Tenormin), and calcium channel blockers such as verapamil (Isoptin).

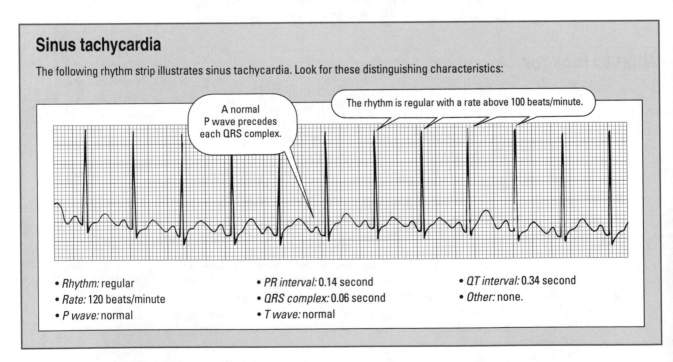

Sinus tachycardia

The following rhythm strip illustrates sinus tachycardia. Look for these distinguishing characteristics:

A normal P wave precedes each QRS complex.

The rhythm is regular with a rate above 100 beats/minute.

- *Rhythm:* regular
- *Rate:* 120 beats/minute
- *P wave:* normal
- *PR interval:* 0.14 second
- *QRS complex:* 0.06 second
- *T wave:* normal
- *QT interval:* 0.34 second
- *Other:* none.

The goal for the patient with sinus tachycardia is to maintain adequate cardiac output and tissue perfusion and to identify and correct the underlying cause.

Getting at the history

Check the patient's medication history. Over-the-counter sympathomimetic agents, which mimic the effects of the sympathetic nervous system, may contribute to the sinus tachycardia. Sympathomimetic agents may be contained in nose drops and cold formulas.

You should also ask about the patient's use of caffeine, nicotine, and alcohol, each of which can trigger tachycardia. Advise him to avoid these substances if he uses them. Ask about the use of such illicit drugs as cocaine or amphetamines, which can cause tachycardia.

More steps to take

Here are other steps you should take for the patient with sinus tachycardia.
• Because sinus tachycardia can lead to injury of the heart muscle, check for chest pain or angina. Also assess for signs and symptoms of CHF, including crackles, an S_3 heart sound, and jugular venous distention.
• Monitor intake and output, along with daily weight.
• Check the patient's level of consciousness to assess cerebral perfusion.
• Provide the patient with a calm environment. Help to reduce fear and anxiety, which can fuel the arrhythmia.
• Teach about procedures and treatments. Include relaxation techniques in the information you provide.
• Be aware that a sudden onset of sinus tachycardia after an MI may signal extension of the infarction. Prompt recognition is vital so treatment can be started.

What happens in tachycardia

Tachycardia can lower cardiac output by reducing ventricular filling time and cutting down the amount of blood pumped by the ventricles during each contraction. Normally, ventricular volume reaches 120 to 130 ml during diastole. In tachycardia, decreased ventricular volume leads to hypotension and decreased peripheral perfusion.

As cardiac output plummets, arterial pressure and peripheral perfusion decrease. Tachycardia worsens myocardial ischemia by increasing the heart's demand for oxygen and reducing the duration of diastole — the period of greatest coronary flow.

Sinus arrest

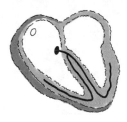

A disorder of impulse formation, sinus arrest is caused by a lack of electrical activity in the atrium, a condition called atrial standstill. (See *Causes of sinus arrest,* page 76.) During atrial standstill, the atria aren't stimulated and an entire PQRST complex will be missing from the ECG strip.

Except for this missing complex, or pause, the ECG usually remains normal. Atrial standstill is called sinus pause when one or two beats aren't formed and sinus arrest when three or more beats aren't formed.

Sinus arrest closely resembles third-degree SA block, also called exit block, on the ECG strip. (See *Understanding sinoatrial blocks.*)

How it happens

Sinus arrest occurs when the SA node fails to generate an impulse. Such failure may result from a number of conditions, including acute infection, heart disease, and vagal stimulation. Sinus arrest may be associated with sick sinus syndrome.

The clinical significance of sinus arrest depends on the patient's symptoms. If the pauses are short and infrequent, the patient will most likely be asymptomatic and not require treatment. He may have a normal sinus rhythm for days or weeks between episodes of sinus arrest. He may not be able to feel the arrhythmias at all.

What's more, pauses of 2 to 3 seconds normally occur in healthy adults during sleep and occasionally in patients with increased vagal tone or hypersensitive carotid sinus disease.

Too many for too long

If sinus arrest is frequent and prolonged, however, the patient will most likely have symptoms. The arrhythmias can produce syncope or near-syncopal episodes usually within 7 seconds of asystole.

During a prolonged pause, the patient may fall and injure himself. Other situations are potentially just as serious. For instance, a symptomatic arrhythmia that occurs while the patient is driving a car could result in a fatal accident.

What to look for

When assessing for sinus pause, you'll find that atrial and ventricular rhythms are regular except for a missing complex at the onset of atrial standstill. (See *Sinus arrest,* page 79.) The atrial and ventricular rates are equal and usually within normal limits. The rate may vary, however, as a result of the pauses.

Causes of sinus arrest

The following conditions can cause sinus arrest:

- sinus node disease, such as fibrosis and idiopathic degeneration

- increased vagal tone, as occurs with Valsalva's maneuver, carotid sinus massage, and vomiting

- digitalis glycosides, quinidine, procainamide and salicylates, especially if given at toxic levels

- excessive doses of beta blockers, such as metoprolol and propranolol

- cardiac disorders, such as chronic coronary artery disease, acute myocarditis, cardiomyopathy, and hypertensive heart disease

- acute inferior wall MI.

Understanding sinoatrial blocks

In sinoatrial (SA) block, the SA node discharges impulses at regular intervals. Some of those impulses, though, are delayed from reaching the atria. Based on the length of the delay, SA blocks are divided into three categories: first-, second-, and third-degree. Second-degree block is further divided into type I (Wenckebach) and type II.

First-degree SA block consists of a delay between the firing of the sinus node and depolarization of the atria. Because the ECG doesn't show sinus node activity, you can't detect first-degree SA block. But you can detect the other three types of SA block.

Second-degree type I block

In this type of SA block, conduction time between the sinus node and the surrounding atrial tissue becomes progressively longer until an entire cycle is dropped. The pause is less than twice the shortest P-P interval.

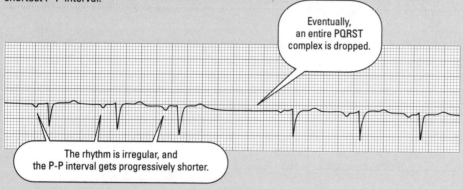

Eventually, an entire PQRST complex is dropped.

The rhythm is irregular, and the P-P interval gets progressively shorter.

Second-degree type II block

The conduction time between the sinus node and atrial tissue is normal until an impulse is blocked. The duration of the pause is a multiple of the P-P interval.

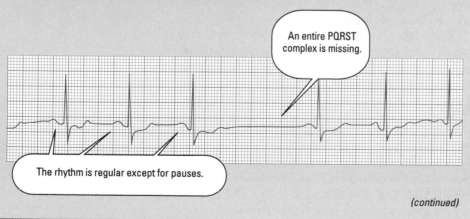

An entire PQRST complex is missing.

The rhythm is regular except for pauses.

(continued)

Understanding sinoatrial blocks *(continued)*

Third-degree block

In this arrhythmia, some impulses are blocked, causing long sinus pauses. The pause isn't a multiple of the sinus rhythm. On an ECG, third-degree SA block looks similar to sinus arrest but results from a different cause.

Third-degree SA block is caused by a failure to conduct impulses; sinus arrest results from failure to form impulses. Failure in each case causes atrial activity to stop.

In sinus arrest, the pause often ends with a junctional escape beat. In third-degree block, the pause lasts for an indefinite period and ends with a sinus beat.

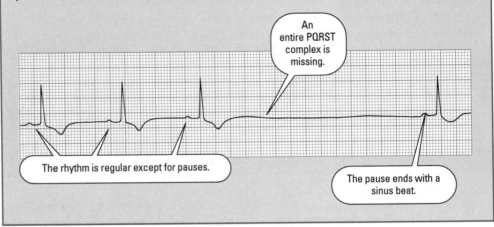

An entire PQRST complex is missing.

The rhythm is regular except for pauses.

The pause ends with a sinus beat.

Of normal size and shape, a P wave precedes each QRS complex but is absent during a pause. The PR interval is normal and constant when the P wave is present and not measurable when absent. The QRS complex, the T wave, and the QT interval are all normal when present and are absent during a pause.

You might see junctional escape beats, including premature atrial, junctional, or ventricular contractions. With sinus arrest, the length of the pause is not a multiple of the previous R-R intervals.

The pause that decreases

You will not be able to detect a pulse or heart sounds when sinus arrest occurs. Usually, the patient will be asymptomatic. Recurrent pauses may cause signs of decreased cardiac output, such as low blood pressure; cool, clammy skin; and altered mental status. The patient also may complain of dizziness or blurred vision.

How you intervene

An asymptomatic patient needs no treatment. For a patient displaying mild symptoms, treatment focuses on maintaining cardiac output and identifying the cause of the sinus arrest. That may involve stopping medications that contribute to SA node suppression, such as digitalis glycosides, beta blockers, and calcium channel blockers.

A patient who develops signs of circulatory collapse needs immediate treatment. As with sinus bradycardia, emergency treatment includes administration of atropine or isoproterenol or insertion of a temporary pacemaker. A permanent pacemaker may be implanted for long-term management.

The goal for the patient with sinus arrest is to maintain adequate cardiac output and perfusion. Be sure to record and document the frequency and duration of pauses. Determine if a pause is the result of sinus arrest or SA block.

Sinus arrest

The following rhythm strip illustrates sinus arrest. Look for these distinguishing characteristics.

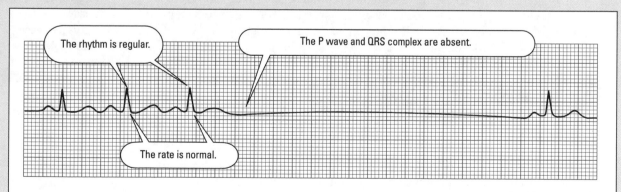

The rhythm is regular.

The P wave and QRS complex are absent.

The rate is normal.

- *Rhythm:* regular, except for the missing PQRST complexes
- *Rate:* 40 beats/minute
- *P wave:* normal; missing during pause
- *PR interval:* 0.20 second
- *QRS complex:* 0.08 seconds, missing during pause
- *T wave:* normal, missing during pause
- *QT interval:* 0.40 second, missing during pause
- *Other:* none.

Don't let sleeping pauses lie

Examine the circumstances under which sinus pauses occur. A sinus pause may be insignificant if detected while the patient is sleeping. If the pauses are recurrent, assess the patient for evidence of decreased cardiac output, such as altered mental status, low blood pressure, and cool, clammy skin.

Ask him if he is dizzy or light-headed or has blurred vision. Does he feel as if he has passed out? If so, he may be experiencing syncope from a prolonged sinus arrest. (See *Syncope and sinus arrest.*)

Document the patient's vital signs and how he feels during pauses, as well as what activities he was involved in at the time. Activities that increase vagal stimulation, such as Valsalva's maneuver or vomiting, increase the likelihood of sinus pauses.

When matters get even worse

Assess for a progression of the arrhythmia. Notify the doctor immediately if the patient becomes unstable. Lower the head of the bed and administer atropine or isoproterenol, as ordered or as your facility's policy directs. Withhold medications that may contribute to sinus pauses, and check with the doctor about whether they should be continued.

If appropriate, be alert for signs of digitalis, quinidine, or procainamide toxicity. Obtain a serum digitalis glycoside level and a serum electrolyte level. If a pacemaker is implanted, give the patient discharge instructions about pacemaker care.

Sick sinus syndrome

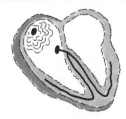

Also called sinus nodal dysfunction, sick sinus syndrome refers to a wide spectrum of SA node abnormalities. The syndrome is caused by disturbances in the way impulses are generated or the inability to conduct impulses to the atrium.

Sick sinus syndrome usually shows up as bradycardia, with episodes of sinus arrest and SA block interspersed with sudden, brief periods of rapid atrial fibrillation. Patients are also prone to paroxysms of other atrial tachyarrhythmias, such as atrial flutter and ectopic atrial tachy-

---

Syncope and sinus arrest

A patient with sinus arrest is at risk for syncope. Ask your patient if he has ever passed out or felt as if he were going to pass out.

Also ask about a history of falls. If he has passed out or if he has a history of falls, obtain a detailed description of each episode, including where and how the syncope occurred.

Asking questions

If possible, check with friends and family members who witnessed the episodes to find out what happened and how long the patient remained unconscious each time.

The information you gather may help determine if a vagal mechanism was involved. The presence of syncope or sinus pauses on an ECG may indicate the need for further electrophysiologic evaluation.

cardia, a condition sometimes referred to as bradycardia-tachycardia (or "brady-tachy") syndrome.

Most patients with sick sinus syndrome are over age 60, but anyone can develop the arrhythmia. It's rare in children except after open heart surgery that results in SA node damage. The arrhythmia affects men and women equally. The onset is progressive, insidious, and chronic.

How it happens

Sick sinus syndrome results either from a dysfunction of the sinus node's automaticity or from abnormal conduction or blockages of impulses coming out of the nodal region. (See *Causes of sick sinus syndrome*.) These conditions, in turn, stem from a degeneration of the area's autonomic nervous system and partial destruction of the sinus node, as may occur with an interrupted blood supply after an inferior wall MI.

Blocked exits

In addition, certain conditions can affect the atrial wall surrounding the SA node and cause exit blocks. Conditions that cause inflammation or degeneration of atrial tissue can also lead to sick sinus syndrome. In many patients, though, the exact cause of sick sinus syndrome is never identified.

Prognosis of the diagnosis

The significance of sick sinus syndrome depends on the patient's age, the presence of other diseases, and the type and duration of the specific arrhythmias that occur. If atrial fibrillation is involved, the prognosis is worse, most likely due to the risk of thromboembolic complications.

If prolonged pauses are involved with sick sinus syndrome, syncope may occur. The length of a pause needed to cause syncope varies with the patient's age, posture at the time, and cerebrovascular status. Consider significant any pause that lasts at least 2 to 3 seconds.

Long-term problems

A significant part of the diagnosis is whether the patient experiences symptoms while the disturbance occurs. Because the syndrome is progressive and chronic, a sympto-

---

Causes of sick sinus syndrome

Sick sinus syndrome may result from:

• conditions leading to fibrosis of the SA node, such as increased age, atherosclerotic heart disease, hypertension, and cardiomyopathy

• trauma to the SA node caused by open heart surgery (especially valvular surgery), pericarditis, or rheumatic heart disease

• autonomic disturbances affecting autonomic innervation, such as hypervagatonia or degeneration of the autonomic system

• cardioactive medications, such as digitalis glycosides, beta blockers, and calcium channel blockers.

matic patient will need life-long treatment. In addition, thromboembolism may develop as a complication of sick sinus syndrome, possibly resulting in stroke or peripheral embolization.

What to look for

Sick sinus syndrome encompasses several potential rhythm disturbances that may be intermittent or chronic. (See *Sick sinus syndrome.*) Those rhythm disturbances include one or a combination of the following:
- sinus bradycardia
- SA block
- sinus arrest
- sinus bradycardia alternating with sinus tachycardia
- episodes of atrial tachyarrhythmias, such as atrial fibrillation or atrial flutter
- failure of the sinus node to increase heart rate with exercise.

Sick sinus syndrome

This rhythm strip illustrates sick sinus syndrome. Look for these distinguishing characteristics:

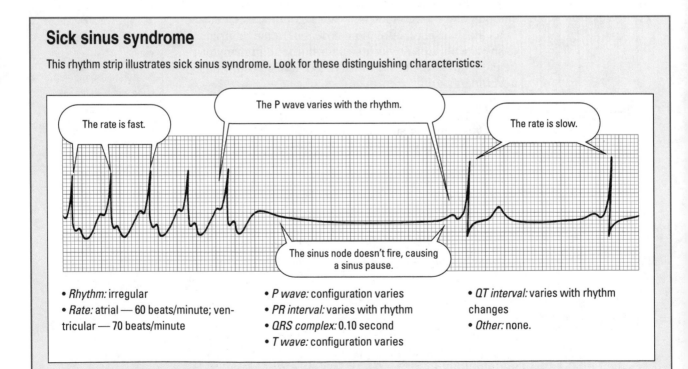

- *Rhythm:* irregular
- *Rate:* atrial — 60 beats/minute; ventricular — 70 beats/minute
- *P wave:* configuration varies
- *PR interval:* varies with rhythm
- *QRS complex:* 0.10 second
- *T wave:* configuration varies
- *QT interval:* varies with rhythm changes
- *Other:* none.

Check for speed bumps

Look also for an irregular rhythm with sinus pauses and abrupt rate changes. Atrial and ventricular rates may be fast, slow, or a combination of both with periods of fast rates and slow rates interrupted by pauses.

The P wave varies with the rhythm and usually precedes each QRS complex. The PR interval is usually within normal limits but varies with changes in the rhythm. The QRS complex and T wave are usually normal, as is the QT interval, which may vary with rhythm changes.

No set pattern

The patient's pulse rate may be fast, slow, or normal, and the rhythm may be regular or irregular. You can usually detect an irregularity on the monitor or when palpating the pulse, which may feel inappropriately slow, then rapid.

If you monitor the patient's heart rate during exercise or exertion, you may observe an inappropriate response to exercise such as a failure of the heart rate to increase. You may also detect episodes of "brady-tachy" syndrome, atrial flutter, atrial fibrillation, SA block, or sinus arrest on the monitor.

Extra sounds

Other assessment findings depend on the patient's condition. For instance, he may have crackles in the lungs, a third heart sound, or a dilated and displaced left ventricular apical impulse if he has underlying cardiomyopathy.

The patient may show signs and symptoms of decreased cardiac output, such as hypotension, blurred vision, and syncope, a common experience with this arrhythmia.

How you intervene

As with other sinus node arrhythmias, no treatment is necessary if the patient is asymptomatic. If the patient is symptomatic, however, treatment aims to alleviate signs and symptoms and correct the underlying cause of the arrhythmia.

Atropine or isoproterenol may be given initially for an acute attack. A pacemaker may be used until the underlying disorder resolves. Tachyarrhythmias may be treated with antiarrhythmic medications, such as propranolol or a digitalis glycoside.

Drugs don't always help

Unfortunately, medications used to suppress tachy-arrhythmias may worsen underlying SA node disease and bradyarrhythmias. The patient may need anticoagulants if he develops sudden bursts, or paroxysms, of atrial fibrillation. The anticoagulants help prevent thromboembolism and stroke, a complication of the condition. (See *Recognizing an embolism*.)

Watch and document

When caring for a patient with sick sinus syndrome, monitor and document all arrhythmias he experiences and signs or symptoms he develops. Assess how his rhythm responds to activity and pain, and look for changes in the rhythm.

Watch the patient carefully after starting beta blockers, calcium channel blockers, or other antiarrhythmic medications. If treatment includes anticoagulant therapy and the insertion of a pacemaker, make sure the patient and his family receive appropriate teaching.

Recognizing an embolism

When caring for a patient with sick sinus syndrome, be alert for signs and symptoms of an embolism, especially if the patient has atrial fibrillation. Any clots that form in the heart can break off and travel through the bloodstream, blocking the blood supply to the lungs, heart, brain, kidneys, intestines, or other organs.

Assess early

Assess the patient for neurologic changes, such as confusion, visual disturbances, weakness, chest pain, dyspnea, tachypnea, tachycardia, and acute onset of pain. Early recognition allows for prompt treatment.

Quick quiz

1. A patient with symptomatic sinus bradycardia at a rate of 40 beats a minute typically experiences:

    A. high blood pressure.
    B. chest pain and dyspnea.
    C. facial flushing and ataxia.

Answer: B. A patient with symptomatic bradycardia suffers from low cardiac output, which may produce chest pain and dyspnea. The patient may also have crackles, an S_3 heart sound, and a sudden onset of confusion.

2. For a patient with symptomatic sinus bradycardia, appropriate nursing interventions include establishing I.V. access to administer:

    A. atropine.
    B. anticoagulants.
    C. a calcium channel blocker.

Answer: A. Atropine or isoproterenol are standard treatments for sinus bradycardia.

3. A monitor shows an irregular rhythm and a rate that increases and decreases in consistent cycles. This rhythm most likely represents:

    A. sinus arrest.
    B. sinus bradycardia.
    C. sinus arrhythmia.

Answer: C. In sinus arrhythmia, common among young people, the heart rate varies with the respiratory cycle and is rarely treated.

4. Treatment for symptomatic sick sinus syndrome includes:

    A. beta blockers.
    B. ventilatory support.
    C. pacemaker insertion.

Answer: C. A pacemaker is often used to maintain a steady heart rate in patients with sick sinus syndrome.

5. Persistent tachycardia in a patient who has had an MI may signal:

    A. chronic sick sinus syndrome.
    B. pulmonary embolism or stroke.
    C. impending CHF or cardiogenic shock.

Answer: C. Sinus tachycardia occurs in about 30% of patients after acute MI and is considered a poor prognostic sign because it may be associated with massive heart damage.

6. Beta blockers, such as metoprolol and atenolol, and calcium channel blockers, such as verapamil, are commonly used to treat the sinus node arrhythmia:
  A. sinus bradycardia.
  B. sinus tachycardia.
  C. sinus arrest.

Answer: B. Beta blockers and calcium channel blockers are commonly used to treat sinus tachycardia.

Test strips

Try these test strips. Answer the questions accompanying each strip; then check your answers with ours.

7. In the rhythm strip below, the rhythm is regular except during a pause; the atrial and ventricular rates are 50 beats/minute; the P wave is of normal size and configuration, except when missing during a pause; the PR interval is 0.16 second; the QRS complex is 0.10 second and is of normal size and configuration, except when missing during a pause; the T wave is normal except when missing during a pause; the QT interval is 0.42 second; and the pause isn't a multiple of a previous sinus rhythm. You would interpret the strip as:
  A. sinus bradycardia.
  B. sinus arrest, or third-degree SA block.
  C. sick sinus syndrome.

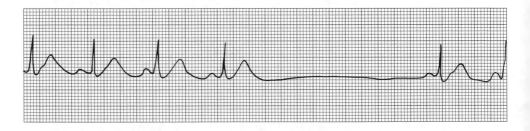

Answer: B. The strip shows sinus arrest, or third-degree SA block.

8. In the strip below, the atrial and ventricular rhythms are regular at 110 beats/minute, the P wave is normal, the PR interval is 0.14 second, the QRS complex is 0.08 second and of normal size and configuration, the T wave is normal, and the QT interval is 0.36 second. You would interpret the rhythm as:

    A. sinus tachycardia.

    B. sinus arrhythmia.

    C. sick sinus syndrome.

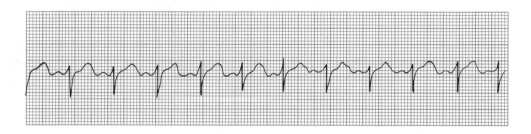

Answer: A. The strip shows sinus tachycardia.

9. Your patient's monitor produces the rhythm strip shown below. After examining its characteristics, you identify the rhythm as:

    A. normal sinus rhythm.

    B. sinus arrhythmia.

    C. sick sinus syndrome.

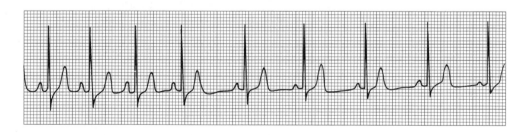

Answer: B. The strip shows sinus arrhythmia. The atrial and ventricular rhythms are irregular with rates of 90 beats/minute, the P wave is normal, the PR interval is 0.12 second, the QRS complex is 0.10 second and normal, the T wave is normal, and the QT interval is 0.30 second.

Scoring

☆☆☆ If you answered all six items correctly and interpreted all three rhythms accurately, *wow!* You deserve to head down to the nearest club and tachy-brady the night away!

☆☆ If you answered four or five correctly and interpreted at least two rhythms accurately, super! When you get to the club, you can lead the dance parade!

☆ If you answered fewer than four correctly and interpreted at least one rhythm accurately, great. A few lessons and you'll be tachy-brading with the best of 'em!

Atrial arrhythmias

Just the facts

This chapter will show you how to identify and care for patients with atrial arrhythmias, including premature atrial contractions, atrial tachycardia, atrial flutter, and atrial fibrillation. In this chapter, you'll learn:

♦ what causes atrial arrhythmias

♦ what the signs and symptoms of atrial arrhythmias are

♦ what effects atrial arrhythmias have on a patient

♦ which nursing interventions and medical treatments are appropriate for atrial arrhythmias.

A look at atrial arrhythmias

Atrial arrhythmias, the most common cardiac rhythm disturbances, result from impulses originating in areas outside the sinoatrial (SA) node. These arrhythmias can affect ventricular filling time and diminish the strength of the atrial kick, a contraction that normally provides the ventricles with about 30% of their blood.

Triple play

Atrial arrhythmias are thought to result from three mechanisms — altered automaticity, circus reentry, and afterdepolarization. Let's take a look at each cause, then review specific atrial arrhythmias.
• *Altered automaticity.* An increase in the automaticity (the ability of cardiac cells to initiate impulses on their own) of the atrial fibers can trigger abnormal impulses. Causes of increased automaticity include extracellular fac-

tors, such as hypoxia, hypocalcemia, and digitalis toxicity, and conditions in which the function of the heart's normal pacemaker, the SA node, is diminished. For example, increased vagal tone or hypokalemia can increase the refractory period of the SA node and allow atrial fibers to fire impulses.

• *Circus reentry*. In circus reentry, an impulse is delayed along a slow conduction pathway. Despite the delay, the impulse remains active enough to produce another impulse during myocardial repolarization. Circus reentry may occur with coronary artery disease or myocardial infarction (MI).

• *Afterdepolarization*. Afterdepolarization can occur with cell injury, digitalis toxicity, and other conditions. An injured cell sometimes only partly depolarizes. Partial depolarization can lead to a repetitive ectopic firing called triggered activity. The depolarization produced by triggered activity is known as afterdepolarization and can lead to atrial or ventricular tachycardia.

Let's examine each atrial arrhythmia in detail.

Premature atrial contraction

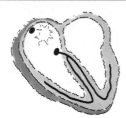

Premature atrial contractions (PACs) originate outside the SA node and usually result from an irritable spot, or focus, in the atria that takes over as pacemaker for one or more beats. The SA node fires an impulse, but then an irritable focus jumps in, firing its own impulse before the SA node can fire again.

PACs may or may not be conducted through the atrioventricular (AV) node and the rest of the heart, depending on their prematurity and the status of the AV and intraventricular conduction system. Nonconducted or blocked PACs don't trigger a QRS complex.

How it happens

PACs, which commonly occur in a normal heart, can be triggered by alcohol, cigarettes, anxiety, fatigue, fever, and infectious diseases. Patients who eliminate or control those factors can correct the arrhythmia.

PACs may also be associated with coronary or valvular heart disease, acute respiratory failure, hypoxia, pulmonary disease, digitalis toxicity, and certain electrolyte imbalances.

PACs are rarely dangerous in patients who don't have heart disease. In fact, they often cause no symptoms and can go unrecognized for years. The patient may perceive PACs as normal palpitations or skipped beats.

Early warning sign

However, in patients with heart disease, PACs may lead to more serious arrhythmias, such as atrial fibrillation and atrial flutter. In a patient with an acute MI, PACs can serve as an early sign of congestive heart failure (CHF) or an electrolyte imbalance. PACs can also result from the release of the neurohormone catecholamine during episodes of pain or anxiety.

What to look for

The hallmark ECG characteristic of a PAC is a premature P wave with an abnormal configuration as compared to a sinus P wave. (See *Nonconducted PACs and second-degree AV block.*) If the PAC occurs soon after the preceding impulse, the atrial P wave may be buried in the T wave, distorting that wave's configuration. (The T wave might be bigger or have an extra bump.)

When the PAC is conducted, the QRS complex appears similar to the underlying QRS complex. PACs are commonly followed by a pause.

The PAC depolarizes the SA node early, causing it to reset itself and disrupt the normal cycle. The next sinus beat occurs sooner than it normally would, causing the P-P interval between two normal beats that have been interrupted by a PAC to be shorter than two consecutive sinus beats, an occurrence referred to as noncompensatory. (See *Premature atrial contractions,* page 92.)

Lost in the T

When examining a PAC on an ECG, look for irregular atrial and ventricular rates. The underlying rhythm may be regular. The P wave is premature and abnormally shaped and may be lost in the previous T wave. Varying configurations of the P wave indicate more than one ectopic site.

Mixed signals

Nonconducted PACs and second-degree AV block

Don't confuse nonconducted PACs with type II second-degree AV block. In type II second-degree AV block, the P-P interval is regular. A nonconducted PAC, however, is an atrial impulse that arrives early to the AV node, when the node isn't yet repolarized.

As a result, the premature P wave fails to be conducted to the ventricle. The rhythm strip below shows a P wave embedded in the preceding T wave.

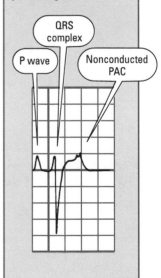

Premature atrial contractions

The following rhythm strip illustrates premature atrial contractions (PACs). Look for these distinguishing characteristics:

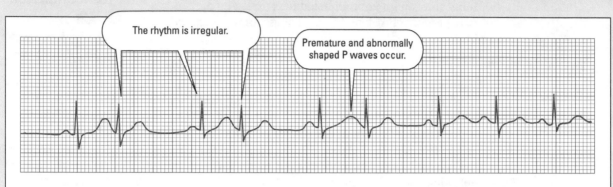

- *Rhythm:* irregular
- *Rate:* 90 beats/minute
- *P wave:* abnormal with PAC; lost in previous T wave

- *PR interval:* 0.16 second
- *QRS complex:* 0.08 second
- *T wave:* abnormal with embedded P waves

- *QT interval:* 0.36 second
- *Other:* none.

The PR interval is usually normal but may be shortened or slightly prolonged, depending on the origin of the ectopic focus. If no QRS complex follows, a nonconducted PAC might have occurred.

PACs may occur in bigeminy (every other beat is a PAC), trigeminy (every third beat is a PAC), or couplets (two PACs at a time).

The patient may have an irregular peripheral or apical pulse rhythm when the PACs occur. He may complain of palpitations, skipped beats, or a fluttering sensation. In a patient with heart disease, signs and symptoms of decreased cardiac output may occur, such as hypotension and syncope.

How you intervene

Most patients who don't have symptoms don't need treatment. If the patient is symptomatic, however, treatment may focus on eliminating the cause, such as caffeine or alcohol. People who have frequent PACs may be treated with drugs that prolong the refractory period. Those drugs include a digitalis glycoside, procainamide, and verapamil.

When caring for a patient with PACs, assess him to help determine what's triggering the ectopic beats. Tailor your patient teaching to help the patient correct or avoid the underlying cause. For example, the patient might need to avoid caffeine or smoking or to learn stress reduction techniques to lessen his anxiety.

If the patient has ischemic heart disease, monitor him for signs and symptoms of CHF, electrolyte imbalances, and the development of more severe atrial arrhythmias.

Atrial tachycardia

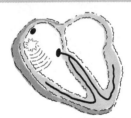

Atrial tachycardia is a supraventricular tachycardia, which means the impulses driving the rapid rhythm originate above the ventricles. Atrial tachycardia has an atrial rate from 150 to 250 beats/minute. The rapid rate shortens diastole, resulting in a loss of atrial kick, reduced cardiac output, reduced coronary perfusion, and ischemic myocardial changes.

Three types of atrial tachycardia exist: atrial tachycardia with block, multifocal atrial tachycardia (or chaotic atrial rhythm), and paroxysmal atrial tachycardia (PAT).

How it happens

Atrial tachycardia can occur in patients with normal hearts. In those cases, the condition is commonly related to excessive use of caffeine or other stimulants, marijuana use, electrolyte imbalances, hypoxia, and physical or psychological stress. However, this arrhythmia is usually associated with primary or secondary cardiac problems.

Cardiac conditions that can cause atrial tachycardia include MI, cardiomyopathy, congenital anomalies, Wolff-Parkinson-White syndrome, and valvular heart disease. This rhythm may also be a component of sick sinus syndrome. Other problems resulting in atrial tachycardia include cor pulmonale, hyperthyroidism, systemic hypertension, and digitalis toxicity, the most common cause of atrial tachycardia. (See *Signs of digitalis toxicity*.)

Signs of digitalis toxicity

With digitalis toxicity, atrial tachycardia isn't the only change you may see in your patient. Be alert for the following signs and symptoms, especially if the patient is taking a digitalis glycoside and his potassium level is low, a combination that can increase the risk of digitalis toxicity.

- *CNS:* fatigue, general muscle weakness, agitation, hallucinations.

- *CV:* arrhythmias (most commonly, conduction disturbances with or without AV block, premature ventricular contractions, and supraventricular arrhythmias), increased severity of CHF, hypotension. *Digitalis glycosides' toxic effects on the heart may be life-threatening and always require immediate attention.*

- *EENT:* yellow-green halos around visual images, blurred vision.

- *GI:* anorexia, nausea.

An ominous sign?

In a healthy person, atrial tachycardia is usually benign. However, this rhythm may be a forerunner of a more serious ventricular arrhythmia, especially if it occurs in a patient with an underlying heart condition.

The increased ventricular rate of atrial tachycardia results in a decrease in the time it takes the ventricles to fill, an increase in myocardial oxygen consumption, and a decrease in oxygen supply. Angina, heart failure, ischemic myocardial changes, and even MI can occur as a result.

What to look for

Atrial tachycardia is characterized by three or more successive ectopic atrial beats at a rate of 150 to 250 beats/minute. The P wave is usually upright, if visible, and followed by a QRS complex.

Keep in mind that atrial beats may be conducted on a 1:1 basis into the ventricles (meaning that each P wave has a QRS complex), so atrial and ventricular rates will be equal. In other cases, atrial beats may be conducted only periodically, meaning a block exists in the AV conduction system. The block keeps the ventricles from receiving every impulse.

Think of the AV node as a gatekeeper or doorman. Sometimes it lets atrial impulses through to the ventricles regularly (every other impulse, for instance), and sometimes it lets them in irregularly (two impulses might get through, for instance, and then three, and then one).

Fast but regular

When assessing a rhythm strip for atrial tachycardia, you'll see that atrial and ventricular rhythms are regular when the block is constant and irregular when it isn't. (See *Atrial tachycardia.*) The rate consists of three or more successive ectopic atrial beats at a rate of 150 to 250 beats/minute. The ventricular rate will vary according to the AV conduction ratio.

The P wave has a 1:1 ratio with the QRS complex, though the P wave may not be discernible due to the rapid rate and may be hidden in the previous ST segment or T wave. You may not be able to measure the PR interval if the P wave can't be distinguished from the preceding T wave.

The QRS complex is usually normal unless the impulses are being conducted abnormally through the ventricles. (See *Identifying types of atrial tachycardia,* pages 96 and 97.) The T wave may be normal or inverted if ischemia is present. The QT interval is usually within normal limits but may be shorter due to the rapid rate. ST-segment and T-wave changes may appear if ischemia occurs with a prolonged arrhythmia.

Check out the outward signs

The patient with atrial tachycardia will have a rapid apical or peripheral pulse rate. The rhythm may be regular or irregular, depending on the type of atrial tachycardia. A patient with paroxysmal atrial tachycardia may complain that his heart suddenly starts to beat faster or that he suddenly feels palpitations. If the tachycardia is persistent or the ventricular rate is rapid, decreased cardiac output can lead to blurred vision, syncope, and hypotension.

Atrial tachycardia

The following rhythm strip shows atrial tachycardia. Look for these distinguishing characteristics:

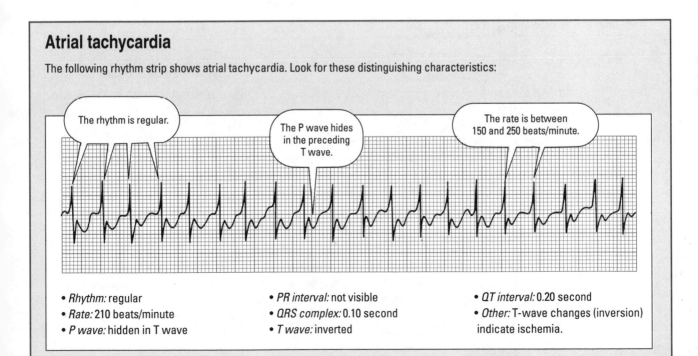

- *Rhythm:* regular
- *Rate:* 210 beats/minute
- *P wave:* hidden in T wave
- *PR interval:* not visible
- *QRS complex:* 0.10 second
- *T wave:* inverted
- *QT interval:* 0.20 second
- *Other:* T-wave changes (inversion) indicate ischemia.

How you intervene

Treatment depends on the type of tachycardia and the severity of the patient's symptoms. Because one of the most common causes of atrial tachycardia is digitalis toxicity, monitor levels of the drug. Measures to produce vagal stimulation, such as Valsalva's maneuver and carotid sinus massage, may be used to treat paroxysmal atrial tachycardia. (See *Understanding carotid sinus massage,* page 98.) These measures lead to slowing of the impulses from the SA and AV nodes, triggering atrial standstill and allowing the SA node to function as the primary pacemaker again.

Identifying types of atrial tachycardia

Atrial tachycardia comes in three varieties. Here's a quick rundown of each.

Atrial tachycardia with block
This arrhythmia is caused by increased automaticity of the atrial tissue. As the atrial rate speeds up and AV conduction becomes impaired, type I (Wenckebach) second-degree AV block may follow.

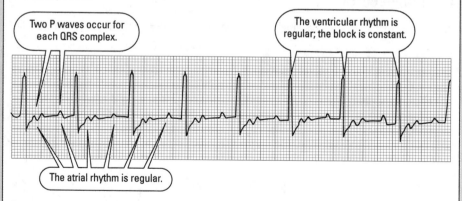

Two P waves occur for each QRS complex.

The ventricular rhythm is regular; the block is constant.

The atrial rhythm is regular.

Interpretation
• *Rhythm:* atrial — regular, ventricular regular if block is constant; irregular if block is variable
• *Rate:* atrial —150 to 250 beats/minute, multiple of ventricular rate; ventricular — varies with block
• *P wave:* slightly abnormal
• *PR interval:* usually normal; may be hidden
• *QRS complex:* usually normal
• *Other:* more than one P wave for each QRS

Identifying types of atrial tachycardia *(continued)*

Multifocal atrial tachycardia (MAT)

In this arrhythmia, atrial tachycardia occurs with numerous atrial foci firing intermittently. MAT produces varying P waves on the strip and occurs most often in patients with chronic pulmonary disease. The irregular baseline in this strip is caused by movement of the chest wall.

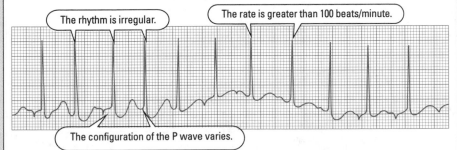

> The rhythm is irregular.

> The rate is greater than 100 beats/minute.

> The configuration of the P wave varies.

Interpretation

- *Rhythm:* both irregular
- *Rate:* atrial rate — 100 to 250 beats/minute; usually under 160; ventricular rate — 100 to 250 beats/minute
- *P wave:* configuration varies; must see at least three different P wave shapes
- *PR interval:* varies
- *Other:* none.

Paroxysmal atrial tachycardia (PAT)

A type of paroxysmal supraventricular tachycardia (PSVT), this arrhythmia features brief periods of tachycardia that alternate with periods of normal sinus rhythm. PAT starts and stops suddenly as a result of rapid firing of an ectopic focus. It often follows frequent PACs, one of which initiates the tachycardia.

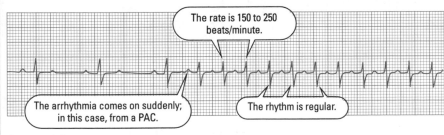

> The rate is 150 to 250 beats/minute.

> The arrhythmia comes on suddenly; in this case, from a PAC.

> The rhythm is regular.

Interpretation

- *Rhythm:* regular
- *Rate:* 150 to 250 beats/minute
- *P wave:* abnormal, possibly hidden in previous T wave
- *PR interval:* identical for each cycle
- *QRS complex:* can be aberrantly conducted
- *Other:* one P wave for each QRS complex.

Understanding carotid sinus massage

Carotid sinus massage may be used to stop paroxysmal atrial tachycardia. Massaging the carotid sinus stimulates the vagus nerve, which then inhibits firing of the SA node and slows AV node conduction. As a result, the SA node can resume its job as primary pacemaker. Risks of the procedure include decreased heart rate, vasodilation, ventricular arrhythmias, and cardiac standstill.

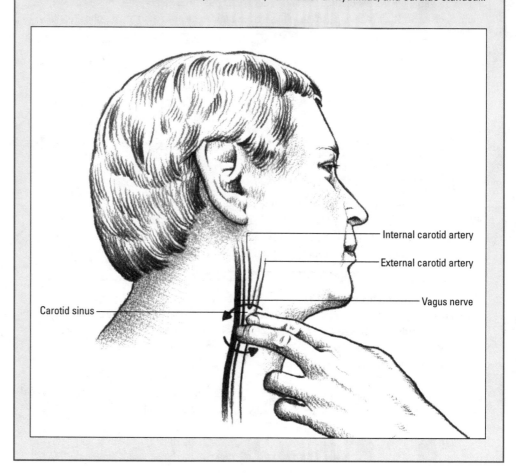

Internal carotid artery

External carotid artery

Vagus nerve

Carotid sinus

Making a bigger block

A patient with atrial tachycardia can be given drugs that increase the degree of AV block, which in turn decreases the ventricular response and slows the rate. Such drugs include digitalis glycosides, propranolol, and verapamil.

In addition, adenosine (Adenocard) can be used to stop atrial tachycardia, and quinidine (Cin-Quin) or procainamide (Pronestyl) can be used to establish normal sinus rhythm. When other treatments fail, synchronized cardioversion may be used. Following open heart surgery, atrial overdrive pacing (also called burst pacing) is often necessary to prevent the arrhythmia. (See *Atrial overdrive pacing.*)

If the arrhythmia is associated with Wolff-Parkinson-White syndrome, catheter ablation (removal of the area causing the arrhythmia) may be used to control recurrent episodes of paroxysmal atrial tachycardia. Because multifocal atrial tachycardia often occurs in patients with chronic pulmonary disease, the rhythm may not respond to treatment. Treatment attempts to correct severe hypoxia when possible.

Monitor the strip

When caring for a patient with atrial tachycardia, carefully monitor the patient's rhythm strips. Doing so may provide information about the cause of atrial tachycardia, which in turn can facilitate treatment.

Be alert to the possibility of digitalis toxicity. Frequent PACs may indicate that tachycardia is caused by reentry and, therefore, can be treated with a vagal maneuver. Remember that vagal stimulation can result in bradycardia, ventricular arrhythmias, and asystole. If vagal maneuvers are used, keep resuscitative equipment readily available.

Monitor the patient for chest pain, indications of decreased cardiac output, and signs and symptoms of heart failure or myocardial ischemia.

Atrial overdrive pacing

Atrial overdrive pacing (also called rapid atrial pacing) can stop atrial tachycardia. In that procedure, the patient's atrial rate is electronically paced slightly higher than the intrinsic atrial rate. With some patients, the atria are paced using much faster bursts or are paced prematurely at a critical time in the conduction cycle.

Whichever variation is used, the result is the same. The pacing interferes with the conduction circuit and renders part of it unresponsive to the reentrant impulse. Atrial tachycardia stops, and the SA node resumes its normal role as pacemaker.

Atrial flutter

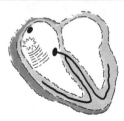

Atrial flutter, a supraventricular tachycardia, is characterized by an atrial rate of 250 to 400 beats/minute, though it's generally around 300 beats/minute. Originating in a single atrial focus, this rhythm results from circus reentry and possibly increased automaticity.

On an ECG, the P waves lose their distinction due to the rapid atrial rate. The waves blend together in a sawtooth appearance and are called flutter waves or F waves. These waves are the hallmark of atrial flutter.

How it happens

Atrial flutter is often associated with second-degree block. In that instance, the AV node fails to allow conduction of all the impulses to the ventricles. As a result, the ventricular rate is slower.

Atrial flutter may be caused by conditions that enlarge atrial tissue and elevate atrial pressures. It is often found in patients with severe mitral valve disease, hyperthyroidism, pericardial disease, and primary myocardial disease. The rhythm is also sometimes encountered in patients with acute MI, chronic obstructive pulmonary disease, and systemic arterial hypoxia. Atrial flutter rarely occurs in healthy people. When it does, it may indicate intrinsic cardiac disease.

Rating the ratio

The clinical significance of atrial flutter is determined by the number of impulses conducted through the node — expressed as a conduction ratio, such as 2:1 or 4:1 — and the resulting ventricular rate. If the ventricular rate is too slow (fewer than 40 beats/minute) or too fast (more than 150 beats/minute), cardiac output can be seriously compromised.

Usually the faster the ventricular rate, the more dangerous the arrhythmia. The rapid rate reduces ventricular filling time and coronary perfusion, which can cause angina, CHF, pulmonary edema, hypotension, and syncope.

What to look for

Atrial flutter is characterized by abnormal P waves that produce a saw-toothed appearance, the hallmark flutter-wave appearance. (See *Atrial flutter*.) Varying degrees of AV block produce ventricular rates one-half to one-fourth of the atrial rate.

The AV node usually won't accept more than 180 impulses per minute and allows every second, third, or fourth impulse to be conducted, the ratio of which determines the ventricular rate.

One of the most common rates is 150 beats/minute. With an atrial rate of 300, that rhythm is referred to as a 2:1 block. (See *Atrial flutter and sinus tachycardia*.)

The QRS complex is usually normal but may be widened if flutter waves are buried in the complex. You won't be able to identify a T wave, nor will you be able to measure the QT interval.

The atrial rhythm may vary between fibrillatory waves and flutter waves, an arrhythmia commonly referred to as atrial fib-flutter.

Misleading pulses

When caring for a patient with atrial flutter, you may note that his peripheral or apical pulse is normal in rate and rhythm. That's because the pulse reflects the number of ventricular contractions, not the number of atrial impulses.

If the ventricular rate is normal, the patient may be asymptomatic. However, if the ventricular rate is rapid, the patient may exhibit signs and symptoms of reduced cardiac output and cardiac decompensation.

How you intervene

Atrial flutter with a rapid ventricular response and reduced cardiac output requires immediate intervention.

Mixed signals

Atrial flutter and sinus tachycardia

Whenever you see sinus tachycardia with a rate of 150 beats/minute, take another look. That rate is a common one for atrial flutter with 2:1 conduction. Look closely for flutter waves, which may be difficult to see if they're hidden in the QRS complex.

Atrial flutter

The following rhythm strip illustrates atrial flutter. Look for these distinguishing characteristics:

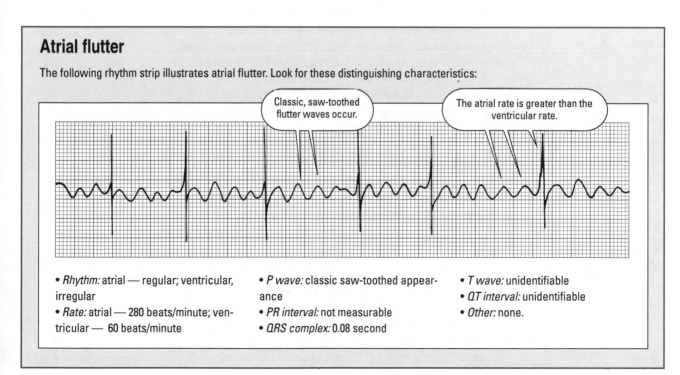

Classic, saw-toothed flutter waves occur.

The atrial rate is greater than the ventricular rate.

• *Rhythm:* atrial — regular; ventricular, irregular
• *Rate:* atrial — 280 beats/minute; ventricular — 60 beats/minute

• *P wave:* classic saw-toothed appearance
• *PR interval:* not measurable
• *QRS complex:* 0.08 second

• *T wave:* unidentifiable
• *QT interval:* unidentifiable
• *Other:* none.

Therapy aims to control the ventricular rate and convert the atrial ectopic rhythm to a normal sinus rhythm. Although stimulation of the vagus nerve may temporarily increase the block ratio and slow the ventricular rate, the effects won't last. For that reason, cardioversion remains the treatment of choice.

Synchronous shock

Synchronized cardioversion delivers an electrical stimulus during depolarization. The stimulus makes part of the myocardium refractory to ectopic impulses and terminates circus reentry movements.

Drug therapy includes digitalis glycosides and verapamil, which rapidly increase AV conduction time. Quinidine may be given to convert flutter to fibrillation, an easier arrhythmia to treat. If digoxin and quinidine therapy is used, the patient must first be given a loading dose of digoxin. Ibutilide fumarate (Corvert) may be used to convert recent-onset atrial flutter to sinus rhythm. If possible, the underlying cause of the atrial flutter should be treated.

Stay alert

Because atrial flutter may be an indication of intrinsic cardiac disease, monitor the patient closely for signs and symptoms of low cardiac output. If cardioversion is indicated, prepare the patient for I.V. administration of a sedative or anesthetic, as ordered. Keep resuscitative equipment at the bedside. Be alert to the effects of digoxin, which depresses the SA node. Be alert for bradycardia as well. Cardioversion can decrease the heart rate.

Atrial fibrillation

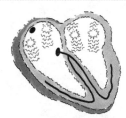

Atrial fibrillation, sometimes called "A-fib," is defined as chaotic, asynchronous, electrical activity in atrial tissue. It stems from the firing of a number of impulses in circus reentry pathways.

Like atrial flutter, atrial fibrillation results in a loss of atrial kick. The ectopic impulses may fire at a rate of 400 to 600 times/minute, causing the atria to quiver instead of contract.

The ventricles respond only to those impulses that make it through the AV node. On an ECG, atrial activity is no longer represented by P waves but by erratic baseline waves called fibrillatory waves, or f waves. This rhythm may be either sustained or paroxysmal (occurring in bursts). It can be preceded by or the result of PACs.

The irregular conduction of impulses through the AV node produces a characteristic irregularly irregular ventricular response. *If you see R waves that look irregularly irregular, suspect atrial fibrillation.*

How it happens

Atrial fibrillation occurs more commonly than atrial flutter or atrial tachycardia. Causes of the arrhythmia include mitral regurgitation, mitral stenosis, hyperthyroidism, infection, coronary artery disease, acute MI, pericarditis, hypoxia, and atrial septal defects.

The rhythm may also occur in a healthy person who uses coffee, alcohol, or cigarettes to excess or who is fatigued and under stress. Certain drugs, such as aminophylline and digitalis glycosides, may contribute to the development of atrial fibrillation.

Where have all the atrial kicks gone?

As with other atrial arrhythmias, atrial fibrillation eliminates atrial kick. That loss, combined with the decreased filling times associated with rapid rates, can lead to clinically significant problems. If the ventricular response is greater than 100 beats/minute—a condition called uncontrolled atrial fibrillation—the patient may develop CHF, angina, or syncope.

Patients with preexisting cardiac disease, such as hypertrophic obstructive cardiomyopathy, mitral stenosis, rheumatic heart disease, or mitral prosthetic valves, tend to tolerate atrial fibrillation poorly and may develop shock and severe CHF.

Left untreated, atrial fibrillation can lead to cardiovascular collapse, thrombus formation, and systemic arterial or pulmonary embolism. (See *Risk of restoring sinus rhythm*.)

What to look for

Atrial fibrillation is distinguished by the absence of P waves and an irregular ventricular response. When a number of ectopic sites in the atria fire impulses, depolariza-

Risk of restoring sinus rhythm

A patient with atrial fibrillation is at increased risk for developing atrial thrombus and systemic arterial embolism. Because the atria don't contract, blood may pool on the atrial wall, and thrombi can form.

If normal sinus rhythm is restored and the atria contract normally, clots can break away and travel through the pulmonary or systemic circulation with potentially disastrous results.

tion can't spread in an organized manner. (See *Atrial fibrillation.*)

Small sections of the atria are activated individually, which results in the atrial muscle quivering instead of contracting. On an ECG, you'll see uneven baseline f waves rather than clearly distinguishable P waves.

That fabulous filter

The AV node protects the ventricles from the 400 to 600 erratic atrial impulses that occur each minute by acting as a filter and blocking some of the impulses. The AV node itself doesn't receive all the impulses, however. If muscle tissue around the AV node is in a refractory state, impulses from other areas of the atria can't reach the AV node, which further reduces the number of atrial impulses conducted through to the ventricles.

Those two factors help explain the characteristic, wide variation in R-R intervals in atrial fibrillation.

Barely measurable

The atrial rate is almost indiscernible but is usually greater than 400 beats/minute. The ventricular rate usual-

---

Atrial fibrillation

The following rhythm strip shows atrial fibrillation. Look for these distinguishing characteristics:

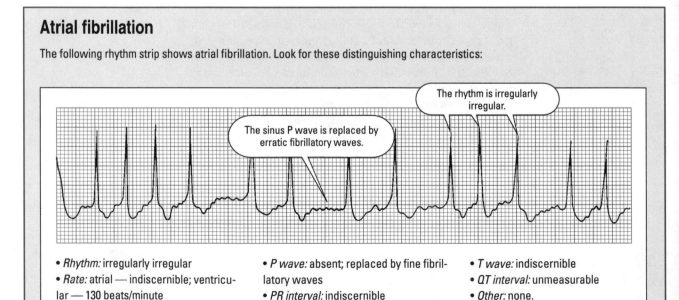

The sinus P wave is replaced by erratic fibrillatory waves.

The rhythm is irregularly irregular.

- *Rhythm:* irregularly irregular
- *Rate:* atrial — indiscernible; ventricular — 130 beats/minute
- *P wave:* absent; replaced by fine fibrillatory waves
- *PR interval:* indiscernible
- *QRS complex:* 0.08 second
- *T wave:* indiscernible
- *QT interval:* unmeasurable
- *Other:* none

ly varies from 100 to 150 beats/minute but can be lower. When the ventricular response rate is below 100, atrial fibrillation is considered controlled. When it exceeds 100, the rhythm is considered uncontrolled.

Atrial fibrillation is called coarse if the f waves are pronounced and fine if they aren't. Atrial fib-flutter may also occur. Look for a configuration that varies between fibrillatory waves and flutter waves.

Pulse differences

When caring for a patient with atrial fibrillation, you may find that the radial pulse rate is slower than the apical rate. That's because the weaker contractions of the heart don't produce a palpable peripheral pulse; only the stronger ones do.

The pulse rhythm will be irregular. If the ventricular rate is rapid, the patient may show signs and symptoms of decreased cardiac output, including hypotension and lightheadedness. His heart may be able to compensate for the decrease if the fibrillation lasts long enough to become chronic. In those cases, however, the patient is at a greater-than-normal risk of developing pulmonary, cerebral, or other emboli and may exhibit signs of those conditions.

How you intervene

The major therapeutic goal in treating atrial fibrillation is to reduce the ventricular response rate to below 100 beats/minute. This may be accomplished either by drugs that control the ventricular response or by cardioversion and drugs in combination to convert the rhythm to sinus.

The ventricular rate may be controlled with such drugs as diltiazem (Cardizem), verapamil (Isoptin), digoxin (Lanoxin), and beta blockers. Ibutilide fumarate (Corvert) may be used to convert new-onset atrial fibrillation to sinus rhythm. Quinidine (Cin-Quin) and procainamide (Pronestyl) can also convert atrial fibrillation to normal sinus rhythm, usually after anticoagulation.

Three critical days

Electrical cardioversion is most successful if used within the first 3 days of treatment and less successful if the rhythm has existed for a long time. If the patient shows signs of more severe angina or of decreased cardiac output, emergency measures are necessary.

When the onset of atrial fibrillation is acute and the patient can cooperate, carotid sinus massage may slow the ventricular response but will not convert the arrhythmia.

Cardioversion

STAT!

A symptomatic patient needs immediate synchronized cardioversion. If possible, anticoagulants should be administered first because cardioversion can cause emboli to form, especially in patients with chronic or paroxysmal atrial fibrillation.

A conversion to normal sinus rhythm will cause forceful atrial contractions to resume abruptly. If a thrombus forms in the atria, the resumption of contractions can result in systemic emboli. (See *How synchronized cardioversion works.*)

Reestablishing its role

Drugs such as digitalis glycosides, procainamide, propranolol (Inderal), quinidine, and verapamil can be given after successful cardioversion to maintain normal sinus

---

How synchronized cardioversion works

A patient whose arrhythmia causes low cardiac output and hypotension may be a candidate for synchronized cardioversion. This procedure may be done electively or as an emergency measure. For instance, it may be used to make a person with atrial fibrillation more comfortable or to save the life of a patient with ventricular tachycardia.

Synchronize the energy
Synchronized cardioversion is similar to defibrillation except that cardioversion generally requires lower energy levels. In synchronized cardioversion, the R wave on the patient's ECG is synchronized with the cardioverter (defibrillator). Once the firing buttons have been pressed, the cardioverter discharges energy when it senses the next R wave.

When the stimulus hits
To stop atrial depolarization and reestablish normal sinus rhythm, stimulation must occur during the R wave. Stimulation that hits a T wave increases the risk of fatal arrhythmias. *Keep in mind— there's a slight delay between the time the firing button is pressed and the moment the energy is actually discharged. Hold the paddles to the patient's chest until the energy is actually discharged.*

Use in digitalis toxicity
Be aware that synchronized cardioversion carries the risk of lethal arrhythmias when used in patients with digitalis toxicity.

rhythm and to control the ventricular rate in chronic atrial fibrillation. Those drugs prolong the atrial refractory period, giving the SA node an opportunity to reestablish its role as the heart's pacemaker. Chronic atrial fibrillation that doesn't respond to routine treatment may be treated with radiofrequency ablation of the bundle of His, followed by insertion of a pacemaker.

When assessing a patient with atrial fibrillation, assess both the peripheral and apical pulses. If the patient is not on a cardiac monitor, be alert for an irregular pulse and differences in the apical and radial pulse rates.

Assess for symptoms of decreased cardiac output and CHF. If drug therapy is used, monitor serum drug levels and observe the patient for evidence of toxicity. Tell the patient to report pulse rate changes, syncope or dizziness, chest pain, or signs of CHF, such as increasing dyspnea and peripheral edema.

Quick quiz

1. The hallmark of a premature atrial contraction is:
   A. a regular atrial rhythm.
   B. a premature, abnormally shaped P wave.
   C. a P wave followed by an aberrantly conducted QRS complex.

Answer: B. Because PACs originate outside the SA node, the P wave comes earlier in the cycle and has a different configuration than the sinus P wave.

2. In atrial flutter, the key consideration in determining treatment is the:
   A. atrial rate.
   B. ventricular rate.
   C. configuration of the flutter waves.

Answer: B. If the ventricular rate is too fast or too slow, cardiac output will be compromised. A rapid ventricular rate may require immediate cardioversion.

3. In controlled atrial fibrillation, the ventricular response rate is:
   A. lower than 60 beats/minute.
   B. lower than 100 beats/minute.
   C. higher than 100 beats/minute.

Answer: B. Atrial fibrillation with a ventricular response rate lower than 100 is considered controlled and often requires no treatment. A rate above 100 is considered uncontrolled and may require cardioversion or other treatment.

4. Carotid sinus massage is used to:
   A. prevent the continued development of PACs.
   B. increase the ventricular rate in AV block.
   C. convert paroxysmal atrial tachycardia to sinus rhythm.

Answer: C. Carotid sinus massage triggers atrial standstill by inhibiting firing of the SA node and slowing AV conduction. This allows the SA node to reestablish itself as the primary pacemaker. In atrial flutter, the technique may increase the block and slow the ventricular rate but won't convert the rhythm.

5. For atrial fibrillation, electrical cardioversion is most successful if used:
   A. during the first 3 days after the onset of the arrhythmia.
   B. during the first 3 weeks of treatment for the arrhythmia.
   C. during the first 3 months after the onset of the arrhythmia.

Answer: A. Electrical cardioversion is most successful if used within the first 3 days of treatment and less successful if the rhythm has existed for a long time.

Test strips

Try out a couple of test strips. Answer the questions accompanying each strip; then check your answers with ours.

6. In the strip shown below, the rhythm is regular, the atrial rate is 310 beats/minute, the ventricular rate is 80 beats/minute, the P wave consists of saw-tooth-shaped waves, the PR interval isn't measurable, the QRS complex is 0.08 second, the T wave isn't identifiable, and the QT interval isn't measurable. You would identify the strip as:
    A. atrial tachycardia.
    B. atrial fibrillation.
    C. atrial flutter.

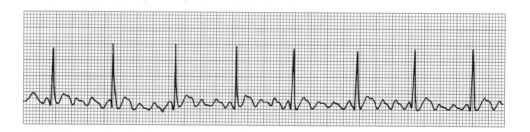

Answer: C. The characteristic saw-toothed appearance of the P waves is a classic indication of atrial flutter.

7. In the ECG strip shown below, the rhythm is irregular, the rate is 80 beats/minute, the P wave is normal, the PR interval is 0.14 second, the QRS complex is 0.08 second, the T wave is normal, and the QT interval is 0.36 second. You would identify the strip as:
    A. atrial fibrillation.
    B. atrial tachycardia.
    C. normal sinus rhythm with PACs.

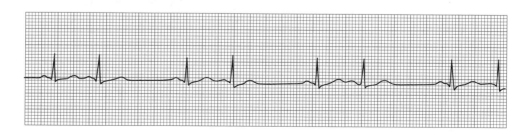

Answer: C. This is normal sinus rhythm with premature atrial contractions occurring after each sinus beat.

8. You notice the following rhythm on the monitor and obtain a rhythm strip. After examining the characteristics of the strip, you identify the rhythm as:

    A. atrial fibrillation.

    B. atrial tachycardia.

    C. normal sinus rhythm with PACs.

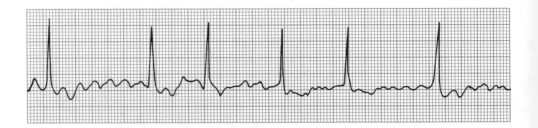

Answer: A. This is coarse atrial fibrillation with aberrant ventricular conduction. The rhythm is irregular, the atrial rate can't be determined, the ventricular rate is 60 beats/minute, the P wave is absent, coarse fibrillatory waves are present, the PR interval is indiscernible, the duration of the QRS complex is 0.12 second, the T wave is indiscernible, and the QT interval is not measurable.

Scoring

☆☆☆   If you answered all eight items correctly, outstanding! You're the MVP of the Atrial World Series!

☆☆   If you answered five to seven correctly, super! You're an up-and-coming power hitter, perhaps destined for the Atrial Hall of Fame!

☆   If you answered fewer than five correctly, hang in there. With a little batting practice, you'll be smacking home runs at Atrial Park in no time!

Junctional arrhythmias

Just the facts

This chapter describes the various types of junctional arrhythmias and how they're treated. In this chapter, you'll learn:

♦ what characteristics junctional arrhythmias have

♦ what causes junctional arrhythmias and which patients are at risk for them

♦ how junctional arrhythmias look on an electrocardiogram (ECG) strip

♦ what assessment findings are associated with certain arrhythmias

♦ how to treat junctional arrhythmias and care for patients who have them.

A look at junctional arrhythmias

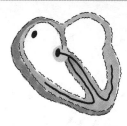

Junctional arrhythmias originate in the atrioventricular (AV) junction — the area around the AV node and the bundle of His. The arrhythmias occur when the sinoatrial (SA) node, a higher pacemaker, is suppressed and fails to conduct impulses or when a block occurs in conduction. Electrical impulses may then be initiated by pacemaker cells in the AV junction.

Just your normal impulse

In normal impulse conduction, the AV node slows transmission of the impulse from the atria to the ventricles, which allows the atria to pump as much blood as they can into the ventricles before the ventricles contract. But impulses aren't always conducted normally. (See *Conduction in Wolff-Parkinson-White syndrome*.)

Because the AV junction is located in the middle of the heart, impulses generated in this area cause the heart to be depolarized in an abnormal way. The impulse moves upward and causes backward, or retrograde, depolarization of the ventricles and inverted P waves in leads II, III, and aV$_F$, leads in which you would normally see upright P waves. (See *Finding the P wave*.)

Which way did the impulse go?

The impulse also moves down toward the ventricles, causing forward, or antegrade, depolarization of the ventricles and an upright QRS complex. Arrhythmias that cause inverted P waves on an ECG may be atrial or junctional in origin.

Conduction in Wolff-Parkinson-White syndrome

Conduction doesn't always take place in a normal way. In Wolff-Parkinson-White syndrome, for instance, a conduction bypass develops outside the atrioventricular (AV) junction and connects the atria with the ventricles, as shown. Wolff-Parkinson-White syndrome is typically a congenital rhythm disorder that occurs mainly in young children and in adults ages 20 to 35.

Rapidly conducted
The bypass formed in Wolff-Parkinson-White syndrome, known as the bundle of Kent, conducts impulses to the atria or the ventricles. Impulses aren't delayed at the AV node, so conduction is abnormally fast. Retrograde conduction, circus reentry, and reentrant tachycardia can result.

Checking the ECG
This syndrome causes a shortened PR interval (less than 0.10 second) and a widened QRS complex (greater than 0.10 second). The beginning of the QRS complex may look slurred because of altered ventricular depolarization. This hallmark sign of Wolff-Parkinson-White syndrome is called a delta wave, shown in the inset.

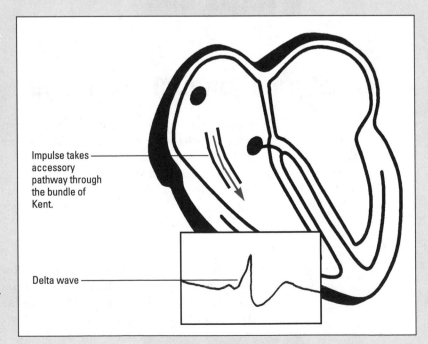

Impulse takes accessory pathway through the bundle of Kent.

Delta wave

Junctional mimic

Atrial arrhythmias are sometimes mistaken for junctional arrhythmias because impulses are generated so low in the

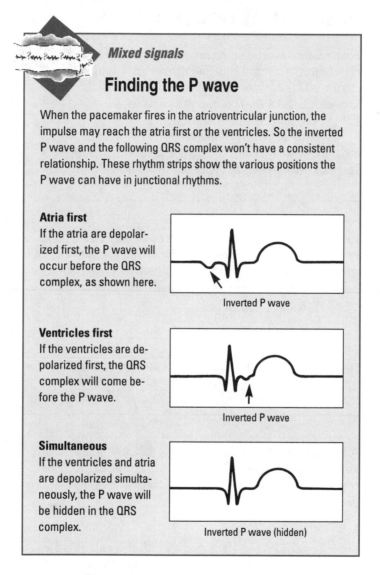

Mixed signals

Finding the P wave

When the pacemaker fires in the atrioventricular junction, the impulse may reach the atria first or the ventricles. So the inverted P wave and the following QRS complex won't have a consistent relationship. These rhythm strips show the various positions the P wave can have in junctional rhythms.

Atria first
If the atria are depolarized first, the P wave will occur before the QRS complex, as shown here.

Inverted P wave

Ventricles first
If the ventricles are depolarized first, the QRS complex will come before the P wave.

Inverted P wave

Simultaneous
If the ventricles and atria are depolarized simultaneously, the P wave will be hidden in the QRS complex.

Inverted P wave (hidden)

atria that they cause retrograde depolarization and inverted P waves. Looking at the PR interval will help you determine whether an arrhythmia is atrial or junctional.

An arrhythmia with an inverted P wave before the QRS complex and a normal PR interval (0.12 to 0.20 second) originated in the atria. An arrhythmia with a PR interval less than 0.12 second originated in the AV junction.

Premature junctional contraction

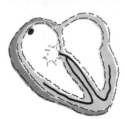

A premature junctional contraction (PJC) is a beat that occurs before a normal beat and causes an irregular rhythm. This ectopic beat occurs when an irritable location within the AV junction acts as a pacemaker and fires either prematurely or out of sequence.

    As with all beats produced by the AV junction, the atria are depolarized in retrograde fashion, causing an inverted P wave. The ventricles are depolarized normally.

How it happens

PJCs may be caused by toxic levels of digoxin (level greater than 2.5 ng/ml), excessive caffeine intake, inferior-wall myocardial infarction (MI), rheumatic heart disease, valvular disease, or swelling of the AV junction after heart surgery.

The beat goes on

Although PJCs themselves usually aren't dangerous, you'll need to monitor the patient carefully and assess him for other signs of intrinsic pacemaker failure.

What to look for

A PJC appears on a rhythm strip as an early beat causing an irregularity. (See *PJC.*) The rest of the strip may show regular atrial and ventricular rhythms, depending on the patient's underlying rhythm.

P wave inversion

Look for an inverted P wave in leads II, III, and aV$_F$. Depending on when the impulse occurs, the P wave may fall before, during, or after the QRS complex. (See *Identifying a PJC.*) If it falls during the QRS complex, it's hidden. If it comes before the QRS complex, the PR interval is less than 0.12 second.

    Because the ventricles are usually depolarized normally, the QRS complex has a normal configuration and a

---

Key characteristics

PJC

- *Rhythm:* irregular with PJC appearance

- *Rate:* varies with underlying rhythm

- *P wave:* inverted; falls before or after or is hidden in QRS complex; may be absent

- *PR interval:* less than 0.12 second or unmeasurable

- *QRS complex:* usually normal

- *T wave:* usually normal

- *QT interval:* usually normal

- *Other:* noncompensatory pause after PJC

normal duration of less than 0.12 second. The T wave and the QT interval are usually normal.

That quickening feeling

The patient may be asymptomatic or he may complain of palpitations or a feeling of quickening in the chest. You may be able to palpate an irregular pulse. If the PJCs are frequent enough, the patient may have hypotension from a transient decrease in cardiac output.

How you intervene

PJCs usually don't require treatment unless symptoms occur. In those cases, the underlying cause should be treated. If digitalis toxicity is the culprit, the medication should be discontinued and serum drug levels monitored.

Don't skip this strip

Identifying a PJC

This ECG strip shows a premature junctional contraction (PJC) — a junctional beat that occurs before a normal sinus beat.

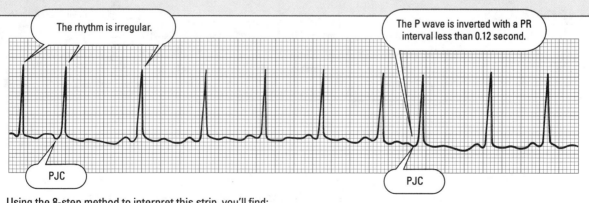

Using the 8-step method to interpret this strip, you'll find:

- *Rhythm:* irregular atrial and ventricular rhythms
- *Rate:* 100 beats/minute
- *P wave:* precedes the QRS complex

- *PR interval:* 0.14 second for the underlying rhythm and 0.06 second for the PJC
- *QRS complex:* 0.06 second

- *T wave:* normal configuration
- *QT interval:* 0.36 second
- *Other:* pause after PJC.

You should also monitor the patient for hemodynamic instability. If ectopic beats are frequent, the patient should decrease or eliminate his caffeine intake. (See *Key facts about PJC*.)

Junctional escape rhythm

A junctional escape rhythm is a string of beats that occurs after a conduction delay from the atria. The normal intrinsic firing rate for cells in the AV junction is 40 to 60 beats/minute.

Remember that the AV junction can take over as the heart's pacemaker if higher pacemaker sites slow down or fail to fire or conduct. The junctional escape beat is an example of this compensatory mechanism. *Because junctional escape beats prevent ventricular standstill, they should never be suppressed.*

Backward and upside-down

In a junctional escape rhythm, as in all junctional arrhythmias, the atria are depolarized by means of retrograde conduction. The P waves are inverted, and impulse conduction through the ventricles is normal.

How it happens

A junctional escape rhythm can be caused by any condition that disturbs SA node function or enhances AV junction automaticity. Causes of the arrhythmia include:
- sick sinus syndrome
- vagal stimulation
- digitalis toxicity
- inferior-wall MI
- rheumatic heart disease.

The great escape

Whether junctional escape rhythm harms the patient depends on how well the patient's heart tolerates a decreased heart rate and decreased cardiac output. The less tolerant the heart is, the more significant the effects of the arrhythmia.

I can't waste time

Key facts about PJC

- The P wave is inverted because of retrograde conduction of the impulse.

- The QRS complex is usually normal.

- The patient is usually asymptomatic.

Key characteristics

Junctional escape rhythm

- *Rhythm:* regular

- *Rate:* 40 to 60 beats/minute

- *P wave:* inverted in leads II, III, and aV$_F$; can occur before, during, or after the QRS complex

- *PR interval:* less than 0.12 second if the P wave comes before the QRS complex

- *QRS:* normal; less than 0.12 second

- *T wave:* normal

- *QT interval:* normal

- *Other:* none

What to look for

A junctional escape rhythm shows a regular rhythm of 40 to 60 beats/minute on an ECG strip. (See *Identifying junctional escape rhythm*.) Look for inverted P waves in leads II, III, and aV$_F$.

The P waves will occur before, after, or hidden within the QRS complex. The PR interval is less than 0.12 second and is measurable only if the P wave comes before the QRS complex.

The rest of the ECG waveform — including the QRS complex, T wave, and QT interval — should appear normal, because impulses through the ventricles are usually conducted normally.

I may be slow, but at least I'm regular

A patient with a junctional escape rhythm will have a slow, regular pulse rate of 40 to 60 beats/minute. The patient may be asymptomatic. However, pulse rates less than

---

Identifying junctional escape rhythm

This ECG strip shows a junctional escape rhythm. Note the inverted P wave.

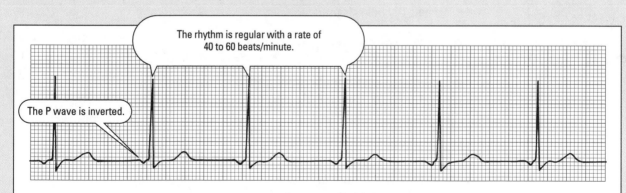

The rhythm is regular with a rate of 40 to 60 beats/minute.

The P wave is inverted.

Using the 8-step method to interpret this strip, you'll find the following distinguishing characteristics:

- *Rhythm:* regular
- *Rate:* 60 beats/minute
- *P wave:* inverted and preceding each QRS complex
- *PR interval:* 0.10 second
- *QRS complex:* 0.10 second
- *T wave:* normal
- *QT interval:* 0.44 second
- *Other:* none.

60 beats/minute may lead to inadequate cardiac output, causing hypotension, syncope, or blurred vision.

How you intervene

Treatment for a junctional escape rhythm involves correcting the underlying cause. Atropine may be given to increase the heart rate, or a temporary or permanent pacemaker may be inserted. (See *Key facts about junctional escape rhythm*.)

Nursing care includes monitoring the patient's serum digitalis glycoside and electrolyte levels and watching for signs of decreased cardiac output, such as hypotension, syncope, or blurred vision. If the patient is hypotensive, lower the head of his bed as far as he can tolerate it and keep atropine at the bedside.

Accelerated junctional rhythm

An accelerated junctional rhythm is caused by an irritable focus in the AV junction that speeds up to take over as the heart's pacemaker. The atria are depolarized by means of retrograde conduction, and the ventricles are depolarized normally. The accelerated rate is usually between 60 and 100 beats/minute.

How it happens

Conditions that affect SA node or AV node automaticity can cause accelerated junctional rhythm. Those conditions include:
- digitalis toxicity
- hypokalemia
- valvular heart disease
- inferior- or posterior-wall MI
- rheumatic heart disease.

Getting a kick out of it

This arrhythmia is significant if the patient has symptoms of decreased cardiac output — hypotension, syncope, and blurred vision. These can occur if the atria are depolarized after the QRS complex, which prevents blood ejection from the atria into the ventricles, or atrial kick.

I can't waste time

Key facts about junctional escape rhythm

- The atrioventricular junction becomes the heart's pacemaker, firing regularly at 40 to 60 beats/minute.

- The P wave is inverted and its location varies in relation to the QRS complex.

- The patient may or may not be symptomatic.

- The rhythm is a protective one and shouldn't be suppressed.

What to look for

With an accelerated junctional rhythm, look for a regular rhythm and a rate of 60 to 100 beats/minute. (See *Identifying accelerated junctional rhythm*.) If the P wave is present, it will be inverted in leads II, III, and aV_F and will occur before or after the QRS complex or be hidden in it.

If the P wave comes before the QRS complex, the PR interval will be less than 0.12 second. The QRS complex, T wave, and QT interval all appear normal.

Low-down, dizzy, and confused

The patient may be asymptomatic because accelerated junctional rhythm has the same rate as sinus rhythm. However, if cardiac output is low, the patient may become dizzy, hypotensive, and confused and have weak peripheral pulses.

Identifying accelerated junctional rhythm

This ECG strip shows an accelerated junctional rhythm.

> The P wave is absent.

> The rhythm is regular with a rate between 60 and 100 beats/minute.

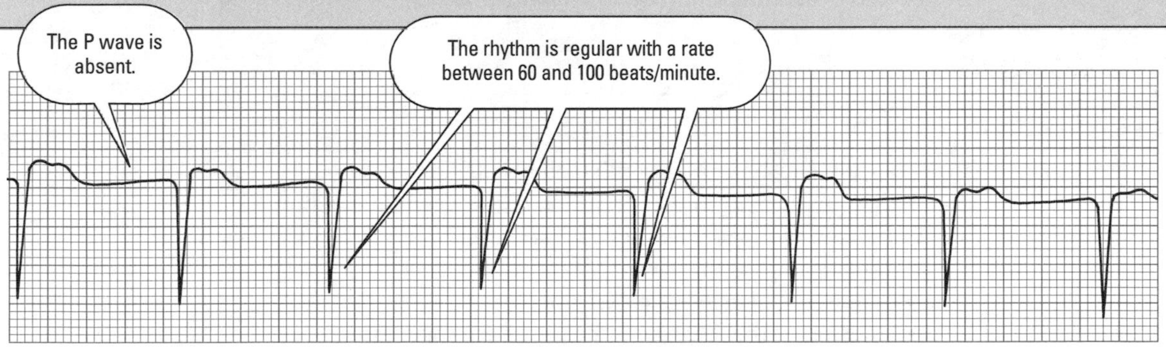

Using the 8-step method to interpret this strip, you'll find the following distinguishing characteristics:

- *Rhythm:* regular
- *Rate:* 80 beats/minute
- *P wave:* absent

- *PR interval:* not measurable
- *QRS complex:* 0.10 second
- *T wave:* normal

- *QT interval:* 0.32 second
- *Other:* none.

How you intervene

Treatment for accelerated junctional arrhythmia involves correcting the underlying cause. Nursing interventions include observing the patient to see how well he tolerates this arrhythmia, monitoring his digitalis glycoside level, and withholding his digitalis glycoside dose, as ordered.

You should also assess the level of potassium and other electrolytes and administer supplements, as ordered; monitor vital signs for hemodynamic instability; and observe for signs of decreased cardiac output. (See *Accelerated junctional rhythm.*)

Junctional tachycardia

In junctional tachycardia, three or more premature junctional contractions occur in a row. This supraventricular tachycardia occurs when an irritable focus from the AV junction has enhanced automaticity, overriding the SA node to function as the heart's pacemaker.

In this arrhythmia, the atria are depolarized by means of retrograde conduction, and conduction through the ventricles is normal. The rate is usually 100 to 200 beats/minute. (See *Identifying junctional tachycardia.*)

How it happens

Possible causes of junctional tachycardia include:
• digitalis toxicity (most common cause), which can be enhanced by hypokalemia
• inferior- or posterior-wall MI or ischemia
• congenital heart disease in children
• swelling of the AV junction after heart surgery.

Compromisin' rhythm

The significance of junctional tachycardia depends on the rate, underlying cause, and severity of the accompanying cardiac disease. At higher ventricular rates, junctional tachycardia may compromise cardiac output by decreas-

---

Key characteristics

Accelerated junctional rhythm

➤ *Rhythm:* regular

➤ *Rate:* 60 to 100 beats/minute

➤ *P wave:* inverted (if present) and occurring before, during, or after QRS complex

➤ *PR interval:* measurable only with P wave that comes before QRS complex; 0.12 second or less

➤ *QRS complex:* usually normal

➤ *T wave:* usually normal

➤ *QT interval:* usually normal

➤ *Other:* none

ing the amount of blood filling the ventricles with each beat. Higher rates also result in the loss of atrial kick.

What to look for

When assessing a rhythm strip for junctional tachycardia, look for a rate of 100 to 200 beats/minute. The P wave is inverted in leads II, III, and aV_F and can occur before, during (hidden P wave), or after the QRS complex. (See *Junctional tachycardia,* page 122.)

Measurement of the PR interval depends on whether the P wave falls before, in, or after the QRS complex. If it comes before the QRS complex, the only time the P wave can be measured, it will always be less than 0.12 second.

The QRS complexes look normal, as does the T wave unless a P wave occurs in it or the rate is so fast that the T wave can't be detected. (See *Junctional and supraventricular tachycardia,* page 122.)

Identifying junctional tachycardia

This ECG strip shows junctional tachycardia.

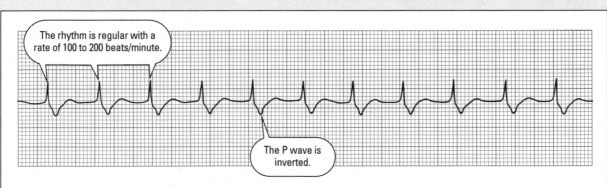

The rhythm is regular with a rate of 100 to 200 beats/minute.

The P wave is inverted.

Using the 8-step method to interpret this strip, you'll find the following distinguishing characteristics:

- *Rhythm:* regular atrial and ventricular rhythms
- *Rate:* atrial and ventricular rates of 115 beats/minute

- *P wave:* inverted, follows QRS complex
- *PR interval:* not measurable
- *QRS complex:* 0.08 second

- *T wave:* normal
- *QT interval:* 0.36 second
- *Other:* none.

Rapid rate = instability

Patients with rapid heart rates may have decreased cardiac output and hemodynamic instability. The pulse will be rapid, and dizziness, low blood pressure, and other signs of decreased cardiac output may be present.

How you intervene

The underlying cause should be treated. If the cause is digitalis toxicity, the digitalis glycoside should be discontinued. Vagal maneuvers and medications such as verapamil may slow the heart rate for the symptomatic patient. (See *Comparing junctional rates.*)

If the patient recently had an MI or heart surgery, he may need a temporary pacemaker to reset the heart's rhythm. Children with permanent arrhythmias may be resistant to drug therapy and require surgery.

Monitor patients with junctional tachycardia for signs of decreased cardiac output. You should also check digitalis glycoside and potassium levels and administer potassium supplements, as ordered. If symptoms are severe and a digitalis glycoside is the culprit, the doctor may order a digitalis glycoside–binding drug.

Junctional tachycardia

- *Rhythm:* regular
- *Rate:* 100 to 200 beats/minute
- *P wave:* usually inverted; location varies around QRS complex
- *PR interval:* shortened at less than 0.12 second or unmeasurable
- *QRS complex:* normal
- *T wave:* usually normal but may contain P wave
- *QT interval:* usually normal
- *Other:* none

Mixed signals

Junctional and supraventricular tachycardia

If a tachycardia has a narrow QRS complex, you may have trouble deciding whether its source is junctional or atrial. Once the rate approaches 150 beats/minute, a formerly visible P wave is hidden in the previous T wave, so you won't be able to use the P wave to figure out where the rhythm originated.

In these cases, call the rhythm *supraventricular* tachycardia, a general term that refers to the origin as being above the ventricles. Examples of supraventricular tachycardia include atrial flutter, multifocal atrial tachycardia, and junctional tachycardia.

Comparing junctional rates

The names given to junctional rhythms vary according to rate. The illustration below shows how the rate of each rhythm correlates with the name of the rhythm.

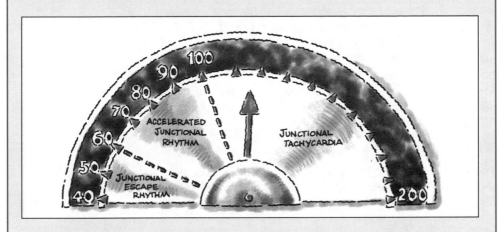

Wandering pacemaker

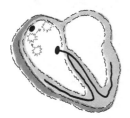

A wandering pacemaker is an irregular rhythm that results when the heart's pacemaker changes its focus from the SA node to another area above the ventricles. The origin of the impulse may wander beat-to-beat from the SA node to other atrial sites or to the AV junction. The P wave and PR interval vary from beat to beat as the pacemaker site changes. (See *Wandering pacemaker.*)

How it happens

Wandering pacemaker may be caused by:
• increased vagal tone
• digitalis toxicity
• organic heart disease such as rheumatic carditis.

The arrhythmia may be normal in young patients and is common in athletes who have slow heart rates. It may be difficult to identify because the arrhythmia is often transient. Although wandering pacemaker is rarely serious, chronic arrhythmias are a sign of heart disease and should be monitored.

Key characteristics

Wandering pacemaker

• *Rhythm:* irregular

• *Rate:* usually normal or below 60 beats/minute

• *P wave:* changes in size and shape

• *PR interval:* varies

• *QRS complex:* usually normal

• *T wave:* normal

• *QT interval:* may vary

• *Other:* none

What to look for

The rhythm on an ECG strip will look slightly irregular because of varying sites of impulse initiation. The rate is usually normal — 60 to 100 beats/minute — but it may be slower. The P waves change shape as the pacemaker site changes. (See *Identifying wandering pacemaker.*)

Impulses may originate in the SA node, atria, or AV junction. If an impulse originates in the AV junction, the P wave may come before, during, or after the QRS complex. The PR interval will also vary from beat to beat as the pacemaker site changes, but it will always be less than 0.20 second.

Mind the PRs and QRSs

The variation in PR interval will cause a slightly irregular R-R interval. (See *Identifying wandering pacemaker.*) If the impulse originates in the AV junction, the PR interval will

---

Identifying wandering pacemaker

This ECG strip shows wandering pacemaker — an atrial arrhythmia with a shifting impulse site. Note the difference in P waves caused by those impulse shifts.

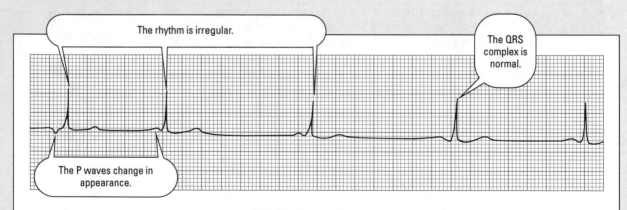

The rhythm is irregular.

The QRS complex is normal.

The P waves change in appearance.

Using the 8-step method to interpret this strip, you'll find the following distinguishing characteristics:

- *Rhythm:* atrial and ventricular rhythms are irregular
- *Rate:* atrial and ventricular rates are 50 beats/minute

- *P wave:* changes in size and shape; first P wave is inverted, second is upright
- *PR interval:* varies

- *QRS complex:* 0.08 second
- *T wave:* normal
- *QT interval:* 0.44 second
- *Other:* none.

be less than 0.12 second. Ventricular depolarization is normal, so the QRS complex will be less than 0.12 second. The T wave and QT interval will usually be normal, although the QT interval can vary.

Patients are generally asymptomatic and unaware of the arrhythmia. (See *Key facts about wandering pacemaker.*) The pulse rate and rhythm may be normal or irregular.

How you intervene

Usually, no treatment is needed. If the patient is symptomatic, however, the underlying cause should be treated.

You'll need to monitor the patient's heart rhythm and assess for signs of hemodynamic instability. Also assess blood pressure, mental status, and skin color.

Quick quiz

1. In a junctional escape rhythm, the P wave can occur:
   A. within the T wave.
   B. on top of the preceding Q wave.
   C. before, during, or after the QRS complex.

Answer: C. In all junctional arrhythmias, the P wave is inverted and may appear before, during, or after the QRS complex.

2. The P wave is inverted in a premature junctional contraction as a result of:
   A. AV block.
   B. antegrade repolarization.
   C. retrograde depolarization.

Answer: C. In all junctional arrhythmias, the atria are depolarized by means of retrograde depolarization. The P waves, if present, are inverted.

3. The inherent rate for the AV junction is:
   A. 20 to 40 beats/minute.
   B. 40 to 60 beats/minute.
   C. 60 to 100 beats/minute.

I can't waste time

Key facts about wandering pacemaker

- The name of this arrhythmia gives a clue as to what happens in it. The origins of the impulses "wander" around the atria and atrioventricular junction.

- You'll see varying P waves on the ECG strip.

- This arrhythmia usually is transient and benign and is common in young children and athletes.

Answer: B. The normal, or inherent, rate for the AV junction is 40 to 60 beats/minute.

4. In an accelerated junctional rhythm, the QRS complex appears:
    A. narrowed.
    B. widened.
    C. normal.

Answer: C. Because the ventricles are usually depolarized normally in this rhythm, the QRS complex has a normal configuration and a normal duration of less than 0.12 second.

5. The normal slowing of impulses as they pass through the AV node allows the atria to:
    A. fill completely with blood from the venae cavae.
    B. pump the maximum amount of blood possible into the ventricles.
    C. remain insensitive to ectopic impulse formation outside the sinus node.

Answer: B. In normal impulse conduction, the AV node slows impulse transmission from the atria to the ventricles and allows the atria to pump as much blood as possible into the ventricles before the ventricles contract.

6. If the ventricles are depolarized first in a junctional rhythm, the P wave will appear:
    A. before the QRS complex.
    B. within the QRS complex.
    C. after the QRS complex.

Answer: C. If the ventricles are depolarized first, the P wave will come after the QRS complex.

Test strips

Here are two test strips. Answer the question accompanying each strip; then check your answers with ours.

7.   In the strip below, the atrial and ventricular rhythms are regular at 47 beats/minute, the P wave is inverted, the PR interval is 0.08 second, the QRS complex is 0.06 second, the T wave is normal, and the QT interval is 0.42 second. You would interpret this rhythm as:
   A.   wandering pacemaker.
   B.   junctional tachycardia.
   C.   junctional escape rhythm.

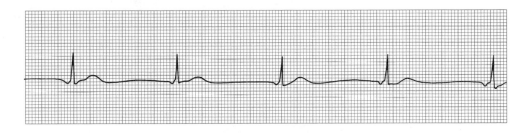

Answer: C. This strip shows junctional escape rhythm.

8.   You would interpret the rhythm shown below as:
   A.   junctional escape rhythm.
   B.   junctional tachycardia.
   C.   sinus bradycardia with a PJC.

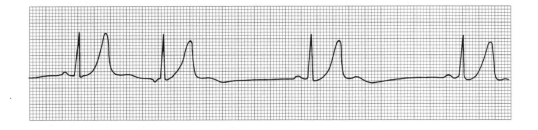

Answer: C. The atrial and ventricular rhythms are irregular at 40 beats/minute, the P wave occurs on the second beat, the PR interval is 0.08 on the second beat and 0.16 second on other beats, the QRS complex is 0.08 second, the T wave is tall and peaked, and the QT interval is 0.48

second. These observations indicate sinus bradycardia with a PJC.

Scoring

☆☆☆   If you answered all eight questions correctly, we're impressed! Turn on your CD player and dance to that hot new band, the Junctional Escape Rhythms!

☆☆   If you answered five to seven questions correctly, wow! You've clearly got that accelerated junctional rhythm!

☆   If you answered fewer than five correctly, don't worry, be tachy!

Ventricular arrhythmias

Just the facts

This chapter discusses the types of ventricular arrhythmias and how each is treated. In this chapter, you'll learn:

♦ where ventricular arrhythmias originate

♦ what characterizes each ventricular arrhythmia

♦ what causes ventricular arrhythmias and which patients are at risk for developing them

♦ how to interpret ventricular arrhythmias on an electrocardiogram (ECG) strip

♦ how to treat, assess, and care for a patient with a ventricular arrhythmia.

A look at ventricular arrhythmias

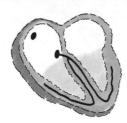

Ventricular arrhythmias originate in the ventricles below the bundle of His. The arrhythmias occur when electrical impulses depolarize the myocardium using a different pathway from normal impulses.

They show up on an ECG in characteristic ways. The QRS complex is wider than normal because of the prolonged conduction time through the ventricles. The T wave and the QRS complex deflect in opposite directions because of the difference in the action potential during ventricular depolarization and repolarization. And the P wave is absent because atrial depolarization doesn't occur.

No kick from the atrium

When electrical impulses are generated from the ventricles instead of the atrium, atrial kick is lost and cardiac output decreases by as much as 30%. As a result, patients with ventricular arrhythmias may show signs and symptoms of cardiac decompensation, including hypotension, angina, syncope, and respiratory distress.

Potential to kill

Although ventricular arrhythmias may be benign, they're potentially deadly because the ventricles are ultimately responsible for cardiac output. Rapid recognition and treatment of ventricular arrhythmias increases the chance for successful resuscitation.

Premature ventricular contraction

A premature ventricular contraction (PVC) is an ectopic beat that may occur in healthy people without causing problems. PVCs may occur singly, in clusters of two or more, or in repeating patterns, such as bigeminy or trigeminy. (See *Identifying PVC*.) When PVCs occur in patients with underlying heart disease, they may indicate impending lethal ventricular arrhythmias.

How it happens

PVCs are usually caused by electrical irritability in the ventricular conduction system or muscle tissue. This irritability may be provoked by anything that disrupts normal electrolyte shifts during cell depolarization and repolarization. Conditions that can disrupt electrolyte shifts include:
• electrolyte imbalances, such as hypokalemia, hypomagnesemia, and hypocalcemia
• metabolic acidosis
• hypoxia
• myocardial ischemia
• drug intoxication, particularly with cocaine, amphetamines, and tricyclic antidepressants
• enlargement of the ventricular chambers
• increased sympathetic stimulation
• myocarditis.

This could get serious

PVCs are significant for two reasons. First, they can lead to more serious arrhythmias, such as ventricular tachycardia or ventricular fibrillation. The risk of developing a more serious arrhythmia increases in patients with ischemic or damaged hearts.

PVCs also decrease cardiac output, especially if the ectopic beats are frequent or sustained. Decreased cardiac output is caused by reduced ventricular diastolic filling time and a loss of atrial kick. The clinical impact of PVCs hinges on how well perfusion is maintained and how long the abnormal rhythm lasts.

What to look for

On the ECG strip, PVCs look wide and bizarre and appear as early beats causing atrial and ventricular irregularity.

Don't skip this strip

Identifying PVC

This ECG strip shows premature ventricular contractions (PVCs) on beats 1, 6, and 11. Note the wide and bizarre appearance of the QRS complex.

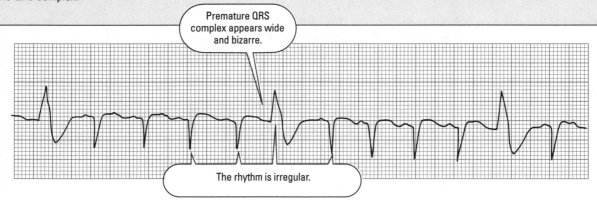

Premature QRS complex appears wide and bizarre.

The rhythm is irregular.

Using the 8-step method to interpret this strip, you'll find these distinguishing characteristics:

- *Rhythm:* irregular
- *Rate:* 120 beats/minute
- *P wave:* none with PVC, but P wave present with other QRS complexes

- *PR interval:* 0.12 second in underlying rhythm
- *QRS complex:* early, with bizarre configuration and duration of 0.14 second in PVC; normal QRS complexes are 0.08 second

- *T wave:* normal; opposite direction from QRS complex
- *QT interval:* 0.28 second with underlying rhythm
- *Other:* none.

The rate follows the underlying rhythm, which is usually regular.

The P wave is absent. Retrograde P waves may be stimulated by the PVC and cause distortion of the ST segment. The PR interval and QT interval aren't measurable on a premature beat, only on the normal beats.

Complex configuration

The QRS complex occurs early. Configuration of the QRS complex is usually normal in the underlying rhythm. The duration of the QRS complex in the premature beat exceeds 0.12 second. The T wave in the premature beat has a deflection opposite that of the QRS complex. (See *PVC*.)

When a PVC strikes on the downslope of the preceding normal T wave — the R-on-T phenomenon — it can trigger more serious rhythm disturbances.

The pause that compensates

A horizontal baseline called a compensatory pause may follow the T wave of the PVC. When a compensatory pause appears, the interval between two normal sinus beats containing a PVC equals two normal sinus intervals. (See *Compensatory pause*.) This pause occurs because the ventricle is refractory and can't respond to the next regularly timed P wave from the sinus node. When a compensatory pause doesn't occur, the PVC is referred to as interpolated.

PVCs all in a row

PVCs that look alike are called unifocal and originate from the same ectopic focus. These beats may also appear in patterns that can progress to more lethal arrhythmias. (See *When PVCs spell danger*.)

Ruling out trouble

To help determine the seriousness of PVCs, ask yourself these questions:
• How often do they occur? As a rule, six or more PVCs per minute require treatment, particularly if they developed recently. In patients with chronic PVCs, an increase in frequency or a change in the pattern of PVCs from the baseline rhythm may signal a more serious condition.
• What pattern do they occur in? If the ECG shows a dangerous pattern — such as paired PVCs, PVCs with more

---

Key characteristics

PVC

- *Rhythm:* irregular during PVC; underlying rhythm may be regular
- *Rate:* follows underlying rhythm
- *P wave:* absent
- *PR interval:* unmeasurable
- *QRS complex:* wide and bizarre
- *T wave:* opposite direction from QRS complex
- *QT interval:* unmeasurable
- *Other:* possible compensatory pause

Compensatory pause

You can determine if a compensatory pause exists by using calipers to mark off two normal P-P intervals. Place one leg of the calipers on the sinus P wave that comes just before the PVC. If the pause is compensatory, the other leg of the calipers will fall precisely on the P wave that comes after the pause.

When PVCs spell danger

Here are some examples of patterns of dangerous premature ventricular contractions (PVCs).

Paired PVCs

Two PVCs in a row are called a pair or couplet (see highlighted areas). A pair can produce ventricular tachycardia because the second contraction usually meets refractory tissue. A salvo — three or more PVCs in a row — is considered a run of ventricular tachycardia.

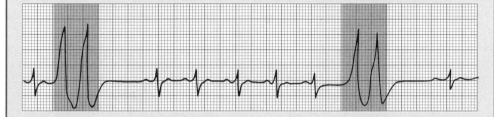

Multiform PVCs

PVCs that look different from one another arise from different sites or from the same site with abnormal conduction (see highlighted areas). Multiform PVCs may indicate severe heart disease or digitalis toxicity.

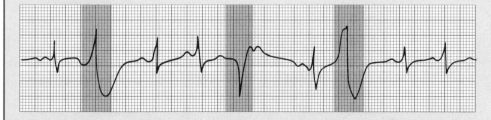

Bigeminy and trigeminy

PVCs that occur every other beat (bigeminy) or every third beat (trigeminy) can result in ventricular tachycardia or ventricular fibrillation (see highlighted areas).

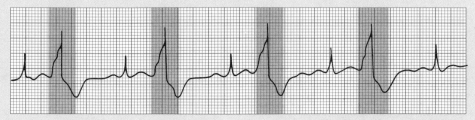

(continued)

When PVCs spell danger (continued)

R-on-T phenomenon
In this phenomenon, the PVC occurs so early that it falls on the T wave of the preceding beat (see highlighted area). Because the cells haven't fully repolarized, ventricular tachycardia or ventricular fibrillation can result.

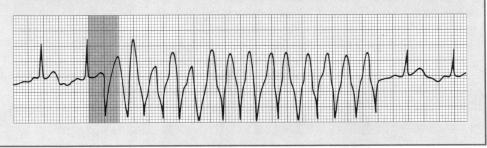

Mixed signals

Deciphering PVCs

To determine whether the rhythm you're assessing is a premature ventricular contraction (PVC) or some other beat, ask yourself the following questions:

• Are you seeing ventricular escape beats rather than PVCs? Escape beats act as a safety mechanism to protect the heart from ventricular standstill.

• Are you seeing normal beats with aberrant ventricular conduction? Some supraventricular impulses may take an abnormal pathway through the ventricular conduction system, causing the QRS complex to appear abnormal.

than one focus, bigeminy, or R-on-T phenomenon — the patient needs immediate treatment.
• Are they really PVCs? Make sure the complex you see is a PVC, not another, less dangerous arrhythmia. (See *Deciphering PVCs.*) Don't delay treatment, however, if the patient is unstable.

Outward signs tell a story

The patient with PVCs will have a much weaker pulse wave after the premature beat and a longer-than-normal pause between pulse waves. At times, you won't be able to palpate any pulse after the PVC. If the carotid pulse is visible, however, you may see a weaker pulse wave after the premature beat. When auscultating for heart sounds, you'll hear an abnormally early heart sound and a diminished amplitude with each premature beat.

Patients with frequent PVCs may complain of palpitations and may also experience hypotension or syncope.

How you intervene

If the patient is asymptomatic, doesn't have heart disease, and doesn't have frequent PVCs, the arrhythmia probably won't require treatment. If he has symptoms or a dangerous form of PVCs, the type of treatment depends on the cause of the problem.

If the PVCs have a cardiac origin, the doctor will order drugs to suppress ventricular irritability. Lidocaine is the drug of choice. Given as an I.V. bolus of 1 to 1.5 mg/kg, lidocaine can be given to a maximum dose of 3 mg/kg followed by a continuous infusion of 1 to 4 mg/minute. Other medications, such as procainamide, may also be given.

When PVCs have a noncardiac origin, treatment is aimed at correcting the cause. This could mean, for example, adjusting drug therapy or correcting acidosis, electrolyte imbalances, hypothermia, or hypoxia.

Stat assessment

Patients who have recently developed PVCs need prompt assessment, especially if they have underlying heart disease or complex medical problems. Those with chronic PVCs should be observed closely for the development of more frequent PVCs or more dangerous PVC patterns. (See *Key facts about PVCs*.)

Until effective treatment is begun, patients with PVCs accompanied by serious symptoms should have continuous ECG monitoring and ambulate only with assistance. If the patient is discharged from the hospital on antiarrhythmic medications, family members should know how to contact the emergency medical system and how to perform cardiopulmonary resuscitation (CPR).

I can't waste time

Key facts about PVCs

- PVCs may be benign or a warning sign of impending lethal arrhythmias.

- The QRS complex is wide and bizarre.

- PVCs have a variety of patterns.

- Treatment for PVCs varies with the cause and the patient's symptoms.

Idioventricular rhythms

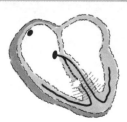

Called the rhythms of last resort, idioventricular rhythms act as safety mechanisms to prevent ventricular standstill when no impulses are conducted to the ventricles from above the bundle of His. The cells of the His-Purkinje system take over and act as the heart's pacemaker to generate electrical impulses.

Idioventricular rhythms can occur as ventricular escape beats, idioventricular rhythm (a term used to designate a specific type of idioventricular rhythm), or accelerated idioventricular rhythm.

How it happens

Idioventricular rhythms occur when all of the heart's other pacemakers fail to function or when supraventricular impulses can't reach the ventricles because of a block in the conduction system. The arrhythmias may accompany third-degree heart block or be caused by:
- myocardial ischemia
- myocardial infarction (MI)
- digitalis toxicity
- pacemaker failure
- metabolic imbalances.

Conduction foibles and pacemaker failures

Idioventricular rhythms signal a serious conduction defect with a failure of the primary pacemaker. The slow ventricular rate of these arrhythmias and the loss of atrial kick markedly reduce cardiac output. (See *Idioventricular rhythm.*) Patients bear close watching because this problem can progress to more lethal arrhythmias. Idioventricular arrhythmias also commonly occur in dying patients.

What to look for

If just one idioventricular beat is generated, it's called a ventricular escape beat. (See *Identifying idioventricular rhythm.*) The beat appears late in the conduction cycle, when the rate drops to 40 beats/minute.

Consecutive ventricular beats on the ECG strip make up idioventricular rhythm. When this arrhythmia occurs, atrial rhythm and rate can't be determined. The ventricular rhythm is usually regular at 20 to 40 beats/minute, the inherent rate of the ventricles. If the rate is faster, it's called an accelerated idioventricular rhythm. (See *Accelerated idioventricular rhythm,* page 138.)

A telltale arrhythmia

Distinguishing characteristics of idioventricular rhythm include an absent P wave or one that can't conduct through to the ventricles. This makes the PR interval unmeasurable.

Because of abnormal ventricular depolarization, the QRS complex has a duration of longer than 0.12 second, with a wide and bizarre configuration. The T-wave deflec-

---

Key characteristics

Idioventricular rhythm

Rhythm: atrial undetermined; ventricular usually regular

Rate: atrial unmeasurable; ventricular 20 to 40 beats per minute

P wave: absent

PR interval: not measurable

QRS complex: wide and bizarre

T wave: deflection opposite that of QRS complex

QT interval: greater than 0.44 second

Other: none

tion may be opposite the QRS complex. The QT interval is usually prolonged, indicating delayed depolarization and repolarization.

The patient may complain of palpitations, dizziness, or light-headedness, or he may have a syncopal episode. If the arrhythmia persists, hypotension, weak peripheral pulses, decreased urine output, or confusion can occur.

How you intervene

Treatment should be initiated immediately to increase the patient's heart rate, improve cardiac output, and establish a normal rhythm. Atropine and isoproterenol may be prescribed to increase the heart rate.

If atropine isn't effective or if the patient develops hypotension or other signs of instability, a pacemaker may

Don't skip this strip

Identifying idioventricular rhythm

This ECG strip shows an idioventricular rhythm.

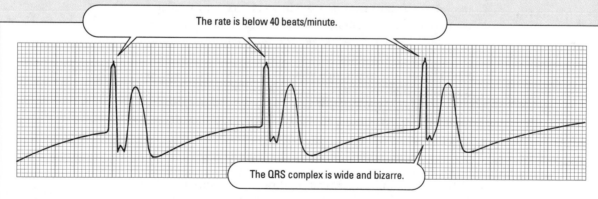

The rate is below 40 beats/minute.

The QRS complex is wide and bizarre.

Using the 8-step method to interpret this strip, you'll find these distinguishing characteristics:

- *Rhythm:* irregular
- *Rate:* unable to determine atrial rate; ventricular rate of 30 beats/minute
- *P wave:* absent

- *PR interval:* not measurable
- *QRS complex:* 0.20 second and bizarre
- *T wave:* directly opposite last part of QRS complex

- *QT interval:* 0.46 second
- *Other:* none.

Accelerated idioventricular rhythm

An accelerated idioventricular rhythm has the same characteristics as an idioventricular rhythm except that it's faster. The rate shown here varies between 40 and 100 beats/minute.

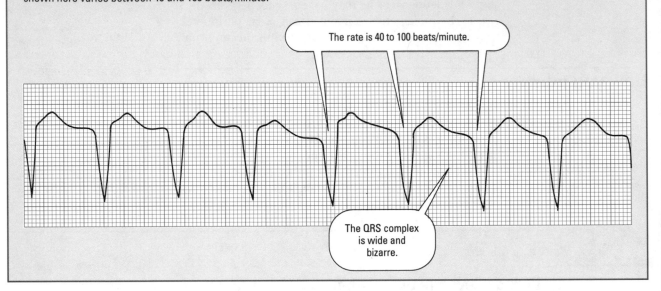

The rate is 40 to 100 beats/minute.

The QRS complex is wide and bizarre.

be needed to reestablish a heart rate that provides enough cardiac output to perfuse organs properly. A transcutaneous pacemaker may be used in an emergency until a temporary or permanent transvenous pacemaker can be inserted. (See *Transcutaneous pacemaker.*)

Remember that the goal of treatment doesn't include suppressing the idioventricular rhythm because it acts as a safety mechanism to protect the heart from standstill. *Idioventricular rhythm should never be treated with lidocaine or other antiarrhythmics that would suppress that safety mechanism.*

Continuous monitoring needed

Patients with idioventricular rhythms need continuous ECG monitoring and constant assessment until treatment restores hemodynamic stability. Keep atropine and pacemaker equipment at the bedside. Enforce bed rest until a permanent system is in place for maintaining an effective heart rate.

Be sure to tell the patient and family members about the serious nature of this arrhythmia and all aspects of treatment. (See *Key facts about idioventricular rhythm.*) If a

Transcutaneous pacemaker

In life-threatening situations in which time is critical, a transcutaneous pacemaker may be used to regulate the heart rate. This device sends an electrical impulse from the pulse generator to the heart by way of two electrodes placed on the front and the back of the patient's chest, as shown.

The electrodes are placed at heart level, on either side of the heart, so the electrical stimulus has only a short distance to travel to the heart. Transcutaneous pacing is quick and effective, but it's used only until transvenous pacing can be started.

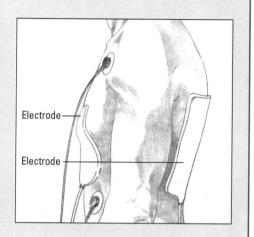

Electrode

Electrode

I can't waste time

Key facts about idioventricular rhythm

- Higher pacemakers fail to conduct impulses to the ventricles, so the ventricles take over.

- The idioventricular rate is generally 20 to 40 beats/minute, though it can be as high as 40 to 100 beats/minute (accelerated idioventricular rhythm).

- QRS complexes are wide and bizarre.

- Patients require treatment because they may become unstable with markedly reduced cardiac output.

permanent pacemaker is inserted, teach the patient and family how it works, how to recognize problems, when to contact the doctor, and how pacemaker function will be monitored.

Ventricular tachycardia

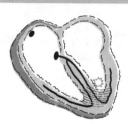

Ventricular tachycardia, commonly called V-tach, occurs when three or more PVCs occur in a row and the ventricular rate exceeds 100 beats/minute. This arrhythmia arises most often at the beginning of cardiac arrest. It usually precedes ventricular fibrillation and sudden cardiac death, especially in patients who aren't in the hospital.

Ventricular tachycardia is an extremely unstable rhythm. It can occur in short, paroxysmal bursts lasting under 30 seconds and causing few or no symptoms. Or it can be sustained, requiring immediate treatment to prevent death, even in patients initially able to maintain adequate cardiac output.

How it happens

This arrhythmia usually results from increased myocardial irritability, which may be triggered by enhanced automaticity or reentry within the Purkinje system or by PVCs

initiating the R-on-T phenomenon. Conditions that can cause ventricular tachycardia include:
- myocardial ischemia
- MI
- coronary artery disease
- valvular heart disease
- heart failure
- cardiomyopathy
- electrolyte imbalances such as hypokalemia
- drug intoxication from digitalis glycosides, procainamide, quinidine, or cocaine.

Unpredictable V-tach

Ventricular tachycardia is significant because of its unpredictability and potential to cause death. A patient may be stable with a normal pulse and adequate hemodynamics or unstable with hypotension and no detectable pulse. Because of reduced ventricular filling time and the drop in cardiac output, the patient's condition can quickly deteriorate to ventricular fibrillation and complete cardiac collapse.

What to look for

On the ECG strip, the atrial rhythm and rate can't be determined. (See *Ventricular tachycardia.*) The ventricular rhythm is usually regular but may be slightly irregular. The ventricular rate is usually rapid — 100 to 200 beats/minute.

The P wave is usually absent but may be obscured by the QRS complex. Retrograde P waves may be present. Because the P wave can't be seen in most cases, you can't measure the PR interval. The QRS complex has a bizarre configuration, usually with an increased amplitude and a duration of longer than 0.12 second.

All about uniformity

QRS complexes in monomorphic ventricular tachycardia have a uniform shape. In polymorphic ventricular tachycardia, the shape of the QRS complex constantly changes. If the T wave is visible, it occurs opposite the QRS complex. The QT interval isn't measurable. (See *Identifying ventricular tachycardia.*)

Torsades de pointes is a special variation of ventricular tachycardia. (See *Torsades de pointes,* page 142.)

Key characteristics

Ventricular tachycardia

Rhythm: unable to determine atrial rhythm; regular or slightly irregular ventricular rhythm

Rate: unable to determine atrial rate; ventricular rate of 100 to 200 beats/minute

P wave: absent

PR interval: unmeasurable

QRS complex: wide and bizarre; duration longer than 0.12 second

T wave: opposite direction of QRS complex

QT interval: unmeasurable

Other: may see torsades de pointes

Quick work prevents collapse

Although some patients have only minor symptoms at first, they still need rapid intervention and treatment to prevent cardiac collapse. Most patients with ventricular tachycardia have weak or absent pulses. Low cardiac output will cause hypotension and a decreased level of consciousness leading to unresponsiveness. Ventricular tachycardia may precipitate angina, congestive heart failure (CHF), or a substantial decrease in organ perfusion.

How you intervene

Treatment depends on whether the patient's pulse is detectable or undetectable. Patients with pulseless ventricular tachycardia receive the same treatment as those with

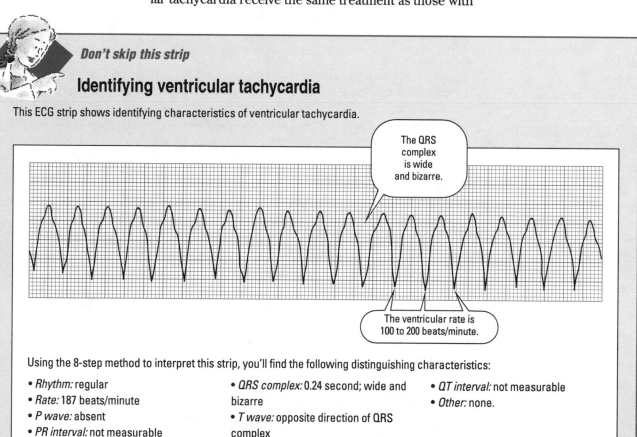

Don't skip this strip

Identifying ventricular tachycardia

This ECG strip shows identifying characteristics of ventricular tachycardia.

The QRS complex is wide and bizarre.

The ventricular rate is 100 to 200 beats/minute.

Using the 8-step method to interpret this strip, you'll find the following distinguishing characteristics:

- *Rhythm:* regular
- *Rate:* 187 beats/minute
- *P wave:* absent
- *PR interval:* not measurable

- *QRS complex:* 0.24 second; wide and bizarre
- *T wave:* opposite direction of QRS complex

- *QT interval:* not measurable
- *Other:* none.

Torsades de pointes

Torsades de pointes, which means "twisting about the points," is a special form of ventricular tachycardia. The hallmark characteristics of this rhythm, shown below, are QRS complexes that rotate about the baseline, deflecting downward and upward for several beats.

The rate is 150 to 250 beats/minute, usually with an irregular rhythm, and the QRS complexes are wide. The P wave is usually absent.

Paroxysmal rhythm
This arrhythmia may be paroxysmal, starting and stopping suddenly, and may deteriorate into ventricular fibrillation. It should be considered when ventricular tachycardia doesn't respond to lidocaine or other treatments.

Reversible causes
The cause of this form of ventricular tachycardia is usually reversible. The most common causes are drugs that lengthen the QT interval, such as the antiarrhythmics quinidine, procainamide, and sotalol. Other causes include myocardial ischemia and electrolyte abnormalities, such as hypokalemia, hypomagnesemia, and hypocalcemia.

Going into overdrive
Torsades de pointes is treated by correcting the underlying cause, especially if the cause is related to specific drug therapy. The doctor may order mechanical overdrive pacing or isoproterenol, which override the ventricular rate and break the triggered mechanism for the arrhythmia. Magnesium sulfate may also be effective. Electrical cardioversion may be used when torsades de pointes doesn't respond to other treatment.

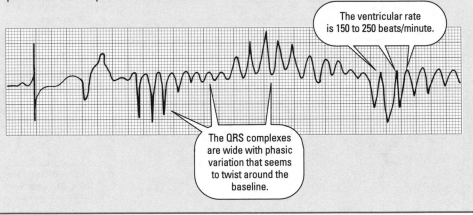

The ventricular rate is 150 to 250 beats/minute.

The QRS complexes are wide with phasic variation that seems to twist around the baseline.

ventricular fibrillation and require immediate resuscitation. Treatment for patients with a detectable pulse depends on whether their condition is stable or unstable.

Unstable patients generally have heart rates greater than 150 beats/minute. They may also have hypotension, shortness of breath, an altered level of consciousness,

CHF, angina, or MI — conditions that indicate cardiac decompensation. These patients are treated immediately with direct-current synchronized cardioversion.

Typical tachycardia complex

A stable patient with a wide QRS complex tachycardia and no signs of cardiac decompensation is treated differently. First, lidocaine is given to try to correct the rhythm disturbance; then other drugs, such as procainamide, are used. If the patient becomes unstable, immediate synchronized cardioversion is performed.

Patients with chronic, recurrent episodes of ventricular tachycardia unresponsive to drug therapy may have a cardioverter-defibrillator implanted. This device is a more permanent solution to recurrent episodes of ventricular tachycardia. (See *Understanding the implantable cardioverter-defibrillator.*)

Always assume the worst

Any wide QRS complex tachycardia should be treated as ventricular tachycardia until definitive evidence is found to establish another diagnosis such as supraventricular tachycardia with abnormal ventricular conduction. *Always assume that the patient has ventricular tachycardia and*

Understanding the implantable cardioverter-defibrillator

The implantable cardioverter-defibrillator has a pulse generator and leads that automatically monitor the heart's activity and deliver electrical shocks as necessary. The surgeon positions a bipolar lead transvenously in the endocardium of the right ventricle. Alternatively, two leads may be placed ⅜" (1 cm) apart on the epicardium of the left ventricle to record the heart rate.

Electrical shocks are delivered by two patch leads sewn on the heart, as shown here, or by one patch lead and a second lead (not shown) placed in the right atrium through the superior vena cava.

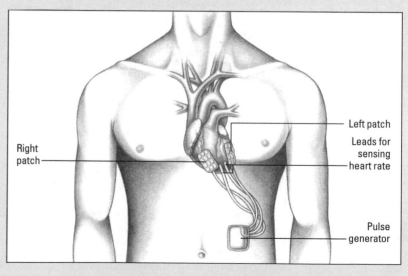

Right patch

Left patch

Leads for sensing heart rate

Pulse generator

treat him accordingly. Rapid intervention will prevent cardiac decompensation or the onset of more lethal arrhythmias.

Teach, teach, teach

Be sure to teach patients and families about the serious nature of this arrhythmia and the need for prompt treatment. (See *Key facts about V-tach*.) If your patient is undergoing cardioversion, tell him he'll be given analgesics and sedatives to help prevent discomfort.

If a patient will be discharged with an implanted defibrillator or a prescription for long-term antiarrhythmic medications, teach his family how to contact the emergency medical system and how to perform CPR.

Ventricular fibrillation

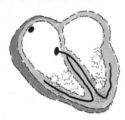

Ventricular fibrillation, commonly called V-fib, is a chaotic pattern of electrical activity in the ventricles in which electrical impulses arise from many different foci. It produces no effective muscular contraction and no cardiac output. Untreated ventricular fibrillation causes most cases of sudden cardiac death in people outside of a hospital.

How it happens

Causes of ventricular fibrillation include:
• myocardial ischemia
• MI
• untreated ventricular fibrillation
• underlying heart disease
• acid-base imbalance
• electric shock
• severe hypothermia
• electrolyte imbalances, such as hypokalemia, hyperkalemia, and hypercalcemia.

Quivering ventricles

With ventricular fibrillation, the ventricles quiver instead of contracting, so cardiac output falls to zero. If fibrillation continues, it leads to ventricular standstill and death.

I can't waste time

Key facts about V-tach

Ventricular tachycardia occurs when three or more premature ventricular contractions occur in a row.

The rate is 100 to 200 beats/minute.

The condition of the patient with this arrhythmia may or may not be stable. The rhythm can severely compromise cardiac output and create an emergency situation.

Treatment varies with the patient's condition. He may be pulseless and require cardiopulmonary resuscitation or he may have a pulse and need medications or cardioversion.

What to look for

On the ECG strip, ventricular activity appears as fibrillatory waves with no recognizable pattern. (See *Ventricular fibrillation.*) Atrial rate and rhythm can't be determined, nor can ventricular rhythm because no pattern or regularity occurs.

As a result, the ventricular rate, P wave, PR interval, QRS complex, T wave, and QT interval can't be determined. Larger, or coarse, fibrillatory waves are easier to convert to a normal rhythm than smaller waves because larger waves indicate a greater degree of electrical activity in the heart. (See *Identifying ventricular fibrillation,* page 148.)

No greater urgency

The patient in ventricular fibrillation is in full cardiac arrest, unresponsive, and without a detectable blood pressure or carotid or femoral pulse. Whenever you see a pattern resembling ventricular fibrillation, check the patient immediately and start treatment.

Be aware, however, that other things can mimic ventricular fibrillation on an ECG strip. Interference from an electric razor is one such mimic, as is muscle movement from shivering.

How you intervene

Defibrillation is the most effective treatment for ventricular fibrillation. (See *Treating ventricular fibrillation or pulseless ventricular tachycardia,* pages 146 and 147.) CPR must be performed until the defibrillator arrives, to preserve oxygen supply to the brain and other vital organs. Drugs such as epinephrine may help the heart respond better to defibrillation. Lidocaine, procainamide, bretylium, and magnesium may be given to decrease heart irritability and prevent a recurrence of ventricular fibrillation.

A shock for life

During defibrillation, electrode paddles direct an electrical current through the patient's heart. The current causes the myocardium to depolarize, which, in turn, encourages the sinoatrial node to resume normal control of the heart's electrical activity.

(Text continues on page 148.)

Key characteristics

Ventricular fibrillation

- *Rhythm:* can't be determined
- *Rate:* can't be determined
- *P wave:* can't be determined
- *PR interval:* can't be determined
- *QRS complex:* duration can't be determined
- *T wave:* can't be determined
- *QT interval:* not applicable
- *Other:* variable size of fibrillatory waves

Treating ventricular fibrillation or pulseless ventricular tachycardia

The following algorithm, based on the most recent information from the American Heart Association, shows the critical steps to take during cardiac arrest caused by ventricular fibrillation (VF) or pulseless ventricular tachycardia (VT).

• Assess airway, breathing, and circulation.
• Perform cardiopulmonary resuscitation (CPR) until the defibrillator is attached.
• Administer a precordial thump *if you witnessed the arrest and the patient has no pulse and if a defibrillator isn't immediately available.*
• Confirm VF or pulseless VT on the defibrillator, and confirm the absence of a pulse.

Defibrillate up to three times (200 joules, 200 to 300 joules, then 360 joules) as needed for persistent VF or pulseless VT.

Determine the heart rhythm.

Pulseless electrical activity is present, including:
• electromechanical dissociation (EMD)
• pseudo-EMD
• idioventricular rhythms
• ventricular escape rhythms
• bradyasystolic rhythms
• postdefibrillation idioventricular rhythms.

Spontaneous circulation returns.
• Assess vital signs.
• Support airway.
• Support breathing.
• Provide medications appropriate for maintaining blood pressure and heart rate and rhythm.

• Continue CPR.
• Intubate at once.
• Establish an I.V. line.
• Assess blood flow using Doppler ultrasound.

Consider possible causes and anticipate treatment. Causes include:
• hypovolemia
• hypoxia
• cardiac tamponade
• tension pneumothorax
• hypothermia
• massive pulmonary embolism
• overdose of drugs, for example, tricyclic antidepressants, digoxin, beta blockers, or calcium channel blockers
• hyperkalemia
• acidosis
• massive acute myocardial infarction.

Asystole is present. Refer to the algorithm on page 151.

Persistent or recurring VF or pulseless VT is present.
• Continue CPR.
• Intubate at once.
• Establish an I.V. line.
• Administer epinephrine, 1 mg I.V. push. Repeat every 3 to 5 minutes.

Defibrillate with 360 joules within 30 to 60 seconds.

Administer prescribed medications, which may include one or more of the following:
• lidocaine, 1.5 mg/kg I.V. push. Repeat every 3 to 5 minutes to a maximum of 3 mg/kg.
• bretylium, 5 mg/kg I.V. push. If VF persists, repeat every 5 minutes with 10 mg/kg to a maximum of 35 mg/kg.
• magnesium sulfate, 1 to 2 g I.V.
• procainamide, 30 mg/minute to a maximum of 17 mg/kg.

Administer epinephrine, 1 mg I.V. push. Repeat every 3 to 5 minutes as needed.

Defibrillate with 360 joules 30 to 60 seconds after each dose of medication. (The pattern should be *drug, shock, drug, shock.*)

For absolute bradycardia (below 60 beats/minute) or relative bradycardia, administer atropine, 1 mg I.V. Repeat every 3 to 5 minutes to a maximum of 0.04 mg/kg.

One paddle is placed to the right of the upper sternum, and one is placed over the fifth or sixth intercostal space at the left anterior axillary line. During cardiac surgery, internal paddles are placed directly on the myocardium.

Automatic external defibrillators are increasingly being used to provide early defibrillation. In this method,

Don't skip this strip

Identifying ventricular fibrillation

The first ECG strip shows coarse ventricular fibrillation; the second shows fine ventricular fibrillation.

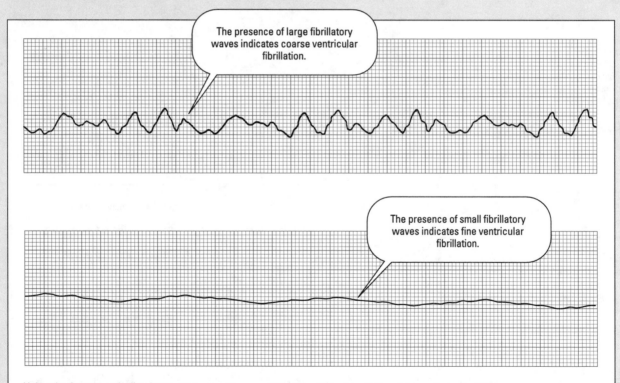

The presence of large fibrillatory waves indicates coarse ventricular fibrillation.

The presence of small fibrillatory waves indicates fine ventricular fibrillation.

Using the 8-step method to interpret these strips, you'll find the following distinguishing characteristics:

- *Rhythm:* chaotic
- *Rate:* undetermined
- *P wave:* absent
- *PR interval:* unmeasurable
- *QRS complex:* indiscernible
- *T wave:* indiscernible
- *QT interval:* not applicable
- *Other:* waveform is a wavy line.

electrode pads are placed on the patient's chest and a microcomputer in the unit interprets the cardiac rhythm, providing the caregiver with step-by-step instructions on how to proceed. These defibrillators can be used by people without medical experience.

Speed is the key

For the patient with ventricular fibrillation, successful resuscitation requires rapid recognition of the problem and prompt defibrillation. (See *Key facts about V-fib.*) Many health care facilities and emergency medical systems have established protocols to help health care workers initiate prompt treatment. Be sure you know where your facility keeps its emergency equipment and how to recognize and deal with lethal arrhythmias.

You'll also need to teach your patient and his family how to contact the emergency medical system. Family members need instruction in CPR. Teach them about long-term therapies that prevent recurrent episodes of ventricular fibrillation, including chronic antiarrhythmic drugs and implantation of a cardioverter-defibrillator.

I can't waste time

Key facts about V-fib

- Ventricular fibrillation is an emergency because cardiac output is absent.
- The fibrillatory pattern may be coarse or fine.
- Immediate cardiopulmonary resuscitation and defibrillation are necessary for the patient's survival.

Asystole

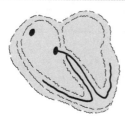

Asystole is ventricular standstill. The patient is completely unresponsive, with no electrical activity in the heart and no cardiac output. This arrhythmia results most often from a prolonged period of cardiac arrest without effective resuscitation.

Asystole has been called the arrhythmia of death. The patient is in cardiopulmonary arrest. Without rapid initiation of CPR and appropriate treatment, the situation quickly becomes irreversible.

How it happens

Anything that causes inadequate blood flow to the heart may lead to asystole, including:
- MI
- severe electrolyte disturbances such as hyperkalemia
- massive pulmonary embolism
- prolonged hypoxemia
- severe, uncorrected acid-base disturbances

- electric shock
- drug intoxication such as cocaine overdose.

What to look for

On the ECG strip, asystole looks like a nearly flat line (except for changes caused by chest compressions during CPR). (See *Key facts about asystole*.) No electrical activity is evident, except possibly P waves for a time. Atrial and ventricular activity is at a standstill, so no intervals can be measured. (See *Identifying asystole*.)

In the patient with a pacemaker, pacer spikes may be evident on the strip, but no P wave or QRS complex occurs in response to the stimulus.

The patient will be unresponsive, without any discernible pulse or blood pressure.

How you intervene

The immediate treatment for asystole is CPR. (See *Treating asystole*.) Start CPR as soon as you determine that the patient has no pulse. Then verify the presence of asystole by checking two different ECG leads. Give repeated doses of epinephrine, as ordered.

I can't waste time

Key facts about asystole

- Ventricular activity is absent, and the patient has no cardiac output.

- Asystole appears as a nearly flat line on the ECG strip.

- This is a medical emergency. Start cardiopulmonary resuscitation and other resuscitation measures immediately.

Don't skip this strip

Identifying asystole

This ECG strip shows asystole, the absence of electrical activity in the ventricles. Except for a few P waves or pacer spikes, nothing appears on the waveform and the line is almost flat.

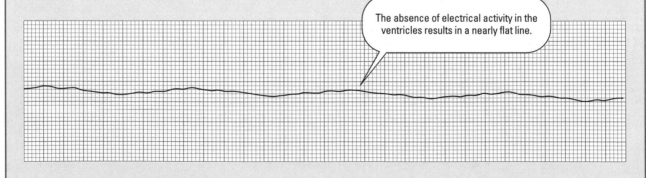

The absence of electrical activity in the ventricles results in a nearly flat line.

Treating asystole

This algorithm for treating asystole is based on the most recent guidelines from the American Heart Association.

- Perform an initial assessment.
- Assess airway, breathing, and circulation.
- Perform cardiopulmonary resuscitation.

- Intubate the patient at once.
- Establish an I.V. line.
- Confirm the diagnosis of asystole in more than one lead.

Consider possible causes:

- hypoxia
- hyperkalemia
- hypokalemia

- preexisting acidosis
- drug overdose
- hypothermia.

Consider performing transcutaneous pacing immediately.

Administer epinephrine, 1 mg I.V. push; repeat every 3 to 5 minutes.

Administer atropine, 1 mg I.V.; repeat every 3 to 5 minutes to a maximum of 0.04 mg/kg.

Consider terminating resuscitation efforts.

Subsequent treatment for asystole focuses on identifying and either treating or removing the underlying cause. Transcutaneous pacing may also be considered.

Slim hope

Your job is to recognize this life-threatening arrhythmia and start resuscitation right away. Unfortunately, most patients with asystole can't be resuscitated, especially after a prolonged period of cardiac arrest.

You should also be aware that pulseless electrical activity can lead to asystole. Know how to recognize this problem and treat it. (See *Pulseless electrical activity*.)

Quick quiz

1. PVCs are most dangerous if they:
A. are multiformed and increase in frequency.
B. appear wide and bizarre.
C. occur after the T wave.

Answer: A. PVCs that have different shapes and increase in frequency may signal severe heart disease or digitalis toxicity and progress to a lethal arrhythmia.

2. The treatment of choice for a patient with ventricular fibrillation is:
A. defibrillation.
B. transesophageal pacing.
C. synchronized cardioversion.

Answer: A. Patients with ventricular fibrillation are in cardiac arrest and require defibrillation.

3. Patients with a slow idioventricular rhythm that doesn't respond to atropine should receive:
A. lidocaine.
B. dobutamine.
C. transcutaneous pacing.

Answer: C. Transcutaneous pacing is a temporary way to increase the rate and ensure an adequate cardiac output. Neither lidocaine nor dobutamine are indicated for a slow idioventricular rhythm.

Pulseless electrical activity

In pulseless electrical activity, the heart muscle loses its ability to contract even though electrical activity is preserved. As a result, the patient goes into cardiac arrest.

On an ECG, you'll see evidence of organized electrical activity, but you won't be able to palpate a pulse or measure the blood pressure.

Causes

This condition requires rapid identification and treatment. Causes include hypovolemia, hypoxia, acidosis, tension pneumothorax, cardiac tamponade, massive pulmonary embolism, hypothermia, hyperkalemia, massive acute MI, and an overdose of drugs such as tricyclic antidepressants.

Treatment

CPR is the immediate treatment, along with epinephrine. Atropine may be given to patients with bradycardia. Subsequent treatment focuses on identifying and correcting the underlying cause.

4. A compensatory pause occurs after a PVC because the:
- A. atria conduct a retrograde impulse.
- B. ventricle is refractory at that point.
- C. bundle of His blocks sinus impulses to the ventricles.

Answer: B. A compensatory pause occurs because the ventricle is refractory and can't respond to the next regularly timed P wave from the sinus node.

5. The term pulseless electrical activity refers to a condition in which there is:
- A. electrical activity in the heart but no actual contraction.
- B. asystole on a monitor or rhythm strip.
- C. an extremely slow heart rate but no pulse.

Answer: B. Pulseless electrical activity is electrical activity without mechanical contraction. The patient is in cardiac arrest, with no blood pressure or pulse.

Test strips

Ready to try a few test strips? Answer the questions below about each strip; then check your answers with ours.

6. In the strip below, the ventricular rhythm is irregular, the ventricular rate is 130 beats/minute, the P wave is absent, the PR interval and QT interval aren't measurable, the QRS complex is wide and bizarre with varying duration, and the T wave is opposite the QRS complex. You would interpret this rhythm as:
- A. ventricular fibrillation.
- B. ventricular tachycardia.
- C. idioventricular rhythm.

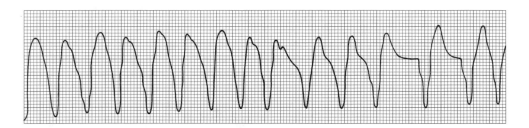

Answer: B. This strip shows ventricular tachycardia.

7. You would interpret the rhythm shown below as:
   A. coarse ventricular fibrillation.
   B. fine ventricular fibrillation.
   C. torsades de pointes.

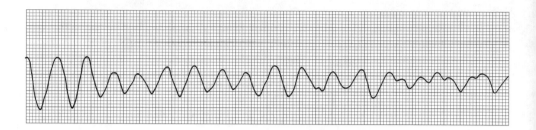

Answer: A. The ventricular rhythm is chaotic, the ventricular rate can't be determined, and the P wave, PR interval, QRS complex, T wave, and QT interval are indiscernible. These observations indicate coarse ventricular fibrillation.

Scoring

☆☆☆ If you answered all seven items correctly, sensational! You're simply the V-best!

☆☆ If you answered four to six correctly, super! You've got a great eye for V-rhythms!

☆ If you answered fewer than four correctly, that's okay. Just monitor your V-heart away!

8

Atrioventricular blocks

Just the facts

This chapter will show you how to identify atrioventricular (AV) block on an electrocardiagram (ECG) and how the arrhythmias are treated. In this chapter you'll learn:

♦ how to identify the various forms of AV block and interpret their rhythms

♦ why AV block is a significant arrhythmia

♦ which patients are at risk for developing AV block

♦ what the signs and symptoms of AV block are

♦ how to care for a patient with AV block.

A look at AV block

AV heart block results from an interruption in the conduction of impulses between the atria and the ventricles. AV block can be total or partial or it may simply delay conduction. The block can occur at the AV node, the bundle of His, or the bundle branches.

The heart's electrical impulses normally originate in the sinoatrial (SA) node, so when those impulses are blocked at the AV node, atrial rates are often normal (60 to 100 beats/minute). The clinical effect of the block depends on how many impulses are completely blocked, how slow the ventricular rate is as a result, and how the block ultimately affects the heart. A slow ventricular rate can decrease cardiac output, possibly causing light-headedness, hypotension, and confusion.

The cause before the block

A variety of factors may lead to AV block, including underlying heart conditions, use of certain drugs, congenital anomalies, and conditions that disrupt the cardiac conduction system. (See *Causes of AV block*.) Typical examples include:

• myocardial ischemia, which impairs cellular function so cells repolarize more slowly or incompletely. The injured cells, in turn, may conduct impulses slowly or inconsistently. Relief of the ischemia can restore normal function to the AV node.

• myocardial infarction (MI), in which cell death occurs. If the necrotic cells are part of the conduction system, they no longer conduct impulses and a permanent AV block occurs.

• excessive dosage of or an exaggerated response to a drug, which can cause AV block or increase the likelihood that a block will develop. Although many antiarrhythmic medications can have this effect, the drugs more commonly known to cause or exacerbate AV blocks include digitalis glycosides, beta blockers, and calcium channel blockers.

• congenital anomalies such as congenital ventricular septal defect that involve cardiac structures and affect the conduction system. Anomalies of the conduction system (such as an AV node that doesn't conduct impulses) can also occur in the absence of structural defects.

Under the knife

AV block can also be caused by inadvertent damage to the heart's conduction system during cardiac surgery. Damage is most likely to occur in operations involving the mitral or tricuspid valve or in the closure of a ventricular septal defect. If the injury involves tissues adjacent to the surgical site and the conduction system isn't physically disrupted, the block may be only temporary. If a portion of the conduction system itself is severed, permanent block results.

Radio blackout

Similar disruption of the conduction system can occur from a procedure called radiofrequency ablation. In this invasive procedure, a transvenous catheter is used to locate the area within the heart that participates in initiating or perpetuating certain tachyarrhythmias.

Causes of AV block

Atrioventricular (AV) blocks can be temporary or permanent. Here's a look at causes of each kind of AV block.

Causes of temporary block
• Myocardial infarction (MI), usually inferior wall
• Digitalis toxicity
• Acute myocarditis
• Calcium channel blockers
• Beta blockers
• Cardiac surgery

Causes of permanent block
• Changes associated with aging
• Congenital abnormalities
• MI, usually anteroseptal
• Cardiomyopathy
• Cardiac surgery

Radiofrequency energy is then delivered to the myocardium through this catheter to produce a small area of necrosis. The damaged tissue can no longer cause or participate in the tachyarrhythmia. If the energy is delivered close to the AV node, bundle of His, or bundle branches, block can occur.

Classes of block

AV blocks are classified according to their severity, not their location. That severity is measured according to how well the node conducts impulses and is separated by degrees — first, second, and third. Let's take a look at them one at a time.

First-degree AV block

First-degree AV block occurs when impulses from the atria are consistently delayed during conduction through the AV node. Conduction eventually occurs; it just takes longer than normal. It's as if a line of people is walking through a doorway, but each person hesitates before crossing the threshold.

How it happens

First-degree AV block may appear normally in a healthy person or result from myocardial ischemia or infarction, myocarditis, or degenerative changes in the heart. The condition may also be caused by medications, such as digitalis glycosides, calcium channel blockers, and beta blockers.

First-degree AV block may be temporary, particularly if it stems from medications or ischemia early in the course of an MI. The presence of first-degree block, the least dangerous type of AV block, indicates some kind of problem in the conduction system. Because first-degree AV block can progress to a more severe block, it should be monitored for changes.

What to look for

In general, a rhythm strip with this block looks like normal sinus rhythm except that the PR interval is longer than normal. (See *First-degree AV block*.) The rhythm will be regular, with one normal P wave for every QRS complex.

The PR interval will be greater than 0.20 second and will be consistent for each beat. The QRS complex is usually normal, although sometimes a bundle-branch block may occur along with first-degree AV block and cause a widening of the QRS complex.

Being without block

Most patients with first-degree AV block show no symptoms of the block because cardiac output is not significantly affected. If the PR interval is extremely long, a longer interval between S_1 and S_2 may be noted on cardiac auscultation.

How you intervene

Usually, just the underlying cause will be treated, not the conduction disturbance itself. Close monitoring helps to detect progression of first-degree AV block to a more serious form of block.

First-degree AV block

The following rhythm strip shows first-degree AV block. Look for these distinguishing characteristics:

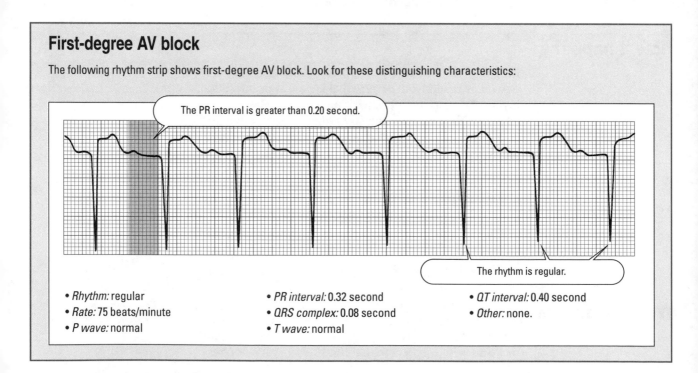

The PR interval is greater than 0.20 second.

The rhythm is regular.

- *Rhythm:* regular
- *Rate:* 75 beats/minute
- *P wave:* normal
- *PR interval:* 0.32 second
- *QRS complex:* 0.08 second
- *T wave:* normal
- *QT interval:* 0.40 second
- *Other:* none.

When caring for a patient with first-degree AV block, evaluate him for underlying causes that can be corrected, such as medications or ischemia. Observe the ECG for progression of the block to a more severe form of block. Administer digitalis glycosides, calcium channel blockers, or beta blockers cautiously.

Type I second-degree AV block

Also called Wenckebach or Mobitz I rhythm, type I second-degree AV block occurs when each successive impulse from the SA node is delayed slightly longer than the previous impulse. That pattern continues until an impulse fails to be conducted to the ventricles, and the cycle then repeats. It's like a line of people trying to get through a doorway, each one taking longer and longer until finally one can't get through.

How it happens

Causes of type I second-degree AV block include coronary artery disease, inferior-wall MI, and rheumatic fever. It may also be due to cardiac medications, such as propranolol (Inderal), digitalis glycosides, and verapamil (Isoptin). Increased vagal stimulation can also cause this block.

Type I second-degree AV block may occur normally in an otherwise healthy person. Almost always temporary, this type of block resolves when the underlying condition is corrected. Although an asymptomatic patient with this block has a good prognosis, the block may progress to a more serious form, especially if the block occurs early during an MI.

What to look for

When monitoring a patient with type I second-degree AV block, you'll note that because the SA node isn't affected by this lower block, it continues its normal activity. As a result, the atrial rhythm is normal. (See *Type I second-degree AV block,* page 160.)

Type I second-degree AV block

The following rhythm strip illustrates type I second-degree AV block. Look for these distinguishing characteristics:

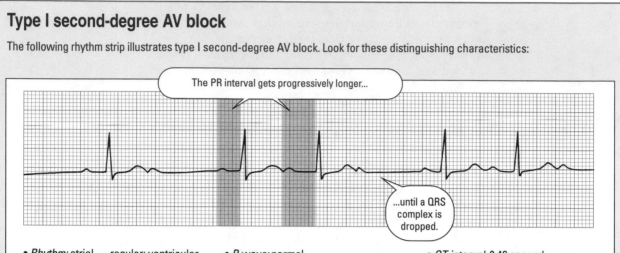

The PR interval gets progressively longer...

...until a QRS complex is dropped.

- *Rhythm:* atrial — regular; ventricular, irregular
- *Rate:* atrial — 80 beats/minute; ventricular — 50 beats/minute

- *P wave:* normal
- *PR interval:* progressively prolonged
- *QRS complex:* 0.08 second
- *T wave:* normal

- *QT interval:* 0.46 second
- *Other:* Wenckebach pattern of grouped beats.

The PR interval gets gradually longer with each successive beat until finally a P wave fails to conduct to the ventricles. This makes the ventricular rhythm irregular, with a repeating pattern of groups of QRS complexes followed by a dropped beat in which the P wave isn't followed by a QRS complex.

Famous footprints

That pattern of grouped beating is sometimes referred to as "the footprints of Wenckebach." (Karel Frederick Wenckebach was a Dutch internist who, at the turn of the century and long before the introduction of the ECG, described the two forms of what is now known as second-degree AV block by analyzing waves in the jugular venous pulse. Following the introduction of the ECG, German cardiologist Woldemar Mobitz clarified Wenckebach's findings as type I and type II. Just thought you might like to know.)

When you're trying to identify type I second-degree AV block, think of the phrase "longer, longer, drop," which describes the progressively prolonged PR intervals and the missing QRS complex. The QRS complexes, by the way, are usually normal because the delays occur in the AV node. (See *Rhythm strip patterns*.)

Lonely Ps, light-headed patients

Usually asymptomatic, a patient with type I second-degree AV block may show signs and symptoms of decreased cardiac output, such as light-headedness or hypotension. Symptoms may be especially pronounced if the ventricular rate is slow.

How you intervene

No treatment is needed if the patient is asymptomatic. For a symptomatic patient, atropine may improve AV node conduction. A temporary pacemaker may be required for long-term relief of symptoms until the rhythm resolves.

When caring for a patient with this block, assess his tolerance for the rhythm and the need for treatment to improve cardiac output. Evaluate the patient for possible

---

Rhythm strip patterns

The more you look at rhythm strips, the more you'll notice patterns. The symbols below represent some of the patterns you might see as you study rhythm strips.

Normal, regular (as in normal sinus rhythm)	♥ ♥ ♥ ♥ ♥ ♥
Slow, regular (as in sinus bradycardia)	♥ ♥ ♥
Fast, regular (as in sinus tachycardia)	♥ ♥ ♥ ♥ ♥ ♥ ♥ ♥ ♥ ♥
Premature (as in a premature ventricular contraction)	♥ ♥ ♥ ♥ ♥ ♥
Grouped (as in type I second-degree AV block)	♥ ♥ ♥ ♥ ♥ ♥ ♥ ♥ ♥
Irregularly irregular (as in atrial fibrillation)	♥ ♥♥ ♥ ♥ ♥♥♥ ♥
Paroxysm or burst (as in paroxysmal atrial tachycardia)	♥ ♥ ♥ ♥♥♥♥♥♥♥

causes of the block, including the use of certain medications or the presence of ischemia.

Check the ECG frequently to see if a more severe type of AV block develops. Make sure the patient has a patent I.V. line. Teach him about his temporary pacemaker, if indicated.

Type II second-degree AV block

Type II second-degree AV block, also known as Mobitz type II block, is less common than type I but more serious. It occurs when occasional impulses from the SA node fail to conduct to the ventricles.

On an ECG, you won't see the PR interval lengthen before the impulse fails to conduct, as you do with type I second-degree AV block. You'll see, instead, consistent AV node conduction and an occasional dropped beat. This block is like a line of people passing through a doorway at the same speed except that periodically, one of them just can't get through.

How it happens

Type II second-degree AV block is usually caused by an anterior-wall MI, degenerative changes in the conduction system, or severe coronary artery disease. The arrhythmia indicates a problem at the level of the bundle of His or bundle branches.

Type II block is more serious than type I because the ventricular rate tends to be slower and the cardiac output diminished. It's also more likely to cause symptoms, particularly if the sinus rhythm is slow and the ratio of conducted beats to dropped beats is low, such as 2:1. Usually chronic, type II second-degree AV block may progress to a more serious form of block. (See *High-grade AV block.*)

What to look for

When monitoring a rhythm strip, look for an atrial rhythm that's regular and a ventricular rhythm that may be regular or irregular, depending on the block. (See *Type II second-degree AV block*, page 164.) If the block is intermittent,

Don't skip this strip

High-grade AV block

When two or more successive atrial impulses are blocked, the conduction disturbance is called high-grade AV block. Expressed as a ratio of atrial-to-ventricular beats, this block will be at least 3:1. With the prolonged refractory period of this block, latent pacemakers can discharge. As a result, you'll often see escape rhythms develop.

Complications

High-grade AV block causes severe complications. For instance, decreased cardiac output and reduced heart rate can combine to cause Stokes-Adams syncopal attacks. In addition, high-grade AV block often progresses quickly to third-degree block.

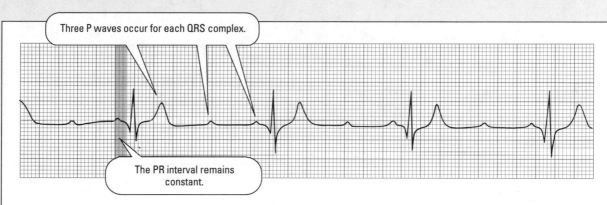

Three P waves occur for each QRS complex.

The PR interval remains constant.

- *Rhythm:* atrial — usually regular; ventricular—usually irregular
- *Rate:* atrial rate exceeds ventricular rate, usually below 40 beats/minute
- *P wave:* usually normal but some not followed by a QRS complex
- *PR interval:* constant but may be normal or prolonged
- *QRS complex:* usually normal, periodically absent
- *Other:* rhythm has appearance of complete AV block except for occasional conducted beat.

the rhythm is irregular. If the block is constant, such as 2:1 or 3:1, the rhythm is regular.

Overall, the strip will look as if someone erased some QRS complexes. The PR interval will be constant for all conducted beats but may be prolonged in some cases. The QRS complex is usually wide, but normal complexes may occur. (See *2:1 AV block,* page 165.)

Jumpin' palpitations!

Most patients who experience a few dropped beats remain asymptomatic as long as cardiac output is maintained. As the number of dropped beats increases, a patient may ex-

Type II second-degree AV block

The following rhythm strip shows type II second-degree atrioventricular (AV) block. Look for these distinguishing characteristics:

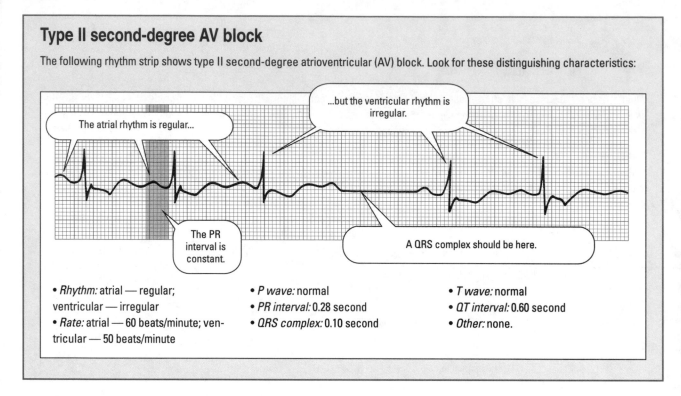

The atrial rhythm is regular...

...but the ventricular rhythm is irregular.

The PR interval is constant.

A QRS complex should be here.

- *Rhythm:* atrial — regular; ventricular — irregular
- *Rate:* atrial — 60 beats/minute; ventricular — 50 beats/minute
- *P wave:* normal
- *PR interval:* 0.28 second
- *QRS complex:* 0.10 second
- *T wave:* normal
- *QT interval:* 0.60 second
- *Other:* none.

perience palpitations, fatigue, dyspnea, chest pain, or light-headedness. On physical examination, you may note hypotension and the pulse may be slow and regular or irregular.

How you intervene

If the dropped beats are infrequent and the patient shows no symptoms of decreased cardiac output, the doctor may choose to only observe the rhythm, particularly if the cause is thought to be reversible. If the patient is hypotensive, treatment aims to improve cardiac output by increasing the heart rate.

Because the conduction block occurs in the His-Purkinje system, drugs that act directly on the myocardium usually prove more effective than those that increase the atrial rate. As a result, isoproterenol (Isuprel) instead of atropine may be ordered to increase the ventricular rate.

Pacemaker Place

Type II second-degree AV block commonly requires placement of a pacemaker. A temporary pacemaker may be used until a permanent pacemaker can be placed.

When caring for a patient with type II second-degree block, assess his tolerance for the rhythm and the need for treatment to improve cardiac output. Evaluate for possible correctable causes such as ischemia.

Keep the patient on bed rest, if indicated, to reduce myocardial oxygen demands. Administer oxygen therapy as ordered. Observe the patient for progression to a more severe form of AV block. Teach the patient and his family about the use of pacemakers if the patient receives one.

Third-degree AV block

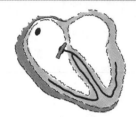

Also called complete heart block, third-degree AV block occurs when impulses from the atria are completely blocked at the AV node and can't be conducted to the ventricles. Maintaining our doorway analogy, this form of block is like one line of people waiting to go through a doorway. In this case, *no one* can go through.

Beats of different drummers

Acting independently, the atria, generally under the control of the SA node, tend to maintain a regular rate of 60 to 100 beats/minute. The ventricular rhythm can originate from the AV node and maintain a rate of 40 to 60 beats/minute or from the Purkinje system in the ventricles and maintain a rate of 20 to 40 beats/minute.

The rhythm strip will look like a strip of P waves laid independently over a strip of QRS complexes. Note that the P wave doesn't conduct the QRS complex that follows it.

How it happens

Third-degree AV block that originates at the level of the AV node is most commonly a congenital condition. This block may also be caused by coronary artery disease, an anterior- or inferior-wall MI, degenerative changes in the heart, digitalis toxicity, or surgical injury. It may be temporary or permanent.

2:1 AV block

In 2:1 second-degree atrioventricular (AV) block, every other QRS complex is dropped, so there are always two P waves for every QRS complex. The resulting ventricular rhythm is regular.

Type I or type II?

To help determine whether a rhythm is type I or type II block, look at the width of the QRS complexes. If they're wide and a short PR interval is present, the block is probably type II.

Keep in mind that type II block is more likely to impair cardiac output, lead to symptoms such as syncope, and progress to a more severe form of block. Be sure to monitor the patient carefully.

Because the ventricular rate is so slow, third-degree AV block presents a potentially life-threatening situation because cardiac output can drop dramatically. In addition, the patient loses his atrial kick, that extra 30% of blood flow pushed into the ventricles by atrial contraction. That happens as a result of the loss of synchrony between the atrial and ventricular contractions. The loss of atrial kick further decreases cardiac output. Any exertion on the part of the patient can worsen symptoms.

What to look for

When analyzing an ECG for this rhythm, you'll note that the atrial and ventricular rhythms are regular. The P and R waves can be "walked out" across the strip, meaning that they appear to march across the strip in rhythm. (See *Third-degree AV block*.)

Some P waves may be buried in QRS complexes or T waves. The PR interval will vary with no pattern or regularity. If the resulting rhythm, called the escape rhythm, originates in the AV node, the QRS complex will be nor-

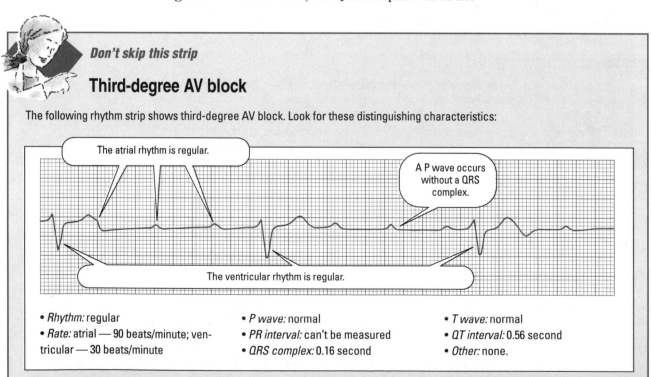

Don't skip this strip

Third-degree AV block

The following rhythm strip shows third-degree AV block. Look for these distinguishing characteristics:

The atrial rhythm is regular.

A P wave occurs without a QRS complex.

The ventricular rhythm is regular.

- *Rhythm:* regular
- *Rate:* atrial — 90 beats/minute; ventricular — 30 beats/minute
- *P wave:* normal
- *PR interval:* can't be measured
- *QRS complex:* 0.16 second
- *T wave:* normal
- *QT interval:* 0.56 second
- *Other:* none.

mal and the ventricular rate will be 40 to 60 beats/minute. If the escape rhythm originates in the Purkinje system, the QRS complex will be wide, with a ventricular rate below 40 beats/minute.

Escape!

The PR interval can't be measured because the atria and ventricles beat independently of each other. The QRS complex is determined by the site of the escape rhythm. Usually, the duration and configuration are normal, but with an idioventricular escape rhythm (an escape rhythm originating in the ventricles), the duration is greater than 0.12 second and the complex is distorted.

While atrial and ventricular rates can vary with third-degree block, they're nearly the same with complete AV dissociation, a similar rhythm. (See *Complete AV dissociation,* page 168.)

Serious signs and symptoms

Most patients with third-degree AV block experience significant symptoms, including severe fatigue, dyspnea, chest pain, light-headedness, changes in mental status, and loss of consciousness. You may note hypotension, pallor, diaphoresis, bradycardia, and a variation in the intensity of the pulse.

A few patients will be relatively free of symptoms, complaining only that they can't tolerate exercise and that they're often tired for no apparent reason. The severity of symptoms depends to a great extent on the resulting ventricular rate.

How you intervene

If cardiac output isn't adequate or the patient's condition seems to be deteriorating, therapy aims to improve the ventricular rate. Atropine or isoproterenol may be given, or a temporary pacemaker may be used to restore adequate cardiac output.

Temporary pacing may be required until the cause of the block resolves or until a permanent pacemaker can be inserted. A permanent block requires placement of a permanent pacemaker.

Don't skip this strip

Complete AV dissociation

With both third-degree AV block and complete AV dissociation, the atria and ventricles beat independently, each controlled by its own pacemaker. But here's the key difference: In third-degree AV block, the atrial rate is faster than the ventricular rate. With complete AV dissociation, the two rates are usually about the same, with the ventricular rate slightly faster.

Rhythm disturbances
Never the primary problem, complete AV dissociation results from one of three underlying rhythm disturbances:
• slowed or impaired sinus impulse formation or SA conduction, as in sinus bradycardia or sinus arrest
• accelerated impulse formation in the AV junction or the ventricular pacemaker, as in junctional or ventricular tachycardia
• AV conduction disturbance, as in complete AV block.

When to treat
The clinical significance of complete AV dissociation — as well as treatment for the arrhythmia — depends on the underlying cause and its effects on the patient. If the underlying rhythm decreases cardiac output, the patient will need treatment to correct the arrhythmia.

   Depending on the underlying cause, the patient may be treated with an antiarrhythmic, such as atropine or isoproterenol, to restore synchrony. Or the patient may be given a pacemaker to support a slow ventricular rate. If drug toxicity caused the original disturbance, the drug should be discontinued.

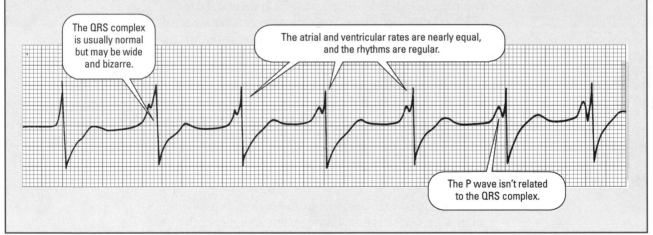

The QRS complex is usually normal but may be wide and bizarre.

The atrial and ventricular rates are nearly equal, and the rhythms are regular.

The P wave isn't related to the QRS complex.

Bundles of troubles

The patient with an anterior wall MI is more likely to have permanent third-degree AV block if the MI involved the bundle of His or the bundle branches than if it involved other areas of the myocardium. Those patients often require prompt placement of a permanent pacemaker.

   An AV block in a patient with an inferior wall MI is more likely to be temporary, as a result of injury to the AV node. Placement of a permanent pacemaker is often delayed in such cases to evaluate recovery of the conduction system.

Check it out...

When caring for a patient with third-degree heart block, immediately assess the patient's tolerance of the rhythm and the need for treatment to support cardiac output and relieve symptoms. Make sure the patient has a patent I.V. line. Administer oxygen therapy, as ordered. Evaluate for possible correctable causes of the arrhythmia, such as medications or ischemia.

If the patient is receiving isoproterenol, keep in mind that the drug raises myocardial oxygen demands and places the patient at risk for developing ventricular arrhythmias. In all cases, minimize the patient's activity and maintain bed rest.

Quick quiz

1. No treatment is necessary if the patient has the form of AV block known as:
   A. first-degree AV block.
   B. type II second-degree AV block.
   C. third-degree AV block.

Answer: A. A patient with first-degree AV block rarely experiences symptoms and usually requires only monitoring for progression of the block.

2. In type I second-degree AV block, the PR interval:
   A. progressively lengthens until a QRS complex is dropped.
   B. varies according to the ventricular response rate.
   C. remains constant despite an irregular ventricular rhythm.

Answer: A. Progressive lengthening of the PR interval creates an irregular ventricular rhythm with a repeating pattern of groups of QRS complexes. Those groups are followed by a dropped beat in which the P wave isn't followed by a QRS complex.

3. Myocardial ischemia may cause cells in the AV node to repolarize:

   A. normally.

   B. faster than normal.

   C. more slowly than normal.

Answer: C. Injured cells conduct impulses slowly or inconsistently. Relief of the ischemia can restore normal function to the AV node.

4. Type II second-degree block is generally considered more serious than type I because in most cases of type II the:

   A. cardiac output is diminished.

   B. ventricular rate rises above 100 beats/minute.

   C. peripheral vascular system shuts down almost as soon as the arrhythmia begins.

Answer: A. This form of AV block causes a decrease in cardiac output, particularly if the sinus rhythm is slow and the ratio of conducted beats to dropped beats is low, such as 2:1.

5. A main component of the treatment for third-degree AV block is:

   A. use of a pacemaker.

   B. administration of calcium channel blockers.

   C. administration of oxygen and antiarrhythmics.

Answer: A. Temporary pacing may be required for this rhythm disturbance until the cause of the block resolves or until a permanent pacemaker can be implanted. Permanent third-degree AV block requires placement of a permanent pacemaker.

Test strips

OK, try out a few test strips. Answer the question accompanying each strip; then check your answers with ours.

6. In the rhythm strip that follows, the atrial and ventricular rhythms are regular, both rates are 75 beats/minute, the P wave is of normal size and configuration, the PR interval is 0.34 second, the QRS complex is 0.08 second, the T wave is of normal configuration, and the QT interval is 0.42 second. You would identify the rhythm as:

A. first-degree AV block.
B. type II second-degree AV block.
C. third-degree AV block.

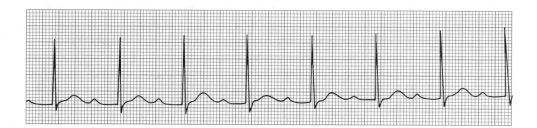

Answer: A. This strip shows sinus rhythm with first-degree AV block.

7. In the following ECG strip, the atrial and ventricular rhythms are regular, the atrial rate is 100 beats/minute, the ventricular rate is 50 beats/minute, the P wave is of normal size and configuration, the PR interval is 0.14 second, the QRS complex is 0.06 second, the T wave is of normal configuration, and the QT interval is 0.44 second. You would identify the rhythm as:
    A. type I second-degree AV block.
    B. type II second-degree AV block.
    C. third-degree AV block.

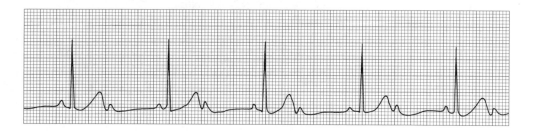

Answer: B. This strip shows type II second-degree AV block.

8. You would identify the rhythm in this strip as:
  A. first-degree AV block.
  B. type I second-degree AV block.
  C. third-degree AV block.

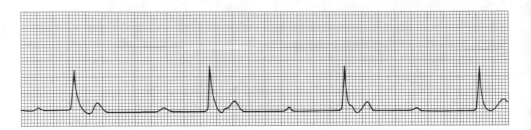

Answer: C. The atrial and ventricular rhythms are regular; the atrial rate is 75 beats/minute; the ventricular rate is 36 beats/minute; the P wave is of normal size and configuration, with no relation to the QRS complex; the QRS complex is 0.16 second, wide, and bizarre; the T wave is of normal configuration, except for the second beat, which is distorted by a P wave; and the QT interval is 0.42 second. These observations indicate third-degree AV block.

Scoring

☆☆☆   If you answered all eight items correctly, way to go! You're clearly Ruler of Noble Node!

☆☆   If you answered five to seven correctly, excellent! You're a Royal Knight of Noble Node!

☆   If you answered fewer than five correctly, that's OK. You're Most High Sheriff of Noble Node!

Part III

Treating arrhythmias

Pacemakers

Just the facts

This chapter provides an overview of pacemakers and will help you recognize malfunctions and respond to them quickly. In this chapter, you'll learn:

♦ what a pacemaker is, what its components are, and how it works

♦ what kinds of pacemakers are available, how they're classified, and how they affect ECG tracings

♦ how to detect, identify, and correct pacemaker malfunctions

♦ how to care for a patient with a pacemaker

♦ what to teach patients about pacemakers.

A look at pacemakers

A pacemaker is an artificial device that electrically stimulates the myocardium to depolarize, which begins a contraction. The device can correct abnormal electrical conduction in patients who have had a myocardial infarction or open heart surgery. It may also be used to complete the cardiac cycle when the heart is unable to do so itself.

Pacemakers may be used when a patient has an arrhythmia, such as certain bradyarrhythmias and tachyarrhythmias, sick sinus syndrome, or atrioventricular (AV) blocks. The device may be temporary or permanent, depending on the patient's condition.

Keeping the beat going

Pacemakers work by generating an impulse from a power source and transmitting that impulse to the heart muscle.

The impulse flows throughout the heart and causes the heart muscle to depolarize. Pacemakers consist of three components: the pulse generator, the pacing leads, and the electrode tip.

Making the pacer work

The pulse generator contains the pacemaker's power source and circuitry. The lithium batteries in a permanent or implanted pacemaker serve as its power source and last about 10 years. The circuitry of the pacemaker is a microchip that guides heart pacing.

A temporary pacemaker, which isn't implanted, is about the size of a small radio or a telemetry box and is powered by alkaline batteries. These units also contain a microchip and are programmed by a touch pad or dials.

A stimulus on the move

An electrical stimulus from the pulse generator moves through wires or pacing leads to the electrode tips. The leads for a pacemaker designed to stimulate a single heart chamber are placed in either the atrium or the ventricle. For dual-chamber, or AV, pacing, the leads are placed in both chambers, usually on the right side of the heart. (See *A look at pacing leads*, page 176.)

Generating the impulse

The electrodes — one on a unipolar lead or two on a bipolar lead — send information about electrical impulses in the myocardium back to the pulse generator. The pulse generator senses the electrical stimulus and then delivers it to the heart muscle.

A unipolar lead system is more sensitive to the heart's intrinsic electrical activity than a bipolar system. A bipolar system isn't as easily affected by electrical activity outside the heart and the generator (for example, from skeletal muscle contraction or magnetic fields). A bipolar system is more difficult to implant, however.

Working with pacemakers

On an ECG, you'll notice a pacemaker spike right away. (See *Pacemaker spikes*, page 177.) It occurs when the pacemaker sends an electrical impulse to the heart muscle. That impulse appears as a vertical line or spike. The col-

A look at pacing leads

Pacing leads have either one electrode (unipolar) or two (bipolar). These illustrations show the difference between the two leads.

Unipolar lead

In a unipolar system, electrical current moves from the pulse generator through the leadwire to the negative pole. From there, it stimulates the heart and returns to the pulse generator's metal surface (the positive pole) to complete the circuit.

Bipolar lead

In a bipolar system, current flows from the pulse generator through the leadwire to the negative pole at the tip. At that point, it stimulates the heart and then flows back to the positive pole to complete the circuit.

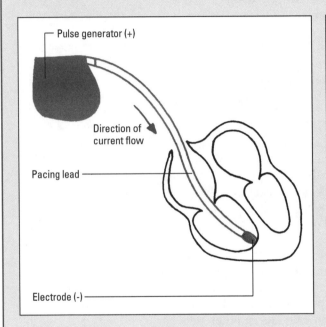

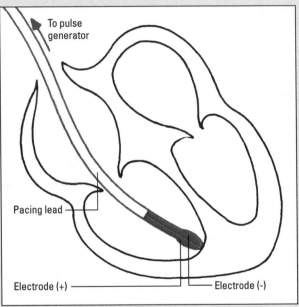

lective group of spikes on an ECG is called pacemaker artifact.

Depending on the position of the electrode, the spike appears in different locations on the waveform.

• When the atria are stimulated by the pacemaker, the spike is followed by a P wave and the patient's baseline QRS complex and T wave. This series of waveforms represents successful pacing, or capture, of the myocardium. The P wave may look different from the patient's normal P wave.

• When the ventricles are stimulated by a pacemaker, the spike is followed by a QRS complex and a T wave. The QRS

complex appears wider than the patient's own QRS complex because of the way the ventricles are depolarized.
• When the pacemaker stimulates both the atria and the ventricles, the spike is followed by a P wave, then a spike, and then a QRS complex. *Be aware that the type of pacemaker used and the patient's condition may affect whether every beat is paced.*

Permanent and temporary pacemakers

Depending on the patient's signs and symptoms, a permanent or a temporary pacemaker can be used to maintain heart rhythm. Lead placement varies according to the patient's specific needs.

Permanent pacemakers

A permanent pacemaker is used to treat chronic heart conditions such as AV block. It's surgically implanted, usually under local anesthesia. The leads are placed transvenously, positioned in the appropriate chambers, and then anchored to the endocardium. (See *Placing pacemaker leads,* page 178.)

Pocket generator

The generator is then implanted in a kind of pocket made from subcutaneous tissue. The pocket is usually constructed under the clavicle. Most permanent pacemakers are programmed before implantation. The programming sets the conditions under which the pacemaker functions and can be adjusted externally if necessary.

Temporary pacemakers

A temporary pacemaker is often inserted in an emergency. The patient may show signs of decreased cardiac output, such as hypotension or syncope. The temporary pacemaker supports the patient until the condition resolves.

A temporary pacemaker can also serve as a bridge until a permanent pacemaker is inserted. Temporary pacemakers are used for patients with low-grade heart block, bradycardia, or low cardiac output. Several types of temporary pacemakers are available, including transvenous, epicardial, and transcutaneous.

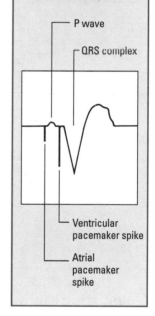

Pacemaker spikes

Pacemaker impulses — the stimuli that travel from the pacemaker to the heart — are visible on the patient's ECG tracing as spikes. Large or small, pacemaker spikes appear above or below the isoelectric line. This example shows an atrial and a ventricular pacemaker spike.

P wave

QRS complex

Ventricular pacemaker spike

Atrial pacemaker spike

Placing pacemaker leads

The surgeon who implants the endocardial pacemaker usually selects a transvenous route and begins lead placement by inserting a catheter percutaneously or by venous cutdown. Then, with a stylet and fluoroscopic guidance, the surgeon threads the catheter through the vein until the tip reaches the endocardium.

Atrial lead
For lead placement in the atrium, the tip must lodge in the right atrium or coronary sinus, as shown here. For placement in the ventricle, it must lodge within the right ventricular apex in one of the interior muscular ridges, or trabeculae.

Implanting the generator
Once the lead is in the proper position, the surgeon secures the pulse generator in a subcutaneous pocket of tissue just below the clavicle. Changing the generator's battery or microchip circuitry requires only a shallow incision over the site and a quick component exchange.

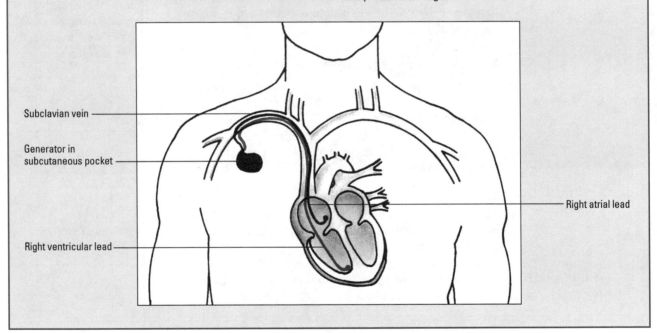

Subclavian vein

Generator in subcutaneous pocket

Right ventricular lead

Right atrial lead

Going the transvenous way

Doctors usually use the transvenous approach — inserting the pacemaker through a vein, such as the subclavian or internal jugular vein — when inserting a temporary pacemaker at the bedside or in other non-surgical environments. The transvenous pacemaker is probably the most common and reliable type of temporary pacemaker. It's usually inserted at the bedside or in a fluoroscopy suite. The leadwires are advanced through a catheter into the right ventricle or atrium and then connected to the pulse generator.

Taking the epicardial route

Epicardial pacemakers are commonly used for patients undergoing cardiac surgery. The doctor attaches the tips of the leadwires to the surface of the heart, then brings the wires through the chest wall, below the incision. They're then attached to the pulse generator. The leadwires are usually removed several days after surgery or when the patient no longer requires them.

Following the transcutaneous path

Use of an external or transcutaneous pacemaker has become commonplace in the past several years. In this noninvasive method, one electrode is placed on the patient's anterior chest wall and a second is applied to his back. An external pulse generator then emits pacing impulses that travel through the skin to the heart muscle.

Transcutaneous pacing is a quick and effective method of pacing the heart rhythm and is often used in emergencies until a transvenous pacemaker can be inserted. However, most alert patients can't tolerate the irritating sensations produced from prolonged pacing at the high energy levels needed to pace the heart externally.

Setting the controls

When your patient has a temporary pacemaker, you'll notice several types of settings on the pulse generator. The rate control regulates how many impulses are generated in one minute and is measured in pulses per minute (ppm). The rate is usually set at 60 to 80 ppm. (See *A look at a pulse generator*, page 180.) The pacemaker fires if the patient's heart rate falls below the preset rate. The rate may be set higher if the patient has a tachyarrhythmia being treated with overdrive pacing.

Measuring the output

The electrical output of a pacemaker is measured in milliamperes (mA). This measurement represents the pacemaker's stimulation threshold, or how much energy is required to stimulate the cardiac muscle to depolarize. The stimulation threshold is sometimes referred to as the energy required for capture.

Sensing the norm

You can also program the pacemaker's sensing threshold, measured in millivolts (mV). Most pacemakers let the

A look at a pulse generator

Below is an illustration of a temporary pulse generator and brief descriptions of its various parts.

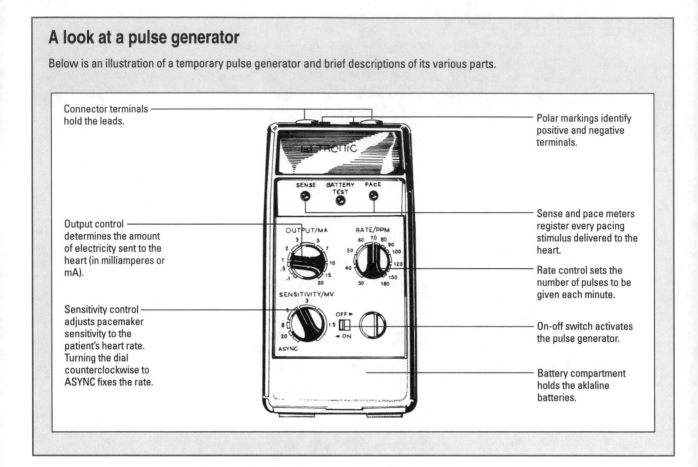

Connector terminals hold the leads.

Polar markings identify positive and negative terminals.

Output control determines the amount of electricity sent to the heart (in milliamperes or mA).

Sense and pace meters register every pacing stimulus delivered to the heart.

Rate control sets the number of pulses to be given each minute.

Sensitivity control adjusts pacemaker sensitivity to the patient's heart rate. Turning the dial counterclockwise to ASYNC fixes the rate.

On-off switch activates the pulse generator.

Battery compartment holds the aklaline batteries.

heart function naturally and assist only when necessary. The sensing threshold allows the pacemaker to do this by sensing the heart's normal activity.

Synchronous and asynchronous pacemakers

Pacemakers can also be classified according to how they stimulate the heart. A synchronous or demand pacemaker responds to the heart's activity by monitoring the intrinsic rhythm and pacing the heart only when it can't do so itself. An asynchronous or fixed rate pacemaker fires at a preset heart rate, regardless of the heart's intrinsic cycle. This type of pacemaker is rarely used. (See *Fixed-rate versus demand pacemakers.*)

Pacemaker codes

The capabilities of pacemakers are described by a five-letter coding system, though three letters are more commonly used. (See *Pacemaker coding system*.)

Introducing letter 1

The first letter of the code identifies the heart chambers being paced. Here are the options and the letters used to signify that option:
- V = Ventricle
- A = Atrium
- D = Dual (ventricle and atrium)
- O = None.

Learning about letter 2

The second letter of the code signifies the heart chamber where the pacemaker senses the intrinsic activity:
- V = Ventricle
- A = Atrium
- D = Dual (ventricle and atrium)
- O = None.

Fixed-rate versus demand pacemakers

Fixed rate, or asynchronous, pacemakers don't take the heart's activity into account. This pacemaker can't sense inherent impulses, so it always tries to deliver a stimulus, whether one is needed or not.

Demand, or synchronous, pacemakers work along with the cardiac rhythm. This pacemaker senses when the heart's inherent rhythm needs help and paces accordingly.

Pacemaker coding system

A coding system for pacemaker functions can provide a simple description of pacemaker capabilities. One commonly used coding system employs three letters to describe functions.

The first letter refers to the chamber paced by the pacemaker. The second refers to the chamber sensed by the pacemaker. The third refers to the pacemaker's response to the sensed event.

In the example shown here, both chambers (represented in the code by *D,* for dual) are paced and sensed, and the pacemaker responds by firing impulses to both chambers.

Chamber paced

Chamber sensed

Response to sensing

Looking at letter 3

The third letter shows the pacemaker's response to the intrinsic electrical activity it senses in the atrium or ventricle:
- T = Triggers pacing (For instance, if atrial activity is sensed, ventricular pacing may be triggered.)
- I = Inhibits pacing (If the pacemaker senses intrinsic activity, it won't fire.)
- D = Dual (The pacemaker can be triggered or inhibited depending on the mode and where intrinsic activity occurs.)
- O = None. (The pacemaker doesn't change its mode in response to sensed activity.)

Figuring out letter 4

The pacemaker's programmability is described by the fourth letter of the code; it tells whether the pacemaker can be modified by an external programming device:
- P = Basic functions programmable
- M = Multiprogrammable parameters
- C = Communicating functions (such as telemetry)
- R = Rate responsiveness (The rate adjusts to fit the patient's metabolic needs and achieve normal hemodynamic status.)
- O = None.

Last but not least, letter 5

The final letter of the code denotes the pacemaker's response to a tachyarrhythmia:
- P = Pacing ability (The pacemaker's rapid bursts pace the heart at a rate above its intrinsic rate to override the source of tachycardia. When the stimulation ceases, the tachyarrhythmia breaks. Increased arrhythmia may result.)
- S = Shock (An implantable cardioverter-defibrillator identifies ventricular tachycardia and delivers a shock to stop the arrhythmia.)
- D = Dual ability to shock and pace
- O = None.

Pacemaker modes

The mode of a pacemaker indicates its functions. Several different modes may be used during pacing, and they may or may not mimic the normal cardiac cycle. Here are four of the more commonly used modes and their three-letter abbreviations. (A three-letter code, rather than a five-letter code, is typically used to describe pacemaker function.)

The AAI mode

The AAI or atrial demand pacemaker is a single-chambered pacemaker that paces and senses the atria. When the pacemaker senses intrinsic atrial activity, it inhibits pacing and resets itself. Only the atria are paced, and the heart remains responsive for the rest of the impulse.

Not in block or brady

Because AAI pacemakers require a functioning AV node and ventricular conduction, they aren't used in AV block or ventricular bradycardia. An AAI pacemaker may be used in patients with sinus bradycardia, which may occur after cardiac surgery, or with sick sinus syndrome as long as the His-Purkinje system isn't diseased.

The VVI mode

The VVI or ventricular demand pacemaker paces and senses the ventricles. (See *AAI and VVI pacemakers*, page 184.) When it senses intrinsic ventricular activity, it inhibits pacing. This single-chambered pacemaker benefits patients with complete heart block and those needing intermittent pacing. Because it doesn't affect atrial activity, it's used for patients who don't need an atrial kick — the extra 30% of cardiac output that comes from atrial contraction.

Unsynchronized activity

If the patient has spontaneous atrial activity, the VVI pacemaker won't synchronize the ventricular activity with it, so tricuspid and mitral regurgitation may develop. Sedentary patients may receive this pacemaker but it won't adjust its rate for more active patients.

DVI mode

The DVI or AV sequential pacemaker paces both the atria and ventricles. (See *DVI pacemaker rhythm strip,* page 185.) However, this dual-chambered pacemaker senses only the ventricles' intrinsic activity, inhibiting its pacing there.

Two types of DVI pacemakers are used:

AAI and VVI pacemakers

Both an AAI and a VVI pacemaker are single-chamber pacemakers. The electrode for an AAI is placed in the atrium; for a VVI, in the ventricle. These rhythm strips show how each pacemaker works.

AAI pacemaker

Note how the AAI pacemaker senses and paces the atria only. The QRS complex that follows occurs as a result of the heart's own conduction.

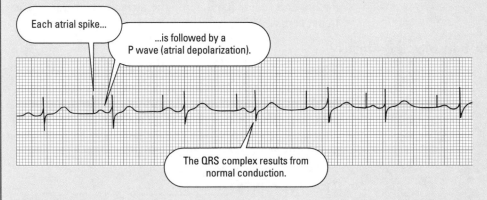

Each atrial spike...

...is followed by a P wave (atrial depolarization).

The QRS complex results from normal conduction.

VVI pacemaker

The VVI pacemaker senses and paces the ventricles. When each spike is followed by a depolarization, as shown here, the rhythm is said to reflect 100% capture.

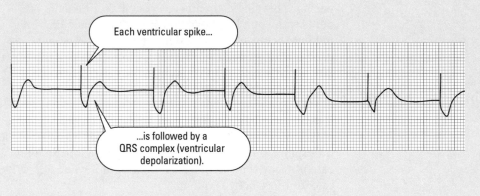

Each ventricular spike...

...is followed by a QRS complex (ventricular depolarization).

• The committed DVI pacemaker doesn't sense intrinsic activity during the AV interval — the time between an atrial and ventricular spike. It generates an impulse even with spontaneous ventricular depolarization.
• The noncommitted DVI pacemaker is inhibited if a spontaneous depolarization occurs within the AV interval.

DVI pacemaker rhythm strip

Here's an ECG tracing from a committed DVI pacemaker, which paces both the atria and the ventricles. The pacemaker senses ventricular activity only. In two of the complexes, the pacemaker didn't sense the intrinsic QRS complex because the complex occurred during the AV interval, when the pacemaker was already committed to fire.

With a noncommitted DVI pacemaker, spikes after the QRS complex wouldn't appear because the stimulus to pace the ventricles would be inhibited.

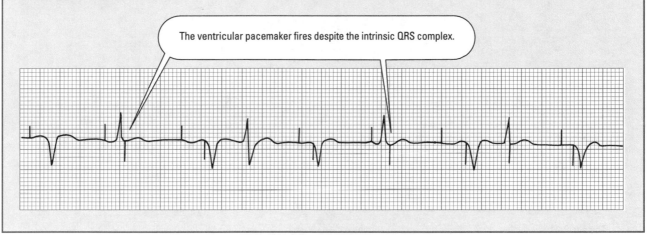

The ventricular pacemaker fires despite the intrinsic QRS complex.

Who's helped

The DVI pacemaker helps patients with AV block or sick sinus syndrome who have a diseased His-Purkinje conduction system. It provides the benefits of AV synchrony and atrial kick, thus improving cardiac output. However, it can't vary the atrial rate and isn't helpful in atrial fibrillation because it can't capture the atria. In addition, it may needlessly fire or inhibit its own pacing.

DDD mode

A DDD or universal pacemaker is used with severe AV block. (See *DDD pacemaker rhythm strip*, page 186.) However, because the pacemaker possesses so many capabilities, it may be hard to troubleshoot problems. Its advantages include its:
• versatility
• programmability
• ability to change modes automatically
• ability to mimic the normal physiologic cardiac cycle, maintaining AV synchrony

DDD pacemaker rhythm strip

On this DDD pacemaker rhythm strip, complexes 1, 2, 4, and 7 reveal the atrial-synchronous mode, set at a rate of 70. The patient has an intrinsic P wave; the pacemaker serves only to make sure the ventricles respond.

Complexes 3, 5, 8, 10, and 12 are intrinsic ventricular depolarizations. The pacemaker senses these depolarizations and inhibits firing. In complexes 6, 9, and 11, the pacemaker is pacing both the atria and the ventricles in sequence. In complex 13, only the atria are paced; the ventricles respond on their own.

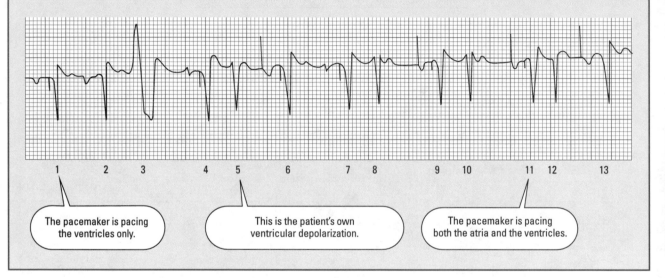

The pacemaker is pacing the ventricles only.

This is the patient's own ventricular depolarization.

The pacemaker is pacing both the atria and the ventricles.

- ability to sense and pace the atria and ventricles at the same time according to the intrinsic atrial rate and the maximal rate limit.

Home, home on the rate range

Unlike other pacemakers, the DDD pacemaker is set with a rate range, rather than a single critical rate. It senses atrial activity and ensures that the ventricles respond to each atrial stimulation, thereby maintaining normal AV synchrony.

Firing and pacing

The DDD pacemaker fires when the ventricle doesn't respond on its own, and paces the atria when the atrial rate falls below the lower set rate. (See *Evaluating a DDD pacemaker rhythm strip*.) In a patient with a high atrial rate, a safety mechanism allows the pacemaker to follow the intrinsic atrial rate only as far as a preset upper limit. That limit is usually set at about 130 beats per minute and helps to prevent the ventricles from following atrial tachycardia or atrial flutter.

Evaluating pacemakers

Now you're ready to find out if your patient's pacemaker is working correctly. To do this, follow the procedure below.

1. Read the records

First, determine the pacemaker's mode and settings. If your patient had a permanent pacemaker implanted before admission, ask him if he has a wallet card from the manufacturer that notes the mode and settings.

If the pacemaker was recently implanted, check the patient's records for information. Don't check only the ECG tracing — you might misinterpret it if you don't know the pacemaker type. For instance, if the tracing has ventricular spikes but no atrial ones, you might guess that it's a VVI pacemaker when it's actually a DVI pacemaker that has lost its atrial output.

2. Look at the leads

Next, review the patient's 12-lead ECG. If it isn't available, examine lead V_1 or MCL_1 instead. Invert the QRS complex here, just as with a left bundle-branch block. *An upright QRS complex may mean that the leadwire is out of position, perhaps even perforating the septum and lodging in the left ventricle.*

3. Scrutinize the spikes

Then select a monitoring lead that clearly shows the pacemaker spikes. Be sure the lead you select doesn't cause the cardiac monitor to mistake a spike for a QRS complex and then double-count the QRS complexes. This may cause the pacemaker alarm to go off, falsely signaling a high heart rate.

4. Mull over the mode

When looking at the ECG tracing of a patient with a pacemaker, consider the pacemaker mode and whether symptoms of decreased cardiac output are present. Then interpret the paced rhythm. Does it match what you know about the pacemaker?

Evaluating a DDD pacemaker rhythm strip

Look for these possible events when examining a rhythm strip showing the activities of a DDD pacemaker.

• *Intrinsic rhythm:* No pacemaker activity occurs because none is needed.

• *Intrinsic P wave followed by a ventricular pacemaker spike:* The pacemaker is tracking the atrial rate and assuring a ventricular response.

• *Pacemaker spike before a P wave, then an intrinsic ventricular QRS complex:* The atrial rate is falling below the lower rate limit, causing the atrial channel to fire. Normal conduction to the ventricles then ensues.

• *Pacemaker spike before a P wave, and a pacemaker spike before the QRS complex:* No intrinsic activity occurs in either the atria or the ventricles.

5. Unravel the rhythm

Look for information that tells you which chamber is paced. Is there capture? Is there a P wave or QRS complex after each atrial or ventricular spike? Or do the P waves and QRS complexes stem from intrinsic activity?

Look for information about the pacemaker's sensing ability. If intrinsic atrial or ventricular activity is present, what is the pacemaker's response? Look at the rate. What is the pacing rate per minute? Is it appropriate given the pacemaker settings? Although you can determine the rate quickly by counting the number of complexes in a 6-second ECG strip, a more accurate method is to count the number of small boxes between complexes and divide this into 1,500.

Troubleshooting problems

Malfunction of a pacemaker can lead to arrhythmias, hypotension, and syncope. (See *When a pacemaker malfunctions*.) Common problems with pacemakers that can lead to low cardiac output and loss of AV synchrony include:
- failure to capture
- failure to pace
- undersensing
- oversensing.

Failure to capture

Failure to capture is indicated on an ECG by a pacemaker spike without the appropriate atrial or ventricular response — a spike without a complex. Think of failure to capture as the pacemaker's inability to stimulate the chamber.

Causes include acidosis, an electrolyte imbalance, fibrosis, an incorrect lead position, a low mA setting, depletion of the battery, a broken or cracked leadwire, or perforation of the leadwire through the myocardium.

Failure to pace

Failure to pace is indicated by no pacemaker activity on an ECG. The problem is caused by battery or circuit failure, cracked or broken leads, or interference between atrial and ventricular sensing in a dual-chambered pacemaker. It can lead to asystole.

Mixed signals

When a pacemaker malfunctions

Occasionally, pacemakers fail to function properly. When that happens, you'll need to take immediate action to correct the problem. The strips shown below are examples of problems that can occur with a temporary pacemaker.

Failure to capture

• If the patient's condition has changed, notify the doctor and ask for new settings.

• If pacemaker settings have been altered by the patient or someone else, return them to their correct positions. Make sure the face of the pacemaker is covered with its plastic shield. Remind the patient not to touch the dials.

• If the heart still doesn't respond, carefully check all connections. You can also increase the mA setting slowly (according to your facility's policy or the doctor's orders), turn the patient from side to side, change the battery, or reverse the cables in the pulse generator so the positive wire is in the negative terminal and vice versa. Keep in mind that the doctor may order a chest X-ray to determine the position of the electrode.

Failure to pace

• If the pacing or indicator light flashes, check the connections to the cable and the position of the pacing electrode in the patient (done by X-ray).

• If the pulse generator is turned on but the indicators aren't flashing, change the battery. If that doesn't help, use a different pulse generator.

Failure to sense intrinsic beats

• If the pacemaker is undersensing (it fires but at the wrong times or for the wrong reasons), turn the sensitivity control completely to the right. If the pacemaker is oversensing (it incorrectly senses depolarization and refuses to fire when it should), turn the sensitivity control slightly to the left.

• Change the battery or pulse generator.

• Remove items in the room that might be causing electromechanical interference. Check that the bed is grounded. Unplug each piece of equipment, and then check to see if the interference stops.

• If the pacemaker is still firing on the T wave and all corrective actions have failed, turn off the pacemaker. Be sure atropine is available in case the patient's heart rate drops, and be prepared to initiate cardiopulmonary resuscitation if necessary.

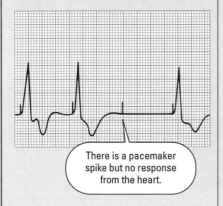

There is a pacemaker spike but no response from the heart.

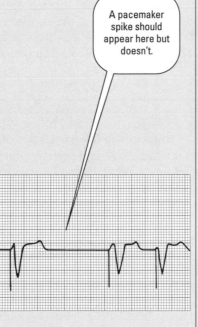

A pacemaker spike should appear here but doesn't.

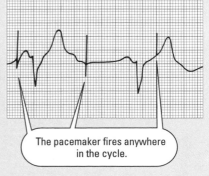

The pacemaker fires anywhere in the cycle.

Failure to sense

Undersensing is indicated by a pacemaker spike when intrinsic cardiac activity is already present. Think of it as help being given when none is needed. In asynchronous pacemakers that have codes such as VOO or DOO, undersensing is a programming limitation.

Spikes out of place

When undersensing occurs in synchronous pacemakers, spikes occur on the ECG where they shouldn't. Although they may appear in any part of the cardiac cycle, the spikes are especially dangerous if they fall on the T wave, where they can cause ventricular tachycardia or fibrillation.

In synchronous pacemakers, the problem is caused by electrolyte imbalances, disconnection or dislodgment of a lead, improper lead placement, increased sensing threshold from edema or fibrosis at the electrode tip, drug interactions, or a depleted or dead pacemaker battery.

Oversensing

If the pacemaker is too sensitive, it can misinterpret muscle movement or other events in the cardiac cycle as depolarization. Then it won't pace when the patient actually needs it, and heart rate and AV synchrony won't be maintained.

How you intervene

Be sure you're familiar with different types of pacemakers and how they function. This will save you time and worry during an emergency. When caring for a patient with a pacemaker, follow these guidelines.

Checks and balances

• Assist with pacemaker insertion, as appropriate.
• Regularly check the patient's pacemaker settings, connections, and functions.
• Monitor the patient to see how well he tolerates the pacemaker.
• Reposition the patient with a temporary pacemaker carefully. Turning may dislodge the leadwire.
• Avoid potential microshocks to the patient by ensuring that the bed is grounded properly.

• Remember that pacemaker spikes on the monitor don't mean your patient is stable. Be sure to check his vital signs and assess for signs and symptoms of decreased cardiac output, such as hypotension, chest pain, dyspnea, and syncope.

On the alert

• Be alert for signs of infection.
• Watch for subcutaneous air around the pacemaker insertion site. Subcutaneous tissue that contains air feels crunchy under your fingers.
• Look for pectoral muscle twitching or hiccups that occur in synchrony with the pacemaker. Both are signs of external cardiac stimulation, which may be serious. Notify the doctor if you note any of those conditions.
• Watch for a perforated ventricle and cardiac tamponade. Signs and symptoms include persistent hiccups, distant heart sounds, pulsus paradoxus (a drop in the strength of a pulse during inspiration), hypotension with narrowed pulse pressure, cyanosis, distended neck veins, decreased urine output, restlessness, and complaints of fullness in the chest. Notify the doctor immediately if you note any of those signs and symptoms.

What to teach the patient

When a patient gets a pacemaker, be sure to cover these points:
• Explain to the patient and family why a pacemaker is needed, how it works, and what they can expect.
• Warn the patient with a temporary pacemaker not to get out of bed without assistance.
• Warn the patient with a transcutaneous pacemaker to expect twitching of the pectoral muscles. Reassure him that he'll receive medication if he can't tolerate the discomfort.
• Instruct the patient not to manipulate the pacemaker wires or pulse generator.
• Give the patient with a permanent pacemaker the manufacturer's identification card, and tell him to carry it at all times.
• Teach the patient and family how to care for the incision, how to take a pulse, and what to do if the pulse drops below the pacemaker rate.

• Advise the patient to avoid tight clothing or other direct pressure over the pulse generator, to avoid magnetic resonance imaging scans and certain other diagnostic studies, and to notify the doctor if he feels confused, light-headed, or short of breath. The patient should also notify the doctor if he has palpitations, hiccups, or a rapid or unusually slow heart rate.

Quick quiz

1. When using an external temporary pacemaker, the energy level should be set at:
    A. the highest mA setting the patient can tolerate.
    B. the lowest mA setting that ensures capture of the myocardium.
    C. an mA setting midway between the setting that causes capture of the myocardium and the setting at which symptoms first appear.

Answer: B. Select the lowest mA setting that causes capture of the myocardium. Higher energy levels will be too irritating for the patient.

2. When a VVI pacemaker senses intrinsic ventricular activity, it responds by:
    A. inhibiting its pacing.
    B. triggering its pacing.
    C. doing nothing.

Answer: A. The third letter of the pacemaker code represents its response to ventricular activity. "I" stands for "inhibited."

3. Severe hiccups in a patient with a temporary transvenous pacemaker are probably due to:
    A. movement of the pacemaker electrode.
    B. the mA being set too low.
    C. tight clothing over the pulse generator.

Answer: A. Hiccups can be triggered by electrode movement, which can cause the pacemaker to stimulate the diaphragm. They can also result from the extracardiac stimulation caused by setting the mA too high, not too low.

4. Failure to capture is represented on the ECG as:
  A. no pacemaker activity.
  B. spikes occurring where they shouldn't.
  C. a spike without a complex.

Answer: C. A spike without a complex indicates the pacemaker's inability to capture or stimulate the chamber.

5. Decreased urine output and distant heart sounds in a patient with a recently implanted pacemaker indicate:
  A. pacemaker failure.
  B. cardiac tamponade.
  C. myocardial infarction.

Answer: B. Decreased urine output and distant heart sounds indicate cardiac tamponade resulting from a perforated ventricle.

6. In a synchronous pacemaker, failure to sense is characterized on the ECG by:
  A. lack of a pacemaker spike.
  B. a pacemaker spike in the presence of intrinsic activity.
  C. a pacemaker spike without evidence of cardiac stimulation.

Answer: B. Undersensing is indicated by a pacemaker spike when intrinsic cardiac activity is present.

Test strip

Time to try out a test strip. Ready? *Go!*

7. In the following ECG strip, the pacemaker is pacing and sensing the ventricles with 100% capture. The mode of response can't be evaluated because of lack of intrinsic activity. You would determine that the patient has a(n):
  A. VVI pacemaker.
  B. DVI pacemaker.
  C. AAI pacemaker.

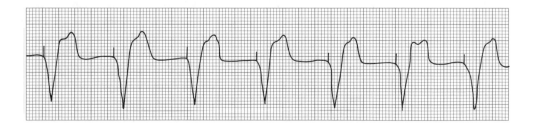

Answer: A. The patient has a VVI or demand pacemaker, which inhibits pacing when it senses ventricular activity.

Scoring

☆☆☆   If you answered all seven items correctly, all right! You're the new leader of the Mighty Myocardial Power Sources!

☆☆   If you answered five or six correctly, terrific! You're first runner-up for the Power Sources and destined to take the lead soon!

☆   If you answered fewer than four correctly, no sweat. You've been voted most likely to generate Power Source impulses!

![10]

Drugs that treat arrhythmias

Just the facts

This chapter provides an overview of the antiarrhythmic drug classification system and gives information on specific drugs within each classification. In this chapter, you'll learn:

♦ how the antiarrhythmic classification system works

♦ what effects antiarrhythmics have on the cardiovascular and other body systems

♦ how to administer various antiarrhythmics and what their adverse effects are

♦ how to care for patients on antiarrhythmic drugs and what to teach them.

A look at antiarrhythmics

Almost half a million Americans die each year from cardiac arrhythmias; countless others suffer symptoms or lifestyle limitations. Along with other treatments, antiarrhythmic drugs can help alleviate symptoms and prolong life.

Antiarrhythmic drugs affect the movement of ions across the cell membrane and alter the electrophysiology of the cardiac cell. They're classified according to their effect on the cell's electrical activity (action potential) and their mechanism of action. (See *Antiarrhythmics and the action potential,* page 196.)

Drugs in the same class are similar in action and adverse effects. When you know where a particular drug fits in the classification system, you'll be better able to remember its actions and adverse effects.

Classifying antiarrhythmics

The classification system divides antiarrhythmic drugs into four classes. Let's take a look at each one.

Class I blocks sodium

Class I drugs block the influx of sodium into the cell during phase 0 of the action potential. This minimizes the

---

Antiarrhythmics and the action potential

Each class of antiarrhythmic drugs acts on a different phase of the action potential of the heart. Here's a rundown on the four classes of antiarrhythmics and how they affect action potential.

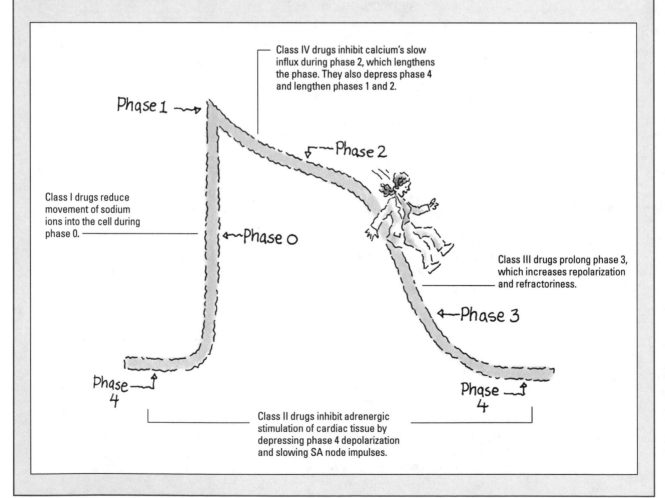

Class IV drugs inhibit calcium's slow influx during phase 2, which lengthens the phase. They also depress phase 4 and lengthen phases 1 and 2.

Phase 1

Phase 2

Class I drugs reduce movement of sodium ions into the cell during phase 0.

Phase 0

Class III drugs prolong phase 3, which increases repolarization and refractoriness.

Phase 3

Phase 4

Phase 4

Class II drugs inhibit adrenergic stimulation of cardiac tissue by depressing phase 4 depolarization and slowing SA node impulses.

chance of sodium reaching its threshold potential and causing cells to depolarize. Because phase 0 is also referred to as the sodium channel or fast channel, these drugs may also be called sodium channel blockers or fast channel blockers.

Antiarrhythmic drugs in this class are further categorized as:

• class Ia: reduce conductivity and prolong repolarization and the action potential
• class Ib: have a local anesthetic effect, don't affect conductivity, and shorten repolarization and the action potential
• class Ic: markedly reduce conduction, are used only for refractory arrhythmias, and are proarrhythmic, meaning they can cause or worsen arrhythmias.

Class II blocks beta receptors

Class II drugs block sympathetic nervous system beta receptors and thereby increase heart rate. These drugs depress sinoatrial (SA) node automaticity and increase atrial and atrioventricular (AV) nodal refractoriness, or resistance to stimulation.

Class III blocks potassium

Class III drugs are called potassium channel blockers because they block the movement of potassium during phase 3 of the action potential and prolong repolarization and the refractory period.

Class IV blocks calcium

Class IV drugs block the movement of calcium during phase 2 of the action potential. Because phase 2 is also called the calcium channel or the slow channel, drugs that affect phase 2 are also known as calcium channel blockers or slow channel blockers. They prolong conductivity and increase the refractory period at the AV node.

Some drugs don't fit

Not all drugs fit neatly into those classifications. For example, sotalol possesses characteristics of both class II and class III drugs. Some drugs used to treat arrhythmias don't fit into the classification system at all. Those drugs include adenosine, digoxin and other digitalis glycosides, atropine, epinephrine, and magnesium. Despite these limitations, the classification system is helpful in understanding how antiarrhythmic drugs prevent and treat arrhythmias.

Drug distribution and clearance

Many patients receive antiarrhythmic drugs by I.V. bolus or infusion because they're more readily available that way than orally. The cardiovascular system then distributes the drugs throughout the body, specifically to the site of action.

Most drugs are changed, or biotransformed, into active or inactive metabolites in the liver. The kidneys are the primary sites for the excretion of those metabolites. *When administering these drugs, remember that patients with impaired heart, liver, or kidney function may suffer from inadequate drug effect or toxicity.*

Antiarrhythmics by class

Broken down by classes, the following section describes commonly used antiarrhythmic drugs. It highlights their dosages, adverse effects, and recommendations for patient care.

Class Ia antiarrhythmics

Class Ia antiarrhythmic drugs are called sodium channel blockers. They include quinidine and procainamide. These drugs reduce the excitability of the cardiac cell, have an anticholinergic effect, and decrease cardiac contractility. (See *Effects of class Ia antiarrhythmics.*) Because the drugs prolong the QT interval, the patient is prone to polymorphic ventricular tachycardia.

Quinidine

Quinidine is used to treat patients with supraventricular and ventricular arrhythmias, such as atrial fibrillation or flutter, paroxysmal supraventricular tachycardia, and premature ventricular contractions (PVCs). The drug comes in several forms, including quinidine sulfate (Cin-Quin) and quinidine gluconate (Duraquin).

How to give it

Here's how to administer quinidine:

• To convert atrial flutter or fibrillation: 200 mg of quinidine sulfate orally every 2 to 3 hours for five to eight doses, with subsequent daily increases until sinus rhythm is restored or toxic effects develop.

• Initial dosage for paroxysmal supraventricular tachycardia: 400 to 600 mg of quinidine sulfate orally every 2 to 3 hours.

• Initial dosage for premature atrial and ventricular contractions: 200 to 300 mg of quinidine sulfate orally three to four times daily; maintenance dosage is 200 to 400 mg orally every 4 to 6 hours.

• For arrhythmias: quinidine gluconate 800 mg (10 ml) added to 40 ml of dextrose 5% in water (D_5W) and infused I.V. at 16 mg/minute (1 ml/minute); given I.V. only in acute situations.

• Maximum dosage: quinidine sulfate not to exceed 4 g daily; quinidine gluconate not to exceed 5 g daily.

Effects of class Ia antiarrhythmics

Class Ia antiarrhythmic drugs — including such drugs as quinidine and procainamide — affect the cardiac cycle in specific ways and lead to specific ECG changes, shown here. Class Ia antiarrhythmics:

• block sodium influx during phase 0, which depresses the rate of depolarization

• prolong repolarization and the duration of the action potential

• lengthen the refractory period
• decrease contractility.

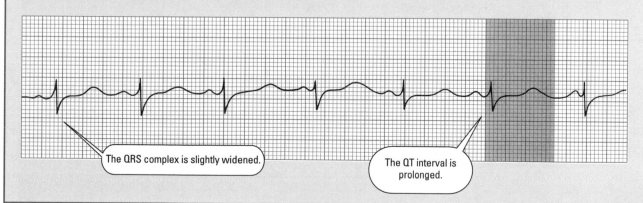

The QRS complex is slightly widened.

The QT interval is prolonged.

What can happen

Adverse cardiovascular effects of quinidine include hypotension, tachycardia, increased ventricular response to atrial fibrillation, atrial flutter, polymorphic ventricular tachycardia, AV block, and heart failure.

How you intervene

Keep the following points in mind when caring for a patient taking quinidine:
• Monitor the patient's ECG, heart rate, and blood pressure closely. Don't give more than 4 g/day. Adjust dosages in patients with heart failure and liver disease. (See *Noncardiac adverse effects of quinidine.*)
• Obtain a baseline QT-interval measurement before the patient begins therapy. Watch for and notify the doctor if the patient develops prolongation of the QT interval, a sign that the patient is predisposed to developing polymorphic ventricular tachycardia. Also notify the doctor if the QRS complex widens by 25% or more.
• Remember that quinidine should be avoided in patients with second- or third-degree AV block who don't have pacemakers. It should also be avoided in patients with profound hypotension, myasthenia gravis, intraventricular conduction defects, or hypersensitivity to the drug. Use it cautiously in elderly patients and in those with renal disease, hepatic disease, or asthma.
• Avoid ventricular tachycardia by administering digitalis glycoside preparations prior to giving quinidine in patients with atrial tachyarrhythmias.
• Monitor patients receiving quinidine and digitalis glycoside preparations closely for signs and symptoms of digitalis toxicity, such as nausea, visual changes, or arrhythmias. Digitalis glycoside levels will be increased.

Procainamide hydrochloride

Procainamide hydrochloride (Pronestyl) is indicated for supraventricular and ventricular arrhythmias. When used for ventricular arrhythmias, it's usually the drug administered when lidocaine fails. It comes in a variety of forms, so dosages differ.

How to give it

Here's how to administer procainamide:

Noncardiac adverse effects of quinidine

In addition to adverse cardiovascular effects of quinidine, other adverse effects include:
• *CNS:* vertigo, confusion, headache, tinnitus, hearing loss, visual disturbances
• *Respiratory:* respiratory arrest
• *GI:* nausea, vomiting, diarrhea, abdominal pain, anorexia, hepatotoxicity
• *Hematologic:* hemolytic anemia, agranulocytosis, allergic reactions including rash, fever, thrombocytopenia, or anaphylaxis.

• Orally: average dose is 250 to 500 mg every 3 hours; sustained-release (Procan SR), 50 mg/kg daily in divided doses every 6 hours.
• I.M.: Initial daily dose is 50 mg/kg divided into equal doses every 3 to 6 hours.
• I.V.: slow injection of 100 mg given no faster than 25 to 50 mg/minute every 5 minutes until one of the following occurs: The arrhythmia is suppressed, the QRS complex widens by 50%, hypotension occurs (often the limiting factor when administering the loading dose), or a total of 1 g has been given.
• I.V. infusion: 2 g mixed in 500 ml (4 mg/ml) of D_5W and infused at 1 to 6 mg/minute for a maintenance dose.

What can happen

Adverse cardiovascular effects of procainamide include bradycardia, tachycardia, hypotension, worsening heart failure, AV block, polymorphic ventricular tachycardia or fibrillation, and asystole.

How you intervene

Keep the following points in mind when caring for a patient taking procainamide:
• Monitor the patient's heart rate, blood pressure, and ECG. Notify the doctor if the patient has hypotension or if you notice widening of the QRS complex by 25% or more. Also report a prolonged QT interval if it's more than half of the R-R interval—a sign that the patient is predisposed to developing polymorphic ventricular tachycardia.
• Warn the patient taking procainamide orally not to chew it, which might cause him to get too much of the drug at once. (See *Noncardiac adverse effects of procainamide*.)
• Monitor serum drug levels. (See *Monitoring procainamide,* page 202.)
• Remember that procainamide should be avoided in patients with second- or third-degree AV block who don't have pacemakers and in patients with blood dyscrasias, thrombocytopenia, myasthenia gravis, profound hypotension, or known hypersensitivity to the drug. Procainamide may also aggravate digitalis toxicity.

> ## Noncardiac adverse effects of procainamide
>
> In addition to adverse cardiovascular effects of procainamide, other dose-related adverse effects include:
> • *CNS:* mental depression, hallucinations, seizures
> • *GI:* anorexia, nausea, vomiting, abdominal pain, diarrhea, bitter taste, hepatic dysfunction
> • *Hematologic:* agranulocytosis, hemolytic anemia, thrombocytopenia, neutropenia
> • *Skin:* rash, urticaria
> • *Other:* fever, lupuslike syndrome in long-term therapy.

Class Ib antiarrhythmics

Class Ib antiarrhythmics include such drugs as lidocaine (Xylocaine) and tocainide (Tonocard). Because of their actions on the heart, these drugs are effective in suppressing ventricular ectopy but aren't used with supraventricular arrhythmias. (See *Effects of class Ib antiarrhythmics.*) They usually don't have major effects on ECG rhythm.

Lidocaine hydrochloride

Because of its affinity for ischemic myocardial tissue, lidocaine is the drug of choice for suppressing ventricular arrhythmias. Generally, a patient is first given a loading dose of the drug and then an infusion of it.

How to give it

Here's how to administer lidocaine:
• I.V. bolus injection: 1 to 1.5 mg/kg (usually 50 to 100 mg) at 25 to 50 mg/minute, repeated every 3 to 5 minutes to a maximum of 300 mg total bolus during a 1-hour period.
• I.V. infusion immediately following the bolus dose: 2 g mixed in 500 ml (4 mg/ml) of D_5W and infused at 1 to 4 mg/minute.

Monitoring procainamide

For patients taking procainamide, you'll need to monitor plasma levels of the drug and its active metabolite *N*-acetylprocainamide (NAPA) to prevent toxic reactions. To suppress ventricular arrhythmias, therapeutic serum concentrations of procainamide should range between 4 and 8 mcg/ml. Therapeutic levels of NAPA should average between 10 and 30 mcg/ml.

Effects of class Ib antiarrhythmics

Class Ib antiarrhythmic drugs—such as lidocaine and tocainide—may affect the QRS complexes as shown on the rhythm strip below. They may also prolong the PR interval. These drugs:

• block sodium influx during phase 0, which depresses the rate of depolarization

• shorten repolarization and the duration of the action potential

• suppress ventricular automaticity in ischemic tissue.

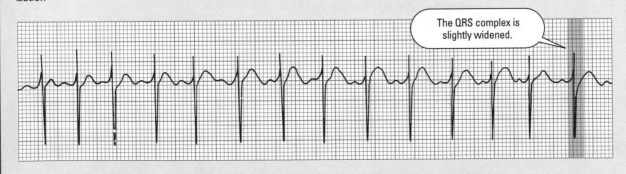

The QRS complex is slightly widened.

What can happen

Cardiovascular adverse effects of lidocaine include AV block, hypotension, bradycardia, new or worsened arrhythmias, and cardiac arrest.

How you intervene

Keep the following points in mind when caring for a patient receiving lidocaine:
• Monitor the patient's heart rate, blood pressure, and ECG.
• Watch for signs and symptoms of drug toxicity. (See *Noncardiac adverse effects of lidocaine.*) The potential for toxicity is increased if the patient has liver disease, is elderly, is taking cimetidine or propranolol, or receives an infusion of the drug for longer than 24 hours.
• Avoid use of the drug in patients known to be hypersensitive to it or in severe SA, AV, or intraventricular block in the absence of an artificial pacemaker.
• Administer cautiously with other antiarrhythmics.

Tocainide hydrochloride

Tocainide is used to suppress life-threatening ventricular arrhythmias such as sustained ventricular tachycardia.

How to give it

The initial dose of tocainide is 400 mg orally every 8 hours. The usual dosage is between 1,200 mg and 1,800 mg daily in three divided doses. The maximum dose is 2,400 mg/day.

What can happen

Adverse cardiovascular effects of tocainide include diaphoresis, bradycardia, hypotension, AV block, palpitations, chest pain, heart failure, and proarrhythmias.

How you intervene

Keep the following points in mind when caring for a patient taking tocainide:
• Monitor the patient's heart rate, blood pressure, and ECG.
• Remember that tocainide should be avoided in patients with second- or third-degree heart block who don't have pacemakers. It should also be avoided in patients with a

---

Noncardiac adverse effects of lidocaine

In addition to adverse cardiovascular effects of lidocaine, other adverse effects (mostly dose-related) include:
• *CNS:* seizures, confusion, drowsiness, dizziness, tremors, restlessness, light-headedness, paresthesia, feeling of dissociation, tinnitus, double vision, agitation
• *Respiratory:* respiratory arrest
• *GI:* nausea, vomiting
• *Other:* anaphylaxis.

history of allergic reactions to local amide-type anesthetics.

• Use with caution with other antiarrhythmics, in elderly patients, in heart failure, or in liver or kidney disease.

• Tell the patient to report dyspnea, cough, signs of infection, and bleeding or bruising. These signs and symptoms may indicate a severe adverse reaction to the drug.

• Keep in mind that the risk of toxicity is greater if the patient is receiving cimetidine (Tagamet) at the same time. (See *Noncardiac adverse effects of tocainide*.)

Class Ic antiarrhythmics

Class Ic antiarrhythmic drugs include flecainide (Tambocor) and propafenone (Rythmol). These drugs slow conduction without affecting the duration of the action potential. (See *Effects of class Ic antiarrhythmics*.) Because of their proarrhythmic potential, these drugs are used only for life-threatening or ventricular arrhythmias.

Effects of class Ic antiarrhythmics

Class Ic antiarrhythmic drugs — including flecainide and propafenone — cause the effects shown below on an ECG by exerting particular actions on the cardiac cycle. Class Ic antiarrhythmics block sodium influx during phase 0, which depresses the rate of depolarization. The drugs exert no effect on repolarization or the duration of the action potential.

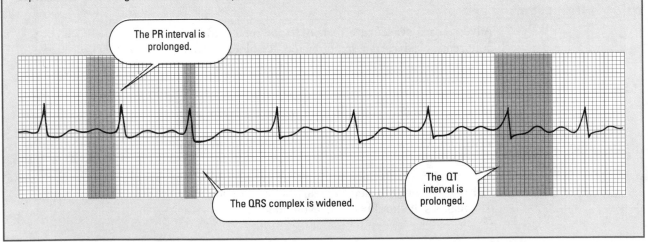

Flecainide acetate

Flecainide is used to treat life-threatening ventricular arrhythmias such as sustained ventricular tachycardia and to prevent paroxysmal supraventricular tachycardia.

How to give it

The dosage for flecainide is 50 to 200 mg orally twice daily, to a maximum of 400 mg/day for life-threatening ventricular arrhythmias and 300 mg/day for the prevention of paroxysmal supraventricular tachycardia.

What can happen

Adverse cardiovascular effects of flecainide include bradycardia, chest pain, palpitations, heart failure, new or worsened arrhythmias, and cardiac arrest.

How you intervene

Keep the following points in mind when caring for a patient taking flecainide:
• Monitor the patient's heart rate, blood pressure, and ECG. Report widening of the QRS complex by 25% or more, and watch closely for signs of heart failure. (See *Noncardiac adverse effects of flecainide,* page 206.)
• Use flecainide cautiously in sick sinus syndrome or in heart, kidney, or liver failure. Avoid its use entirely in second- or third-degree AV block, in bifascicular blocks, and when the patient doesn't have a pacemaker.
• Administer flecainide cautiously in patients receiving amiodarone, cimetidine, digoxin, or a beta blocker.
• Correct electrolyte imbalances before starting flecainide therapy.

Propafenone hydrochloride

Propafenone is used only for life-threatening ventricular arrhythmias.

How to give it

The usual dosage of propafenone is 150 to 300 mg orally three times daily, to a maximum of 900 mg/day.

What can happen

Propafenone's adverse effects on the cardiovascular system include heart failure, AV block, chest pain, bradycardia, atrial fibrillation, bundle-branch block, hypotension,

---

Noncardiac adverse effects of tocainide

In addition to adverse cardiovascular effects of tocainide, other adverse effects include:
• *CNS:* mood changes, headache, dizziness, paresthesia, tremors, confusion, blurred or double vision, seizures, coma
• *Respiratory:* respiratory arrest, pulmonary fibrosis, pneumonitis, pulmonary edema
• *GI:* nausea, vomiting, diarrhea, anorexia, abdominal pain
• *Hematologic:* fever, chills, thrombocytopenia, aplastic anemia, agranulocytosis
• *Skin:* rash.

and such proarrhythmias as ventricular tachycardia, ventricular fibrillation, and PVCs.

How you intervene

Keep the following points in mind when caring for a patient taking propafenone:
• Monitor the patient's heart rate, blood pressure, and ECG. Report widening of the QRS complex greater than 25%. If widening occurs, the dosage may need to be reduced. Monitor the patient closely for heart failure.
• Remember that propafenone should be avoided in patients with heart failure, cardiogenic shock, sick sinus syndrome without a pacemaker, bronchospastic disorders, hypotension, or SA, AV, or bifascicular blocks.
• Administer propafenone cautiously in patients also receiving cimetidine, other antiarrhythmics such as quinidine, or a beta blocker. (See *Noncardiac adverse effects of propafenone*.)
• Be aware that patients receiving a digitalis glycoside along with propafenone might have increased plasma concentration of the glycoside, leading to digitalis toxicity.
• Use cautiously in patients also taking an oral anticoagulant because propafenone can increase the plasma concentration of the drug.
• Correct electrolyte imbalances before starting propafenone therapy.
• Instruct the patient to report recurrent or persistent infections.

Class II antiarrhythmics

Class II antiarrhythmic drugs are used to treat supraventricular and ventricular arrhythmias, especially those caused by excess catecholamines. The drugs are called beta blockers because they block beta receptors in the sympathetic nervous system. (See *Effects of class II antiarrhythmics*.)

Two types of beta receptors exist: beta$_1$ and beta$_2$. Beta$_1$ receptors increase heart rate, contractility, and conductivity. Blocking those receptors decreases the actions listed above.

Beta$_2$ receptors relax smooth muscle in the bronchi and blood vessels. Keep in mind that blocking these receptors may result in vasoconstriction and bronchospasm.

Noncardiac adverse effects of flecainide

In addition to adverse cardiovascular effects of flecainide, other adverse effects include:
• *CNS:* headache, drowsiness, dizziness, syncope, fatigue, blurred vision, tremor
• *Respiratory:* dyspnea
• *GI:* dry mouth, nausea, vomiting, constipation, abdominal pain.

Noncardiac adverse effects of propafenone

In addition to adverse cardiovascular effects of propafenone, other adverse effects include:
• *CNS:* dizziness, blurred vision, fatigue, headache, paresthesia
• *Respiratory:* dyspnea
• *GI:* unusual taste, nausea, vomiting, dyspepsia, constipation, diarrhea
• *Hematologic:* anemia, bruising.

Effects of class II antiarrhythmics

Class II antiarrhythmic drugs — including such beta-adrenergic blockers as propranolol, esmolol, acebutolol, and sotalol — cause certain effects on an ECG (as shown here) by exerting particular actions on the cardiac cycle. Class II antiarrhythmics:

- depress SA node automaticity
- shorten the duration of the action potential

- increase the refractory period of atrial and AV junctional tissues, which slows conduction

- inhibit sympathetic activity.

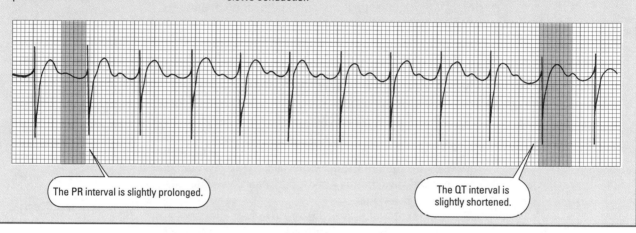

The PR interval is slightly prolonged.

The QT interval is slightly shortened.

Beta blockers that block only beta$_1$ receptors are referred to as cardioselective. Those that block both beta$_1$ and beta$_2$ receptors are referred to as noncardioselective.

Beta blockers

The following beta blockers are FDA-approved for use as antiarrhythmics:

- acebutolol (Sectral). This drug is classified as cardioselective. The normal dosage is 200 mg orally twice daily, increased as needed to a usual dosage of 600 to 1,200 mg daily.
- propranolol (Inderal). This drug is classified as noncardioselective. It may be given orally or I.V. The oral dosage is 10 to 30 mg three or four times daily. The I.V. dosage is 1 to 3 mg, at a rate not to exceed 1 mg/minute, repeated after 2 minutes and again after 4 hours, if necessary.
- esmolol (Brevibloc). This drug is a short-acting cardioselective drug administered by I.V. titration. The loading dose is 500 mcg/kg over 1 minute, then 50 mcg/kg/minute for 4 minutes, titrated until the desired effect is achieved.

• sotalol (Betapace). This drug is a noncardioselective drug that also has class III characteristics. The initial dosage is 80 mg orally twice daily. Most patients respond to 160 to 320 mg/day divided into two or three doses.

What can happen

The adverse effects of beta blockers on the cardiovascular system may vary, but they include bradycardia, hypotension, AV block, heart failure, chest pain, and palpitations.

How you intervene

Keep the following points in mind when caring for a patient taking a beta blocker:
• Monitor the patient's heart rate, blood pressure, and ECG.
• Remember that beta blockers should be avoided in patients with bradycardia, second- or third-degree AV block, heart failure, and shock. Use them cautiously in patients with diabetes mellitus, kidney disease, hyperthyroidism, liver disease, myasthenia gravis, peripheral vascular disease, and hypotension.
• Keep in mind that noncardioselective beta blockers are contraindicated in patients with asthma or other bronchospastic disease. (See *Noncardiac adverse effects of class II beta blockers.*)
• Remember that beta blockers diminish the patient's ability to withstand exercise because the heart rate can't increase. These drugs also block sympathetic response to shock.
• Correct electrolyte imbalances before starting therapy with a beta blocker.

> ### Noncardiac adverse effects of class II beta blockers
>
> In addition to adverse cardiovascular effects of class II beta blockers, other adverse effects include:
> • *CNS:* insomnia, syncope, mental depression, emotional lability, fatigue, headache, and dizziness
> • *Respiratory:* dyspnea, bronchospasm, especially in patients with asthma or other bronchospastic disease
> • *Hematologic:* thrombocytopenia, agranulocytosis, alterations in blood sugar level
> • *Skin:* rash.

Class III antiarrhythmics

Class III antiarrhythmics are called potassium channel blockers. (See *Effects of class III antiarrhythmics.*) They include bretylium (Bretylol), amiodarone (Cordarone), and ibutilide fumarate (Corvert). Sotalol has qualities of both class II and class III antiarrhythmics.

Bretylium tosylate

Bretylium is used to treat ventricular fibrillation and other ventricular arrhythmias. It's especially helpful in treating arrhythmias that don't respond to lidocaine.

Effects of class III antiarrhythmics

Class III antiarrhythmic drugs — including bretylium, amiodarone, sotalol, and ibutilide — cause the effects shown below on an ECG by exerting particular actions on the cardiac cycle. Class III antiarrhythmics:

• block potassium movement during phase 3

• increase the duration of the action potential

• prolong the effective refractory period.

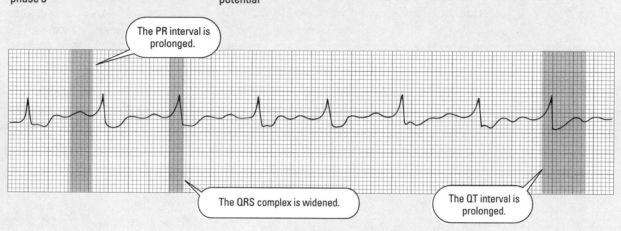

The PR interval is prolonged.

The QRS complex is widened.

The QT interval is prolonged.

How to give it

Here's how to administer bretylium:
• I.V. injection: 5 mg/kg I.V. bolus over 1 minute, then increase to 10 mg/kg. May be repeated every 15 to 30 minutes to a maximum of 35 mg/kg.
• I.V. infusion: 2 g mixed in 500 ml (4 mg/ml) of solution and infused at a rate of 1 to 2 mg/minute.

What can happen

Adverse cardiovascular effects of bretylium include transient tachycardia and hypertension followed by flushing, bradycardia, severe hypotension, AV block, chest pain, and heart failure.

How you intervene

Keep the following points in mind when caring for a patient receiving bretylium:
• Monitor the patient's heart rate, blood pressure, and ECG.
• Keep the patient supine to avoid sudden postural hypotension.

• Remember that bretylium should be avoided in patients with digitalis toxicity, aortic stenosis, pulmonary hypertension, or heart failure and in patients known to be hypersensitive to the drug. Use the drug cautiously in patients with renal disease and adjust the dosage as needed. (See *Noncardiac adverse effects of bretylium*.)

• Keep in mind that bretylium may add to the effects of catecholamines.

Amiodarone

Amiodarone is used to treat supraventricular arrhythmias, paroxysmal supraventricular tachycardia caused by ventricular arrhythmias, and accessory pathway conduction such as Wolff-Parkinson-White syndrome. Use of amiodarone is limited because of its adverse effects. (See *Noncardiac adverse effects of amiodarone*.)

Take care not to confuse amiodarone with amrinone (Inocor), which is a positive inotropic agent.

How to give it

Here's how to administer amiodarone:
• Orally: 800 to 1,600 mg daily for 1 to 3 weeks, followed by 600 to 800 mg/day for 4 weeks, followed by 200 to 600 mg/day as a maintenance dosage.
• I.V. infusion: 150 mg mixed in 100 ml D_5W and infused over 10 minutes (15 mg/minute); then 900 mg mixed in 500 ml D_5W with 360 mg infused over the next 6 hours (1 mg/minute), followed by 540 mg infused over 18 hours (0.5 mg/minute). After the first 24 hours, a maintenance I.V. infusion of 720 mg/24 hours (0.5 mg/minute) should be continued.

What can happen

Adverse effects of amiodarone given by I.V. infusion include bradycardia, hypotension, ventricular tachycardia, AV block, cardiogenic shock, heart failure, asystole, and pulseless electrical activity.

Long-term oral therapy is associated with bradycardia, sinus arrest, SA block, AV block, and hypotension.

How you intervene

Keep the following points in mind when caring for a patient taking amiodarone:
• Monitor the patient's vital signs, ECG, and respiratory status.

Noncardiac adverse effects of bretylium

In addition to adverse cardiovascular effects of bretylium, other adverse effects include:
• *CNS:* vertigo, dizziness, light-headedness, syncope (usually secondary to hypotension)
• *GI:* severe nausea, vomiting (with rapid infusion).

Noncardiac adverse effects of amiodarone

In addition to adverse cardiovascular effects of amiodarone, other adverse effects include:
• *CNS:* malaise, fatigue, dizziness
• *Respiratory:* pulmonary toxicity (progressive dyspnea, cough, fever, pleuritic chest pain)
• *GI:* nausea, vomiting, constipation.

- Monitor laboratory test results, such as electrolyte levels, liver function studies, pulmonary function studies, and chest X-rays.
- Check for signs of digitalis toxicity or increased prothrombin time. Amiodarone can increase the serum levels of digitalis glycosides and oral anticoagulants.
- Remember that amiodarone should be avoided in patients with hypersensitivity to the drug, cardiogenic shock, marked sinus bradycardia, and second- or third-degree AV block without a pacemaker. Use the drug cautiously in patients with cardiomegaly, preexisting bradycardia or sinus node disease, conduction disturbances, or depressed ventricular function.
- Be aware that the drug has a long half-life (56 days), so it takes a long time for the drug to reach therapeutic levels and to be cleared by the body.

Ibutilide fumarate

Ibutilide fumarate (Corvert) is becoming increasingly popular for the rapid conversion of recent-onset atrial fibrillation or flutter to sinus rhythm. The drug increases atrial and ventricular refractoriness.

How to give it

If your adult patient weighs 132 lb (60 kg) or more, he'll receive 1 mg of ibutilide fumarate I.V. over 10 minutes. If he weighs less than 132 lb, the dose is 0.01 mg/kg.

Ibutilide fumarate may be diluted in 50 ml of normal saline or 5% dextrose solution. Should the arrhythmia still be present 10 minutes after the infusion is complete, the dose may be repeated.

What can happen

Adverse cardiovascular effects of ibutilide fumarate include premature ventricular contractions, ventricular tachycardia, sustained polymorphic VT, hypotension, bundle-branch block, atrioventricular block, hypertension, bradycardia, tachycardia, palpitations, and lengthening of the QT interval. Noncardiac adverse effects include headache and nausea.

How you intervene

Keep these points in mind when giving ibutilide fumarate:
- Monitor the patient's vital signs and ECG continuously

during the infusion and for at least 4 hours afterward. The infusion will be stopped if the arrhythmia terminates or if the patient develops ventricular tachycardia (VT) or marked prolongation of the QT interval, which signals the possible development of polymorphic ventricular tachycardia.

• Have emergency equipment and medication nearby for the treatment of sustained ventricular tachycardia.

• Ibutilide fumarate is not recommended for patients with a history of polymorphic ventricular tachycardia.

• The drug should be used cautiously in patients receiving digoxin (Lanoxin) because it can mask signs and symptoms of cardiotoxicity associated with excessive digoxin levels.

• Don't administer ibutilide fumarate at the same time or within 4 hours of class Ia or other class III antiarrhythmics.

• Don't give ibutilide fumarate with other drugs that prolong the QT interval, such as phenothiazines, tricyclic or tetracyclic antidepressants, or antihistamines such as terfenadine (Seldane) and astemizole (Hismanal).

Class IV antiarrhythmics

Class IV antiarrhythmic drugs are called calcium channel blockers. They include verapamil (Calan) and diltiazem (Cardizem). These drugs prolong conduction time and the refractory period in the AV node. (See *Effects of class IV antiarrhythmics.*)

Other calcium channel blockers, including nifedipine (Procardia), don't cause electrophysiologic changes and aren't used as antiarrhythmics.

Verapamil hydrochloride

Verapamil is used for paroxysmal supraventricular tachycardia because of its effect on the AV node. It also slows the ventricular response in atrial fibrillation and flutter.

How to give it

Here's how to administer verapamil:
• Orally for chronic atrial fibrillation: 80 to 120 mg three or four times a day to a maximum of 480 mg/day.
• I.V. injection for supraventricular arrhythmias: 0.075 to 0.15 mg/kg (usually 5 to 10 mg) over 2 minutes; may repeat in 30 minutes as a 10-mg dose if no response occurs.

What can happen

Cardiovascular adverse effects of verapamil include bradycardia or tachycardia, AV block, hypotension, heart failure, edema, flushing, and ventricular fibrillation.

How you intervene

Keep the following points in mind when caring for a patient taking verapamil:
• Monitor the patient's heart rate, blood pressure, and ECG. Also monitor liver function studies. (See *Noncardiac adverse effects of verapamil*.)
• Note that calcium may be given before verapamil to prevent hypotension.
• Advise the patient to change position slowly to avoid postural hypotension.
• Remember that verapamil should be avoided in sick sinus syndrome or second- or third-degree AV block without a pacemaker and in atrial fibrillation or flutter due to Wolff-Parkinson-White syndrome. It also should be avoided in patients with hypersensitivity to the drug, advanced heart failure, cardiogenic shock, profound hypotension, acute myocardial infarction (MI), or pulmonary edema.

Noncardiac adverse effects of verapamil

In addition to adverse cardiovascular effects of verapamil, other adverse effects include:
• *CNS:* headache, dizziness
• *Respiratory:* dyspnea
• *GI:* nausea, constipation, elevated liver enzymes
• *Skin:* rash.

Effects of class IV antiarrhythmics

Class IV antiarrhythmic drugs — including such calcium channel blockers as verapamil and diltiazem — affect the cardiac cycle in specific ways and may lead to the ECG change shown here. Class IV antiarrhythmics:

• block calcium movement during phase 2

• prolong the conduction time and increase the refractory period in the AV node

• decrease contractility.

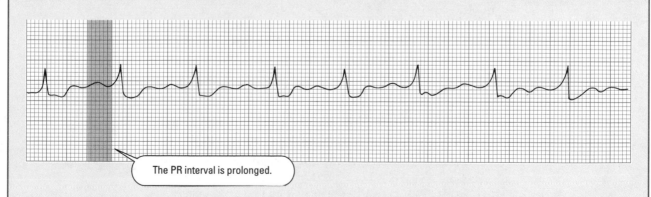

The PR interval is prolonged.

• Give the drug cautiously to patients receiving digitalis glycosides or oral beta blockers, elderly patients, and patients with heart failure, hypotension, liver disease, and kidney disease. Don't give verapamil to patients receiving I.V. beta blockers.

Diltiazem hydrochloride

Diltiazem is administered I.V. to treat paroxysmal supraventricular tachycardia and atrial fibrillation or flutter. Diltiazem is also used to treat angina and hypertension, but those uses won't be discussed here.

How to give it

Here's how to give diltiazem:
• I.V. injection: 0.25 mg/kg (usually 20 mg) over 2 minutes; may repeat in 15 minutes at 0.35 mg/kg (usually 25 mg) over 2 minutes.
• I.V. infusion: 125 mg mixed in 100 ml normal saline solution or D_5W for a total volume of 125 ml (1 mg/ml) of solution and infused at a rate of 5 to 15 mg/hour (usually 10 mg/hour).

What can happen

Adverse cardiovascular effects of diltiazem include edema, flushing, bradycardia, hypotension, heart failure, arrhythmias, conduction abnormalities, sinus node dysfunction, and AV block.

How you intervene

Keep the following points in mind when caring for a patient receiving diltiazem:
• Monitor the patient's heart rate, blood pressure, and ECG.
• Diltiazem should be avoided in patients with sick sinus syndrome or second- or third-degree AV block without a pacemaker, atrial fibrillation or flutter due to Wolff-Parkinson-White syndrome, advanced heart failure, cardiogenic shock, profound hypotension, acute MI, pulmonary edema, or sensitivity to the drug.
• Use cautiously in elderly patients; in patients with heart failure, hypotension, or liver or kidney disease; and in

those receiving digitalis glycosides or beta blockers. (See *Noncardiac adverse effects of diltiazem.*)
• Don't give to patients receiving I.V. beta blockers.
• Advise the patient to change position slowly to avoid postural hypotension.

Unclassified antiarrhythmics

Some antiarrhythmic drugs defy categorization. Let's look at some of those drugs, called unclassified or miscellaneous antiarrhythmic drugs.

Adenosine

Adenosine is a naturally occurring nucleoside used to treat paroxysmal supraventricular tachycardia. It acts on the AV node to slow conduction and inhibit reentry pathways. (See *Adenosine and the heart.*) It's also useful in treating paroxysmal supraventricular tachycardia associated with Wolff-Parkinson-White syndrome.

Although adenosine isn't effective for atrial fibrillation or atrial flutter, it does slow the rate in paroxysmal supraventricular tachycardia enough to determine the rhythm so that a more appropriate agent such as verapamil can be used.

How to give it

Administer 6 mg of adenosine I.V. over 1 to 2 seconds, immediately followed by a rapid flush with normal saline solution. The drug's half-life is less than 10 seconds, so it needs to reach the circulation quickly. Repeat with an injection of 12 mg of adenosine if the rhythm doesn't convert within 1 to 2 minutes. The 12-mg dose may be repeated once.

What can happen

Adverse cardiovascular effects of adenosine include transient arrhythmias such as a short asystolic pause at the time of conversion. Other adverse effects include hypotension if large doses are used, facial flushing, diaphoresis, chest pressure, and recurrence of the arrhythmia. (See *Noncardiac adverse effects of adenosine.*)

How you intervene

Keep the following points in mind when caring for a patient receiving adenosine:

Adenosine and the heart

Adenosine affects the heart by:
• prolonging the AV node refractory period
• decreasing SA node automaticity and slowing the sinus rate.

Noncardiac adverse effects of diltiazem

In addition to adverse cardiovascular effects of diltiazem, other adverse effects include:
• *CNS:* headache, drowsiness, dizziness, weakness
• *GI:* nausea, transient elevation of liver enzymes, constipation, abdominal discomfort
• *Skin:* rash.

Noncardiac adverse effects of adenosine

In addition to adverse cardiovascular effects of adenosine, other adverse effects include:
• *CNS:* apprehension, light-headedness, burning sensation
• *Respiratory:* dyspnea
• *GI:* nausea.

• Monitor the patient's heart rate, blood pressure, ECG, ventilatory rate and depth, and breath sounds for wheezes.
• Remember that adenosine should be avoided in patients with hypersensitivity to the drug, second- or third-degree AV block, or sick sinus syndrome without a pacemaker. Use cautiously in older adults and in patients with asthma or those receiving dipyridamole (Persantine) or carbamazepine (Tegretol).
• Store adenosine at room temperature.
• The patient may require a higher dose or not respond to therapy at all if he is also taking aminophylline or another xanthine derivative.

Atropine sulfate

Atropine is an anticholinergic drug that blocks vagal effects on the SA node. (See *Atropine and the heart.*) This enhances conduction through the AV node and speeds the heart rate. Atropine is used to treat symptomatic bradycardia and asystole.

How to give it

Administer atropine by a 0.5- to 1-mg I.V. injection repeated as needed at 3- to 5-minute intervals, to a maximum dose of 0.04 mg/kg. The initial dose for asystole is 1 mg. The maximum dose is 3 mg.

What can happen

Adverse cardiovascular effects of atropine include tachycardia, palpitations, bradycardia if given slowly or in a dose of less than 0.5 mg, hypotension, and chest pain and increased myocardial oxygen consumption in patients with coronary artery disease.

How you intervene

Keep the following points in mind when caring for a patient receiving atropine:
• Monitor the patient's heart rate, blood pressure, ECG, urine output, and bowel sounds. (See *Noncardiac adverse effects of atropine.*)
• Remember that atropine should be avoided in patients with hypersensitivity to belladonna, acute-closure glaucoma, GI obstruction, obstructive uropathy, myasthenia gravis, and tachyarrhythmias.

Atropine and the heart

Atropine increases the heart rate by blocking parasympathetic nervous system effects. Blocking those effects increases the firing rate of the SA node and improves conduction through the AV node.

Noncardiac adverse effects of atropine

In addition to adverse cardiovascular effects of atropine, other adverse effects include:
• *CNS:* headache, restlessness, insomnia, dizziness, blurred vision, dilated pupils, photophobia
• *GI:* dry mouth, constipation, paralytic ileus
• *GU:* urine retention.

• Use atropine cautiously in patients with renal disease, heart failure, hyperthyroidism, hepatic disease, hypertension, and acute MI. Don't give atropine for bradycardia unless the patient is symptomatic. Increasing the heart rate in these patients can lead to increased myocardial oxygen consumption and a worsening of the infarction.

Digoxin

Digoxin (Lanoxin) is used to treat paroxysmal supraventricular tachycardia and atrial fibrillation and flutter, especially in patients with congestive heart failure. It provides antiarrhythmic effects by enhancing vagal tone and acting on the SA and AV nodes. (See *Digoxin and the heart.*) It also strengthens myocardial contraction.

How to give it

To administer digoxin rapidly and orally by tablet, give a digitalizing dose of 0.75 to 1.25 mg divided into two or more doses every 6 to 8 hours. The usual maintenance dosage is 0.125 to 0.5 mg daily.

To administer digoxin I.V., give a digitalizing dose of 0.4 to 0.6 mg, with additional doses of 0.1 to 0.3 mg administered every 4 to 8 hours. The usual maintenance dose for I.V. administration is 0.125 to 0.5 mg daily in divided doses or as a single dose.

What can happen

Too much digoxin in the body causes toxicity. Toxic cardiac effects include SA and AV blocks and junctional and ventricular arrhythmias. Digitalis toxicity is treated by discontinuing digoxin; correcting oxygenation and electrolyte imbalances; treating arrhythmias with phenytoin, lidocaine, atropine, or a pacemaker; giving digoxin immune fab (Digibind) to reverse life-threatening arrhythmias or blocks (occurs within 30 to 60 minutes); and correcting the potassium level before giving digoxin immune fab.

How you intervene

Keep the following points in mind when caring for a patient receiving digoxin:

Digoxin and the heart

Digoxin affects the heart by:
• slowing conduction through the AV node
• prolonging the AV node refractory period
• decreasing SA node automaticity and slowing the sinus rate.

• Check for signs of digitalis toxicity, especially in patients with hypokalemia, hypocalcemia, hypercalcemia, or hypomagnesemia. Monitor serum electrolyte levels, as ordered.

• Monitor the patient's apical heart rate and ECG. A heart rate below 60 beats per minute or a change in rhythm can signal digitalis toxicity. If this occurs, withhold digoxin and notify the doctor. (See *Noncardiac adverse effects of digoxin*.)

• Remember that digoxin should be avoided in patients with known hypersensitivity to the drug, sick sinus syndrome, SA or AV block, ventricular tachycardia, hypertrophic cardiomyopathy, or Wolff-Parkinson-White syndrome. Use cautiously in older adults and in patients with acute MI, liver or kidney disease, or hypothyroidism.

• Withhold digoxin for 1 to 2 days before performing electrical cardioversion.

Epinephrine

Epinephrine is a naturally occurring catecholamine. It acts directly on alpha- and beta-adrenergic receptor sites of the sympathetic nervous system and is used to help restore cardiac rhythm in cardiac arrest and to treat symptomatic bradycardia. Its actions include increasing the blood pressure, heart rate, and cardiac output.

How to give it

To restore sinus rhythm in cardiac arrest in adults, administer epinephrine by I.V. injection as a 0.5- to 1-mg dose (5 to 10 ml of 1:10,000 solution). Doses may be repeated every 3 to 5 minutes as needed. (Some clinicians advocate doses of up to 5 mg, especially for patients who don't respond to the usual I.V. dose.) After initial I.V. administration, an infusion may be given at 1 to 4 mcg/minute.

To treat symptomatic bradycardia in patients not in cardiac arrest, administer epinephrine by I.V. infusion at an initial rate of 1 mcg/minute, and then adjust the dose according to the patient's response. The usual range for a positive response is 2 to 10 mcg/minute.

What can happen

Adverse cardiovascular effects include palpitations, hypertension, tachycardia, ventricular fibrillation, anginal pain, and ECG changes, including a decreased T-wave amplitude.

Noncardiac adverse effects of digoxin

In addition to adverse cardiovascular effects of digoxin, other adverse effects resulting from toxicity include:

• *CNS:* headache, visual disturbances, hallucinations, fatigue, muscle weakness, agitation

• *GI:* anorexia, nausea, vomiting, diarrhea.

Noncardiac adverse effects of epinephrine

In addition to adverse cardiovascular effects of epinephrine, other adverse effects include:

• *CNS:* nervousness, tremor, dizziness, headache, disorientation, agitation, fear, pallor, weakness, cerebral hemorrhage; in patients with Parkinson's disease, increased rigidity and tremor

• *Respiratory:* dyspnea

• *GI:* nausea, vomiting.

How you intervene

Keep these points in mind when administering epinephrine:
• Be sure to note the concentration of the epinephrine solution used. (Remember that 1 mg equals 1 ml of 1:1,000 or 10 ml of 1:10,000 concentration.)
• When administering I.V. epinephrine, monitor the patient's heart rate, ECG rhythm, and blood pressure throughout therapy.
• Don't mix the drug with alkaline solutions. Use D_5W, lactated Ringer's solution, or normal saline solution or a combination of dextrose and saline solution.
• Some epinephrine products contain sulfites. Use of those products normally should be avoided in patient's with sulfite allergies. The only exception is when epinephrine is being used in an emergency.
• Remember that the use of epinephrine with digoxin (Lanoxin) or such general anesthetics as cyclopropane or a halogenated hydrocarbon like halothane (Fluothane) may increase the risk of ventricular arrhythmias.
• Avoid giving epinephrine with other drugs that exert a similar effect. Doing so can cause severe adverse cardiovascular effects.

Magnesium sulfate

Magnesium sulfate is used to treat ventricular arrhythmias, especially polymorphic ventricular tachycardia. It's also used as a preventive measure in acute MI. Magnesium sulfate decreases myocardial cell excitability and conduction. (See *Magnesium sulfate and the heart.*)

How to give it

To administer magnesium sulfate, give 2 to 6 g I.V. over several minutes. This dose may be followed by a continuous I.V. infusion of 3 to 20 mg/minute for 5 to 48 hours. The dosage and duration of therapy depend on the patient's response and serum magnesium levels. The optimum dosage is still under study.

What can happen

Adverse cardiovascular effects of magnesium sulfate include diaphoresis, flushing, depressed cardiac function, bradycardia, hypotension, and circulatory collapse.

Magnesium sulfate and the heart

Magnesium sulfate acts in a way similar to class III antiarrhythmic drugs because it:
• slows conduction through the AV node
• prolongs the refractory period in the atria and ventricles.

How you intervene

Keep the following points in mind when caring for a patient receiving magnesium sulfate:
• Monitor the patient's heart rate, blood pressure, ventilatory rate, ECG, urine output, deep tendon reflexes, and mental status. (See *Noncardiac adverse effects of magnesium sulfate*.)
• Remember that magnesium sulfate should be avoided in patients with renal disease. Use it cautiously in patients with renal insufficiency and in those taking digitalis glycosides.
• Monitor closely for signs and symptoms of hypermagnesemia, such as hypotension, AV block, central nervous system depression, depressed or absent deep tendon reflexes, muscle weakness or paralysis, and respiratory arrest.
• Have I.V. calcium available to counteract the effects of hypermagnesemia.
• Have intubation equipment and a mechanical ventilator available.

> **Noncardiac adverse effects of magnesium sulfate**
>
> In addition to adverse cardiovascular effects of magnesium sulfate, other adverse effects include:
> • *CNS:* drowsiness, depressed reflexes, flaccid paralysis, hypothermia
> • *Respiratory:* respiratory paralysis
> • *Other:* hypocalcemia.

Teaching about antiarrhythmics

Here are some important points to emphasize to a patient when teaching about antiarrhythmic drugs:
• Take the drug exactly as prescribed. Stress also that patients should not stop taking the drugs on their own.
• Call the doctor if chest pain, shortness of breath, coughing, palpitations, dizziness, fatigue, a weight gain of more than 2 lb (0.9 kg) a day, a very fast or slow heart rate, a change in the regularity of the heartbeat, or persistent changes you feel might be related to drug therapy occur.
• See your doctor for regular checkups, as scheduled. Periodic physical examinations, ECGs, chest X-rays, and laboratory studies will help evaluate the effectiveness of therapy.

Quick quiz

1. Antiarrhythmic drugs that depress the rate of depolarization belong to class:

    A. I.

    B. II.

    C. III.

Answer: A. Class I antiarrhythmic drugs block sodium influx during phase 0, depressing the rate of depolarization.

2. The antiarrhythmic drug used to treat PVCs or ventricular tachycardias that don't respond to lidocaine is:

    A. atropine.

    B. procainamide.

    C. magnesium sulfate.

Answer: B. Procainamide is used to treat PVCs or ventricular arrhythmias that don't respond to lidocaine.

3. The drug that blocks vagal stimulation and increases the heart rate is:

    A. atropine.

    B. diltiazem.

    C. verapamil.

Answer: A. Atropine blocks vagal effects on the SA node, enhances conduction through the node, and speeds the heart rate. The drug is used to treat symptomatic bradycardia.

4. Because of bretylium's effect on blood pressure, you would advise a patient taking the drug to:

    A. avoid undue stress.

    B. change positions slowly.

    C. take the drug on an empty stomach.

Answer: B. Bretylium can cause postural hypotension, so you should advise the patient to change position slowly.

5. The drugs known for lowering the resting heart rate are:

    A. beta blockers.

    B. potassium channel blockers.

    C. sodium channel blockers.

Answer: A. Beta blockers block sympathetic nervous system beta receptors and lower heart rate, contractility, and conduction.

Scoring

☆☆☆   If you answered all five items correctly, just say *wow!*
        You're the antiarrhythmic drug czar!

☆☆   If you answered three or four correctly, great job!
        You're the deputy antiarrhythmic drug czar!

☆   If you answered fewer than three correctly, no worries.
        You're the antiarrhythmic drug czar's sergeant at
        arms!

Part IV

The 12-lead ECG

Obtaining a 12-lead ECG

Just the facts

This chapter focuses on the 12-lead electrocardio-gram (ECG), which gives a more complete view of the heart's electrical activity than a rhythm strip. In this chapter you'll learn:

♦ how the 12-lead ECG helps diagnose pathologic conditions

♦ how the heart's electrical axis relates to the 12-lead ECG

♦ how to prepare your patient, place the electrodes, and record the ECG

♦ what the diagnostic purposes of the posterior-lead ECG and the right chest lead ECG are

♦ what the function of a signal-averaged ECG is.

A look at the 12-lead ECG

The 12-lead ECG is a diagnostic test that helps identify pathologic conditions, especially angina and acute myocardial infarction (MI). It gives a more complete view of the heart's electrical activity than a rhythm strip and can be used to assess left ventricular function. Patients with other conditions that affect the heart's electrical system may also benefit from a 12-lead ECG. (See *Why a 12-lead ECG?* page 226.)

Interdependent evidence

Like other diagnostic tests, a 12-lead ECG must be viewed alongside other clinical evidence. So always correlate the patient's ECG results with his history, physical assessment findings, laboratory results, and medication regimen.

Remember, too, that an ECG can be done in a variety of ways, including over a telephone line. (See *Transtelephonic cardiac monitoring*.) Transtelephonic monitoring, in fact, has become increasingly important as a tool for assessing patients at home and in other nonclinical settings.

Transtelephonic cardiac monitoring

Using a special recorder-transmitter, patients at home can transmit electrocardiograms (ECGs) by telephone to a central monitoring center for immediate interpretation. This technique, called transtelephonic cardiac monitoring (TTM), reduces health care costs and is gaining widespread use.

Nurses play an important role in TTM. Besides performing extensive patient and family teaching, they may run the central monitoring center and help interpret ECGs sent by patients.

TTM allows the health care professional to assess transient conditions that cause such symptoms as palpitations, dizziness, syncope, confusion, paroxysmal dyspnea, and chest pain. Such conditions, which often don't show themselves while the patient is in the presence of a health care professional, can make diagnosis difficult and costly.

With TTM, the patient can transmit an ECG recording from his home when the symptoms appear, avoiding the need to go to the hospital for diagnosis and offering a greater opportunity for early diagnosis. Even if symptoms don't appear often, the patient can keep the equipment for long periods of time, which further aids in the diagnosis of the patient's condition.

Home care

TTM can also be used by patients having cardiac rehabilitation at home. You'll call the patient regularly during this period to receive transmissions and assess progress. Because of this continuous monitoring, TTM can help reduce the anxiety felt by many patients and their families after discharge, especially if the patient suffered a myocardial infarction.

TTM is especially valuable for assessing the effects of drugs and for diagnosing and managing paroxysmal arrhythmias. In both cases, TTM can eliminate the need for admitting the patient for evaluation and a potentially lengthy hospital stay.

Understanding TTM equipment

TTM requires three main pieces of equipment: an ECG recorder-transmitter, a standard telephone line, and a receiver. The ECG recorder-transmitter converts electrical activity picked up from the patient's heart into acoustic waves. Some models contain built-in memory that stores a recording of the activity so the patient can transmit it later.

A standard telephone line is used to transmit information. The receiver converts the acoustic waves transmitted over the telephone line into ECG activity, which is then recorded on ECG paper for interpretation and documentation in the patient's chart. The recorder-transmitter uses two types of electrodes applied to the finger and chest. These electrodes produce ECG tracings similar to those of a standard 12-lead ECG.

Credit card-size recorder

One recently developed recorder operates on a battery and is about the size of a credit card. When a patient becomes symptomatic, he holds the back of the card firmly to the center of his chest and pushes the start button. Four electrodes located on the back of the card sense electrical activity and record it. The card can store 30 seconds of activity and can later transmit the recording across phone lines for evaluation by a clinician.

How leads work

The 12-lead ECG records cardiac activity using a series of electrodes placed on the patient's extremities and chest wall. The 12 leads include three bipolar limb leads (I, II, III), three unipolar augmented limb leads (aV_R, aV_L, and aV_F), and six unipolar precordial, or chest, leads (V_1, V_2, V_3, V_4, V_5, and V_6). These leads provide 12 different views of the heart's electrical activity. (See *A look at the leads*.)

Up, down, and across

Scanning up, down, and across the heart, each lead transmits information about a different area. The waveforms obtained from each lead vary depending on the location of the lead in relation to the wave of depolarization, or electrical stimulus, passing through the myocardium.

Limb leads

The six limb leads record electrical activity in the heart's frontal plane. This plane is a view through the middle of the heart from top to bottom. Electrical activity is recorded from the anterior to the posterior axis.

Precordial leads

The six precordial leads provide information on electrical activity in the heart's horizontal plane, a transverse view through the middle of the heart, dividing it into upper and lower portions. Electrical activity is recorded from either a superior or an inferior approach.

The electrical axis

Besides assessing 12 different leads, a 12-lead ECG records the heart's electrical axis. The axis is a measurement of electrical impulses flowing through the heart.

As impulses travel through the heart, they generate small electrical forces called instantaneous vectors. The mean of these vectors represents the force and direction of the wave of depolarization through the heart. That mean is called the electrical axis. It's also called the mean instantaneous vector and the mean QRS vector.

Havin' a heart wave

In a healthy heart, impulses originate in the sinoatrial (SA) node, travel through the atria to the atrioventricular

---

Why a 12-lead ECG?

A 12-lead ECGs is usually performed on patients having an MI. In addition, this diagnostic test may be ordered for patients with the following conditions that also affect the heart's electrical system:

• heart chamber enlargement

• digitalis glycoside or other drug toxicity

• electrolyte imbalances

• pulmonary embolism

• pericarditis

• hypothermia.

A look at the leads

Each of the 12 leads views the heart from a different angle. These illustrations show the direction of each lead relative to the wave of depolarization (shown in color) and list the 12 views of the heart.

Views reflected on a 12-lead ECG

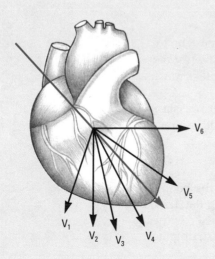

Leads	View of heart
Standard limb leads (bipolar)	
I	lateral wall
II	inferior wall
III	inferior wall
Augmented limb leads (unipolar)	
aV_R	no specific view
aV_L	lateral wall
aV_F	inferior wall
Precordial, or chest, leads (unipolar)	
V_1	anteroseptal wall
V_2	anteroseptal wall
V_3	anterior wall
V_4	anterior wall
V_5	lateral wall
V_6	lateral wall

(AV) node, and then to the ventricles. Most of the movement of the impulses is downward and to the left, the direction of a normal axis.

Swingin' on an axis

In an unhealthy heart, axis direction varies. That's because the direction of electrical activity swings away from areas of damage or necrosis. Knowing the normal deflection of each lead will help you evaluate whether the electrical axis is normal or abnormal.

Obtaining a 12-lead ECG

You may be required to obtain an ECG in an emergency. In order to obtain the ECG, you'll need to:
- gather the appropriate supplies
- explain the procedure to the patient
- attach the electrodes properly
- know how to use an ECG machine
- interpret the recordings.

Let's take a look at each aspect of the procedure.

Preparing for the recording

First, gather all the necessary supplies, including the ECG machine, recording paper, electrodes, and gauze pads. Take them to the patient's bedside. Then perform the following actions.

Explain the procedure

Next, tell the patient that the doctor has ordered an ECG, and explain the procedure. Emphasize that the test takes about 10 minutes and that it's a safe and painless way to evaluate cardiac function.

Answer the patient's questions, and offer reassurance. Preparing him well helps alleviate anxiety and promote cooperation.

Prepare the patient

Ask the patient to lie supine in the center of the bed with his arms at his sides. If he can't tolerate lying flat, raise the head of the bed to semi-Fowler's position. Ensure privacy, and expose the patient's arms, legs, and chest, draping him for comfort.

Select electrode sites

Select the areas where you'll attach the electrodes. Choose spots that are flat and fleshy, not muscular or bony. Shave the area if it's excessively hairy. Clean excess oil or other substances from the skin to enhance electrode contact. *Remember — the better the electrode contact, the better the recording.*

Making the recording

The 12-lead ECG offers 12 different views of the heart, just as 12 photographers snapping the same picture would produce 12 different snapshots. To help ensure an accurate recording — or set of "pictures" — the electrodes must be applied correctly. Inaccurate placement of an electrode by greater than $\frac{3}{5}''$ (1.5 cm) from its standardized position may lead to inaccurate waveforms and an incorrect ECG interpretation.

The 12-lead ECG requires four electrodes on the limbs and six across the front of the chest wall.

Going out on a limb lead

To record the bipolar limb leads I, II, and III and the unipolar limb leads aV_R, aV_L, and aV_F, place electrodes on both of the patient's arms and on his left leg. The right leg also receives an electrode, but that electrode acts as a ground and doesn't contribute to the waveform.

Where the wires go

Finding where to place the electrodes on the patient is easy because each leadwire is labeled or color coded. (See *Monitoring the limb leads*, pages 230 to 231.) For example, a wire — usually white — might be labeled "RA" for right arm. Another wire — usually red — might be labeled "LL" for left leg. Precordial leads are also labeled or color coded according to which wire corresponds to which lead.

No low leads allowed

To record the six precordial leads (V_1 through V_6), position the electrodes on specific areas of the anterior chest wall. (See *Positioning precordial electrodes*, page 232.) If they're placed too low, the ECG tracing will be inaccurate.
• Place lead V_1 over the fourth intercostal space at the right sternal border. To find the space, locate the sternal

(Text continues on page 232.)

Monitoring the limb leads

These diagrams show electrode placement for the six limb leads. RA indicates right arm; LA, left arm; RL, right leg; and LL, left leg. The plus sign (+) indicates the positive pole, the minus sign (-) indicates the negative pole, and G indicates the ground. Below each diagram is a sample ECG recording for that lead.

Lead I
This lead connects the right arm (negative pole) with the left arm (positive pole).

Lead II
This lead connects the right arm (negative pole) with the left leg (positive pole).

Lead III
This lead connects the left arm (negative pole) with the left leg (positive pole).

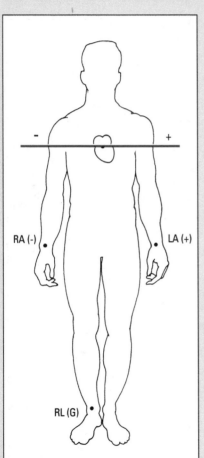

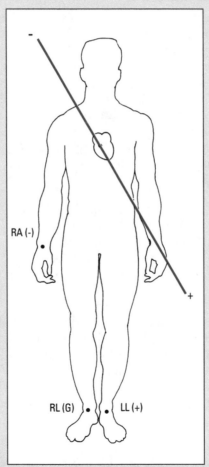

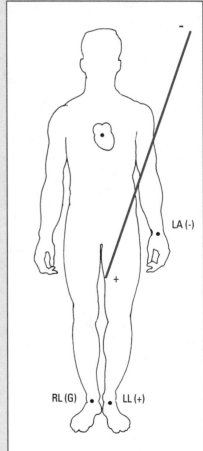

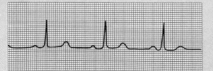

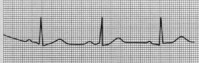

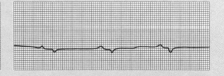

Lead aV_R

This lead connects the right arm (positive pole) with the heart (negative pole).

Lead aV_L

This lead connects the left arm (positive pole) with the heart (negative pole).

Lead aV_F

This lead connects the left leg (positive pole) with the heart (negative pole).

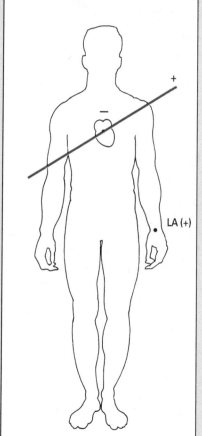

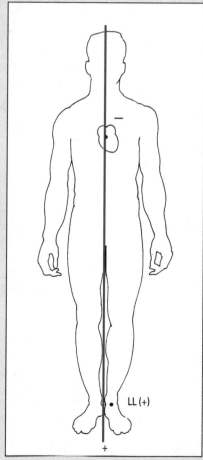

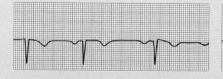

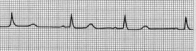

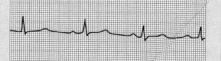

Positioning precordial electrodes

The precordial leads complement the limb leads to provide a complete view of the heart. To record the precordial leads, place the electrodes as shown below.

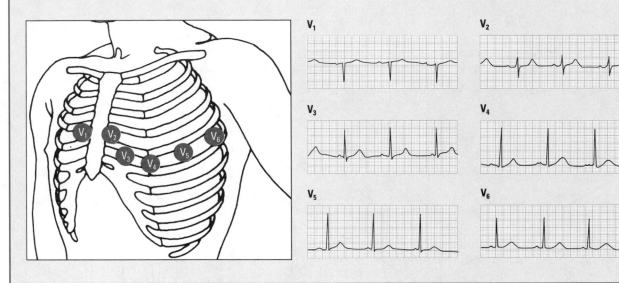

notch at the second rib and feel your way down along the sternal border until you reach the fourth intercostal space.

- Place lead V_2 just opposite V_1, over the fourth intercostal space at the *left* sternal border.
- Place lead V_3 midway between V_2 and V_4.
- Place lead V_4 over the fifth intercostal space at the left midclavicular line. *Tip:* Placing lead V_4 before lead V_3 makes it easier to see where to place lead V_3.
- Place lead V_5 over the fifth intercostal space at the left anterior axillary line.
- Place lead V_6 over the fifth intercostal space at the left midaxillary line. If you've placed leads V_4 through V_6 correctly, they should line up horizontally.

Give me more electrodes!

In addition to the 12-lead ECG, two other ECGs may be used for diagnostic purposes: the posterior-lead ECG and the right chest lead ECG. These ECGs use chest leads to assess areas standard 12-lead ECGs can't.

Seeing behind your back

Because of lung and muscle barriers, the usual chest leads can't "see" the heart's posterior surface to record myocardial damage there. So some doctors add three posterior leads to the 12-lead ECG: leads V_7, V_8, and V_9. These leads are placed opposite anterior leads V_4, V_5, and V_6, on the left side of the patient's back, following the same horizontal line.

On rare occasions, a doctor may request right-sided posterior leads. These leads are labeled V_7R, V_8R, and V_9R and are placed on the right side of the patient's back. Their placement is a mirror image of the electrodes on the left side of the back. This type of ECG provides information on the right posterior area of the heart.

Checking out the right chest

The usual 12-lead ECG evaluates only the left ventricle. If the right ventricle needs to be assessed for damage or dysfunction, the doctor may order a right chest lead ECG. For example, a patient with an inferior wall MI might have a right chest lead ECG to rule out right ventricular involvement.

With this type of ECG, the six leads are placed on the right side of the chest in a mirror image of the standard precordial lead placement. Electrodes start at the left sternal border and swing down under the right breast area.

Know your machine

Once you understand how to position the electrodes, familiarize yourself with the ECG machine. Machines come in two types: multichannel recorders and single-channel recorders.

With a multichannel recorder, you'll attach all electrodes to the patient at once and the machine prints a simultaneous view of all leads. With a single-channel recorder, you'll obtain a strip for one lead at a time by attaching and removing electrodes and stopping and starting the tracing each time. To begin recording the patient's ECG, follow these steps:

• Plug the cord of the ECG machine into a grounded outlet. If the machine operates on a charged battery, it may not need to be plugged in.
• Place one or all of the electrodes on the patient's chest, based on the type of machine you're using.

• Make sure all leads are securely attached, and then turn on the machine.

• Instruct the patient to relax, lie still, and breathe normally. Ask him not to talk during the recording to prevent distortion of the ECG tracing.

• Set the ECG paper speed selector to 25mm/second. If necessary, enter the patient's identification data. Then calibrate or standardize the machine according to the manufacturer's instructions.

• Press the AUTO button and record the ECG. If you're performing a right chest lead ECG, select the appropriate button for recording.

• Observe the quality of the tracing. When the machine finishes the recording, turn it off.

• Remove the electrodes and clean the patient's skin.

Interpreting the recording

ECG tracings from multichannel and single-channel machines look the same. (See *Multichannel ECG recording*.) The printout will show the patient's name and room number and, possibly, his medical record number. At the top of the printout, you'll see the patient's heart rate and wave durations, measured in seconds.

Some machines are also capable of recording ST-segment elevation and depression. The name of the lead will appear next to each 6-second strip.

Get out your pen

Make sure to write this information on the printout: date, time, doctor's name, and special circumstances. For example, you might record an abnormal electrolyte level, related drug treatment, abnormal placement of the electrodes, or the presence of an artificial pacemaker or chest pain.

Remember: ECGs are legal documents. They belong on the patient's chart and must be saved for future reference and comparison with baseline strips.

Signal-averaged ECG

Although most patients will be tested with a 12-lead ECG, some may benefit from being tested with a signal-averaged ECG. This simple, noninvasive test helps identify pa-

Multichannel ECG recording

The top of a 12-lead ECG recording usually shows patient identification information along with the interpretation done by the machine. A rhythm strip is often included at the bottom of the recording.

Standardization

Look for the standardization marks on the recording, normally 10 small squares high. If the patient has high voltage complexes, the marks will be half as high. You'll also notice that lead markers separate the lead recordings on the paper and that each lead is labeled.

Also familiarize yourself with the order in which the leads are arranged on the ECG tracing. Getting accustomed to the layout of the tracing will help you interpret the ECG more quickly and accurately.

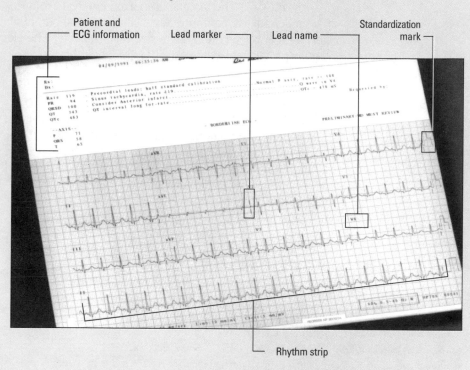

Patient and ECG information — Lead marker — Lead name — Standardization mark

Rhythm strip

tients at risk for sudden death from sustained ventricular tachycardia.

The test uses a computer to identify late electrical potentials — tiny impulses that follow normal depolarization. Late electrical potentials can't be detected by a 12-lead ECG.

Who gets the signal?

Patients prone to ventricular tachycardia — those who've had a recent MI or unexplained syncope, for example— are good candidates for a signal-averaged ECG. Keep in mind that 12-lead ECGs should be done when the patient is free of arrhythmias.

Noise free

A signal-averaged ECG is a noise-free, surface ECG recording taken from three specialized leads for several hundred heartbeats. (See *Electrode placement for a signal-averaged ECG*.) The test takes approximately 10 minutes. The machine's computer detects late electrical potentials and then enlarges them so they're recognizable. The electrodes for a signal-averaged ECG are labeled X-, X+, Y-, Y+, Z- , Z+, and ground.

The machine averages signals from those leads to produce one representative QRS complex without artifacts. This process cancels noise, electrical impulses that don't occur as a repetitious pattern or with the same consistent timing as the QRS complex. That additional noise is filtered out so late electrical potentials can be detected. Muscle noise can't be filtered, however, so the patient must lie still for the test.

Electrode placement for a signal-averaged ECG

Positioning electrodes for a signal-averaged ECG is much different than for a 12-lead ECG. Here's one method:

1. Place the positive X electrode at the left fourth intercostal space, midaxillary line.
2. Place the negative X electrode at the right fourth intercostal space, midaxillary line.
3. Place the positive Y electrode at the left iliac crest.
4. Place the negative Y electrode at the superior aspect of the manubrium of the sternum.
5. Place the positive Z electrode at the fourth intercostal space left of the sternum.
6. Place the ground (G) on the lower right at the eighth rib.
7. Reposition the patient on his side, or have him sit forward. Then place the negative Z electrode on his back (not shown), directly posterior to the positive Z electrode.
8. Attach all the leads to the electrodes, being careful not to dislodge the posterior lead. Now, you can obtain the tracing.

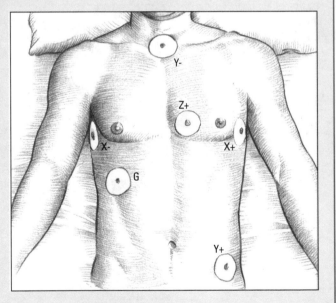

Quick quiz

1. The precordial leads are placed:
   A. on the anterior chest starting with the fourth intercostal space at the right sternal border.
   B. on the lateral chest starting with the fourth intercostal space at the left midaxillary line.
   C. on the posterior chest wall starting with the fourth intercostal space at the midscapular line.

Answer: A. Lead V_1 is placed anteriorly between the fourth and fifth ribs at the right sternal border. Leads V_2 to V_6 are then placed accordingly.

2. A signal-averaged ECG measures:
   A. electrical impulses from the SA node.
   B. late electrical potentials throughout the heart.
   C. action potentials of individual cardiac cells.

Answer: B. Signal-averaged ECGs measure late electrical potentials, tiny electrical impulses that occur after depolarization and can cause ventricular tachycardia.

3. A posterior-lead ECG is used to assess:
   A. posterior myocardial damage.
   B. inferior myocardial damage.
   C. damage to the interventricular septum.

Answer: A. This ECG assesses damage to the posterior surface of the heart, an area a standard 12-lead ECG can't detect.

4. The difference between a multichannel 12-lead ECG and a single-channel ECG is that a single-channel ECG:
   A. requires 15 leads.
   B. can't be used at the bedside.
   C. requires rearranging electrodes for each lead.

Answer: C. A single-channel ECG must be obtained lead by lead.

5. A 12-lead ECG is used to assess function of the:
   A. right ventricle.
   B. left ventricle.
   C. right and left ventricle simultaneously.

Answer: B. A 12-lead ECG gives a more complete view of the heart's electrical activity than a rhythm strip and is used to assess left ventricular function.

Scoring

☆☆☆   If you answered all five items correctly, great job! You're the new leader of the 12-lead ECG pack!

☆☆   If you answered three or four correctly, we're impressed! Your leadership qualities are obvious, and you're next in line for a top job!

☆   If you answered fewer than three correctly, that's cool. You're a promising leader-in-training.

Interpreting a 12-lead ECG

Just the facts

This chapter describes how to interpret a 12-lead electrocardiogram (ECG). By providing 12 different views of the heart's electrical activity, this test helps diagnose serious cardiac conditions. In this chapter, you'll learn:

♦ how to examine each lead's waveforms for abnormalities

♦ how to determine the heart's electrical axis

♦ what ECG changes occur in the patient with angina

♦ how to differentiate the types of acute myocardial infarction (MI) using a 12-lead ECG

♦ what 12-lead ECG changes occur with bundle-branch block.

A look at interpreting a 12-lead ECG

To interpret a 12-lead ECG, use the systematic approach outlined here.

1. Check the ECG tracing to see if it's technically correct. Make sure the baseline is free from electrical interference and drift.

2. Scan the limb leads I, II, and III. The R-wave voltage in lead II should equal the sum of the R voltage in leads I and III. Lead aV_R should always be negative. If these rules aren't met, the tracing may be recorded incorrectly.

3. Locate the lead markers on the waveform. Lead markers are the points where one lead changes to another.

4. Check the standardization markings to make sure all leads were recorded with the ECG machine's amplitude at the same setting. Standardization markings are usually located at the beginning of the strip.

5. Assess the heart rate and rhythm as you learned in earlier chapters.

6. Determine the heart's electrical axis. Use either the quadrant method or the degree method, described later in this chapter.

7. Examine limb leads I, II, and III. The R wave in lead II should be taller than in lead I. The waves in lead III should be smaller versions of the waves in lead I. The P wave or QRS complex may be inverted. Each lead should have flat ST segments and upright T waves and Q waves should be absent.

8. Examine limb leads aV_L, aV_F, and aV_R. The tracings from leads aV_L and aV_F should be similar, but aV_F should have taller P and R waves. Lead aV_R has no diagnostic value. Its P wave, QRS complex, and T wave should be deflected downward.

9. Examine the R wave in the precordial leads. Normally, the R wave — the first positive deflection of the QRS complex — gets progressively taller from lead V_1 to lead V_5. Then it gets slightly smaller in lead V_6. (See *R-wave progression.*)

10. Examine the S wave — the negative deflection after an R wave — in the precordial leads. It appears extremely deep in lead V_1 and becomes progressively more shallow, usually disappearing at lead V_5.

All about waves

As you examine each lead, note where changes occur so you can identify the area of the heart affected. Remember that P waves should be upright; however, they may be inverted in lead aV_R or biphasic or inverted in leads III, aV_L, and V_1.

PR intervals should always be constant, just like QRS-complex durations. QRS-complex deflections will vary. Observe for pathologic Q waves.

Elevated one minute, depressed the next

ST segments should be isoelectric or have minimal deviation. ST-segment elevation greater than 1 mm above the baseline and ST-segment depression greater than 0.5 mm below the baseline are considered abnormal. Leads facing an injured area will have ST-segment elevations, and leads facing away will display ST-segment depressions.

That old, changeable T wave

The T wave normally deflects upward in leads I, II, and V_3 through V_6. It's inverted in lead aV_R and variable in the other leads. T-wave changes have many causes and aren't always a reason for alarm. Excessively tall, flat, or inverted T waves occurring with symptoms such as chest pain indicate ischemia.

Split-second duration

A normal Q wave generally has a duration of less than 0.04 second. An abnormal Q wave has either a duration of more than 0.04 second, a depth greater than 4 mm, or a height one-third of the R wave.

Abnormal Q waves indicate myocardial necrosis. These waves develop when depolarization can't take its normal path due to damaged tissue in the area. *Remember that lead aV_R normally has a large Q wave, so disregard this lead when searching for abnormal Q waves.*

Finding the electrical axis

The electrical axis is the average direction of the heart's electrical activity during ventricular depolarization. Leads

R-wave progression

These waveforms show normal R-wave progression through the precordial leads. Note that the R wave is the first positive deflection in the QRS complex. Also note that the S wave gets smaller, or regresses, from V_1 to V_6 until it finally disappears.

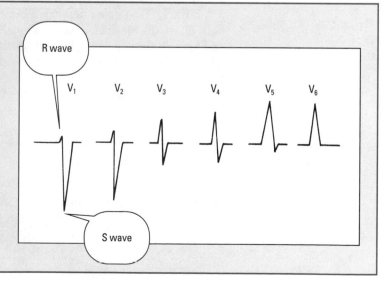

placed on the body sense the sum of the heart's electrical activity and record it as waveforms.

Cross my heart

You can determine your patient's electrical axis by examining the waveforms recorded from the six frontal plane leads: I, II, III, aV_R, aV_L, and aV_F. Imaginary lines drawn from each of the leads intersect the center of the heart and form a diagram known as the hexaxial reference system. (See *Hexaxial reference system.*)

Where the axis falls

An axis that falls between 0 and +90 degrees is considered normal. An axis between +90 and +180 degrees indicates right axis deviation, and one between 0 and -90 degrees indicates left axis deviation. An axis between -180 and -90 degrees indicates extreme axis deviation and is called an indeterminate axis.

To determine your patient's electrical axis, use one of the two methods described below.

Quadrant method

The quadrant method, a fast, easy way to plot the heart's axis, involves observing the main deflection of the QRS complex in leads I and aV_F. (See *Quadrant method,* page 244.) Lead I indicates whether impulses are moving to the right or left, and lead aV_F indicates whether they're moving up or down.

If the QRS-complex deflection is positive or upright in both leads, the electrical axis is normal. If lead I is upright and lead aV_F points down, left axis deviation exists.

Right on and right in

When lead I points downward and lead aV_F is upright, right axis deviation exists. Both waves pointing down signal indeterminate axis deviation.

Degree method

A more precise axis calculation, the degree method gives an exact degree measurement of the electrical axis. (See *Degree method,* page 245.) It also allows you to determine the axis even if the QRS complex isn't clearly positive or negative in leads I and aV_F. To use this method, follow these steps.

Memory jogger

Think of the QRS-complex deflections in leads I and aV_F as thumbs pointing up or down. Two thumbs up is normal; anything else is abnormal.

Hexaxial reference system

The hexaxial reference system consists of six bisecting lines, each representing one of the six limb leads, and a circle, representing the heart. The intersection of all lines divides the circle into equal, 30-degree segments.

Shifting degrees

Note that + 0° appears at the 3 o'clock position (positive pole lead I). Moving counterclockwise, the degrees become increasingly negative, until reaching ± 180°, at the 9 o'clock position (negative pole lead I).

The bottom half of the circle contains the corresponding positive degrees. However, a positive-degree designation doesn't necessarily mean that the pole is positive.

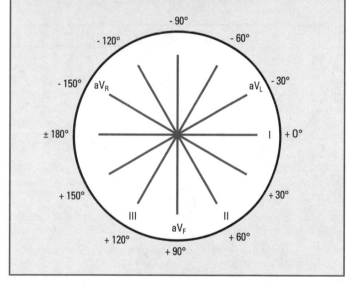

1. Review all six leads, and identify the one that contains either the smallest QRS complex or the complex with an equal deflection above and below the baseline.

2. Use the hexaxial diagram to identify the lead perpendicular to this lead. For example, if lead I has the smallest QRS complex, then the lead perpendicular to the line representing lead I would be lead aV$_F$.

3. After you've identified the perpendicular lead, examine its QRS complex. If the electrical activity is moving toward the positive pole of a lead, the QRS complex deflects up-

Quadrant method

This chart will help you quickly determine the direction of a patient's electrical axis. Just observe the deflections of the QRS complexes in leads I and aV$_F$. Then check the chart to determine whether the patient's axis is normal or has a left, right, or extreme axis deviation.

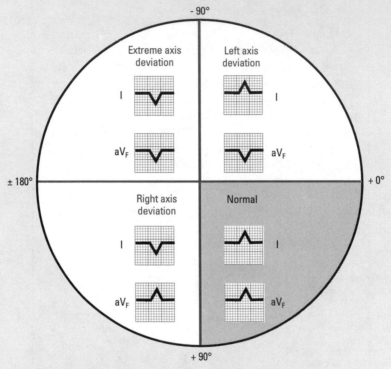

ward. If it's moving away from the positive pole of a lead, the QRS complex deflects downward.

4. Plot this information on the hexaxial diagram to determine the direction of the electrical axis.

Axis deviation

Finding a patient's electrical axis can help confirm a diagnosis or narrow the range of possible diagnoses. (See *Causes of axis deviation*, page 246.) Factors that influence the location of the axis include the heart's position in the chest, the heart's size, the patient's body size or type, the conduction pathways, and the force of the electrical impulses being generated.

Degree method

The degree method of determining axis deviation allows you to identify a patient's electrical axis by degrees on the hexaxial system, not just by quadrant. To use this method, take the following steps.

Step 1

Identify the lead with the smallest QRS complex or the equiphasic QRS complex. In this example, it's lead III.

Lead I 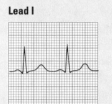 **Lead II** 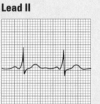 **Lead III** 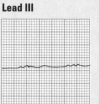 **Lead aV$_R$** 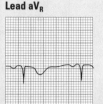 **Lead aV$_L$** 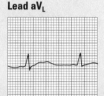 **Lead aV$_F$**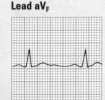

Step 2

Locate the axis for lead III on the hexaxial diagram. Then find the axis perpendicular to it, which is the axis for lead aV$_R$.

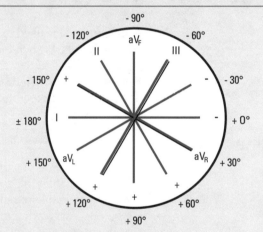

Step 3

Now, examine the QRS complex in lead aV$_R$, noting whether the deflection is positive or negative. As you can see, the QRS complex for this lead is negative. This tells you that the electric current is moving toward the negative pole of aV$_R$, which, on the hexaxial diagram, is in the right lower quadrant at + 30°. So the electrical axis here is normal at + 30°.

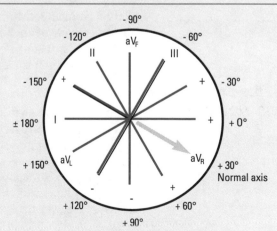

Remember that electrical activity in the heart swings away from areas of damage or necrosis, so the damaged part of the heart will be the last area to be depolarized. For example, in right bundle-branch block, the impulse travels quickly down the normal left side and then moves slowly down the damaged right side. This shifts the electrical forces to the right, causing right axis deviation.

No worries

Axis deviation isn't always cause for alarm, and it isn't always cardiac in origin. For example, infants and children normally have right axis deviation. Pregnant women normally have left axis deviation.

Disorders affecting 12-lead ECGs

A 12-lead ECG is used to diagnose such conditions as angina, bundle-branch block, and MI. By reviewing sample ECGs, you'll know what classic signs to look for. Here's a rundown on those three common cardiac conditions and what 12-lead ECG signs to look for.

Angina

During an episode of angina, the myocardium demands more oxygen than the coronary arteries can deliver. The arteries are unable to deliver enough blood, most often as a result of a narrowing of the arteries from coronary artery disease, a condition that may be complicated by platelet clumping, thrombus formation, or vasospasm.

An episode of angina usually lasts between 2 and 10 minutes. The closer to 30 minutes the pain lasts, the more likely the pain is from an MI rather than angina.

Stable or unstable?

You may hear the term *stable angina* applied to certain conditions and *unstable angina* applied to others. In stable angina, pain is triggered by exertion or stress and is often relieved by rest. Each episode follows the same pattern.

Unstable angina, on the other hand, is more easily provoked, often waking the patient. It's also unpredictable and worsens over time. The patient with unstable angina

---

Causes of axis deviation

This list covers common causes of right and left axis deviation.

Left
- Normal variation
- Inferior wall MI
- Left anterior hemiblock
- Wolff-Parkinson-White syndrome
- Mechanical shifts (ascites, pregnancy, tumors)
- Left bundle-branch block
- Left ventricular hypertrophy
- Aging

Right
- Normal variation
- Lateral wall MI
- Left posterior hemiblock
- Right bundle-branch block
- Emphysema
- Right ventricular hypertrophy

is treated as a medical emergency. The onset of unstable angina often portends MI.

In addition to the ECG changes noted below, the patient with unstable angina will complain of chest pain that may or may not radiate. The pain is generally more intense and lasts longer than the pain of stable angina. The patient may also be pale, clammy, nauseous, and anxious.

Fleeting change of heart

Most patients with either form of angina show ischemic changes on the ECG only during the angina attack. (See *ECG changes associated with angina*.) Because these changes may be fleeting, always obtain an order for, and perform, a 12-lead ECG as soon as the patient reports chest pain.

The ECG will allow you to analyze all parts of the heart and pinpoint which area and coronary artery are involved. By recognizing danger early, you may be able to prevent an MI or even death.

Drugs are a key component of anginal treatment and may include nitrates, beta blockers, calcium channel blockers, and aspirin to reduce platelet aggregation.

Bundle-branch block

One potential complication of an MI is a bundle-branch block. In this disorder, either the left or the right bundle branch fails to conduct impulses. A bundle-branch block

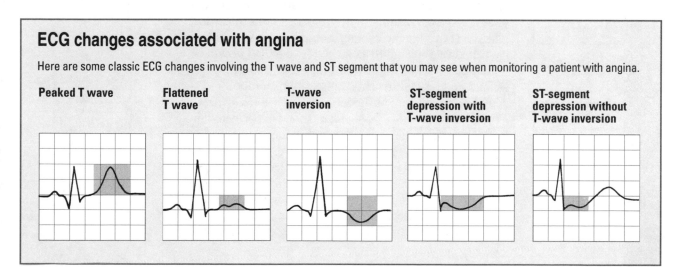

ECG changes associated with angina

Here are some classic ECG changes involving the T wave and ST segment that you may see when monitoring a patient with angina.

Peaked T wave **Flattened T wave** **T-wave inversion** **ST-segment depression with T-wave inversion** **ST-segment depression without T-wave inversion**

that occurs farther down the left bundle, in the posterior or anterior fascicle, is called a hemiblock.

Some blocks require treatment with a temporary pacemaker. Others are monitored only to detect whether they progress to a more complete block.

Impulsive behavior

In a bundle-branch block, the impulse travels down the unaffected bundle branch and then from one myocardial cell to the next to depolarize the ventricle.

Because this cell-to-cell conduction progresses much more slowly than the conduction along the specialized cells of the conduction system, ventricular depolarization is prolonged.

Wide world of complexes

Prolonged ventricular depolarization means the QRS complex will be widened. The normal width of the complex is 0.06 to 0.10 second. If the width increases to greater than 0.12 second, a bundle-branch block is present.

Once you identify a bundle-branch block, examine lead V_1, which lies to the right of the heart, and lead V_6, which lies to the left of the heart. You'll use these leads to determine whether the block is in the right or the left bundle.

Right bundle-branch block

Right bundle-branch block (RBBB) occurs with such conditions as anterior wall MI, coronary artery disease, and pulmonary embolism. It may also occur without cardiac disease. If this block develops as the heart rate increases, it's called rate-related RBBB. (See *How RBBB occurs*.)

In this disorder, the QRS complex is greater than 0.12 second and has a different configuration, sometimes resembling rabbit ears or the letter "M." (See *Recognizing RBBB,* page 250.) Septal depolarization isn't affected in lead V_1, so the initial small R wave remains.

The R wave is followed by an S wave, which represents left ventricular depolarization, and a tall R wave (called R prime, or R′), which represents late right ventricular depolarization. The T wave is negative in this lead. However, that deflection is called a secondary T-wave change and is of no clinical significance.

How RBBB occurs

In right bundle-branch block (RBBB), the initial impulse activates the interventricular septum from left to right, just as in normal activation (arrow 1). Next, the left bundle branch activates the left ventricle (arrow 2). The impulse then crosses the interventricular septum to activate the right ventricle (arrow 3).

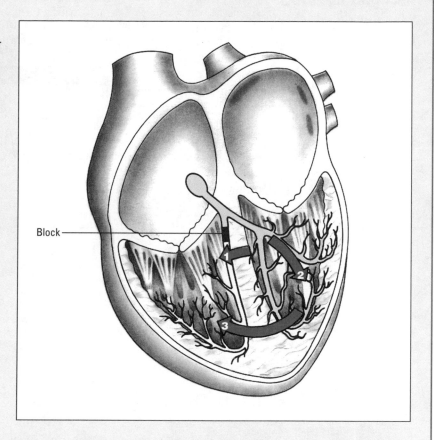

Block

Opposing moves

The opposite occurs in lead V_6. A small Q wave is followed by depolarization of the left ventricle, which produces a tall R wave. Depolarization of the right ventricle then causes a broad S wave. In V_6, the T wave should be positive.

Left bundle-branch block

Left bundle-branch block (LBBB) never occurs normally. This block is usually caused by hypertensive heart disease, aortic stenosis, degenerative changes of the conduction system, or coronary artery disease. (See *How LBBB occurs,* page 251.) When it occurs along with an anterior wall MI, it usually signals complete heart block, which requires insertion of a pacemaker.

Recognizing RBBB

This 12-lead ECG shows the characteristic changes of right bundle-branch block (RBBB). In lead V_1, note the rsR´ pattern and T-wave inversion. In lead V_6, see the widened S wave and the upright T wave. Also note the prolonged QRS complexes.

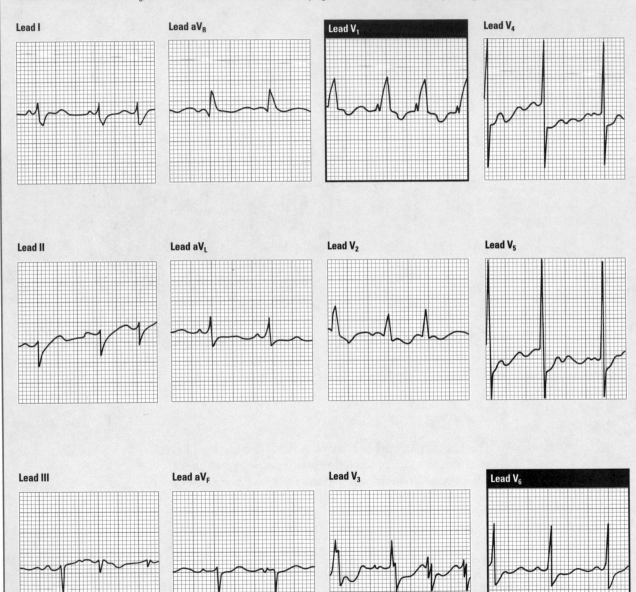

How LBBB occurs

In left bundle-branch block, the impulse first travels down the right bundle branch (arrow 1). Then the impulse activates the interventricular septum from right to left (arrow 2), the opposite of normal activation. Finally, the impulse activates the left ventricle (arrow 3).

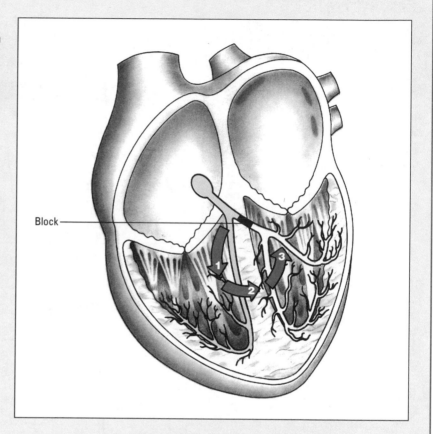

Block

One ventricle after another

In LBBB, the QRS complex will be greater than 0.12 second because the ventricles are activated sequentially, not simultaneously. (See *Recognizing LBBB,* page 252.) As the wave of depolarization spreads from the right ventricle to the left, a wide S wave is produced in lead V_1, with a positive T wave. The S wave may be preceded by a Q wave or small R wave.

Slurring your R waves

In lead V_6, no initial Q wave occurs. A tall, notched R wave, or a slurred one, is produced as the impulse spreads from

Recognizing LBBB

This 12-lead ECG shows characteristic changes of a left bundle-branch block (LBBB). All leads have prolonged QRS complexes. In lead V_1, note the QS wave pattern. In lead V_6, you'll see the slurred R wave and T-wave inversion. The elevated ST segments and upright T waves in leads V_1 to V_4 are also common in LBBB.

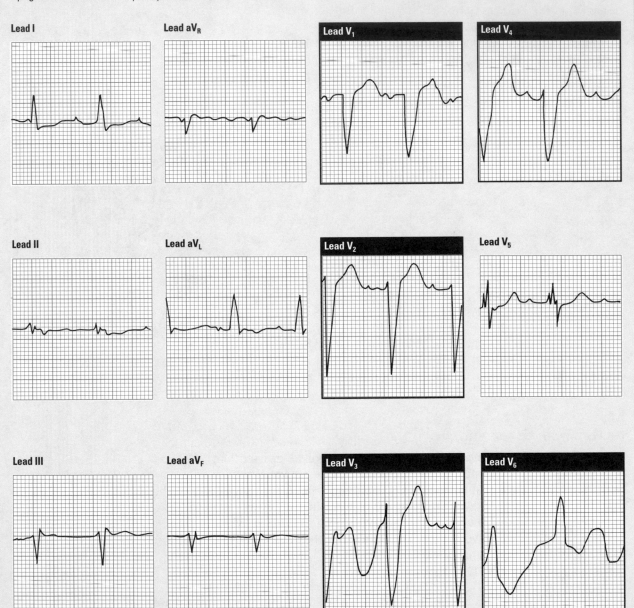

right to left. This initial positive deflection is a sign of LBBB. The T wave is negative.

Myocardial infarction

Unlike angina, pain from an MI lasts for at least 20 minutes, may persist for several hours, and is unrelieved by rest. MI usually occurs in the left ventricle, though the location varies depending on the coronary artery affected.

For as long as the myocardium is deprived of an oxygen-rich blood supply, an ECG will reflect the three pathologic changes of an MI: ischemia, injury, and infarction. (See *Reciprocal changes in an MI,* page 254.)

Zone of infarction

The area of myocardial necrosis is called the zone of infarction. Scar tissue eventually replaces the dead tissue, and the damage caused is irreversible.

The ECG change associated with a necrotic area is a pathologic Q wave, which results from lack of depolarization. Such Q waves are permanent. MIs that don't produce Q waves are called non–Q wave MIs.

Zone of injury

The zone of infarction is surrounded by the zone of injury, which shows up on an ECG as an elevated ST segment. ST-segment elevation results from a prolonged lack of blood supply.

Zone of ischemia

The outermost area is called the zone of ischemia and results from an interrupted blood supply. This zone is represented on an ECG by T-wave inversion. Changes in the zones of ischemia or injury are reversible.

From ischemia to injury

Generally, as an MI occurs, the patient experiences chest pain and an ECG shows such changes as ST-segment elevation, which indicates that myocardial injury is occurring. You'll also typically see T waves flatten and become inverted.

Rapid treatment can prevent myocardial necrosis. However, if symptoms persist for more than 6 hours, little can be done to prevent necrosis. That's one of the reasons patients are advised to seek medical attention as soon as symptoms begin.

Reciprocal changes in an MI

Ischemia, injury, and infarction — the three I's of myocardial infarction (MI) — produce characteristic ECG changes. Changes shown by the leads that reflect electrical activity in damaged areas are shown on the right.

Reciprocal leads, those opposite the damaged area, will show opposite ECG changes, as shown to the left of the illustration.

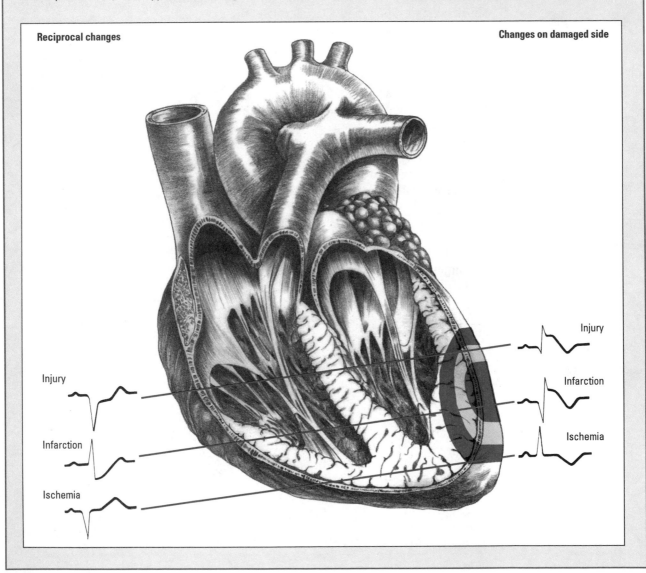

Reciprocal changes

Injury

Infarction

Ischemia

Changes on damaged side

Injury

Infarction

Ischemia

The telltale Q wave

Q waves can appear hours to days after an MI and signify that an entire thickness of the myocardium has become necrotic. Tall R waves in reciprocal leads can also develop. This type of MI is called a transmural, or Q-wave, MI.

Back to baseline

Knowing how long such changes last can help you determine how long ago an MI occurred. ST segments return to baseline within a few days to 2 weeks. Inverted T waves may persist for several months. Although not every patient who has had an MI develops Q waves, those who do keep them on their ECGs indefinitely.

What to do for an MI

The most important thing you can do for a patient with an MI is to remain vigilant about detecting changes in his condition and in his ECG. (See *Monitoring MI patients*.)

The primary goal of treatment for an MI is to limit the size of the infarction by decreasing cardiac workload and increasing oxygen supply to the myocardium. (See *Improving blood flow*, page 256.) Besides rest, pain relief, and supplemental oxygen, such medications as nitroglycerin, morphine sulfate, beta blockers, calcium channel blockers, angiotensin-converting enzyme (ACE) inhibitors, and antiarrhythmics are used. Thrombolytic therapy also may be prescribed to dissolve a thrombus occluding a coronary artery.

Mixed signals

Monitoring MI patients

Remember that specific leads monitor specific walls of the heart. Here's a quick overview of those leads.

• For an anterior wall MI, monitor lead V_1.
• For a septal wall MI, monitor lead V_1 or MCL_1 to pick up hallmark changes.
• For a lateral wall MI, monitor lead V_6 or MCL_6.
• For an inferior wall MI, monitor lead II.

Identifying types of an MI

The location of the MI is a critical factor in determining the most appropriate treatment and predicting probable complications. Characteristic ECG changes that occur with each type of MI are localized to the leads overlying the infarction site. (See *Locating myocardial damage*, page 256.) Here's a look at characteristic ECG changes that occur with different types of MIs.

Improving blood flow

Increasing the blood supply to the heart of a patient who has had an MI can help prevent further damage to his heart. Besides medications, blood flow to the heart can be improved by:

• intra-aortic balloon pump
• percutaneous transluminal coronary angioplasty
• atherectomy
• laser treatment
• stent placement
• coronary artery bypass graft.

Locating myocardial damage

After you've noted characteristic lead changes of an acute myocardial infarction, use this chart to identify the areas of damage. Match the lead changes in the second column with the affected wall in the first column and the artery involved in the third column. Column four shows reciprocal lead changes.

Wall affected	Leads	Artery involved	Reciprocal changes
Inferior (diaphragmatic)	II, III, aV$_F$	Right coronary artery	aV$_L$
Lateral	I, aV$_L$, V$_5$, V$_6$	Circumflex artery, branch of left anterior descending (LAD) artery	V$_1$, V$_2$
Anterior	V$_2$ to V$_4$	Left coronary artery, LAD artery	II, III, aV$_F$
Posterior	V$_1$, V$_2$	Right coronary artery, circumflex artery	R wave greater than S wave; depressed ST segments; elevated T wave
Anterolateral	I, aV$_L$, V$_4$ to V$_6$	LAD artery, circumflex artery	II, III, aV$_F$
Anteroseptal	V$_1$ to V$_3$	LAD artery	None

Anterior wall MI

The left anterior descending artery supplies blood to the anterior portion of the left ventricle. The artery supplies blood to the ventricular septum and portions of the right and left bundle-branch systems.

When the anterior descending artery becomes occluded, an anterior wall MI occurs. (See *Recognizing an anterior wall MI.*) Complications of an anterior wall MI include varying degrees of heart block, ventricular irritability, and left ventricular failure.

Recognizing an anterior wall MI

This 12-lead ECG shows typical characteristics of an anterior wall myocardial infarction (MI). Note that the R waves don't progress through the precordial leads. Also note the ST-segment elevation in leads V_2 to V_3. As expected, the reciprocal leads II, III, and aV_F show slight ST-segment depression. Axis deviation is normal at + 60 degrees.

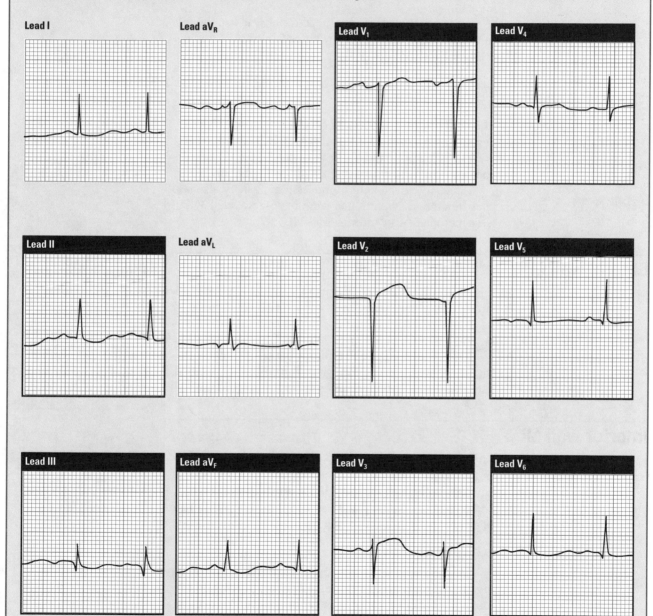

Changing the leads

An anterior wall MI causes characteristic ECG changes in leads V_2 to V_4. The precordial leads show poor R-wave progression because the left ventricle can't depolarize normally. ST-segment elevation and T-wave inversion are also present.

The reciprocal leads for the anterior wall are the inferior leads II, III, and aV_F. They show tall R waves and depressed ST segments.

Septal wall MI

The patient with a septal wall MI is at increased risk for developing a ventricular septal defect. ECG changes are present in leads V_1 and V_2. In those leads, the R wave disappears, the ST segment rises, and the T wave inverts.

Because the left anterior descending artery also supplies blood to the ventricular septum, a septal wall MI often accompanies an anterior wall MI.

Lateral wall MI

A lateral wall MI is usually caused by a blockage in the left circumflex artery and shows characteristic changes in the left lateral leads I, aV_L, and V_5 to V_6. The reciprocal leads for a lateral wall infarction are V_1 and V_2.

This type of infarction typically causes premature ventricular contractions and varying degrees of heart block. A lateral MI usually accompanies an anterior or inferior MI.

Memory jogger

To remember which leads are critical in diagnosing a lateral wall MI, think of the *l*'s in lateral MI and left lateral leads.

Inferior wall MI

An inferior wall MI is usually caused by occlusion of the right coronary artery and produces characteristic ECG changes in the inferior leads II, III, and aV_F and reciprocal changes in the lateral leads I and aV_L. (See *Recognizing an inferior wall MI*.) It's also called a diaphragmatic MI because the inferior wall of the heart lies over the diaphragm.

Patients with inferior wall MI are at risk for developing sinus bradycardia, sinus arrest, heart block, and premature ventricular contractions. This type of MI occurs alone, with a lateral wall MI, or with a right ventricular MI.

Recognizing an inferior wall MI

This 12-lead ECG shows the characteristic changes of an inferior wall myocardial infarction (MI). In leads II, III, and aV$_F$, note the T-wave inversion, ST-segment elevation, and pathologic Q waves. In leads I and aV$_L$, note the slight ST-segment depression, a reciprocal change. This ECG shows left axis deviation at -60 degrees.

Lead I
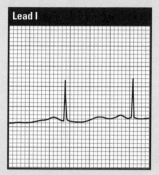

Lead aV$_R$
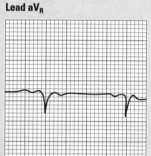

Lead V$_1$
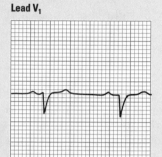

Lead V$_4$
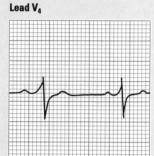

Lead II
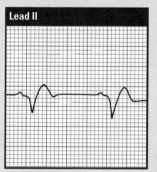

Lead aV$_L$
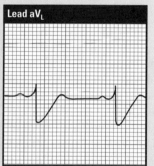

Lead V$_2$
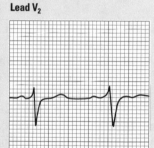

Lead V$_5$
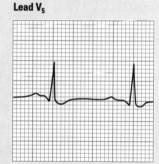

Lead III
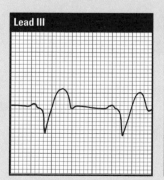

Lead aV$_F$
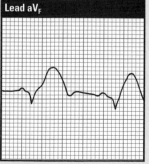

Lead V$_3$
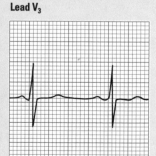

Lead V$_6$
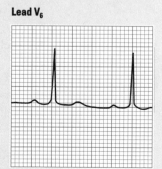

Right ventricular MI

A right ventricular MI usually follows occlusion of the right coronary artery. This type of MI rarely occurs alone. In fact, 40% of all patients with an inferior wall MI also suffer a right ventricular MI.

A right ventricular MI can lead to right ventricular failure or right bundle-branch block. The classic changes are ST-segment elevation, pathologic Q waves, and inverted T waves in the right precordial leads V_2R to V_6R.

Take the right lead

Identifying a right ventricular MI is difficult without information from the right precordial leads. If those leads aren't available, you can observe leads II, III, and aV_F or watch leads V_1, V_2, and V_3 for elevated ST segments. If a right ventricular MI has occurred, use lead V_1 to monitor for further damage.

Posterior wall MI

A posterior wall MI is caused by occlusion of either the right coronary artery or the left circumflex arteries. This MI produces reciprocal changes on leads V_1 and V_2.

Classic ECG changes for a posterior wall MI include tall R waves, ST-segment depression, and upright T waves. Posterior infarctions usually accompany inferior infarctions. Information about the posterior wall and pathologic Q waves that might occur can be obtained from leads V_7 to V_9 using a posterior ECG.

Quick quiz

1. Your patient's ECG shows positively deflected QRS complexes in leads I and aV$_F$. Using the four-quadrant method for determining axis, you determine that he has:
- A. a normal axis.
- B. left axis deviation.
- C. right axis deviation.

Answer: A. If the QRS-complex deflection is positive or upright in both leads, the electrical axis is normal.

2. Your patient's ECG shows a negatively deflected QRS complex in lead I and a positively deflected one in lead aV$_F$. Using the four-quadrant method for determining axis, you determine that he has:
- A. a normal axis.
- B. left axis deviation.
- C. right axis deviation.

Answer: C. When lead I points downward and lead aV$_F$ is upright, right axis deviation exists. Both waves pointing down signals indeterminate axis deviation.

3. If your patient has T-wave inversion, ST-segment elevation, and pathologic Q waves in leads II, III, and aV$_F$, suspect an acute MI in the:
- A. anterior wall.
- B. inferior wall.
- C. lateral wall.

Answer: B. Leads II, III, and aV$_F$ face the inferior wall of the left ventricle, so the ECG changes there are indicative of an acute inferior wall MI.

4. If a patient's QRS complex has an R′ wave in V$_1$, suspect:
- A. right ventricular hypertrophy.
- B. left ventricular hypertrophy.
- C. RBBB.

Answer: C. In RBBB, depolarization of the right ventricle takes longer than normal, thereby creating an R′ wave in lead V$_1$.

5. Myocardial injury is represented on an ECG by the presence of:

    A. T-wave inversion.

    B. ST-segment elevation.

    C. a pathologic Q wave.

Answer: B. ST-segment elevation is the ECG change that corresponds with myocardial injury. It's caused by a prolonged lack of blood supply.

6. On a 12-lead ECG, a posterior wall infarction produces:

    A. deep, broad Q waves in leads V_1 through V_3.

    B. inverse or mirror image changes in V_1 and V_2.

    C. raised ST segments in all leads.

Answer: B. Leads V_1 and V_2 show reciprocal changes when a posterior MI occurs. Look at the mirror images of these leads to determine the presence of a posterior MI.

7. The appearance of Q waves in the aftermath of an MI signify that:

    A. the interventricular septum has become injured.

    B. an entire thickness of the myocardium has become necrotic.

    C. a superficial layer of the myocardium has become ischemic.

Answer: B. Q waves can appear hours to days after an MI and signify that an entire thickness of the myocardium has become necrotic.

8. An ST segment located 1.5 mm above the baseline is considered:

    A. normal.

    B. slightly depressed.

    C. abnormally elevated.

Answer: C. ST segments should be isoelectric or have minimal deviation. ST-segment elevation greater than 1 mm above the baseline is considered abnormal.

Test strips

Okay, it's time to try out a couple of test ECGs.

9. In the 12-lead ECG below, you'll see an rsR′ pattern in lead V_1, as well as T-wave inversion. Looking at lead V_6, you'll note a widened S wave and an upright T wave. These changes indicate:

    A. right ventricular MI.
    B. LBBB.
    C. RBBB.

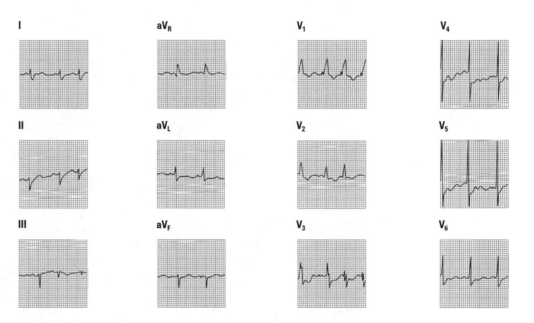

Answer: C. The rsR′ configuration in lead V_1 and the wide S wave in V_6 indicate RBBB.

10. Your patient says he thinks he might have had a heart attack about 3 years ago but, because he never went to the doctor, he doesn't know for sure. Looking at his admission ECG, you think he definitely had an MI at some point. You base your assessment on the presence of:

A. pathologic Q waves in leads II, III, and aV_F.

B. inverted T waves in leads I, aV_L, and V_6.

C. depressed ST segments in leads II, aV_L, and V_5.

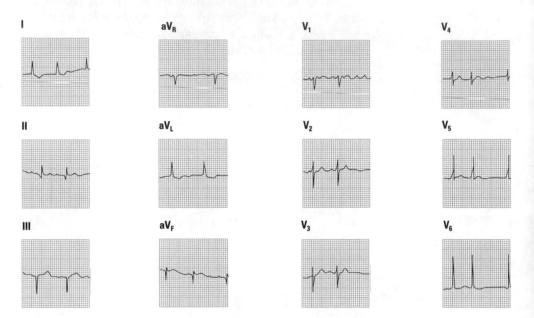

Answer: A. Old damage to the myocardium is indicated by the presence of pathologic Q waves, in this case in leads II, III, and aV_F. Those findings lead you to suspect the patient suffered an inferior wall MI at some point.

Scoring

☆☆☆ If you answered all ten items correctly, wow! You've graduated (with honors) from the School of 12-Lead ECG Interpretation!

☆☆ If you answered six to nine correctly, super! You're ready to take a graduate course on 12-lead ECG interpretation!

☆ If you answered five or fewer correctly, you're definitely on the right track. Just review your notes from 12-Lead ECG Interpretation 101!

Glossary and index

Glossary

aberrant conduction: abnormal pathway of an impulse traveling through the heart's conduction system

ablation: surgical or radio-frequency removal of an irritable focus in the heart; used to prevent tachyarrhythmias

afterload: resistance that the left ventricle must work against to pump blood through the aorta

amplitude: height of a waveform

arrhythmia: disturbance of the normal cardiac rhythm from the abnormal origin, discharge, or conduction of electrical impulses

artifact: waveforms in an ECG tracing that don't originate in the heart

atrial kick: amount of blood pumped into the ventricles as a result of atrial contraction; contributes approximately 30% of total cardiac output

automaticity: ability of a cardiac cell to initiate an impulse on its own

bigeminy: premature beat occurring every other beat; alternates with normal QRS complexes

biotransformation: series of chemical changes of a substance as a result of enzyme activity; end result of drug biotransformation may be active or inactive metabolites

biphasic: complex containing both an upward and a downward deflection; usually seen when the electrical current is perpendicular to the observed lead

bundle-branch block: slowing or blocking of an impulse as it travels through the bundle branches

capture: successful pacing of the heart, represented on the ECG tracing by a pacemaker spike followed by a P wave or QRS complex

cardiac output: amount of blood ejected from the left ventricle per minute; normal value is 4 to 8 L/minute

cardioversion: restoration of normal rhythm by electric shock or drug therapy

carotid sinus massage: manual pressure applied to the carotid sinus to slow the heart rate

circus reentry: delayed impulse in a one-way conduction path in which the impulse remains active and reenters the surrounding tissues to produce another impulse

compensatory pause: period following a premature ventricular contraction during which the heart regulates itself, allowing the sinoatrial node to resume normal conduction

conduction: transmission of electrical impulses through the myocardium

conductivity: ability of one cardiac cell to transmit an electrical impulse to another cell

contractility: ability of a cardiac cell to contract after receiving an impulse

couplet: pair of premature beats occurring together

defibrillation: termination of fibrillation by electrical shock

deflection: direction of a waveform, based on the direction of a current

depolarization: response of a myocardial cell to an electrical impulse that causes movement of ions across the cell membrane, which triggers myocardial contraction

diastole: phase of the cardiac cycle when both atria (atrial diastole) or both ventricles (ventricular diastole) are at rest and filling with blood

ECG complex: waveform representing electrical events of one cardiac cycle; consists of five main waveforms (labeled P, Q, R, S, and T), a sixth waveform (labeled U) that occurs under certain conditions, the PR and QT intervals, and the ST segment

ectopic beat: contraction that occurs as a result of an impulse generated from a site other than the sinoatrial node

electrical axis: direction of the depolarization waveform as seen in the frontal leads

enhanced automaticity: condition in which pacemaker cells increase the firing rate above their inherent rate

excitability: ability of a cardiac cell to respond to an electrical stimulus

extrinsic: not inherently part of the cardiac electrical system

indicative leads: leads that have a direct view of an infarcted area of the heart

intrinsic: naturally occurring electrical stimulus from within the heart's conduction system

inverted: negative or downward deflection on an ECG

late electrical potentials: cardiac electrical activity that occurs after depolarization; predisposes the patient to ventricular tachycardia

lead: perspective of the electrical activity in a particular area of the heart through the placement of electrodes on the chest wall

monomorphic: form of ventricular tachycardia in which the QRS complexes have a uniform appearance from beat to beat

multiform or multifocal: type of premature ventricular contractions that have differing QRS configurations as a result of their originating from different irritable sites in the ventricle

nonsustained ventricular tachycardia: ventricular tachycardia that lasts less than 30 seconds

pacemaker: group of cells that generates impulses to the heart muscle or a battery-powered device that delivers an electrical stimulus to the heart to cause myocardial depolarization

paroxysmal: episode of an arrhythmia that starts and stops suddenly

polymorphic: type of ventricular tachycardia in which the QRS complexes change from beat to beat

preload: stretching force exerted on the ventricular muscle by the blood it contains at the end of diastole

proarrhythmia: rhythm disturbance caused or made worse by drugs or other therapy

quadrigeminy: premature beat occurring every fourth beat that alternates with three normal QRS complexes

reciprocal leads: leads that take a view of an infarcted area of the heart opposite that taken by indicative leads

reentry mechanism: failure of a cardiac impulse to follow the normal conduction pathway; instead it follows a circular path

refractory: arrhythmia that doesn't respond to usual treatment measures

refractory period: brief period during which excitability in a myocardial cell is depressed

repolarization: recovery of the myocardial cells after depolarization during which the cell membrane returns to its resting potential

retrograde depolarization: depolarization that occurs backward toward the atrium instead of downward toward the ventricles; results in an inverted P wave

rhythm strip: length of ECG paper that shows multiple ECG complexes representing a picture of the heart's electrical activity in a specific lead

Stokes-Adams attack: sudden episode of light-headedness or loss of consciousness caused by an abrupt slowing or stopping of the heartbeat

sustained ventricular tachycardia: type of ventricular tachycardia that lasts longer than 30 seconds

systole: phase of the cardiac cycle when both of the atria (atrial systole) or the ventricles (ventricular systole) are contracting

trigeminy: premature beat occurring every third beat that alternates with two normal QRS complexes

triplet: three premature beats occurring together

uniform or unifocal: type of premature ventricular contraction that has the same or similar QRS configuration and that originates from the same irritable site in the ventricle

vagal stimulation: pharmacologic or manual stimulation of the vagus nerve to slow the heart rate

Valsalva's maneuver: technique of forceful expiration against a closed glottis; used to slow the heart rate

Index

i refers to an illustration; t refers to a table

i refers to an illustration; t refers to a table

i refers to an illustration; t refers to a table

i refers to an illustration; t refers to a table

i refers to an illustration; t refers to a table

i refers to an illustration; t refers to a table

i refers to an illustration; t refers to a table

i refers to an illustration; t refers to a table

i refers to an illustration; t refers to a table

i refers to an illustration; t refers to a table

i refers to an illustration; t refers to a table